Duped

Duped

Truth-Default Theory
and the Social Science
of Lying and Deception

Timothy R. Levine

The University of Alabama Press   Tuscaloosa

The University of Alabama Press
Tuscaloosa, Alabama 35487-0380
uapress.ua.edu

Typeface: Scala and Scala Sans

Cover image: Woodcut style expressionist image of the Greek Trojan Horse © Jeffrey
Thompson at www.123RF.com
Cover design: David Nees

Cataloging-in-Publication data is available from the Library of Congress.
ISBN: 978-0-8173-2041-6 (cloth)
ISBN: 978-0-8173-5968-3 (paper)
E-ISBN: 978-0-8173-9271-0

Contents

Illustrations

Figures

Preface

DURING THE 2016 US PRESIDENTIAL election, fact-checking revealed that only one out of every six of the winning candidate's statements was rated as honest or mostly honest. Yet fact-checking apparently held little sway with millions of voters who saw the candidate whose statements were more factually aligned as the less trustworthy of the two. How could this be? Despite the post-election soul searching of political pundits, this pattern is far from unique. Across a host of issues such as the advent of fake news, climate-science denial, and Bernie Madoff's appeal to investors, people can be astonishingly gullible. There are people who come off as authentic and sincere even when the facts discredit them. People fall victim to conspiracy theories and economic scams that should be dismissed as obviously ludicrous.

Many people, especially academics, see widespread gullibility as stemming from an unengaged and ill-informed public: If only people were better educated, surely they would be better at correctly distinguishing fact from fiction. Yet simple fact-checking coupled with public-education campaigns is unlikely to provide adequate solutions. Why? Because day in and day out, we spend our lives within a mind-set that can be characterized as a "truth-default." We uncritically accept virtually all of the communication messages we receive as "honest." Think about it: how many tweets, posts, articles, texts, e-mails, phone calls, and spoken declarative sentences do you receive each day? Now ask yourself: How many of those do you question in terms of honesty? Chances are, the answer is near zero. This is a near-universal human tendency. We all are perceptually blind to deception. We are hardwired to be duped. The question is, can anything be done to militate against our vulnerability to deception without further eroding the trust in people and social institutions that we so desperately need in civil society?

But there is a second critical point. Even though we have a strong tendency toward unquestioning belief, sometimes we do suspect deception. There are situations in which we abandon our truth-default. But, even when people are on guard for deception, folk wisdom about deception leads to predictable er-

rors in judgment. In the most recent presidential campaign, blurting out politically incorrect statements was understood by many Americans as evidence
of authenticity. Appearing confident was interpreted as a sign of honesty. Alternatively, speaking like a politician with carefully chosen words signaled that
the candidate was not to be trusted. Rather than questioning whether the candidate's statements actually aligned with known facts, assessments of honesty and sincerity were based on the candidate's demeanor. The problem is,
demeanor is highly misleading. Appearing honest and being honest are usually unrelated.

My objectives here are ambitious and radical. I want to start a revolution. I
seek to overthrow existing deception theory and provide a new, coherent, and
data-consistent approach to understanding deception and deception detection.
For more than twenty-five years, I have seen a need for a new theory of deception and deception detection. Ekman's idea of leakage was hugely influential, but the deficiencies were apparent almost immediately. His focus shifted
over time from the leakage hierarchy to a focus on the face and microexpressions. But my read of the ensuing literature reveals more excuses for why the
data do not seem to support his theory than solid, replicated, affirmative scientific support. Interpersonal deception theory is even less viable. It is logically incoherent, and I knew it to be empirically false four years before it was
eventually published. The new cognitive load approach in criminal and legal
psychology does not seem to be the path forward either, for the theoretical reasons identified by Steve McCornack, as well as weak, inconsistent, and just
plain odd empirical findings. The need is clear. Existing theory does not cut
it. A new perspective is needed.

Duped: Truth-Default Theory and the Social Science of Lying and Deception tells
the story of my program of research culminating in my new theory of deception: truth-default theory (TDT). Approximately sixty original studies and experiments are summarized and woven together within the TDT framework.
I detail where the ideas came from, how ideas were tested, and how the findings combine to produce a coherent new understanding of human deception
and deception detection.

The story begins in 1989, when I coauthored my first deception detection
experiment as a graduate student. The experiment brought college-student dating couples into the lab, and my professor and I looked at how the closeness
of the communicators' relationship and how prompting suspicion affected
our research subjects' ability to tell whether their partners were lying. The big
finding was that even when we tried to make them highly suspicious, our subjects still tended to believe their partners regardless of their partners' actual

honesty. This finding was called *truth-bias*, and it has turned out to be a very robust finding. Since then I have collected data in countries around the world and recruited a wide variety of research subjects, including college students, university professors, police detectives, customs agents, and professional spy catchers. Truth-bias has been a constant finding. I have never found people to be otherwise. Over time I have pieced together coherent understandings of truth-bias, how best to catch lies, and the interplay between the two.

TDT proposes that the content of incoming communication is usually uncritically accepted as true, and most of the time this is a good thing for us. One of the most surprising new insights is that truth-bias and truth-default work well for us. I argue that the tendency to believe others is an adaptive product of human evolution that enables efficient communication and social coordination. The truth-default allows humans to function socially. Further, because most deception is enacted by a few prolific liars, the so-called truth-bias is not really a bias after all. Passive belief makes us right most of the time. The catch is that it also makes us vulnerable to occasional deceit.

Importantly, TDT also challenges current social-scientific and folk views of deception that prioritize nonverbal and linguistic behavior as the keys to lie detection. According to TDT, the path to improved human lie detection involves listening to what is said, rather than to how it is said. As previously mentioned, the recent US election provides an excellent example of a situation where confidence and belligerence were decoded as authenticity and were often mistaken for honesty. More broadly, research shows that using evidence and skilled question asking produces much better outcomes than passive observation of deception cues like gaze aversion, facial expressions, body language, pronoun usage, or decontextualized counts of details.

My research on lie detection and truth-bias has produced many provocative new findings over the years. For example, we have uncovered what makes some people more believable than others (a believability quotient) and have discovered several ways to improve lie-detection accuracy. I directed a team of researchers (funded by the FBI and involving agents from the NSA) that produced the highest lie-detection accuracy ever published. Truth-default theory weaves together all these findings under a common framework. The evidence is organized and presented all in one place.

This book's perspective is best described as quantitative, experimental, multidisciplinary social science. My academic home discipline is communication. Consequently, deception and deception detection are first and foremost understood as communicative processes. The focus is more social and interpersonal than intrapsychic. Theoretically, TDT integrates ideas from a variety of academic disciplines such as evolutionary biology (Robert Trivers), social psychology (Dan Gilbert), and the philosophy of language (Paul Grice). Structurally, the book is modeled on classics in experimental social psychology such as Latane and Darley's (1970) *The Unresponsive Bystander*, presenting a logical series of original experiments.

The research subjects in TDT experiments range from college-student dating couples to nationally representative samples of US adults to elite NSA agents. Data collections span five continents. Every major TDT claim is scientifically tested and replicated. Small chunks of TDT ideas and results have been appearing in peer-reviewed academic journal articles for more than two decades. The book shows how all those findings and ideas fit together into a coherent package. The book also showcases for students, young professors, and social science aficionados what can be achieved with long, sustained, ambitious, programmatic, multimethod research. The applications are diverse, ranging from deception in romantic relationships to catching terrorists to criminal interrogation.

My approach might be described as abductive science. I don't see what I do as either dust bowl empiricism or as exclusively hypothetico-deductive theory testing. The theory building presented in this book is not of the abstract, armchair, speculative sort. The propositions are all data based, and the explanations were articulated so as to offer a coherent account of the existing scientific data. I did not seek to publish my theory until I had original research to support and replicate every major claim. I have that evidence now, and it is presented in the pages that follow.

But my intent is not just post hoc explanation. Good theory must also be generative. It needs to lead to new predictions that no one would think to make absent the theory. In line with Imre Lakatos, I want to propose a theory that is out in front of the data, not always chasing from behind to try and catch up.

A final feature of my theory is that it is modular. Truth-default theory is a collection of quasi-independent minitheories, models, or effects that are joined by an overarching logic. The parts can stand on their own, but they also fit together to provide a bigger picture.

Stylistically, the text shifts between first-person storytelling, objective scientific narration, and editorializing. The book provides an engaging read targeted to a diverse audience. I strove to be accessible to the novice while also providing valuable insights for even the most sophisticated and informed reader. I aim to provide an engaging, fun, interesting read without sacrificing scholarly rigor. The result is a book that can be read and appreciated at different levels by different audiences.

Acknowledgments

THERE ARE SEVERAL INDIVIDUALS WITHOUT whom this book would not have happened, and many of the ideas presented here are not all my own. First, there is my good friend Steve McCornack, who, to my knowledge, first coined the term "truth-bias." Perhaps no other idea has played a more prominent role in my thinking. Without Steve, it is unlikely I would have ever done a deception experiment. As I explain in chapter 1, I got my start in deception research as Steve's lab assistant. My first several published articles on deception were all collaborations with Steve. His ideas regarding truth-bias, suspicion, probing, information manipulation, and the problems with cognitive load all influenced my thinking in important ways. I am grateful for Steve's friendship as well as his intellectual contributions.

Another absolutely critical influence was Hee Sun Park. Besides being my spouse, she came up with the ideas for the veracity effect, the Park–Levine probability model of base-rate effects, and the "How People Really Detect Lies" study. Each of these ideas is a key part of truth-default theory (TDT). Without these critical pieces of the puzzle, I would not have a coherent theory of deception.

A third key contributor was J. Pete Blair. Prior to earning his PhD, Pete was a professional investigator and interviewer-interrogator. He has brought a more applied flavor to my research, and many of the ideas regarding improving accuracy (e.g., content in context, expertise, question effects) are, at least in part, Pete's. Pete has become a highly valued collaborator and a good friend.

Three of my former graduate students deserve special mention. Ms. Rachel Kim was my chief lab assistant and collaborator on the creation of the NSF tapes, as well as experiments on base-rates, suspicion, deception motives, and projected motives. I owe Rachel much, and it was a pleasure having her on the team. When Rachel left MSU, I was exceptionally fortunate to have David Clare step into the role as my chief lab assistant. David was there for many of the more recent data collections (e.g., demeanor, experts, interactive base-rates, and the FBI expert experiment), and he was a fabulously reliable research assistant and a great student. David's preliminary PhD paper provides key evidence for the central premise of the theory. Kim Serota played an important role in the "few prolific liars" program of research, the demeanor studies, some of the base-rate studies, and the *Lie to Me* experiment. Amongst many assets, Kim has a real gift for the visual depiction of data. Kim created or formatted several of the figures presented in the book. He continues to be a valued friend and coauthor and has taken the lead in the lie prevalence research. His restaurant recommendations are spot-on too.

A number of other students, from high school students to PhD candidates, have contributed in various ways to the research reported here. These include (but are not limited to) Yasuhiro Daiku, Hillary Shulman, Allison Shaw, Doug Messer, Frankie Carey, Kelli Asada, Mikala Hughes, Dave DeAndrea, Chris Carpenter, Alex Davis, Darcy Dietrich, April Li, David Yuan, Tracie Greene, Eric Jickling, and the students of my Com 399 and UGS200H deception classes. Yasuhiro made many of the high-resolution figures for the book.

Thanks also to the National Security Agency, the Baton Rouge District Attorney's Office, and the US Customs and Border Protection office in Detroit for their involvement in the research. Dan Baxter was especially helpful. Big thanks to the National Science Foundation for the initial funding and to the FBI for additional financial support.

Much of my own work summarized in this book originally appeared in journal articles over the past twenty-eight years. Numerous journal editors and journal reviewers have provided invaluable feedback over the years. Credit is given to specific journals in notes and the bibliography. Here, I express my appreciation and recognition to all the journals, editors, and reviewers who contributed to the ideas, presentation, and dissemination of TDT and research behind it.

My friend Tom Hove provided valuable feedback on many of the ideas presented in the book. Dave DeAndrea has also read early drafts, provided wonderful feedback, and even assigned drafts in his classes. Torsten Reimer coined the terms "truth-default" and "trigger." Mark Knapp, Michael Beatty, and Howie Giles have been very supportive of my work and my career. Harry David provided initial editing and proofreading.

Dan Waterman is my editor at the University of Alabama Press. Dan has been terrifically supportive and helpful. He really got behind the project. I am very fortunate to have Dan as an editor. Thanks for everything, Dan!

Credit also goes to former professors who taught me well: Buddy Wheeless, Jim McCroskey, G. R. Miller, Frank Boster, and Jack Hunter. Finally, credit also goes to four individuals who have especially influenced me through their wonderful scholarship: Paul Meehl, Gerd Gigerenzer, Bob Cialdini, and Dan Gilbert.

TIM LEVINE
BIRMINGHAM, ALABAMA

List of Studies and Experiments

Chapter Eight
  IMT Study One: The First IMT Study
  IMT Study Two: Replication and Inclusion of a Dichotomous Assessment
  IMT Study Three: Effects of Deception Severity
  IMT Study Four: Relationship among IMT Dimensions

Chapter Nine
  TDT Study One: The Prevalence of Lying in America
  TDT Study Two: Diary Studies Reexamined
  TDT Study Three: A Replication with College Students
  TDT Study Four: Teens Lie a Lot
  TDT Study Five: The Prevalence of Lying in the UK

Chapter Ten
  TDT Experiment Six: Selecting Truths and Lies
  TDT Experiment Seven: Generating Truths and Lies
  TDT Experiment Eight: Introducing the NSF Cheating Experiments
  TDT Study Nine: Toward a Pan-Cultural List of Deception Motives
  TDT Experiment Ten: Projected Motives One
  TDT Experiment Eleven: Projected Motives Two
  TDT Experiment Twelve: Projected Motives Three

Chapter Eleven
  TDT Experiment Thirteen: Lovers Just Aren't Leery
  TDT Experiment Fourteen: Rachel Kim and Suspicion Redux
  TDT Experiment Fifteen: David Clare and Evidence for the Truth-Default
  TDT Experiment Sixteen: David Clare and Evidence for the Truth-Default Two

Chapter Twelve
  TDT Experiment Seventeen: The First Base-Rate Experiment
  TDT Experiment Eighteen: Accuracy Is a Predictable Linear Function of
    Base-Rates

PART I

The Social Science of Deception

1

The Science of Deception

On the morning of July 19, 2012, I listened with interest as two former CIA agents, Philip Houston and Michael Floyd, were interviewed during an episode of *The Diane Rehm Show* on National Public Radio about their new book, *Spy the Lie*.[1] The book was a popular-press attempt to share the secrets of lie detection with the book-buying public. It seemed to me that some of what they were saying was right on target, while some of their other advice was pure bunk. What really caught my ear, however, was their response to one particular caller who asserted that we might not be able to detect lies very well. Some liars, this caller said, were really good at lying. The caller referenced Robert Hanssen, the FBI agent who spied against the United States for Russia and successfully evaded detection for more than twenty years. Didn't Robert Hanssen exemplify our inability to catch some lies and liars?

The authors replied that their approach to detecting lies was not based on scientific research but on anecdotes and personal experience. Experience had taught them that their approach was highly effective.

Wow! I found this response really curious. First, the caller had not referenced academic research. The caller's comments involved anecdote, not science. As we will see in chapter 3, much research shows that people are poor lie detectors. Science clearly contradicts some of these authors' assertions. But why bring scientific research up at that time? Second, I did not expect the authors to volunteer information implying that their view might contradict scientific evidence, and to openly express their hopeful desire that listeners trust their anecdotes over science. Is that really persuasive? Presumably, they were on the radio to promote their book. To my ear, they had just undercut themselves. Third, while they might have had good reasons to believe that the lies they detected were valid, how could they have known how many lies they had missed? They had no way of knowing how often they had been suckered. The best lies are never detected. In the lab, researchers know what is truth and what is lie. In everyday life, we often cannot know what is truth and what is lie with 100 percent certainty. Sometimes we are wrong and never know we are wrong. This was the caller's point, and it was a good one. As we will see in chapter 13, some liars are really good at telling convincing lies.

Here is an observation from my own research that applies to using examples as evidence for what works in lie detection. From 2007 to 2010, I had funding from the National Science Foundation to create a collection of videotaped truths and lies for use in deception detection research. I ended up creating more than three hundred taped interviews during that time. (I have made more since then with funding from the FBI.) I have watched these three hundred interviews many times over the years. For every liar you can point to multiple things that seem to give the lie away. If you watch the tapes carefully, the clues are almost always there to see.

There are, however, a couple important catches. First, what gives away one liar is usually different from the signals that reveal the next liar. The signs seem to be unique to the particular lie, and the science discussed later in the book backs this up. Second, if you go through the tapes carefully, for every liar who seems to be exposed by a telltale sign or collection of clues, there are honest people who act the same way and do the same things. That is, most of the behaviors that seem to give away liars also serve to misclassify honest people.

That honest people can appear deceptive is one of the many insights I have gained from watching so many tapes where the actual truth (called "ground truth" by researchers) is known for certain. If you know some statement is a lie, you can usually point to clues indicating deceit. That is because of hindsight.[2] Pointing out clues with hindsight is one thing. Using those same behaviors to correctly distinguish truthful from deceptive communication is quite another. Different liars do different things, and some honest people do those things too. When I watch tapes of truths and lies without knowing in advance which is which, whether some behavior indicates a lie is not entirely clear. I find that when I don't know who is a liar beforehand, I miss some lies, and I falsely suspect some honest people of deceit. Many times, I am just not sure one way or the other. Cherry-picking examples is easy and makes for persuasive and appealing anecdotes. Cherry-picked examples informed by hindsight do not lead to useful knowledge and understanding that extend beyond the specific example.

This makes me suspicious of knowledge by common sense, anecdote, and personal experience. I want scientifically defensible evidence. If what I think does not mesh with the data, we have to question what I think. This principle, by the way, is not only useful in assessing the quality of advice. It is also a good way to detect lies. There is much more on the use of evidence in lie detection in chapter 14.

What the scientific research says (at least up through 2006; current findings are more nuanced) is that people are typically not very good at accurately distinguishing truths from lies. The research behind this conclusion is extensive and solid, and that will be covered in chapter 3.

Nevertheless, we should not be too quick to dismiss professionals with expertise in interrogation and interviewing who believe there are ways to catch liars and detect lies. Just because their evidence is anecdotal does not mean that it is false or necessarily incorrect. In fact, my research described in this book is, in part, an effort to use science to reconcile research findings with practitioners' experience. That is, rather than trying to debunk practitioners, as so many of my fellow academics try to do, I began designing experiments to explain the differences between successful interrogations and typical deception detection laboratory experiments. Much of the research, I have come to believe, tells us more about lie detection in the lab than in real life.[3]

A more accurate scientific conclusion is that people were not very good at detecting lies in lie-detection experiments published prior to 2006. The research did not prove that lies can't be detected! The research showed that lies cannot be accurately detected *in the type of experiments that were used to study lie detection.* Conclusions from research are always limited by how the research was done. In the case of research on the accuracy of deception detection, I have come to believe that this is a critical, game-changing point (see chapters 12, 13, and 14, and compare the research reviewed in chapter 14 to that reviewed in chapter 3).

I have come to believe that many approaches to lie detection are ineffectual, especially those that involve what I call "cues." Some approaches do have more promise. Improving accuracy involves understanding what works, what does not work, and why. Because I am a social scientist, anecdotes, yarns, and good stories are not going to cut it as evidence. Scientific evidence is required. Real-world observations are critical in generating the ideas that I research, but such observations are only the starting point. I prove my points with controlled experiments. I insist that my results replicate. I think my readers should expect this. And it is this insistence on scientific evidence that can be replicated that makes my approach better than the alternative approaches and theories out there.

This, however, does not mean I have an aversion to good stories. I began the chapter with a story about listening to the radio one morning. Then there was a second story about my repeated viewing of the NSF deception tapes. Stories are great for explaining ideas, making ideas understandable, and generating research ideas. Stories are essential for making points interesting and engaging. I will tell plenty of stories throughout the book. I will also present hard data that are scientifically defensible and have passed the dual tests of replication and publication in peer-reviewed academic journals. At the end of the day, I am doing science, and this book is about a scientific approach to deception and deception detection.

Speaking of stories, here is another, and while it is a digression, I think it addresses a question many readers may have at the outset. People tend to find deception interesting. People are naturally curious about lies and lie detection. And it's not every day that people meet a deception detection researcher. Actually, there are not many of us around to meet. People who have sustained careers studying the social science of deception probably number less than two or three dozen worldwide. Anyway, when people find out that I study deception, one common question is how and why I got into deception research. This is a question that I have been asked too many times to count, and this is a good time and place to answer it.

The truth is that I stumbled into deception research. I became a deception researcher largely out of serendipity. Remaining a deception researcher was opportunistic. Back in grade school, I was very interested in the physical sciences. Other little kids wanted to be policemen or firemen or astronauts, but I wanted to be a geologist when I grew up. That changed in junior high and high school. I had a strong fascination for why people did things and with social dynamics. One of my nicknames in high school was Freud; but I wasn't interested in psychological disorders. I was curious about normal, everyday social behavior. And I still am. What I call *truth-default theory* (TDT) is about deception in the lives of normal people in their everyday social interactions.

When I was in high school, it was unclear whether I could go to college. I'm dyslexic. A psychologist told my parents it would be a waste of money to send me to college. I was sure to flunk out. Fortunately for me, my grades were good enough, and I scored well enough on the ACT test, to be admitted to all the colleges to which I applied. My parents agreed to give me a chance, as long as I selected a public, in-state university with low tuition. I chose Northern Arizona University.

When I went off to college, I knew I would be a psychology major. As I learned more, I gravitated toward persuasion as a topic. I grew up the son of a real estate salesperson, and sales and social influence intrigued me. During my third year in college, I learned that persuasion was a topic of research, and when I went on to graduate school, that was the topic that drew me in. I switched from psychology to communication mostly for practical reasons. It was easier to get into top-rated graduate programs with full-ride funding in communication than in the more competitive field of psychology. I did both my MA thesis and my PhD thesis on the topic of persuasion. I teach classes on persuasion to this day. It was early in graduate school that I started picking up interpersonal-communication processes as a second area of focus.

By the time I finished my first semester of graduate school, I pretty much knew my career choice was in academia and that I wanted to be a professor.[4] It turned out that I had some talent in research and that I enjoyed teaching. I managed to get into the highly regarded PhD program at Michigan State University, where two leaders in persuasion (Gerry Miller and Frank Boster) were on the faculty. Miller's health was in decline, and I ended up studying under Boster.

About halfway through my PhD studies, Michigan State hired a new professor by the name of Steve McCornack. Steve and I were nearly the same age, and we had much in common. More than that, I was really impressed by Steve. I thought (and still do) that he was really smart. I like smart people. As an undergraduate student, Steve had done a research project on deception that had won an international award and been published.[5] Writing and publishing an award-winning research paper as an undergraduate—wow! Even more than just the award and publication, his ideas and findings were really cool.

Prior to Steve's, there had been only one other study on lie detection among people who knew each other.[6] The prevailing wisdom at the time was that the better you knew someone, the better you would be at detecting their lies. Knowledge of another person was expected to enhance deception detection accuracy. Steve, however, predicted the exact opposite. The better you know someone, the more you tend to think you can tell when they lie, but also the more you think they wouldn't lie to you. Relationship closeness, according to Steve, makes us truth-biased. This was intriguing. I read Steve's research, I heard him present his research, and I knew this was someone I wanted to collaborate with and learn from.

When Steve joined the faculty at Michigan State, I arranged to be assigned as his research assistant. My advisor, Frank Boster, was graduate director, and getting the assignment to Steve as his assistant was a simple matter. Over the next couple of years, we did a number of studies together.[7] I just got sucked into deception research. Each study led to more questions. The more I learned about deception, the more a set of challenging puzzles became apparent to me.

One thing led to another, and now I am writing this book twenty-five years later. It took a quarter century, but I now have answers that hold up and are worth sharing.

What I like most about deception research, and probably the biggest reason I stuck with it, is that in the realm of deception research, most things are not what they seem. Common sense is often wrong, and surprising twists come one after another. Too much social science is content with documenting the obvious. Deception research, in contrast, presents a challenging set of puzzles to solve.

What drew me to deception research is similar to what attracts my wife and me to certain television dramas. We get bored quickly with series that are conventional and predictable. We like complex plotlines and unanticipated developments. This is what I really like about *Game of Thrones* (both the HBO series and the books) and *Lonesome Dove* (book and miniseries).

The other thing that has kept me doing deception research is that the need and potential for improvement have been apparent to me since my first involvement as a graduate student. It seemed to me that deception research could do better. The theory needed improvement, the methodology could be made better, and the findings could be stronger and more coherent. In short, there was plenty of opportunity to make a scientific splash. So many areas of social science research evolve into super-specialized endeavors looking at ever-more microscopic issues of little interest to anyone outside the sub-sub-subspecialty. But this was not the case in deception research. So I stuck with deception as a topic and gradually solved one puzzle after another.

PRIOR DECEPTION RESEARCH AND THE NEED FOR A NEW APPROACH TO DECEPTION

This book offers a new approach to understanding deception and deception detection: truth-default theory. The main impetuses behind the theory and this book were my growing dissatisfaction with the prevailing theory and my desire to solve some challenging puzzles stemming from the research findings. What was needed to really understand deception and deception detection was a new theory. It has taken much research, much persistence, some talented and insightful collaborators, and more than a little luck to get to this point.

I have several goals for TDT besides just offering an explanation of deception and deception detection. For one, the theory needs to solve some persistent mysteries. There are a number of odd things in the existing scientific literature that (until TDT) did not seem to make much sense. A coherent way to make sense of the literature is needed. Second, there is a need for a coherent logic that points in new directions and yields new findings. Much deception research seems to be spinning its wheels, so to speak. The research needs to get out of an intellectual rut. Most of all, the theory needs to make predictions that turn out to be right. It seems to me that older theories are better at excuse generation than accurate prediction. Findings really don't support the older theories, but the failures are either ignored or explained away. I want a theory that when put to the test will clearly and unequivocally pass. In short, the aim is to provide a theory of deception that makes past findings coherent, leads to interesting new discoveries, and, most of all, passes scientific muster.

The previous research on deception is diverse. In this and the next two chapters, I will focus on four interrelated questions that have received large amounts of attention. As research has progressed, well-documented answers have emerged. The four questions are as follows:

1. What do people look for in order to distinguish between whether someone else is honest or lying?
2. What, if any, specific behaviors actually distinguish truthful communication from lies?
3. How accurate are people at distinguishing truths from lies?
4. Under what conditions are people more accurate or less accurate at lie detection, and what types of people, if any, are more skilled or less skilled lie detectors?

Here is a sneak peek at the short answers to the four key questions above.

When explicitly asked, the thing that people most often believe gives away lies is that liars won't look you in the eye.[8] Interestingly, this belief appears cross-cultural.[9] Also, it appears that eye contact has no validity as a reliable indicator of deception.[10] There is no scientific evidence that liars look in some particular direction when lying.[11] Zero.

People look for more than just a lack of eye contact when deciding whether someone is to be believed. My research has found a constellation of interrelated behaviors and impressions that people associate with honesty and deceit.[12] People who seem nervous, anxious, hesitant, and uncertain and who lack confidence are likely to be doubted, while people who come off as friendly, composed, confident, and engaged tend to be believed. Based on these packages of behaviors and impressions, we can predict well who will be believed and who is more likely to be seen as a liar. Further, we have found a number of other interesting things about these believability markers. First, they are highly intercorrelated, they occur in combination, and they are perceived as gestalts. Second, they are not language dependent and appear to be cross-cultural. Finally, while these behaviors strongly determine believability, they are unrelated to actual honesty. Chapter 13 covers the details of my work on honest demeanor. I believe I have discovered what amounts to a "believability quotient."

Research looking for specific cues that actually distinguish truths from lies has identified numerous candidate behaviors. At the level of the results of the individual published study, there is strong evidence for specific behaviors (cues) that differentiate liars from honest speakers. However, as research has progressed, findings typically have failed to be replicated, or completely opposite findings have been obtained. The net result is that as evidence has accumulated, the evidence for cues has become weaker.[13] The more each given cue has been researched, the less it has seemed to distinguish between truths and lies. This trend has held over time. So, the answer to whether there are specific behaviors that actually distinguish truths and lies appears mostly negative. Taken as a whole, the evidence suggests that such cues exist but are ephemeral and lack the potency and consistency to be of much practical value.[14]

Given that research shows that what people look for in detecting lies is not very strongly linked to actual lying, it should now be no surprise that people tend to be poor lie detectors. Literally hundreds of studies have exposed people to truths and lies and asked them to make a decision about which is which. When the results of these experiments are scored as the percentage correct and averaged across studies, what we get is just under 54%.[15] People have a better than fifty-fifty chance of detecting lies, but the odds are not much better than chance.

Finally, research has looked for exceptions to the conclusion of 54%, slightly-better-than-chance accuracy. Until very recently, research has not found many. It does not seem to matter whether the lies are read, seen, or heard.[16] Video-taped lies yield about the same accuracy as face-to-face communication. It does not seem to matter whether the judges are college students, police, friends, romantic partners, or intelligence agents.[17] The 54% accuracy result has been remarkably stable, and most studies produce accuracy levels between 44 and 64%.[18]

To summarize, people have a constellation of behaviors that they look for when assessing whether someone is lying. The behaviors people look for, however, do not seem to be behaviors that actually distinguish truths from lies. Seemingly as a result, people are poor lie detectors. Forty years of research failed to provide a reliable path to improved accuracy that has met the scientific standard of replication.

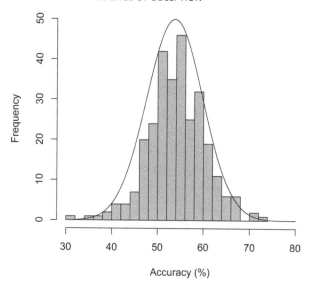

Figure 1.1. Accuracy in deception detection experiments prior to 2006.

Although the research findings just described are very well supported, they are not very satisfying: "People are poor lie detectors. They look for the wrong things. But there really aren't any right things. All is hopeless." This is not exactly an encouraging, feel-good message. There is no TED Talk in my future for that kind of conclusion. Rather than just give up and find a better topic for research, I opted to try to discover a new way of understanding deception that would make apparent that which had been missing. We, after all, do sometimes catch others in lies. How is this done? Past research told us much about what does not seem to work. Research is needed that shows what does work. Chapter 14 summarizes my research addressing this need.

Besides the practical goal of improved accuracy, a viable theory also needs to solve two puzzles. I call these the mystery of normally distributed, slightly-better-than-chance accuracy, and the mystery of deception accuracy in research not about deception. From an academic and theoretical standpoint, these are two places where existing theories come up short. These nevertheless are empirical facts that any good theory must make understandable.

One of the things about deception research that had really puzzled me is the mystery of normally distributed, slightly-better-than-chance accuracy. I have already explained that average accuracy in prior deception detection experiments is 54%. Most findings fall between 44% and 64%. As shown in figure 1.1, I took each of the 289 findings included in the Bond and DePaulo (2006)

meta-analysis of deception detection accuracy and graphed them with statistical software. The percentage correct found in each study is arrayed along the
horizontal axis. The number of studies finding a particular level of accuracy
forms the vertical axis. As you can see, the findings are neatly and normally
distributed around the average finding.[19] I ask the reader to take a moment
to consider why this might be the case and why I find this graph odd and in
need of explanation.

Here is why I find this odd. For one thing, real findings from real research
in the social sciences are seldom this consistent and this orderly. What findings this consistent and this orderly mean is that all the studies are finding
the same thing but varying by some small random amount. Usually, of course,
findings vary from study to study not only because of random error but also
because of a number of nonrandom things such as who the subjects were, the
nature of the research design, other variables included in the study, and the
like. All this creates variability in results from study to study. Some studies
converge on stronger effects than other studies. In the language of social science, most areas of research have *moderators*. Moderators are other variables
that impact the nature of findings. They make things work differently. Moderators make findings conditional. The existence of moderators in a literature
functions to spread the findings out. Moderators are very common in social
science, and it is odd that the literature on deception detection accuracy is so
devoid of substantial moderators.

Another thing is that if people could not detect lies at all, findings would
be distributed around fifty-fifty chance. They are not. Look at figure 1.1. Findings are not centered on 50 percent. Accuracy is better than chance. So, it's
not that people are totally incapable. At the same time, people do not seem to
be much better than chance. This too seems odd to me. Why are people only
a little better than chance—not more, not less? What can account for this robust finding of only slightly better than chance? I do not believe past theory
(see chapter 4) has a credible explanation. I will explain why the findings are
the way they are in chapter 13.

The second puzzle is that of deception accuracy in research not about deception. Among my many interests is a long-held affinity for classic old experiments in social science. One well-known example is Stanley Milgram's famous
experiments on obedience to authority.[20] Readers who are up on social science
will know this, but I will briefly summarize the study for those less familiar
with Milgram's research. Subjects come into the lab with another person they
believe to be another subject. The study is ostensibly about the effects of punishment on learning. One subject is the learner, and the other is the teacher.

The learner must learn some word pairs, and the teacher is told to deliver an electric shock to the learner whenever there is an error. Each error is to be punished with an increasingly intense shock starting at 15 volts and increasing in 15-volt increments to 450 volts. If the teacher objects to zapping the learner (who frets, screams, complains of a heart condition, and finally stops responding altogether), an experimenter in a white lab coat calmly tells the teacher to continue. This goes on until the subject absolutely refuses to continue, or until the 450-volt shock is delivered thrice. What Milgram found, of course, is that a majority of subjects (65 percent) went all the way—delivering the maximum shock to the poor victim. This study is considered to provide strong evidence for the power of authority. The subjects were just following orders, and a majority did so in spite of the brutality and the learner's protests.

This study was also a deception detection experiment, although it is usually not thought of as such. The learner was really an actor; the only one actually shocked was the teacher-subject, to convince them that the shock generator was real. Otherwise, everything was pretty much all staged. Just how likely is it that some Ivy League professor is going to electrocute members of the public in some on-campus torture chamber by getting other members of the public to flip the switch? Yet apparently, no subject recognized the deception. Accuracy was zero. All the subjects were sucked into the storyline, and no one saw through the ruse. That is not consistent with 54% accuracy in deception detection experiments. What gives?

Here is another famous example that is even more informative. Asch conducted a famous series of experiments on conformity.[21] In these experiments, subjects judged the lengths of lines. There was a standard line, and then, as if on a multiple-choice test, there were three comparison lines labeled A, B, and C. Subjects were asked which of the three comparison lines (A, B, or C) was the same length as the standard. The subjects were asked to make these judgments either alone or in groups. When they were in groups, other group members would sometimes all give the same incorrect answer. When all the others gave the wrong answer, the subject faced a choice as to whether to give the answer that looked right to him, or to go along with the group and provide an incorrect answer. When alone, people were able to choose the correct answer with more than 99% accuracy. After witnessing unanimous group errors, subjects gave the same erroneous answer as the group 36.8% of the time. The results of this study are typically seen as strong evidence for the power of conformity to group pressure. Again, although not typically considered in this way, these results also tell us about deception detection.

The groups' errors were, of course, preplanned and part of the experiment.

They were flat-out lies. The incorrect answers were knowingly and intentionally false statements meant to mislead the real subject. What's more, they were clearly and obviously objectively false. Subjects could see the right answers with their own eyes. Responses in the control group verified that the truth was obvious. Yet few if any of the subjects came to the seemingly obvious conclusion that the group errors were simply lies. As Asch described: "Instances of suspicion were rather infrequent. One would expect distrust to grow as the majority continued to err. [But] before his [the subject's] suspicions had the opportunity to take root, he had unwittingly come to doubt himself and to seek explanations in other directions. . . . Most subjects did not suspect that the majority judgments were not genuine. Suspicion at times occurred only as an hypothesis which, like many others, was rejected"[22] (29, 31). So, as with Milgram's experiments, Asch's also documented 0.00% lie-detection accuracy.

These two findings are far from unusual. Much experimental social science uses research confederates (i.e., people who appear to be other subjects but who are really working for the research team and are acting out a contrived role) and other types of deception. In my own research, confederates are identified as such by research subjects less than 1.0% of the time.

So I ask you: Why is accuracy so reliably 54% in studies of deception detection designed to be about deception detection, yet near zero in studies that involve deception but are not about deception? This too is a puzzle that a viable theory of deception needs to solve. I think I have solved this mystery too, and the answer is provided in chapters 10 and 11.

A QUICK GLANCE AHEAD

This first chapter is meant as a teaser. We look here at how isolated examples can be misleading and the advantages of systematic scientific investigation. A few provocative findings are described, and some interesting mysteries presented. The rest of the book provides much more detail about social science theory and research on the topic of deception. This book is about where deception theory and research has been and where it needs to go. I hope you will read on.

The first half of the book (part 1) introduces readers to deception theory and research. Part 1 does two big things. First, readers are provided with a detailed and authoritative history and description of the social science of deception. The next three chapters in particular provide what might be thought of as "Deception 101." What is known about deception is summarized. How the facts are most often framed and understood is explained. In short, readers are provided with all the prior knowledge needed to really understand TDT and the scholarly environment that predated it. Second, part 1 makes the case for why TDT is needed. To preview my argument over the next four chapters, there exists an unacceptably large mismatch between the understandings provided by previous theories and the results of prior research. Simply put, previous theories run afoul of data in important ways. Bringing theory more in line with findings is among TDT's more compelling selling points, and the need for theory-data consistency provides the primary rationale for TDT and for this book. That is, TDT does a better job of predicting and explaining facts than its rivals do, and this more than anything else makes TDT valuable.

To these ends, chapters 2 and 3 summarize some of the most important and most central areas of prior deception research. Chapter 2 focuses on "cues." We will take a close look at the research on (a) the behaviors that people think distinguish truths and lies, (b) the behaviors that people actually rely on in distinguishing truths from lies, and (c) the behaviors that do and do not actually distinguish truths from lies. Chapter 3 examines people's ability to distinguish truths from lies in traditional deception detection experiments. In both, priority is given to meta-analysis, looking at trends across larger numbers of studies rather than at the findings of individual studies. I strive to provide a coherent picture of what we know by focusing on findings that reliably replicate and by describing the big-picture implications of those results.

The fourth chapter is titled "Rivals," and it takes a historical look back at the other important theories of deception that precede TDT. Chapter 5 critiques those theories and provides a detailed rationale for the book and TDT. If prior theory were adequate and sufficient, there would be little to be gained from yet another theory. The case is made that prior theories have serious deficiencies and that the need for TDT is real and pressing.

Part 2 of the book shifts the focus from prior theory and research to TDT. Here, I explicate it and describe my program of research leading to, testing, and replicating TDT.

Chapter 6 provides a succinct and rough summary of TDT. Key definitions are provided. TDT is modular, by which I mean that it is an organized collection of stand-alone mini-theories, hypotheses, and effects. Each of the modules is briefly described, and the propositional structure weaving them together laid out. But the chapter just provides an outline, with little explanation. The detail comes in chapters 7 through 14.

Chapters 7 and 8 provide a careful conceptual analysis of deceptive communication. Chapter 7 takes a close look at issues in defining deception from the TDT perspective. The eighth chapter examines deception as information manipulation. TDT's companion theories by Steve McCornack, information manipulation theory (IMT) and information manipulation theory 2 (IMT2), are summarized. Beginning in chapter 8, a series of numbered original empirical studies are summarized testing relevant theoretical predictions. In chapter 8, a series of four IMT studies are detailed. In chapters 9 through 14, TDT studies and experiments one through fifty-five are described. The TDT studies are ordered to reflect the logical flow of the theory rather than chronological order. The aim is to showcase TDT's extensive and robust empirical foundation and its predictive power.

Chapter 9 explicates TDT's first two propositions and the Few Prolific Liars module. The empirical support is detailed. Why people lie is examined in the tenth chapter, which delves into proposition five and the People Lie for a Reason module. And it provides the first part of the answer to the mystery of accuracy in research that uses deception but is not about deception.

Chapter 11 gets to the core of TDT, focusing on *truth-bias* and *the truth-default* and summarizing my research on them. The existence of the truth-default and the idea of triggers provide additional insight into the mystery of accuracy in research that uses deception but is not about deception. Chapter 12 focuses on two important implications of truth-bias, namely, *the veracity effect* and *the Park–Levine Probability Model*. The focus is on the empirical evidence supporting these modules and proposition three. Chapter 12 explains why base-rates are so important.

The focus in chapter 13 shifts to offering a coherent explanation for the prior detection-accuracy findings described in chapters 1 and 3. The companion modules A Few Transparent Liars and Sender Honest Demeanor are explicated, and the evidence consistent with proposition eleven is described. The mystery of normally distributed slightly-better-than-chance accuracy is solved.

Improving accuracy is the topic of chapter 14. How People Really Detect Lies is described, along with the Content-in-Context, Question Effects, and Expertise modules. In the process, evidence for the twelfth, thirteenth, and fourteenth propositions is provided.

Finally, chapter fifteen wraps things up.

2

Cues

THIS CHAPTER AND THE NEXT review the prior research on deception and deception detection. The topic of deception is expansive, and the prior research extensive. This review is therefore selective. My goal is not to cover everything, but instead to give the reader a deep understanding of the most informative and influential prior findings relevant to assessing the empirical adequacy of the theories reviewed in chapter 4, as well as TDT. Research more germane to specific subtopics falling under the umbrella of TDT is covered in part 2 rather than here.

The research reviewed focuses on answering four long-standing and central questions. Research on the first two questions is covered in this chapter, and the research on the third and fourth questions in the next. To review, these four key questions are:

1. What do people look for in order to distinguish whether someone else is honest or lying?
2. What, if any, specific behaviors actually distinguish truthful communication from lies?
3. How accurate are people at distinguishing truths from lies?
4. Under what conditions (if any) are people more accurate or less accurate at lie detection, and what types of people (if any) are more skilled or less skilled lie detectors?

In answering these questions, I rely on meta-analysis rather than on the results of individual primary studies. For readers not familiar with meta-analysis, it is a set of statistical procedures used for summarizing prior findings across many studies. The results of individual studies become the data points in meta-analysis, and trends across studies are examined.

It is my impression that my reliance on meta-analysis may be controversial within some scholarly circles. When I have sought to publish individual papers in peer-reviewed journals, one or more reviewers typically find fault with my reliance on meta-analysis, asserting that my approach to reviewing the past literature is problematic because I failed to mention some specific finding or another favored by the reviewer. Because this is such a common criticism, I start here by explaining the several reasons I have adopted an approach that prioritizes meta-analysis over specific findings from primary studies.

First, a number of high-quality meta-analyses on the topics covered here enable us to see trends across large numbers of studies. I believe it would be remiss not to rely on these meta-analyses. Surely better conclusions are obtained from reliance on vastly larger samples. Second, reliance on individual studies creates the risk of either cherry-picking results that support one's own favored conclusion or concluding that the results are just a confusing jumble of contradictory findings. The thing is, individual studies or findings can be cited to support pretty much all the claims put forth by the various theorists and researchers. At the same time, individual findings can also be cited that seem to disprove just about any claim or theory. For just about every claim or finding, there is a seemingly contradictory finding. When there are literally hundreds of previous findings to pick and choose from, it is not surprising that lists of citations can be provided in support of any number of contradictory claims. Competently conducted meta-analysis avoids cherry-picking by including large numbers of studies selected by study features rather than by study results. Meta-analysis also allows us to see trends across studies, making convergence in results visible. It reveals idiosyncratic findings as just that. Apparently contradictory results can be seen in the context of more general patterns. Finally, meta-analysis provides a big-picture overview of research that often cannot be seen when looking at individual results. It provides a context for understanding specific findings. For these reasons and more (e.g., greater statistical power, increased precision in point estimation, detection of publication bias and other artifacts), meta-analyses are given priority in this review.

Even with meta-analysis, however, caution is still needed in the interpretation research findings. If all studies share a common feature or practice, the trend across studies will reflect that commonality. Results are always constrained by the methods used to produce the findings, and until new methods are tried, limitations that extend across literatures can be invisible. Such is almost certainly the case with the research reviewed in this chapter and the next.

It is not so much that the findings are flawed or invalid. Instead, findings and conclusions are limited by constraints imposed by the research methods that have become conventional over time, and by what I believe are theoretically myopic understandings of deception. As the book progresses, I will point out some of these limitations, their implications, ways to overcome them, and empirical evidence that once overcome, new insights are gained. For now, let me lead you through a tour of the historical mainstays of prior deception research.

DECEPTION CUES

By *deception cues* I mean objective, observable, parsed or delineated behaviors that are statistically associated with (a) folk wisdom regarding what liars do, (b) people's truth–lie assessments, and/or (c) the act of lying as opposed to telling the truth. That is, deception cues are specific behaviors thought to, or used to, rightly or wrongly distinguish truths from lies. Research has shown that folk wisdom regarding deception cues does not neatly map onto what people actually rely on when making truth–lie judgments and that none of these corresponds fully with the behaviors that do and do not actually differentiate honest messages from lies. But these three sets of cues are not totally independent either. This chapter considers separately the issues of folk beliefs, relied-upon cues, and the actual utility of cues, while also considering the overlap between these sets of behaviors.

Examples of cues include nonverbal behaviors such as direction of gaze, self-touching, foot wiggling, particular facial expressions, and tone of voice. Cues can also be verbal-linguistic, such as pronoun usage, negations, or the number of details provided in an account of an event. Obviously, human behavior can be categorized or scaled in any number of different ways, and thus the number of different cues that can be studied is large. One meta-analysis, for example, identified 158 different cues that had been investigated in research prior to 2003.[1] A more recent meta-analysis of just linguistic cues found 202 such cues including 79 that were nonredundant and studied in at least four prior independent investigations.[2]

Although cues can be verbal or nonverbal, nonverbal cues have clearly been the primary focus of prior cue research, especially prior to 2000. I think there are two interrelated reasons for the historical emphasis on nonverbal cues. First, folk wisdom about deception detection holds that nonverbal behaviors are useful in spotting liars. Second, and perhaps as a result, a disproportionate number of the researchers who have studied deception over the years happen also to have long-standing interests in nonverbal communication. Leading deception researchers such as Paul Ekman, Bella DePaulo, and Judee Burgoon are known not only for their deception research but also for more general work on nonverbal communication. It is natural that they would integrate their thinking on nonverbal communication and deception. But, because of pervasive folk beliefs and because influential researchers were especially interested in nonverbal communication, the research has skewed in that direction.

It is worth emphasizing that the cues discussed in this chapter are probabilistically related to deception and perceptions of deception rather than necessarily or invariably linked to deception or veracity assessment. That is, the research tells us about statistical trends over large numbers of people rather than about the behaviors, perceptions, or beliefs of specific people. For example, vocal pitch appears to be one of the more reliable cues to actual deception.[3] On average, liars tend to have more highly pitched voices when they are lying than the voices of people who are speaking honestly. This does not mean that people with high voices lie more than people with deeper voices or that if someone's vocal pitch increases, they are beginning to tell a lie. On average, lies are slightly but significantly more highly pitched than honest statements, all else being equal.

It is very common in the social sciences, and deception research is no exception, to focus on "significant differences." A result that is labeled "statistically significant" is one where the extent of difference or statistical association is improbable (usually, 5% or less) assuming no difference or association at all. Statistical significance refers to the probability of a finding conditional on the statistical nil-null hypothesis being true. This means that presuming there was just one focal test conducted, there is a 95% or better chance that the finding would not have been obtained if there were really no difference or association. In terms of effect size, which is discussed below, a result that is significant is unlikely to be a difference of exactly $d = 0.00$.[4]

It is good and useful to know that some finding is not literally zero, but such knowledge is very limited, and it can be misleading to make the inferential leap from not-zero to something important. If you have one penny, you are not flat broke, but that penny will not take you very far or buy you much. Having a few dollars and being a millionaire are very different economic situations even though both are not zero money. So, if some finding is not zero, we want to know how big the finding is, and statistical significance does not tell us this. For this reason, in understanding statistical trends or probabilistic relationships, perhaps the most critical consideration is effect size.

Effect sizes tell us the strength of statistical association. In the case of deception cues, effect sizes tell us how much difference there is in the observation of the cue between truths and lies. Obviously, the larger the effect size associated with a given cue, the more useful that cue. A nondeception example of a very large effect size is that men tend to be taller than women. One source lists the sex difference in height as $d = 1.72$.[5] Even the strongest deception cues are much, much weaker than this. The difference in vocal pitch, for example, is $d = 0.21$.[6] But even a difference as large as the difference in height between men and women is still probabilistic if we want to apply the general trend to specific people. For example, if we know there are two people in a room, and we know that one is taller than the other, how likely is it that the taller person is male and the shorter person is female? We can't be sure, right? Both could be males, both could be females, or there could be one male and one female. All we know is that the two people are not the same height and that, on average, men are taller than women. From this information we can only play the odds, and we might guess that the taller person is male and the shorter person female. We also need to remember that this is a guess based on probabilistic information and that some women are tall, some men are short, and some women are taller than some men. And vocal pitch (or any other deception cue) is much less informative about honesty than height is about the biological sex of a human. Using cues as the basis for deciding that a particular person is lying about something is a tenuous and error-prone business at best.

Understanding the size of an effect size requires some context. Researchers talk about small, medium, and large effects in abstract senses, but to understand how big a difference is, it helps to ask, "Compared to what?" Let me give two real examples from deception research where I think a failure to put effect sizes in context may lead to some potentially misleading research claims.

The first example involves two experiments that were published in *Psychological Science* reporting evidence for unconscious lie detection.[7] Both experiments showed that measures of unconscious lie detection were significantly better than chance, and significantly better than an explicit lie detection task. The effect sizes for the efficacy of unconscious lie detection relative to chance were reported as $d = 0.32$ in the first experiment and $d = 0.27$ in the second experiment.

The second example is a relatively recent meta-analysis of the effectiveness of deception detection training.[8] Training improved accuracy over no training, $d = 0.50$.

Now let's provide some context. The average accuracy in deception detection experiments is 54%, a value significantly better than chance at $d = 0.42$.[9] A previous meta-analysis of deception detection training reported that training improved accuracy from 54% to 58%, and the effect size for that improvement was $r = 0.20$.[10] An effect size of $r = 0.2$ converts to $d = 0.41$. Research also shows a placebo effect for deception detection training.[11] Even bogus training can improve accuracy over a no-training control.

Put into context, the evidence for the efficacy of unconscious lie detection is actually weaker than the accuracy obtained in the average explicit deception detection task.[12] Unconscious lie detection may have been better than explicit detection in Ten Brinke's two experiments, but unconscious lie detection is less impressive than the 54% average that we will look at in the next chapter.

A training effect of $d = 0.5$ seems like a pretty substantial effect, but it is not that different from what was found in a previous meta-analysis, and in terms of bottom-line accuracy, that's an improvement from about 54% accuracy in no-training controls to about 59% accuracy with training. Further, that gain is over no training, not a placebo control. In both cases the findings are statistically significant and the effect sizes look ample, but accuracy still falls within the slightly-better-than-chance range, training or not, conscious or unconscious.

Before we get into specific findings from cue research, it is also important to remember that cues are not enacted in isolation, even though they are often treated this way in the literature. That is, cues are often discussed, and treated statistically, as if they are independent from one another.[13] But cues can be highly intercorrelated, and they present as constellations of cues and are interpreted by others as a package. I call these constellations of cues that create impressions *demeanor*.[14] Demeanor is discussed in greater detail in chapter 13. For now, keep in mind that when we talk about this cue or that cue, cues do not travel alone but instead in groups, and people's impressions and judgments rest more on overall demeanor than on any specific cue.

Folk Beliefs about Deception Cues

The definitive research study of the cues that people associate with deception was done by Charlie Bond.[15] Bond's study was a truly amazing undertaking, both in its scope and in its findings. He investigated the stereotypes and folk beliefs people hold about liars and deception cues. With the help of eighty-nine co-researchers from around the world, data were collected in seventy-five different countries using forty-three different languages. In all, data were collected from 4,840 subjects across two studies.

In the first study, forty subjects (twenty males and twenty females) from each of fifty-eight different countries were surveyed and asked a simple open-ended question: "How can you tell when people are lying?" In locations where English was not the dominant language, the question was translated into the local language, and the answers were translated back to English. Multiple answers were allowed. The 2,320 subjects gave 11,157 responses that were classified into one of 103 different categories of answers.

Far and away, the most frequent answer was that a liar won't look you in the eye, or in other words, liars avert their gaze. Nearly two-thirds of the people (63.7%) mentioned eye behavior of this type as a signal to deception. The next-most-common answer was nervousness, mentioned by a mere 28% of the people. Behaviors such as incoherent speech, body movements, facial expressions, speech errors, logical inconsistencies, blushing, and pauses and delayed speech were listed by between 15% and 25% of those surveyed.

The findings were remarkably consistent across the different countries. Gaze aversion was listed as the top-ranked response in fifty-one of the fifty-eight countries, and gaze aversion was listed as a cue in every country where the data were collected. The cross-country reliability of the responses was an astounding $\alpha = .98$.

Some responses were surprisingly uncommon. Fewer than 1% of respondents gave answers that involved group membership (politicians, ethnic minorities, etc.), motivational factors, or confessions. These last two are striking, because experimental work shows that motivation and confessions strongly impact assessments of honesty and dishonesty.[16] However, as we will see in the next section, folk beliefs do not map perfectly onto cue reliance or cue utility.

In their second study, a survey was constructed with close-ended questions and was distributed to forty men and women in each of sixty-three different countries. Research subjects were presented with a list of cues and asked whether liars, compared to honest people, do such things more often, less frequently, or about the same. Again, gaze aversion was the number one most common deception belief, with 71.5% of people worldwide agreeing that liars have less eye contact. Approximately two-thirds of subjects also answered that liars shift their posture more than usual, liars touch and scratch themselves (these are "adaptors" in the nonverbal literature), and liars talk too much. About half of the people thought liars act nervous.

There are a number of striking aspects of these results. I think the finding that will be the most surprising for most people is the degree of convergence across cultures. Even people who know very little about nonverbal communication and cross-cultural communication know that nonverbal communication is culturally dependent. But, when it comes to deception, research shows more cross-cultural similarity than differences. In my work on honest demeanor, I too have found an amazing degree of similarity in the nonverbal styles of believable and deceptive-looking people across language and country.[17]

A second noteworthy finding is that people everywhere believe that deception cues are mostly nonverbal. Although verbal cues such as logical inconsistencies are mentioned, the primacy of nonverbal behaviors (eyes, face, body,
hands, and voice) is clear and pronounced. This primacy of nonverbal folk cues
was also evident in an earlier meta-analysis of beliefs about deception.[18] In
that analysis, strong beliefs (effect sizes $d > 1.00$) included liars (compared to
honest speakers) doing more self-touching, making more speech errors, talking faster, and making more posture shifts, more pausing, and less eye contact. Thus, from the vantage of folk wisdom, people believe that observation
of nonverbal behavior is the best way to tell whether someone is lying or not.
From a research marketing point of view, social scientists arguing for nonverbal deception cues, as well as pop-psych lie detection gurus, have an easy sales
pitch when claiming nonverbal cues as the path to lie detection.

A third interesting observation is that changing up the question asked to
participants produces very different sorts of answers. Bond asked people, "How
can you tell when people are lying?" When the question is changed to something like "Think of a time when you found out you were lied to. How did you
discover the lie?" the answers shift to verbal signals like confessions and content inconsistency with knowledge.[19] Thus, there seems to be a strong discon-
nect between folk beliefs about what liars do and what people actually do to
catch liars. There is more on how people really detect deception in chapter 14.

A final point to make about Bond's findings is that even though avoiding
eye contact is the most widely held belief about deception, it holds no actual
utility as a deception cue. Its validity is zero. The amount of eye contact is unrelated to actual lying ($d = 0.01$).[20] This, of course, raises the question, Why
are people's folk beliefs about deception so very wrong?

Cues Linked with Judgments of Truths and Lies

Unlike folk beliefs of deception cues, where there is a single, go-to study with
simple and clear findings, the empirical story of cues linked with veracity assessment is more complex and multifaceted. Research on folk cues generally
uses survey methods where people are asked what they think liars do. Research
on cues linked with judgments, in contrast, tends to be experimental and behavioral. In a prototypical experiment, people might be shown several videotaped statements (some of which are actually honest, and others are lies) and
asked to make a judgment about which are true and which are lies. The behaviors of the senders (people making the statements) can then be coded for cues
by the researchers. How much eye contact did they have? Did they act nervous?
Researchers then look at what the senders were doing in relation to how of-

TABLE 2.1. CUES THAT AFFECT TRUTH-LIE JUDGMENTS

Cue	Zuckerman et al. (1981)	Hartwig and Bond (2011)
Gaze	0.45 (H)	0.30 (H)
Posture shifts	0.50 (L)	0.18 (L)
Response latency	0.36 (L)	0.37 (L)
Speech rate	0.67 (L)	0.43 (L)
Speech errors	0.27 (L)	0.52 (L)
Speech hesitations	0.58 (L)	0.56 (L)
Plausibility	—	1.06 (H)
Logical coherence	—	0.72 (H)
Involvement	—	0.93 (H)
Vocal uncertainty	—	0.95 (L)
Friendliness	—	0.74 (H)
Cooperation	—	0.90 (H)
Nervousness	—	0.63 (L)

Note: Numerical findings are the effect size *d* for each cue. (H) indicates cues where increases are linked to judgments of honesty and (L) cues are associated with lie judgments. The dashes were not included in the earlier meta-analysis. All reported effects are statistically significant at $p < .05$.

Sources: Maria Hartwig and Charles Bond, "Why Do Lie-Catchers Fail? A Lens Model Meta-analysis of Human Lie Judgments," *Psychological Bulletin* 137, no. 4 (July 2011): 643–59, http://dx.doi.org:10.1037/a0023589; Miron Zuckerman, Bella M. DePaulo, and Robert Rosenthal, "Verbal and Nonverbal Communication of Deception," in *Advances in Experimental Social Psychology* 14, edited by Leonard Berkowitz, 1–59 (New York: Academic Press, 1981).

ten a sender was seen as honest or deceptive by judges. Sender behaviors that predict judges' truth-deception assessments are cues linked with judgments.

When considering specific cues linked with judgments, there are two meta-analyses on the topic, and even though the two meta-analyses were published thirty years apart, the findings are reasonably consistent.[21] Table 2.1 list cues and impressions that are associated with truth and lie judgments across studies as of 1981 and 2011. People are more likely to attribute deceit to speakers who avoid eye contact, shift posture more often, take longer to respond, talk faster, make more speech errors, have more pauses and hesitations, have less plausible content, contradict themselves, are less conversationally involved, convey uncertainty in their voices, are less friendly and cooperative, and act nervous.

There are many similarities between the folk-wisdom cues and the judged-as-deception cues, but there are also some interesting differences. Cues like eye contact, nervousness, speech errors, coherence, response latencies, and hesitations show up in both sets. Plausibility shows up as the strongest cue affecting judgments, however, and gaze avoidance loses its prominence. Also, judgments seem to be influenced more strongly by gestalt impressions (involved and engaged, friendly, cooperative, confident, calm rather than nervous) than specific cues (avoids eye contact, shifts posture, makes speech errors). In my own research on demeanor,[22] I have found that these gestalt impressions and specific cues tend to be highly intercorrelated with one another, and it is behaviors in combination that really matter. That is, people who are believable enact the believable-appearing behaviors as a package or a set, while people who tend to be judged as deceptive do many things in combination that make them less believable. In our first demeanor experiment (TDT experiment twenty-nine, described in chapter 13), for example, the difference in truth–lie judgments between the honest and the deceptive demeanor senders was a whopping $d = 2.58$! It is constellations of behaviors that influence the honesty and deception judgments, and the impact of these constellations is massive, vastly stronger than the impact of even the most potent single cue in isolation.

Further, assessments of honesty–deception rest not only on the number of cues but also on how the cues change (or not) over time. In one of my favorite studies that is almost never cited, Henningsen and colleagues (including a friend of mine from graduate school, Mike Cruz) showed research subjects videotapes of mock witnesses being questioned by an attorney.[23] The content of the testimony was constant, but the nonverbal cues of the witnesses were varied. Some witnesses exhibited consistent folk deception cues (adaptors, gaze aversion, nonfluent speech), some avoided these deception cues, and some were inconsistent in their nonverbal presentation, showing the cues for some answers and not others. Inconsistent nonverbal performances were seen as more deceptive than consistent performances, even performances that were consistently deceptive looking ($d = 0.63$).

Behaviors That Actually Distinguish Truths and Lies

The third set of cues to discuss is probably of the most interest to many readers. These are cues that do or do not actually distinguish truths and lies. There is plenty of prior research on cues' actual validity-utility in distinguishing truths and lies, and this research has been summarized in four different meta-analyses. The first meta-analysis, published in 1981,[24] examined nineteen different cues that had been studied anywhere between two and sixteen times each. This first meta-analysis found that eight of the nineteen cues showed statistically significant differences between truths and lies. For more than twenty years, the 1981 meta-analysis was the go-to source for deception cues. In 2003 deception cues were again assessed, this time by Bella DePaulo and her colleagues.[25] The 2003 meta-analysis examined 158 cues or impressions from 120 different samples. Individual cues had been studied anywhere from three to forty-nine times. Two additional meta-analyses were published in 2006 and 2007 but were smaller in scale than the 2003 analysis.[26]

The results across the four meta-analyses are summarized in Table 2.2. Cues are split into three groups: cues that show consistent differences between truths and lies across meta-analyses, cues that are significant in one meta-analysis but not others, and cues where the meta-analyses all agree that there is little difference between truths and lies.

Looking across the four meta-analyses, two cues have consistently been found to distinguish lies from truth. Liars exhibit higher vocal pitch and increased pupil dilation. There were huge effects for these cues in 1981, but as the research has progressed, the cumulative effects have diminished and are no longer large. Thus, the best scientific evidence to date suggests that vocal pitch and pupil dilation are small but real cues to deception.[27]

There is also a set of cues that show up as statistically significant in one meta-analysis but not the others. It is hard to know what to make of some of these inconsistencies. Take, for example, hand movements. In 2003 the effect is $d = 0.00$. In 2007 the effect is reported as $d = 0.38$. This is not a large effect, but it was bigger than most (and was in fact the largest effect reported in that particular meta-analysis), and it was highly statistically significant, $p < .001$. It is hard to reconcile how the cumulative across-study evidence can point to both zero and significantly not-zero. If pushed, we might guess that maybe a lot of supportive evidence accumulated between 2003 and 2007 to push the effect from 0.00 to 0.38. A closer look at the details of the studies producing these conflicting findings shows that this cannot be the case. The 2003 $d = 0.00$ effect is based on 951 subjects from twenty-nine studies, while the 2007 $d = 0.38$ effect is based on 308 subjects from just five prior studies. We see the same pattern for response latency. The smaller effect in 2003 is based on more evidence than the larger effect in 2006 and 2007. Still, the pattern is not consistent across cues.

Methodological choices may explain some of the differences between the DePaulo and the Sporer–Schwandt meta-analyses. It is an unfortunate fact that many published articles do not report statistical findings in sufficient detail for use in meta-analysis, and the different meta-analyses dealt with the problem differently. The DePaulo meta-analysis threw a very wide net and included

TABLE 2.2. VALIDITY OF DECEPTION CUES IN SIGNALING ACTUAL DECEPTION

Cue	Zuckerman et al.	DePaulo et al.	Sporer and Schwandt
Consistent Differences between Truths and Lies			
Pupil dilation	1.49*	.39*	—
Pitch	2.26*	.21*	.18*
Mixed findings			
Adaptors	.40*	.01	.04
Head nods	—	.01	.18*
Hand movements	—	.00	.38*
Foot and leg movements	.06	.09	.13*
Response latency	.13	.02	.21*
Illustrators	.12	.14*	.03
Repetitions	—	.21*	.17
Shrugs	.48*	.04	—
Speech errors	.23*	.17	.08
Consistent No-Difference			
Eye contact/gaze	.11	.01	.02
Blinks	.61	.07	.01
Head movements	.27	.02	.12
Smile	.09	.00	.06
Posture shift	.08	.05	.02
Response length	.12	.03	.08
Speech rate	.02	.07	.02
Filled pauses	—	.00	.08
Unfilled pauses	—	.04	.03

Note: Findings are the absolute value of the effect size *d*. * are findings that are statistically significant at $p < .05$. The results are from Miron Zuckerman, Bella M. DePaulo, and Robert Rosenthal, "Verbal and Nonverbal Communication of Deception," in *Advances in Experimental Social Psychology* 14, ed. Leonard Berkowitz (New York: Academic Press, 1981), 1–59; Bella M. DePaulo, James J. Lindsay, Brian E. Malone, Laura Muhlenbruck, Kelly Charlton, and Harris Cooper. "Cues to Deception," *Psychological Bulletin* 129, no. 1 (January 2003): 74–118, http://dx.doi:10.1037/0033–2909.129.1.74; Siegfried Ludwig Sporer and Barbara Schwandt, "Moderators of Nonverbal Indicators of Deception: A Meta-analytic Synthesis," *Psychology, Public Policy, and Law* 13, no. 1 (February 2007): 1–34, https://doi.org/10.1037/1076–8971.13.1.1, and "Paraverbal Indicators of Deception: A Meta-analytic Synthesis," *Applied Cognitive Psychology* 20, no. 4 (May 2006): 421–46, https://doi.org/10.1002/acp.1190.

studies where effect sizes could not be measured precisely. Findings that were "non-significant" with no other information were considered to have zero effect. Studies where the direction of effect but not size of effect were discerned were given the smallest possible non-zero effect ($d = \pm 0.01$). This made the DePaulo meta-analysis much more extensive in that it included many more prior findings but it also biased the results downward to some unknown extent. The extent of the bias likely varies from cue to cue, but as many as 41% of the estimates may have been underestimates. Thus, the DePaulo meta-analysis is best considered a lower-bound estimate.[28]

Sporer–Schwandt, in contrast, used only estimates of effects that could be estimated precisely and thus included a much smaller slice of the prior research. The nature of reporting practices is such that detailed findings are more likely to be reported when findings are "significant" than when they are not. Thus, larger findings were more likely to find their way into the Sporer–Schwandt analysis. Therefore, while Sporer–Schwandt provides a more precise estimate of the effects that can be precisely estimated, it is very likely that those meta-analyses overestimate cues' effects (because smaller findings are less likely to be included). For this reason, the Sporer–Schwandt results are probably best considered an upper-bound estimate. In cases where Sporer–Schwandt provides larger estimates than DePaulo, my best guess is that the truth lies somewhere in between. In the cases where DePaulo found larger effects, there was presumably little downward bias, and those numbers might provide the best estimate given the larger sample.

The inconsistencies also point to something I have long observed. Cue findings are ephemeral. They are highly significant in one study, only to vanish or even reverse in the next. And, the trend is, the more evidence, the smaller the effect. We will explore this in more detail in the next section, on the decline effect.

The third set of cues produces a consistent lack of difference between truths and lies. Cues like eye contact, smiling, posture shifts, and speech rate show no significant differences and small effects across meta-analyses. It is scientifically safe to conclude that these behaviors do not signal honesty or deceit. Although in statistics we do not accept the literal null hypothesis of $d = 0.00$, we can have a high degree of confidence that the true population effect is near zero.

Table 2.3 lists all the cues from the DePaulo meta-analysis that had been studied at least ten times. The criterion of ten or more prior studies is arbitrary, but because cue findings are shifty, I just don't have much confidence in findings based on fewer data than that. Table 2.3 lists some statistically sig-

TABLE 2.3. ASSOCIATIONS BETWEEN CUES AND ACTUAL LYING

Cue	Number Prior Studies	Effect Size (d)	Heterogeneous
Details	24	−.30*	Yes
Verbal-vocal uncertainty	10	+.30*	No
Nervousness	16	+.27*	Yes
Vocal tension	10	+.26*	Yes
Vocal pitch	21	+.21*	Yes
Fidgeting	14	+.16*	Yes
Illustrators	16	−.14*	No
Facial pleasantness	13	−.12*	Yes
Foot and leg movements	28	−.09	
Speech rate	23	+.07	
Blinking	17	+.07	
Nonverbal immediacy	11	−.07	
Posture shifts	29	+.05	
Response length	49	−.03	
Self-references	12	−.03	
Response latency	32	+.02	
Head movements	14	−.02	
Relaxed posture	13	−.02	
Eye contact	32	+.01	
Self-fidgeting	18	−.01	
Head nods	16	+.01	
Silent pauses	15	+.01	
Hand movements	29	.00	
Smiling	27	.00	
Non-ah speech errors	17	.00	
Filled pauses	16	.00	

Note: * p < .05.

Note: Cues studied at least ten times.

Source: Bella M. DePaulo, James J. Lindsay, Brian E. Malone, Laura Muhlenbruck, Kelly Charlton, and Harris Cooper. "Cues to Deception," *Psychological Bulletin* 129, no. 1 (January 2003): 74–118, http://dx.doi:10.1037/0033-2909.129.1.74

nificant cue effects, but most cues are not significant (even cumulated across ten or more studies), and those that are significant typically show small and heterogeneous effects. Heterogeneous effects are those that vary significantly from study to study.

A Decline Effect for Cues

I have long noticed that cue findings are erratic. As a graduate student, I was especially impressed by one particular cue experiment by deTurck and Miller.[29] They used an unusually realistic method for generating truths and lies, and also developed a way to control for nondeception arousal. The results showed six cues that differentiated not only between truths and lies but also between aroused truths and lies. The six cues were adaptors, hand gestures, speech errors, pauses, response latencies, and message duration. What's more, the effect sizes ranged from $d = 0.72$ to $d = 1.18$. These were big, strong effects! But I was also aware of the meta-analysis findings at the time.[30] Cumulative findings across studies were uniformly weaker in meta-analysis, and the response latency and duration findings did not hold up as significant in meta-analysis. So, which findings should we believe? When the 2003 DePaulo meta-analysis was eventually published, its findings discredited both prior candidates.[31] The trend was clear: effect sizes for cues get smaller over time as evidence accumulates. Maybe the careful reader already noticed this trend in Table 2.2.

Then, several years ago, I read a popular press news story that gave me a label for what I was observing: the "decline effect."[32] The title of the article is "The Truth Wears Off," and the subtitle asks, "Is There Something Wrong with the Scientific Method?" The article recounts several documented cases of once-good findings that became harder and harder to replicate. I was sure this was happening in the deception cue literature. Then a new meta-analysis was published that conveniently listed side by side the average effect sizes and the number of studies comprising the average effect.[33] I did the correlation. It was significant and negative.[34] I contacted the authors of that new meta-analysis, and we reanalyzed their data.[35] The decline effect is real, and the effect shows up both cross-sectionally and longitudinally. This decline effect in deception cue research is graphed in figure 2.1. Each dot is a different cue. The average effect size (d) for each cue is plotted on the vertical axis, and the number of studies (k) investigating the cue is the horizontal axis. The size of the dot is proportional to the combined sample size. Larger dots correspond to larger samples. Small dots are findings based on few subjects. As you can see, the trend is very clear once graphed. As time goes by, as evidence accumulates, and as the sheer quantity of data increases, cues get weaker and weaker.

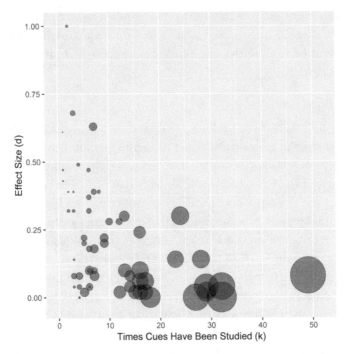

Figure 2.1. The relationship between the number of times a cue has been studied
(*k*) and its cumulative effect size (*d*) weighted by sample size.

Primary Studies Tell a Different Story than Meta-Analyses

Recent evidence suggests that it would be wrong to conclude that cues do not
distinguish truths from lies. A recent meta-analysis looked at the combined
predictive power of multiple cues for distinguishing truths from lies in 125
prior research reports yielding 144 statistical predications.[36] The findings were
unexpected, given the findings of previous meta-analyses, and very provocative.

The results were expressed in units of the multiple correlation coefficient,
R, which reflects the combined predictive power of all the cues in a given
study. The average *R* was .52, which was highly significant and substantial.
This translates to a percent-correct rate of 67.9%. Clearly, cues do distinguish
truths from lies in most studies.

The extent of predictive power varied quite a bit from study to study. The
multiple correlations uncovered ranged from near zero (*R* = .01) to almost
perfect prediction (*R* = .87). The middle 50% of findings fell between .37 and
.70, with a median of .48. Despite the variation, the results were stable across
a number of considerations. Student samples did not differ from non-student
data. The motivation to lie did not affect cue utility, and neither did the pres-

ence or absence of interaction or whether the lies were about feelings or facts. Curiously, predictability was not affected by number of cues to make the prediction or the nature of the cues (visible, written, content, vocal, or global impression). Further, most of the predictive power was carried by a single cue (r = .43 for single strongest cue, R = .52 for combined effects).

These findings seem hard to reconcile with findings that focus on the utility of specific cues. The r = .43 for the average effect for the strongest cue is equivalent to d = 0.95. As shown in Table 2.3, however, there is no evidence that any specific cue is anywhere near this strongly associated with honesty and deceit. That discrepancy is odd indeed.

I have some findings that may shed light on how cues can be predictive of deceit in specific studies, while specific cues are not consistently predictive across studies. The study was a placebo-control experiment testing the effectiveness of training people to deception detection with nonverbal cues.[37] The training findings are described toward the end of the next chapter, but here I will focus on the cue findings and the story behind the results. For our initial "valid training" condition, we picked four cues that past literature suggested were associated with deception; for our placebo training, we picked four cues that past research indicated as unrelated to deception. Subjects were trained to look for either the valid cues, the placebo cues, or no cues at all (no-training control). The results were not what we expected and were initially inexplicable. The placebo group performed better than the no-training control, but the valid training group did the worst! We then coded the truths and lies that the subjects had viewed for the cues that we had trained them in. Three of the four "valid" cues were significantly related to deception, but in the opposite way that one would have anticipated based on past research. The cues were highly "significant," but they flipped sign.

In the stimulus messages used in the bogus training experiment, we had two senders who produced four truths and four lies each. Four of eight cues showed significant differences for honesty, with effect sizes ranging from d = 0.20 to d = 0.35. But these differences were small compared to the differences between the senders. The senders differed on seven of eight cues (d = 0.41 to d = 2.72). Senders also differed in their cues from message to message within truths and within lies on four of the eight cues (d = .41 to d = 0.84). Further, there were statistically significant interactions between sender, message, and actual honesty on twenty-nine of the thirty-two possible interactions.

Consider the implications! There are cues differences, but sometimes they flip sign. What signals deception in some studies signals honesty in others. Further cues differ from person to person much more than they differ between truths and lies. And specific individuals differ from honest statement to honest statement and lie to lie. This makes trying to get a valid baseline problematic if not impossible. People are not constant in the cues over time.

The conclusion that I draw from these findings and from the various cue meta-analyses is that compelling evidence exists for the ephemeral nature of cues. At the level of the individual study investigating some set of deception cues, cues are statistically useful in distinguishing truths from lies. Cue studies reliably find cue effects that both are statistically significant and have moderate to large effect sizes, and this is true regardless of the demographics of the liar, the topic of the lies, the motivation of the liar, what the lie was about, or the particular cues studied. Yet, when specific cues are studied again, the findings do not replicate. That is, there are always cues in almost all data sets, but what those cues tell us changes from study to study, and as research accumulates over time, the utility of specific cues regresses toward zero.

SUMMARY

The purpose of this chapter is to summarize findings of prior research on deception cues, with emphasis on conclusions drawn from meta-analysis so that we might focus on the big picture and trends over time, rather than getting caught up in idiosyncratic findings. The review and discussion are organized around two key questions.

What do people look for in order to distinguish whether someone else is honest or lying? People pay much attention to nonverbal behavior when assessing honesty and deceit. In terms of specific cues, there is a worldwide, cross-cultural consensus in the folk belief that liars avoid eye contact. But when behaviors that actually influence honesty assessments are analyzed, perceptions of plausibility, logical consistency, confidence, friendliness, and conversational involvement are quite important. What's more, cues are not used in isolation, nor are they uncorrelated. Constellations of cues combine to create an honest or dishonest demeanor that guides people's decisions about whether or not someone is honest. (There is more on this in chapter 13 when sender demeanor and the BQ [believability quotient] are discussed.)

What, if any, specific behaviors actually distinguish truthful communication from lies? The short answer is, not many. The only two cues that hold up consistently across various meta-analyses are that liars have larger pupils and higher pitch, on average, than honest senders. The differences are not large enough to have much practical use in lie detection. In general, there are few behavioral differences that distinguish truths from lies, and the differences that are there are not large, are inconsistent, and tend to diminish as scientific evidence accumulates.

The next chapter addresses two additional questions:

- How accurate are people at distinguishing truths from lies?
- Under what conditions (if any) are people more accurate or less accurate at lie detection, and what types of people (if any) are more skilled or less skilled lie detectors?

3

Deception Detection Accuracy

IN 1941 FAY AND MIDDLETON conducted what might be the first modern deception detection experiment.[1] Six speakers were each asked ten personal questions about factual matters. Right before each answer, the speaker was instructed with a flash card to lie or tell the truth. All answers were delivered over a public address system. Forty-seven students listened to each answer and were instructed to make a determination of truth or lie for each answer. Over the sixty answers and forty-seven listener-judges, 55.6% were judged correctly. The just slightly-better-than-fifty-fifty finding was the case for both male and female speakers, both male and female listeners, and same- and opposite-sex combinations of speakers and listeners.

Deception detection research really didn't take off until the 1970s, but Fay and Middleton's experiment foreshadowed the hundreds of experiments that would follow. For one thing, their results were only a couple of percentage points off the eventual across-study average, and their conclusion of only slightly-better-than-chance accuracy would be replicated over and over and over for the next seventy-five years.

Another important aspect of the Fay–Middleton study is that their method would become a prototype for how to study deception detection accuracy. In most of the studies that were to follow, there would be senders who created truthful and/or deceptive communications that would be received by people (I'll call them judges) who evaluated the messages as honest or lies. Typically, an equal number of truths and lies were presented, and accuracy was calculated as the percentage of correct judgments across truths and lies. Variations on this basic theme were accomplished by changing the nature of truths and lies being judged (e.g., topic of the lie, sender motivation, spontaneous lies vs. planned lies, etc.), changing the mode of communication (e.g., face-to-face, videotape, text messaging), or changing the judges (e.g., students, police, psychiatrists). The sender and the judges might be strangers or friends, and the sender might or might not be directly questioned by either the judge or an interviewer, and so forth. As the research progressed, more and more variations were tried, with the goal of finding what might lead to improved accuracy. The range of variations was vast, but most deception detection experiments can be understood as variants of the same theme, and most studies found results remarkably similar to those of Fay and Middleton. Improving upon slightly-better-than-chance accuracy proved elusive, at least until a few years ago. And even now that a handful of approaches to improved accuracy have been documented, most findings still have just slightly-better-than-chance accuracy.

In this chapter, my goal is simply to demonstrate the remarkable pervasiveness, tenacity, and robustness of the slightly-better-than-chance accuracy findings. I also point out several features of slightly-better-than-chance accuracy that I find provocative. I ask the reader to keep in mind that a viable scientific theory of deception must provide a coherent account of the findings described here and that a viable theory cannot be contradicted by reliable empirical findings. Thus, the findings described here provide standards for assessing the empirical adequacy of the theories and approaches explained in subsequent chapters.

It is helpful to be explicit up front about how outcomes are typically scored in most deception detection experiments: messages are either honest or outright lies, and judges are asked to judge each message as either honest or lie. The task and the scoring are very much like a true-false test. Honest messages judged as honest, and lies judged as lies, are scored as correct. Honest messages scored as lies, and lies scored as honest, are incorrect. Overall raw accuracy, or just "accuracy," for short, is the percentage of judgments that are correct averaged across all messages. That is, accuracy is the percentage of correct truth–lie classifications. Truth accuracy and lie accuracy refer to scores for just the truthful messages or only the lies, respectively. Finally, truth-bias is the percent of messages judged as honest.

There are several meta-analyses of deception detection accuracy.[2] Of these, the one I find most useful is the 2006 Bond and DePaulo meta-analysis. It summarized almost three hundred findings cumulated from 206 works involving almost 25,000 judgments of over four thousand senders. It is very thorough, and its findings are widely accepted. It offers a clear picture of the sixty-four years of research from the publication of Fay and Middleton's study through 2006. Other meta-analyses shed additional light on some specific issues, but the Bond and DePaulo 2006 analysis gives us the clearest view of the big picture.

Bond and DePaulo document and summarize strong evidence for the robust nature of the slightly-better-than-chance accuracy finding in deception detection experiments. The mean percentage of truth–lie judgments that were correct was 53.98% unweighted and 53.46% when weighted by the number of judgments constituting each sample. The population standard deviation was estimated to be 4.52%, and the 95% confidence interval around the weighted mean was 53.3% to 53.6%. In terms of the spread of findings, the first and third quartiles were 50.0% and 58.0%, meaning that half of all findings fell within this narrow range. Ninety percent of all findings fell within 45% and 64%, and findings below 39% and above 67% were in the bottom and top 1%, respectively. The distribution of these findings is graphed in figure 1.1 in the first chapter. As it illustrates, most prior results fall closely around the across-study average. "Slightly-better-than-chance" concisely yet accurately describes the large number of findings summarized by the Bond and DePaulo meta-analysis.

Although the 54% average clearly reflects poor performance, accuracy is nevertheless statistically significantly better than chance. The null hypothesis of fifty-fifty mere chance can be ruled out with a high degree of statistical confidence ($p < .0001$). People are better than chance in deception detection experiments, and the effect size for the difference between the average accuracy and chance is about $d = 0.40$.

The statistical conclusion that accuracy is substantially better than chance seems incongruous with the substantive conclusion that accuracy is poor. This apparent paradox causes much confusion in the literature, and it requires explanation. Why this is the case may not be obvious or intuitive. For the record, here is what is actually going on. The calculation of statistical differences (both statistical significance and effect size) involves the ratio of the size of the difference relative to variability. Large effects can be "large" because the differences (in this case, between observed accuracy and chance) are big or because variability is small (i.e., everyone performs similarly). In terms of statistical significance, the difference between observed accuracy and chance (typically 3% or 4%) is divided by the standard error of the difference. This standard error is, in turn, determined by the sample size and the standard deviation. In most areas of social scientific research, individual variation is substantial, so small differences can be significant only when the sample size is large.

Deception detection is different.[3] There is typically not much individual variation in deception detection experiments, so the standard deviation of accuracy tends to be small. Because the standard deviation is small, the standard error is small, and the ratio of the difference from chance to the standard error is large. Consequently, differences of 3% or 4% that are small in an absolute sense are large in the statistical sense of being much larger than the differences expected by chance given the minuscule variability in individual performance. Stated differently, individual variability is minimal, so even small differences are statistically significant even with small samples.

A similar explanation accounts for the effect size associated with the difference between obtained accuracy and chance. Effect sizes are some ratio of "effect variance" to "total variance," where the total is "effect variance" plus "error variance." In deception detection experiments, the lack of "within variance" associated with difference in individual performance makes error variance small and the effect-to-total ratio relatively large.

The apparent paradox of small absolute differences that are statistically large creates much confusion. Researchers often rely on statistical significance as the standard for scientific evidence and are quick to make the leap from a statistically significant difference to a pragmatically useful difference, even though the second does not necessarily follow from the first. Confusion is further created by arbitrary rules of thumb where $d = 0.4$ is a "medium" effect size. The result is incoherent thinking in which 54% accuracy is dismissed as not much better than a coin flip, while findings that are $p < .001$ or $d = 0.4$ are heralded as strong evidence for important effects, even though the 54% is $p < .0001$ and $d = 0.42$. The confusions are compounded when the focus is on the findings of individual experiments without placing results into the larger context of the research literature.

As a result, there are a number of variables that make a "statistically significant difference" in terms of accuracy, but few of these make more than a few percentage points' difference or produce findings other than slightly-better-than-chance accuracy. The research literature is full of "significant differences" between trivial gradations of slightly-better-than-chance accuracy. Table 3.1 lists the accuracy associated with several well-researched potential moderators of deception detection accuracy.

MEDIUM/MODALITY

Communication medium and the related ideas of cue availability-exposure and media affordances have probably been the single most often studied class of predictor variable in the deception detection accuracy literature. Many deception theories specify that deception can be detected based on various types of deception cues. The key idea is that not all types of cues are available in all

TABLE 3.1. SLIGHTLY-BETTER-THAN-CHANCE DECEPTION DETECTION ACCURACY

Across-Study Average	53.46%[1]
Video only	50.4%[1]
Audio only	53.8%[1]
Audio-visual	54.0%[1]
Little sender motivation	53.4%[1]
Motivated senders	53.3%[1]
Spontaneous lies	53.1%[1]
Planned lies	53.8%[1]
No exposure to baseline honest behaviors	53.0%[1]
Exposure to an honest baseline	54.6%[1]
Student and non-expert samples	53.3%[1]
Students as judges	54.2%[2]
Expert judges	53.8%[1]
Expert judges	55.5%[2]

[1] Charles F. Bond Jr. and Bella M. DePaulo, "Accuracy of Deception Judgments," *Personality and Social Psychology Review* 10, no. 3 (August 2006): 214–34, https://doi.org/10.1207/s15327957pspr1003_2.

[2] Michael G. Aamodt and Heather Custer, "Who Can Best Catch a Liar?" *Forensic Examiner* 15, no. 1 (Spring 2006): 6–11.

[3] Maria Hartwig, Pär Anders Granhag, Leif A. Strömwall, and Aldert Vrij, "Police Officers' Lie Detection Accuracy: Interrogating Freely versus Observing Video," *Police Quarterly* 7, no. 4 (December 2004): 429–456, https://doi.org/10.1177/1098611104264748.

[4] Norah E. Dunbar, Matthew L. Jensen, Judee K. Burgoon, Katherine M. Kelley, Kylie J. Harrison, Bradley J. Adame, and Daniel Rex Bernard, "Effects of Veracity, Modality, and Sanctioning on Credibility Assessment during Mediated and Unmediated Interviews," *Communication Research* 42, no. 5 (July 2015): 649–74, https://doi.org/10.1177/0093650213480175.

[5] Steven A. McCornack and Malcolm R. Parks, "Deception Detection and Relationship Development: The Other Side of Trust," in *Communication Yearbook 9*, edited by Margaret L. McLaughlin, 377–89 (Beverly Hills: Sage, 1986).

[6] Steven A. McCornack and Timothy R. Levine, "When Lovers Become Leery: The Relationship between Suspicion and Accuracy in Detecting Deception," *Communication Monographs* 57, no. 3 (September 1990): 219–30.

[7] Timothy R. Levine, David D. Clare, Tracie Green, Kim B. Serota, and Hee Sun Park, "The Effects of Truth-Lie Base Rate on Interactive Deception Detection Accuracy, *Human Communication Research* 40, no. 3 (July 2014): 350–372, https://doi.org/10.1111/hcre.12027.

TABLE 3.1 CONTINUED

Expert questioning in Hartwig et al. (2004)	56.7%[3]
Expert questioning in Dunbar et al. (2013)	59.0%[4]
Romantic partners	59.0%[5]
	58.4%[6]
Friends	64.2% to 65.4%[7]
No interaction	52.6%[1]
Observed interaction with third party	54.0%[1]
Mere interaction with judge	52.8%[1]
Probing questions	49.0% to 57%[8]
Cognitive load inductions	
reverse order	58%[9]
keep eye contact	53.5%[10]
unanticipated questions	58.7%[11]
Nonverbal training to detect lies	58.0%[12]
Placebo training to detect lies	55.9%[13]

[8] Timothy R. Levine and Steven A. McCornack, "Behavioral Adaptation, Confidence, and Heuristic-Based Explanations of the Probing Effect," *Human Communication Research* 27, no. 4 (October 2001): 471–502.

[9] Aldert Vrij, Samantha A. Mann, Ronald P. Fisher, Rebecca Milne, and Ray Bull, "Increasing Cognitive Load to Facilitate Lie Detection: The Benefit of Recalling an Event in Reverse Order," *Law and Human Behavior* 32, no. 3 (June 2008): 253–65, https://doi.org/10.1007/s10979-007-9103-y.

[10] Aldert Vrij, Samantha Mann, Sharon Leal, and Ronald Fisher, "'Look into My Eyes': Can an Instruction to Maintain Eye Contact Facilitate Lie Detection?" *Psychology, Crime & Law* 16, no. 4 (2010): 327–48, https://doi.org/10.1080/10683160902740633.

[11] Meiling Liu, Pär Anders Granhag, Sara Landstrom, Emma Roos af Hjelmsater, Leif Strömwall, and Aldert Vrij, "'Can You Remember What Was in Your Pocket When You Were Stung by a Bee?' Eliciting Cues to Deception by Asking the Unanticipated," *Open Criminology Journal* 3, no. 3 (June 2010): 31–36, https://doi:10.2174/1874917801003010031.

[12] Mark G. Frank and Thomas Hugh Feeley, "To Catch a Liar: Challenges for Research in Lie Detection Training," *Journal of Applied Communication Research* 31, no. 1 (February 2003): 58–75, https://doi.org/10.1080/00909880305377.

[13] Timothy R. Levine, Thomas Hugh Feeley, Steven A. McCornack, Mikayla Hughes, and Chad M. Harms, "Testing the Effects of Nonverbal Training on Deception Detection Accuracy with the Inclusion of a Bogus Training Control Group," *Western Journal of Communication* 69, no. 3 (July 2005): 203–17, https://doi.org/10.1080/10570310500202355.

types of media. For example, vocal pitch is not available in text-based communication, and body language is not available in audio-only or text-based media. Thus, many theories predict differences in deception detection accuracy depending on the type of medium because different media have different affordances that provide access to different types of deception cues.

More recently, with the advent of the internet, social networks, smartphones, and various other new media, interest in media differences has been renewed and intensified. The presumption seems to be that new media have changed everything in communication. Each medium has different affordances, and conclusions from one medium may not apply to other media. The lack of differences observed in various old media has not deterred reexamination with various new media.[4]

Historically, Maier and Thurber were among the first to investigate media differences in deception detection.[5] They reported much higher accuracy for text and audio-only communication (77%) than for audio-visual communication (58%). They proposed that being able to see visual cues distracted would-be lie detectors, and advised against direct visual observation in lie detection.

By the time the first meta-analysis was reported in 1981, however, the issue of media effects and cue exposure became more complex, and the differences between media were smaller.[6] Accuracy was above chance across media with the exception of video-only, face-only presentations. Across conditions, accuracy was better than chance at $d = 0.68$.[7] Generally, exposure to the face reduced accuracy (with face, $d = 0.60$; without face, $d = 0.75$; face-only, $d = 0.05$). In contrast, visual exposure to the sender's body improved accuracy from $d = 0.53$ to $d = 0.82$. Exposure to speech (audio and content) had the largest effects, with access to speech leading to much-improved accuracy ($d = 1.14$) relative to visual-only conditions ($d = 0.21$). Access to tone of voice only ($d = .20$) and transcripts-only ($d = .70$) were also above chance, with transcripts-only yielding accuracy below full-audio ($d = 1.14$). The highest accuracy was obtained from speech-and-body-without-face ($d = 1.49$). The conclusions were that media made a difference, and that verbal content, vocal and paralinguistic information, and the observation of body language all improved accuracy. Only observation of the face was unhelpful.

Over time, however, those effects mostly dissipated. By the time of the 2006 Bond–DePaulo meta-analysis, only one difference mattered. Visual-only detection was no better than chance, while the slightly-better-than-chance accuracy conclusion held otherwise. As we can see in Table 3.1, when comparing the 54% across-study average, accuracy is (with rounding) 54% with audio-only, 54% with audio-visual, 53% with face-to-face communication and 53% with no interaction.

COMMUNICATION DURATION

Conceptually similar to the thinking regarding media/modality effects, arguments are sometimes made for interview duration.[8] Just as some media allow for more cues than others, longer communication duration allows for more cues to emerge. This line of reasoning holds that poor accuracy is expected from brief communications, but improved accuracy is possible in longer, more cue-rich communications. At least in my own research, however, interview duration is not correlated with accuracy.[9] Longer exposure to a greater number of cues does not improve accuracy if those cues have little diagnostic value.[10]

LIE STAKES

Key theories also predict that sender motivation, or "stakes," is a critical factor in lie detection. An influential theory specifies stakes as a critical prerequisite for deception detection accuracy. The logic holds that deception cues arise from lies of consequence. The deception detection research community has accepted this claim uncritically. Yet accuracy rounds to 53% for both motivated senders and unmotivated senders.[11] The existing evidence does not support the idea that lie stakes meaningfully affect accuracy.

PLANNING

One might think that planned lies would be different than spontaneous lies. Planning and preparation might make lies harder to detect, while spontaneous lies might be more transparent. Yet this does not seem to be the case either. Planned lies are detected with 54% accuracy, compared to 53% for spontaneous lies.[12] Again, accuracy is slightly better than chance regardless of planning and preparation.

BASELINE BEHAVIORS

Cue-based approaches to deception detection also predict that prior exposure to honest baseline communication should improve deception detection accuracy. The idea is that individuals have different communication styles, and assessing a person's behaviors while they're being honest enables the observation of later changes attributable to the act of lying. Observation of baseline behaviors significantly improves accuracy ($d = 0.24$), but in terms of raw accuracy, that is an improvement from 53% to 55%.[13] Again, the trend holds.

Accuracy is slightly-better-than-chance regardless of prior exposure to baseline honest behavior.

STUDENTS VS. EXPERTS

I wish I had a dollar for every time I have heard the "used-college-students-as-research-subjects" criticism applied to some social scientific finding or another. There is often a concern that findings originating from college student samples will not generalize to the broader population. In deception detection experiments, however, the characteristics of research subjects making the judgments make little difference in accuracy. I mentioned previously that individual differences in performance were small, leading to small standard errors and highly significant effects. This is true both within and across samples of judges. One meta-analysis estimates that individual differences in lie detection ability make less than a 1% difference in the percent-correct accuracy scores across studies.[14] A second meta-analysis found that judge age, experience, education, and personality were not associated with deception detection accuracy.[15] That same meta-analysis found no sex differences in lie detection ability and that students were not any different from people with careers in law enforcement. A third meta-analytic test reported mixed findings.[16] In twenty experiments involving head-to-head comparisons between expert and nonexpert judges, no differences were observed ($d = -0.03$). However, forty-two samples of expert judges produced slightly but statistically significant ($p < .05$) higher accuracy (55%) than 250 samples involving nonexpert judges (53%). In a couple experiments where experts actually did the questioning, accuracy was higher still (57% and 59%) but remained in the range of slightly-better-than-chance accuracy that typifies the larger literature.[17]

RELATIONSHIP BETWEEN THE LIAR AND THE JUDGE

The issue of the relationship between the sender and the judge has been studied and presents something of a paradox. Common sense and folk wisdom tell us that knowing a sender should facilitate deception detection accuracy. When we know another person and we know how they usually act, we may know how they act when they are lying (presuming the existence of idiosyncratic deception cues that would be invisible to meta-analysis), and we have knowledge about people we know that may make communication content useful.[18] But, as McCornack and Parks pointed out, relationships involve trust, and trust can blind us to lies.[19]

The goal of their experiment was to assess how relational closeness affected deception detection accuracy. They predicted that as people became closer,

Figure 3.1. McCornack and Parks's model of relational
closeness and deception detection.

they became more confident in their ability to read their partners. The increase in confidence produced truth-bias, that is, a tendency to believe their
partner. Truth-bias lowered accuracy. This series of causal links has come to be
known as the McCornack and Parks Model of Relationship Deception, which
is depicted in figure 3.1.

McCornack and Parks brought dating partners into the lab, separated them,
and made one the sender. The sender was videotaped making honest and deceptive answers to a series of opinion questions. The other partner, the judge,
then watched the videotaped answers, made a truth–lie judgment for each,
and also rated how confident they were in each judgment. In line with the
model, the closer the relationship, the higher the ratings of confidence; the
more confident, the greater the proportion of messages judged as honest, and
the more truth-bias was negatively associated with the percent of judgments
that were correct. These findings were subsequently replicated,[20] and the links
in the model have been supported by meta-analysis.[21] McCornack and Parks's
model is well-documented.

There is, however, a catch. In the McCornack and Parks model, relationship
closeness, albeit indirectly, reduces accuracy. Experiments using dating couples
often report accuracy levels above the meta-analysis average. For example, accuracy was 59% in the McCornack and Parks original, and 58% in a follow-up
McCornack and I did using dating partners as subjects.[22] And, in a recent series of experiments involving friends and strangers in a face-to-face lie detection task, friends (64% to 65%) performed substantially better than strangers
(48% to 55%).[23] I am not entirely sure what to make of this. Accuracy is still
in the slightly-better-than-chance range, but it seems consistently better than
the 54% average, even though the closeness-trust link is well-documented.[24]

INTERACTION BETWEEN LIAR AND DUPE

Yet another variable that had been investigated with respect to accuracy is
whether or not there is conversational back-and-forth between the sender and
the judge. Meta-analysis finds little difference in accuracy between no interaction (53%), interaction between sender and judge (53%), and a judge ob-

serving interaction between the sender and some other person (54%).[25] Several studies have investigated the related issue of asking probing questions.[26] The research consistently finds that merely asking probing questions (or hearing probing questions asked) does not affect accuracy either way, but the probed senders are more likely to be believed than senders who are not questioned. Steve McCornack and I call this finding "the probing effect," and we spent much time early in our research careers testing various explanations for the effect.[27] For the present discussion, however, it is sufficient to note that mere interaction and mere question asking have negligible impact on deception detection accuracy.

TRAINING

Various approaches have been used to train people to be better lie detectors, and three meta-analyses summarize the evidence for the efficacy of deception detection training.[28] All three meta-analyses conclude that training significantly improves accuracy over no-training controls. In the 2003 analysis, accuracy in controls matched the 54% accuracy in the literature as a whole compared to 58% for trained judges. The effect size for the improvement was $d = 0.41$. In the 2012 meta-analysis, the effect size was slightly larger ($d = 0.50$). The evidence, however, might be construed as suggesting that training just made judges more cynical. Accuracy for lies-only improved from 49% to 55% with training, but accuracy on truths dipped slightly, from 58% to 56%.[29] The most recent analysis, too, found that gains were limited to accuracy for lies; there was no improvement for truth accuracy.[30] I have found this in my own experiments.[31]

Thus, evidence suggests that training improves accuracy by 4% or 5%, but there are three big caveats. First, if the improvement from training is taken at face value, accuracy remains well within the slightly-better-than-chance range that is typical with training or not. This is a difference between getting eleven out of twenty right compared to twelve out of twenty correct. It is not very impressive. Second, training appears to affect cynicism more than ability, a finding which I find worrisome (more on this point shortly). Third, the gains are improvements over no-training controls. A more scientifically defensible design might involve a placebo control.

In 2005 I published one of my favorite deception experiments (actually, a series of experiments) testing my concerns about the deception detection training evaluation literature.[32] The experiments compared three groups of judges. Some judges received no training, some got valid training, and others were assigned to a placebo training control group. Valid training and placebo training were created in two ways: either based on the research at the time or based on coding of the cues that were actually in the specific truths and lies that composed the test materials. Valid training improved accuracy only when the training was based on cues actually present in and idiosyncratic to the materials used in the experiment. Training based on prior research findings did not help. In the case where valid training was effective, it produced an eight-point gain in accuracy over the no-training control (50% to 58%), but only a marginal improvement of the placebo control (56% vs. 58%). Further, my suspicions about training producing skepticism were borne out. Both valid training and bogus training produced a greater proportion of lie judgments than the no-training controls ($d = 0.81$). Just as in the Frank–Feeley and Hauch meta-analyses, training improvements emerged only for lies, not for truths.

TRUTH AND LIE ACCURACY

The training literature raises an important issue that I have so far skirted. When we have been talking about "deception detection accuracy," we have been talking about the percentage of correct truth–lie classifications averaged across truths and lies. This can be quite misleading, because the percentage correct for truths is often quite different from the percentage correct for lies. This is because people are typically truth-biased. We will spend much of chapters 11 and 12 on the topic of truth-bias, its causes, and its implications. For now, I need to mention that any variable that affects truth-bias will likely affect truth accuracy and lie accuracy in the opposite ways. As the proportion of messages judged as true increases, truth accuracy increases, and accuracy for lies decreases.[33] And, while overall accuracy is pretty stable from study to study, truth-bias fluctuates more substantially.[34] For this reason, when reporting raw accuracy (percentage correct), I often find it useful to present total accuracy, truth-bias, accuracy for truths only, and accuracy for lies only.

Recall that in meta-analysis the average accuracy across truths and lies is 54%. For truths only, accuracy improves to 61%; and for lies only, it dips to 47%.[35] Note that the average of truth and lie accuracy (61 + 47 = 108; 108 ÷ 2 = 54) is the overall average, and the overall average masks the difference between truths and lies. This observation led to the "veracity effect," which is the focus of chapter 12.

SIGNAL DETECTION

Because raw accuracy conflates the ability to correctly discriminate truths and lies with bias, some researchers prefer to report findings in metrics from signal detection theory. Deception detection using signal detection measures typically reports "hits," "false alarms," d' (d-prime, or sensitivity), and bias. Hits are correctly identified lies, which are identical to what I call lie accuracy. False alarms are erroneously classified truths (or 1 minus truth accuracy). Sensitivity, or d', is a statistical measure of accuracy controlling for bias and chance. Bias is a measure of the extent to which errors tip in the direction of false positives or false negatives.

In deception detection research, the average d' is .24, and d' correlates with raw percentage correct at r = .99.[36] I prefer raw accuracy (qualified by truth-bias and truth and lie accuracy scored separately) because I think it makes research findings more understandable. If I say accuracy is 54%, that is more meaningful to most people than saying accuracy is d' = .24. Further, if I report my results in signal detection metrics only, then readers who don't know signal detection math are disenfranchised. But if I report truth and lie accuracy, people who actually know and understand signal detection have all the information they need to calculate their preferred metrics. Because signal detection sensitivity and raw accuracy are so highly correlated in deception detection literature, I see little to gain from signal detection.

SCALING HONESTY AND DECEIT

Another way accuracy can be obscured is by scaling honesty ratings rather than using dichotomous truth–lie measures. With dichotomous, forced-choice truth–lie assessment, overall accuracy, accuracy for truths only, accuracy for lies only, and truth-bias (percentage true) are easily scored and interpreted (or converted to signal detection metrics if that is preferred). Some research, however, has people rate messages on scales from honest to deceptive. If people rate honest messages as more honest than lies, then they are to some extent accurate. It is hard to know how accurate. So, for example, if ratings are on a seven-point scale, where 1 is totally lying and 7 is completely honest, the average for honest messages is 5.8, and the average for lies is 5.2, and these two means are significantly different, then are people good at lie detection? Other times, researchers will ask senders to rate their own honesty, and the judge's ratings will be subtracted from sender ratings to measure accuracy. How accurate is a discrepancy score of 1.8?

The reason I think scaling honesty obfuscates findings is that it allows researchers to pass off statistical differences that might translate into very small differences in percentage correct without putting the differences into a well-understood metric or into the context of the larger literature. With percentage correct, we can compare outcomes not only to chance but also against the 54%

across-study average and the 45% to 65% range within which most results fall. With scaled honesty, we need to calculate effect sizes, and convert effect sizes into comparable units, and only then can we put findings into perspective.

I have other objections to scaling honesty in deception detection experiments beyond just clarity and transparency. I think scaling honesty tends to confound several conceptually distinct ideas. I worry that such scaling conflates perceptions of honesty with confidence, and both of these with judgments of moral condemnation. I also worry that scaled honesty measures further conflate message features (e.g., proportion of message content that is false or misleading) with perceptions of deceptive intent. So, for example, on the 1 to 7 scale (7 honest), if a subject rates a message as "3," what does that mean? Does it mean that they think it might be a lie but are not very sure? Does it mean that it is a lie, but not a big, bad lie? Does it mean that it is partly false and partly true? It could, I believe, mean any of these things, and research consumers should be highly skeptical of research claims based on ambiguous scaling of this sort.

It has been asserted for reasons that have never made sense to me that low accuracy in deception detection experiments may be a measurement artifact of dichotomous truth–lie judgments and that using honesty scaling produces higher accuracy.[37] It might be that using scaled honesty lets research find "significant results" without having to acknowledge the 50-something-percent accuracy. But, as a matter of empirical fact, accuracy is actually lower with scales than dichotomous truth–lie assessments.[38] The mean effect size reflecting improvement over chance is .42 for dichotomous measures and .34 for rating scales, a difference that is statistically significant at $p < .05$!

UNCONSCIOUS AND INDIRECT LIE DETECTION

A belief similar to the idea that accuracy is higher when scaled is the idea of implicit, indirect, less-conscious lie detection. So far we have been discussing explicit or direct lie detection experiments in which people are instructed to assess messages for honesty, most often with an either/or, truth–lie choice. As we know, accuracy in such experiments hovers around 54% and is not very impressive. The idea behind implicit deception is that while people may be poor lie detectors in direct lie detection tasks, maybe they are better at some quasi-conscious or unconscious level. In the language of Daniel Kanheman,[39] maybe system two (slow, deliberate, analytical) is a poor lie detector, but maybe system one (fast, intuitive, largely unconscious) picks up on lie clues that system two misses.

To my knowledge, the first suggestion for the superiority of implicit lie detection was Bella DePaulo's 1997 meta-analysis of confidence and deception detection accuracy. That meta-analysis found that people rated themselves as more confident in their assessments when judging truths than lies. DePaulo and colleagues describe their findings and conclusions this way:

> We also tested the hypothesis that feelings of confidence might function as measures of indirect deception detection, in that they might differentiate truths from lies. The meta-analysis of eight tests of this hypothesis produced support for this idea. Judges were substantially more confident when judging truths than lies. . . . Measures of indirect deception detection hold great promise in this field in which explicit measures of deception detection often yield unimpressive levels of accuracy. Judges who appear totally unable to distinguish truths from lies based on their explicit judgments may show some evidence of accurate discrimination based on indirect measures. Such judges may not realize that the discriminations they are making are relevant to deception, or they may simply be unwilling to explicitly call another person a liar.[40]

Since then, many authors have asserted the superiority of indirect over direct measures of deception detection.[41] Recently, an article in *Psychological Science* concluded: "Across two experiments, indirect measures of accuracy in deception detection were superior to traditional, direct measures. These results provide strong evidence for the idea that although humans cannot consciously discriminate liars from truth tellers, they do have a sense, on some less-conscious level, of when someone is lying."[42]

I am skeptical of the superiority of indirect lie detection. Both quotes above conclude that direct deception is no better than chance. This is just false. It is a straw man argument. People can directly and consciously discriminate between truths and lies with a great degree of statistical certainty. What I think is going on is an apples-and-oranges comparison. Indirect measures of accuracy are being evaluated based on significance tests. Statistically significant differences are found between truths and lies with a variety of indirect measures. Direct measures, on the other hand, are evaluated on the basis of percentage right. Fifty-four percent seems pretty darn poor. People forget that there are substantial statistical differences between 50% chance and 54%, and accuracy based on direct assessments gets morphed from the factually accurate "slightly-better-than-chance" to the empirically false "totally unable."

Along with Charlie Bond and Maria Hartwig, I recently looked at indirect lie detection effects with meta-analysis.[43] Based on 130 different estimates spanning twenty-four different indirect measures, indirect detection was significantly better than chance ($d = .23$), but it was not better than direct measures ($d = .42$). Based on these data, Charlie Bond and I wrote a reply to the *Psychological Science* article touting the advantage of indirect detection.[44]

MERE MEASUREMENT RELIABILITY

Here is another of those unappreciated but important findings. In the 2006 Bond–DePaulo meta-analysis, the best predictor by far of the accuracy reported in any given experiment was the number of judgments upon which the finding was based. The big predictor was not some theoretically important variable like cue availability, extent of interaction, sender stakes, or judge expertise. The best predictor was a methodological consideration. The greater the number of judgments in an experiment, the more closely the results approached the across-study mean of 54% accuracy. All the findings that are on the tails of the distribution in figure 1.1 have one thing in common. They are all based on a relatively few number of judgments.[45]

When plotting findings by the number of judgments, as Bond and DePaulo did, the resulting graph is called a funnel plot. To the extent that study-to-study differences are just random fluctuations, such plots look like a funnel. The principle is that there is more random variability in small sample data than in large sample data. This is related to the idea popularly known as the Law of Large Numbers.[46] Random error, however, does not show a linear decrease as sample size increases. It is more of a curve (standard error involves the square root of N, the sample size). Deception detection findings, when graphed in this way, form a nicely symmetrical funnel. The differences in findings from study to study are mostly just random noise. This finding as much as any other poses a huge challenge for deception theory. Why don't variables such as cue availability, extent of interaction, sender motivation, or judge expertise matter much? Why is slightly-better-than-chance accuracy so darn pervasive? This should also make us skeptical of non-normative accuracy findings based on small numbers of judgments.[47]

DISPERSION IN DETAIL

So far, we have been discussing accuracy mostly in terms of central tendency; that is, the average accuracy is such-and-such under this or that condition or circumstance. Our discussion of prior accuracy findings closes with thinking about deception detection in terms of variability or dispersion. In my view,

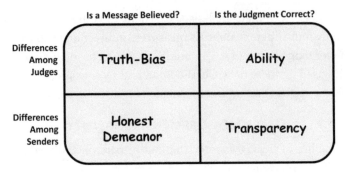

Figure 3.2. Variability in judgments of honesty and deception.

thinking about sources or components of variation in truth and lie judgments provides important and underappreciated clues about what is going on in deception detection experiments.

We know that on average people are more likely to believe others than to infer a lie (truth-bias) and that people are correct, on average, about 54% of the time. If we believe someone when they tell us something, we might believe them because we tend to believe others, or we might believe them because they seem honest. When we think someone might be lying, that might be because of us (how we are seeing things), or it might be because the liar did something that made them seem dishonest. When we correctly distinguish truth from lie, it could be because we have some skill at lie detection, or it might be because the person we are observing is a poor liar. In short, both belief and accuracy can vary due to either the sender or the person judging the sender.

I use the terms "ability" and "truth-bias" to describe differences among judges, and the terms "transparency" and "honest demeanor" to describe differences among senders. Differences in accuracy could be because of judge ability or sender transparency. Differences in honest and lie assessments might be because of judge truth-bias or sender honest demeanor. The four sources of variability are mapped out in figure 3.2

As it turns out, these four dimensions of variability differ a lot from one another in the amount they vary.[48] Generally, senders vary more than judges. Also, the proportions of messages judged as honest or deceptive vary more than the proportions of judgments that are correct or incorrect. So, the most variance is observed in sender honest demeanor, and the least amount of variance is in judge ability. Variance in truth-bias and transparency falls in between these two. This means that there are big differences in how believable some senders are. Some people are almost always believed, others are seen as dishonest, and these differences have nothing to do with actual honesty. There are some differences in how gullible judges are and some difference in how inscrutable senders are. These differences are quite a bit less pronounced than the differences in honest demeanor, but they are quite a bit larger than the differences in judge ability. As mentioned previously, differences in judge ability contribute very little to accuracy results. The lack of judge variation in ability comports with the small standard errors in deception detection research that were mentioned at the beginning of this chapter.

Understanding differences in variability provides critical insight into how we might best explain prior findings. As a general scientific rule, where there is variance, there is the potential for cause and effect. The variance is where the action is. Since the variance is more in senders than in judges, attention might be placed there for clues as to what is going on.

SUMMARY

The purpose of chapters 2 and 3 is to summarize findings of prior research on deception detection. Emphasis is on conclusions drawn from meta-analysis, so that we might focus on the big picture and trends over time, rather than getting caught up in idiosyncratic findings. This chapter answered two important questions:

How accurate are people at distinguishing truths from lies? People are slightly better than chance at distinguishing truths from lies in deception detection experiments. Accuracy is better than chance, but not by much. The across-study average is about 54% correct truth–lie discrimination.

Under what conditions (if any) are people more accurate or less accurate at lie detection, and what types of people (if any) are more skilled or less skilled lie detectors? The slightly-better-than-chance accuracy is remarkably robust and invariant. Some things make a difference of a few percentage points this way or that, but the slightly-better-than-chance holds across a wide range of conditions and methods.

Besides answering these two critical questions, this chapter also highlights some important but underappreciated findings. One of these is the small standard errors in deception detection experiments involving multiple judgments per judge. The implication is that even small differences in raw accuracy can be statistically significant with ample effect sizes. Findings need to be understood in context. Second, the number of judgments strongly impacts the results, making unusual results based on small data untrustworthy. Third, raw accuracy (i.e., correct truth–lie discrimination) and accuracy for lies are not the same thing. The implication is that if people are better than chance at truth–

lie discrimination, this does not mean that they are better than chance at recognizing lies per se. Finally, there is much more variability in senders than in judges. This suggests that viable explanations for findings need to account for both sender variability and judge constancy.

In chapter 4, various prior theories of deception and deception detection are reviewed. We can see how well these theories align with the actual findings on cues and accuracy.

4

Rivals

THIS CHAPTER AND THE NEXT describe and evaluate prior deception theory. Six prior theories of deception detection are summarized in this chapter. These are Ekman's original leakage theory, Ekman's updated perspective, four-factor theory, Bella DePaulo's self-presentation perspective, interpersonal deception theory, and Aldert Vrij's cognitive load approach. Each of these theories is reviewed chronologically, showing how ideas have evolved over time. In the next chapter, each of these theories is evaluated in relation to the prior research described in chapters 2 and 3. Also in the next chapter, I offer the catchall-umbrella idea of cue theories as a way to show the commonalities in the logic behind many of the prominent deception theories and to show how theory has shaped research priorities and design. This chapter along with the next, I hope, will make clear the need for a new theory which I, not coincidentally, offer.

Two additional deception theories, information manipulation theory (IMT) and its update, IMT2, are presented in chapter 8. IMT and IMT2 are companion theories rather than rivals and therefore are discussed elsewhere. As we will see in the next chapter, I do not consider DePaulo's self-presented perspective either a cue theory or a rival. But- her self-presentation work marked an important point in the chronology of how deception theory has evolved over time. Thus coverage of self-presentation seemed essential for telling a complete story. Consequently, even though it is not a rival, it fit well within the narrative of this chapter.

MAJOR THEORIES OF DECEPTION AND DECEPTION DETECTION

Ekman, Friesen, and Leakage

The first and perhaps the most influential theory of deception was originally described by Paul Ekman and Wallace Friesen in their 1969 article titled "Nonverbal Leakage and Clues to Deception."[1] Ekman's ideas and research have shaped deception research ever since. Most of the subsequent theories can be understood as extensions of, or variations on, the ideas of leakage and deception clues. The research designs used to examine deception-linked behaviors and deception detection accuracy were also profoundly influenced by Ekman and Friesen.[2]

Ekman's work has had the greatest impact outside academic research circles. The television drama *Lie to Me*[3] offered a fictional portrayal of lie detection closely modeled on Ekman's theory and research.[4] Readers who travel by air in the United States have probably been screened by the TSA (Transportation Security Administration) using SPOT (Screening Passengers by Observation Technique). As you approach a screening checkpoint at the airport, you may see a TSA agent just standing off to the side watching people as they approach. They are practicing SPOT, and SPOT is based, at least in part, on Ekman's theory.[5]

According to the original Ekman and Friesen articulation, a key distinction is made between *deception clues* and *leakage*.[6] Deception clues signal that deception is in progress but are not informative about the information being concealed. Leakage, in contrast, gives away the concealed information. The truth leaks out, so to speak.

For example, imagine that a witness to a crime is being interviewed by the police. The witness falsely denies seeing anything. Because the witness is nervous about lying to the police, the witness might wring his or her hands. The nervous hand-wringing behavior is a deception clue, because it signals that the person is lying, but it is uninformative about what is being concealed. Alternatively, if the hands and arms are swaying back and forth unconsciously, it might mean that he or she saw the suspect run away. This is an example of leakage. The knowledge that the suspect was seen running away leaked out.

Both leakage and deception clues may occur in both self- and other-deception. In the case of other-deception, the liar is aware of what he or she wants to conceal, and of the need not to give him or herself away. So, there will be both conscious attempts to appear honest while conveying false information and unconscious indications of deceit, because not all of our actions are completely controllable. In self-deception, people may unconsciously give the truth away, but they do not consciously convey false information.

A key aspect of Ekman's theory is that it focuses only on *high-stakes lies* and not on inconsequential or white lies. The lie must produce an emotional response in a liar to be signaled behaviorally, and this is expected only for lies

of consequence. As we will see, the theoretical requirement of high stakes became a critical issue as research progressed.

How lies are signaled is a function of the nonverbal sending capacity of a
body part and how much feedback we get regarding communication involving
that body part. Sending capacity has to do with how much can be communicated in a particular way. According to Ekman, the face is very expressive and
communicative and thus has the most nonverbal sending capacity. The hands
have less sending capacity than the face, and the feet have less still. The same
order is true about feedback. We are more likely to be conscious of our face
than our hands and more conscious of our hands than our feet.

With regard to deception clues and leakage, there are two key types of nonverbal displays: affect displays and adaptors. Affect displays, as the name implies, convey emotional states. Affect is displayed mostly on the face. With regard to deceptive affect displays, one can intensify, de-intensify, neutralize, or
substitute one emotion for another. That is, I can make my face appear hap-
pier than I really am or less happy than I really am. I can convey a lack of emotion, or I can appear happy when I am really irritated.

Emotions can also be shown in *micro facial expressions*. Microexpressions
are so brief that they are barely perceptible, and they are not fully under conscious control. Micro facial expressions can supposedly be seen by trained observers or by watching video in slow motion or frame by frame.

Adaptors are habituated body movements learned early in life when they
were adaptive and served some function. In adulthood they are enacted as fragments of the original behavior. They are done habitually and unconsciously,
and they appear to be random behaviors. Examples of adaptors include fidgeting or unconsciously playing with the self or objects.

Since the face is most expressive, with the greatest sending capacity, and is
also where we get the most feedback about our nonverbal communication performance, the face is most likely to convey deceptive messages by suppress-
ing, intensifying, or conveying faked emotion. The exception is micro facial
expressions, which can slip out and honestly express felt emotions. As Ekman
and Friesen assert, "The face is equipped to lie the most and leak the most,
and thus can be a very confusing source of information during deception."[7]
They continue that "one would expect the usual observer of the face typically
to be misled. One would expect the keen observer, on the other hand, to receive contradictory information from facial cues: simulated messages, micro
leakage of information which contradicts the simulations, and deception clues
of squelched displays and improperly performed simulations."[8]

The hands are suggested to be less under conscious control than the face and to be ill equipped to enact deception. The hands, however, can give deception away. Adaptors, especially self-adaptors, can be a sign of leakage. For example, a liar may be smiling to convey happiness, but the hands may be suggesting anxiety or defensiveness. Self-adaptors can also function as deception clues.

According to Ekman and Friesen, the legs and feet "are a primary source of both leakage and deception clues."[9] "Leakage in the legs/feet could include aggressive foot kicks, flirtatious leg displays, autoerotic or soothing leg squeezing, abortive restless flight movements. Deception clues can be seen in tense leg positions, frequent shift of leg posture, and in restless or repetitive leg and foot acts."[10] This is because although the legs have limited sending capacity, we are less aware of what our feet are doing.

This reasoning gave rise to the idea of the *leakage hierarchy*, which is at the core of Ekman and Friesen's original theory. As they describe:

> To summarize, the availability of leakage and deception clues reverses the pattern described for differences in sending capacity, internal feedback, and external feedback. The worst sender, the legs/feet, is also the least responded to and the least within ego's [self] awareness, and thus a good source for leakage and deception clues. The best sender, the face, is most closely watched by alter [other person], most carefully monitored by ego [self], most subject to inhibition and dissimulation, and thus the most confusing source of information during deception; apart from micro expressions, it is not a major source of leakage and deception clues. The hands are intermediate on both counts, as a source of leakage and deception clues, and in regard to sending capacity and internal and external feedback.[11]

Finally, Ekman and Friesen offer the caveat that their theory does not apply to everyone. They speculate that there are some people who do not leak very much and who are highly convincing nonverbal liars.

To summarize the original leakage theory, there are two types of nonverbal behaviors, leakage and deception clues, that can be used to detect deception. The usefulness of these nonverbal deception signals rests on the extent to which they are under conscious control. Leakage and deception clues are most apparent in the legs and feet and in micro facial expressions, and the least apparent in non-micro facial behavior. No attention was given to the voice.

Leakage and deception clues are expected only in high-stakes deception, and, even then, not by everyone.

As time has progressed, the original distinction between leakage cues and deception clues has faded for all but Ekman. "Leakage" has come to be used more generally as interchangeable with "deception clues," and deception clues are now often called deception cues.

However, the main idea that honest senders and liars exhibit different nonverbal behaviors and that nonverbal behavior provides the path to lie detection was incredibly influential and guided the direction of subsequent theory and research for the next forty-plus years. In the theory and research that followed, it was theorists and researchers trained primarily in nonverbal communication who contributed the most. Deception was therefore researched and understood as first and foremost a nonverbal phenomenon, and this traces directly to Ekman and Friesen.

EKMAN UPDATED

Ekman's theoretical perspective has evolved over time, and his ideas have been periodically updated in the four editions of his book *Telling Lies*, as well as in various other journal articles and book chapters.[12] The core ideas have mostly remained intact, and most of the evolution in Ekman's thinking has been in further elaboration and refinement of his ideas. The preface of the third edition of his book states that he did not believe there were any errors in previous editions. He contends that while research findings over the past forty-five years were generally supportive, new results have also provided important new insights.

Much of Ekman's more recent research on deception was done in collaboration with professors Maureen O'Sullivan and Mark Frank, who are Ekman protégés. Relative to other camps of deception theorists, Ekman and colleagues have published relatively few peer-reviewed original research studies testing their ideas. Much of what they have published has proven controversial within the deception-research community.

Perhaps the biggest change in thinking from the original 1969 theoretical statement to more recent articulations relates to the leakage hierarchy and the utility of different parts of the body in signaling deceit. In the original version, legs and feet were held to be most informative. Over time, the role of leg and foot movements lost prominence, and the focus moved increasingly to the face, especially to microexpressions, which became the primary source of leakage and deception clues. Verbal content (e.g., slips of the tongue, inconsistent content) and the voice (especially pitch) are recognized in more recent writings as sources of leakage and deception clues.[13]

Despite the changes in what is most and least informative, Ekman has retained the distinction between leakage and deception clues, and he has remained steadfast in the core idea that deception is signaled behaviorally and nonverbally. He is unequivocal about this, and he states that his confidence in the utility of behavioral observation as a deception detection method has increased over time. He also claims to have provided clear scientific-empirical support of this in his own research.[14]

Emotion has always played a key role in Ekman's thinking, and if anything, the centrality of emotion in his theoretical stance has intensified over time. Ekman contends that three emotions in particular are linked with deception: fear of being caught, guilt about lying, and "duping delight" (the positive emotional state prompted by fooling another person).

Besides leaked emotions, a second reason Ekman believes that some lies fail is because the liar has not adequately planned his or her lie. In such cases, liars often contradict themselves, and verbal content is a source of deception clues. Unprepared liars can also be tripped up with unanticipated questions.

Ekman is careful to add the qualification that, at least in regard to deception clues, behaviors are not signs of deception per se. Instead, they are signs of emotions that are typically linked with deception. People can experience fear, guilt, and delight for reasons other than deception. Honest people can contradict themselves. Thus, deception clues should be considered "hot spots" rather than sure-fire signs of deceit. Deception clues are not definitive, and failure to understand this leads to the Othello error, which rests on the failure to realize that an honest person may show the same signs of emotion as a liar.[15] So, for example, a crime witness who seems scared might be scared of testifying rather than because he or she is lying.

Stakes have remained a critical element in the Ekman perspective over time. Stakes refer to the consequences of success or failure of a lie. The greater the consequences, the greater the link between deception and emotions, and consequently, the greater the likelihood of leakage and deception clues. The most critical element in stakes according to Ekman is when the liar expects punishment from a failed lie. Ekman and colleagues are steadfast in their contention that stakes make a critical difference, and they are quick to dismiss findings from low-stakes, everyday lies as irrelevant to their approach.[16] Frank and Ekman state their view clearly: "In a low-stakes lie—wherein one gains nothing for successfully lying and loses nothing for unsuccessfully lying—one would expect very little emotion to be elicited in the liar, although the cognitive overload clues may still occur. However, if a lie situation has high stakes, one would expect a great deal of emotion elicited in the liar, along with the cognitive overload clues. . . . It is the presence of these emotions that is central to a liar's fear of getting caught, guilt over lying, or even enjoyment or excitement of getting away with a lie. Research has shown that facial signs of fear, distress, or enjoyment can and do betray deception."[17]

Besides a greater focus on the face as a source of leakage and deception clues, the other major transformation in Ekman's perspective has been an increased focus on individual differences both in liars and, especially, in lie detectors. Not all liars are thought to be leaky,[18] and people who are believed in one situation tend to be believed in a second situation.[19] As to lie detectors, Ekman and colleagues believe that some people have a knack for lie detection; others don't.[20]

Individual differences in senders can give rise to errors in deception detection. The Brokaw Hazard occurs when a liar does not show a clue, but an honest person does show the clue.[21] For example, imagine that two people are interviewed about a crime. One of the two people is a nervous type who always seems tense. The other person is laid back, almost always calm. It is a mistake to presume that the more nervous person is lying. To overcome the Brokaw Hazard and to guard against individual differences in sender demeanor, Ekman advocates reliance on baseline honest behaviors. He suggests it is wise to assess how a person acts in everyday conversation and then look for changes in deception clues when the person might be lying.[22]

Individual differences in deception detection ability have also come to play an increasingly important role in Ekman and colleagues' more recent thinking. In 1991 Ekman and O'Sullivan published a deception detection study testing several groups of subjects: Secret Service officers, federal polygraphers (from the CIA, NSA, FBI, and the military), judges, police, psychiatrists, adults interested in deception, and students.[23] The Secret Service group (average accuracy = 64.1%) did better than the other groups (who ranged from 57.6% to 52.8%, with students scoring the lowest). In 1999 Ekman and his colleagues reported a similar test of lie-detector groups, this time including federal officers (mostly CIA), sheriffs, mixed law-enforcement officers, federal judges, clinical psychologists, and academic psychologists.[24] Whereas the 1991 study involved detecting lies about felt emotions, the 1999 study involved lies about opinions. The results again showed variation among the groups. The federal officers (73%) did the best, followed by some of the clinical psychologists (67.5%) and the sheriffs (66.7%). The mixed law-enforcement group did the worst (50.8%).

More recently still, the idea of the *deception detection wizard* has been ad-

vanced.[25] The claim is that a very small proportion of the population is exceptionally adept at distinguishing truths from lies. This select group performs
at rates better than 80% or 90% across three sets of videotaped truths and lies.
In an independent test of the wizard idea, Gary Bond tested 112 experts and
122 students on a lie detection task.[26] Overall, students and experts did not differ from each other or from the slightly-better-than-chance accuracy levels reported by meta-analysis. Eleven (10%) of the experts, however, obtained levels
of accuracy over 80%. No student did that well. When tested again, two of
the eleven experts again preformed at better than 90%. Although most well-
performing lie detectors regressed to the mean, some small number of experts
exhibit strings of successful judgments that appear statistically improbable.

The most recent iteration of the "a few can detect lies" claim combines individual differences in lie detection ability with stakes.[27] The idea is that at
least some experts are adept at detecting deception under conditions of consequential, high-stakes lies. That is, lie stakes and expertise statistically interact
such that high accuracy is observed only for experts judging high-stakes lies.
When either student samples are used, or when experts judge low-stakes lies,
accuracy is just slightly above chance. Meta-analyses showing poor accuracy
and a lack of effects for expertise are acknowledged, but those findings are dismissed. According to O'Sullivan and colleagues: "This [accuracy is slightly better than chance as reported in meta-analysis] mistaken conclusion may have
resulted from the disproportionate representation of college students in most
lie detection research. Given that college-age students are significantly less accurate than adults older than twenty-two [self-citation to an unpublished poster
is provided], when college students contribute the bulk of the data examined
in a meta-analysis, their chance scores will swamp the statistically significant
results reported for police groups in several countries"[28]

In support of their conclusions, O'Sullivan and her colleagues reviewed
twenty-three studies examining thirty-one police groups in deception detection tasks. Each accuracy task was coded as involving high- or low-stakes lies.
They report eleven accuracy results at 60% or above. Ten of the eleven findings above 60% accuracy were coded as high-stakes lies. The sixteen results at
or below the meta-analysis average of 54% were coded as low-stakes lies. They
report that the (unweighted) mean accuracy for experts judging high-stakes
lies was 67.2%, compared to 55.2% accuracy for low-stakes lies.[29]

Taken at face value, O'Sullivan et al.'s literature review appears to offer strong
and compelling support for the expertise by stakes interaction argument. However, this paper (as well as the idea of wizards) has been widely criticized in

the deception-research community. I will simply say that I find their claims and analysis unconvincing.

To summarize Ekman's view, the focus is on emotions and facial expressions in high-stake lies. Lies can be detected by observing behavioral clues and leakage, and some people are very good lie detectors.

I will close my discussion of Ekman with a quote that succinctly conveys the contrast between his view and my own theory. According to Ekman: "[The] reason why most people do so poorly in judging deceit is that they rely too much upon what people say and ignore the discrepancies between the expressive behaviors and what is said."[30] I, in contrast, believe almost the exact opposite: The reason why most people do so poorly in distinguishing truths from lies is that they rely too much upon demeanor and expressive behavior and pay too little attention to the content of what people say.

FOUR-FACTOR THEORY

In the years that followed the publication of Ekman and Friesen's leakage theory, research on deception and deception detection increased dramatically. Much of this research tried to isolate nonverbal behaviors that distinguished lying from honest communication. Research also sought to assess people's ability to detect lies under different conditions (e.g., from the face alone, from just the body, from the body and the face, etc.).

In 1981 Zuckerman, DePaulo, and Rosenthal summarized the then-new literature of deception and deception detection.[31] By the time of their analysis, some behaviors (e.g., smiling, gaze, response length) had been investigated by as many as fifteen or sixteen separate studies. There were also fifteen available studies of deception detection accuracy. Zuckerman et al. employed the then-new technique of meta-analysis to aid their summary.

The reason Zuckerman et al. is covered here is not because of their results, but instead because of how they chose to frame their results. They introduced a framework that has since come to be known as "four-factor theory." Four-factor theory substantially extended Ekman and Friesen's ideas about deception clues and the internal psychological processes that might produce them. Four-factor theory guided thinking about deception and deception detection for twenty-plus years, until the DePaulo cue meta-analysis was published in 2003.

According to four-factor theory, deception is not directly associated with specific verbal and nonverbal behaviors. Instead, deception is associated with four internal, psychological factors or processes that influence specific behaviors. The four include felt emotions, arousal, cognitive effort, and attempted behavioral control. For those readers familiar with social science–speak, four mediators were specified. Mediators are variables that come in the middle. They are caused by some more distal cause or causes, and, in turn, cause some outcome. The cause flows through them, so to speak. In four-factor theory, deception causes emotions, arousal, cognitive effort, and attempted behavioral control, each of which, in turn, gives rise to behavioral differences that indirectly and probabilistically distinguish truths from lies.

First, consistent with Ekman, deception is thought to produce emotional responses in liars. Liars should feel guilty and should fear detection. These emotions that result from deception might be conveyed nonverbally. For example, less-pleasant facial expressions may result when someone is lying. Or a liar who is feeling guilty might avert his or her gaze.

Second, it was widely believed that deception, relative to honest communication, is physiologically arousing. It is this arousal, in fact, that a polygraph measures. Arousal is reflected in increased heart rate, blood pressure, and skin conductance. The increased arousal associated with deception is thought to produce recognizable behavioral displays such as pupil dilation, more eye blinking, higher-pitched speech, and more fidgeting and nervous behaviors.

Third, many researchers believed (and still do) that deception is more cognitively difficult and demanding than being honest. Liars need to make up the content of their lies while trying to keep their stories consistent. This increased cognitive effort should lead to longer response latencies, more pauses, more speech errors and disfluencies, and fewer gestures.

Fourth, attempted control leads deceivers to try to avoid those behaviors that might give their lies away, and to present behaviors that appear honest. The net result can be behavior that appears stiff and rehearsed or too slick and rehearsed, or that leads to a discrepancy between what one part of the body and another are doing.

Taken together, these four factors provide the basis for predicting the sorts of behavioral differences (cues) that might be useful in lie detection. These factors also offer explanations for why nonverbal deception cues exist and provide a rationale for further research on the topic. Next to the original Ekman and Friesen work, four-factor theory probably has been the second-most theoretically influential perspective on deception.

BELLA DEPAULO AND SELF PRESENTATION

In 1992 Bella DePaulo offered a view of deception quite different from that of Ekman or four-factor theory.[32] Prior to this, theory had predicted and provided explanations for observable behavioral differences between honest and deceptive communication. DePaulo's self-presentation view, in contrast, provides a theoretical logic for predicting few behavioral differences. A second major departure is that while Ekman's work focused on high-stakes lies, DePaulo's thinking was much more centered on what might be called everyday lies, or lies in everyday life. A third shift in focus was from uncontrollable, unconscious behaviors to purposeful and strategic actions.

By "self-presentation," DePaulo meant a person controlling his or her own behavior to create a desired impression on others. People are strategic and goal-directed in the image they convey publicly. Self-presentation can, but need not be, deceptive. Rather than conveying an overtly false impression, subtle editing and packaging is more common.

DePaulo's self-presentation perspective is sketched as follows:[33]

- People try to regulate their nonverbal behaviors rather than allowing their nonverbal behaviors to be fully spontaneous and unconscious expressions of their internal states.
- Regulation of nonverbal behaviors is guided by self-presentation goals. People want others to believe what they say- and for others to see them in a positive light.
- As situations create different demands for self-presentation, nonverbal behaviors will shift accordingly.
- The regulation of nonverbal self-presentation behaviors is learned but also affected by personality. Some people are more concerned with impressions than others.
- Adults generally have the skills necessary to successfully regulate their nonverbal behavior to meet their self-presentation goals.
- How successful people are in conveying impressions depends on a presenter's skill, but even more on (a) the lack of skill in perceivers, and (b) in perceivers' willingness to go along with the presentation and accept other's self-presentations.[34]
- The range of impressions people can successfully convey is limited. For example, shy people may have difficulty maintaining the image of the social butterfly. Deceptive presentations are more believable when they are subtle shadings than when they are outrageous falsifications.

According to DePaulo, people see their everyday lies as of little consequence, and they experience little anxiety, guilt, regret, or fear of detection. Liars need and want to be believed, but so do truth tellers. Nevertheless, sometimes lies are not as convincing as truths, and sometimes liars' performances are more deliberate and prepackaged. As DePaulo puts it: "Our self-presentational perspective has led us to reject the view that lie telling is typically a complicated, stressful, guilt-inducing process that produces clear and strong cues. Instead, we believe that most deceptive presentations are so routinely and competently executed that they leave only faint behavioral residues."[35] And "Behavioral cues that are discernible by human perceivers are associated with deceit only probabilistically. To establish definitively that someone is lying, further evidence is needed.[36]

INTERPERSONAL DECEPTION THEORY (IDT)

Proceeding in chronological order of origination, the next theory is Buller and Burgoon's (1996) interpersonal deception theory (IDT).[37] IDT can be understood as an ambitious and extensive merging of ideas from Ekman, four-factor theory, and the self-presentation views with speculation advanced in a 1986 article by Jim Stiff and G. R. Miller.[38] Several additional variables that Steve McCornack and I were researching at the time (e.g., relational closeness, suspicion, truth-bias, information manipulation dimensions) were (often after renaming) thrown into the mix for added complexity.[39] However, in combining of these different views, the continuity and nuance of each is lost. Thus, IDT represents a relabeling and repackaging of many earlier ideas by others that are mixed together and thrown into a complex, convoluted, and opaque amalgamation.

Stiff and Miller's article is a good place to start in understanding the ideas that would give rise to IDT.[40] These two authors made the important observation that in most research that preceded their experiment, deception detection was limited to the passive observation of behavior. There was no interaction between the potential liar and the person assessing honesty. Coming from the communication discipline,[41] Stiff and Miller thought it obvious that in situations involving interpersonal communication, people can question one another, and that interaction might affect deception detection accuracy. They called these questions or requests for additional information "probes," and they reasoned that interactive deception was likely different from noninteractive deception, in part because probing questions might change how things go during a communication exchange.

One might guess that asking probing questions would be predicted to enhance deception detection accuracy. Questioning should help us get at the truth, right? This is the presumption behind cross-examining a witness in a court of law or a reporter's asking the tough questions during an interview.

Stiff and Miller's thinking was more nuanced and not so conventional. Influenced by the theories discussed previously, they thought that asking suspicious questions would make the potential liar more anxious and aroused and consequently make the person appear more deceptive. The opposite was expected for supportive questions. People who asked friendly, trust-implying questions would appear more honest. So suspicious questions would lead to improved accuracy for liars but to worsened accuracy for honest senders, while supportive questions would produce higher accuracy for honest senders and lower accuracy for liars. At least that is what Stiff and Miller initially predicted.

Stiff and Miller tested their predictions with an experiment. Honest and deceptive senders were questioned with either supportive (positive probes) or suspicion-implying questions (negative probes). These interactions were videotaped, and the actual questioning was edited out so that only the answers remained. In this way, only the honest and deceptive answers resulting from the question, and not the questions themselves, might affect judgments. The videotaped truths and lies were examined for nineteen potential deception cues, and the tapes were also shown to college students who judged each as a truth or a lie so that accuracy could be calculated.

The results were not what Stiff and Miller expected. For accuracy, the biggest effect (by far) was for the honesty of the sender ($r = .61$), which was much higher for truths than lies.[42] But this was of no interest to the authors. The nature of the probes did not affect accuracy at all ($r = .00$). Probing, however, did affect perceptions of honesty. The effect was not big ($r = .14$, $d = 0.28$), but it was statistically different from zero. Communicators who were probed with the suspicious probing questions were believed more often than those who were probed with supportive, positive questions, even though the people judging the messages did not hear the probes. This was unexpected, and it caught Stiff and Miller's attention.

Of the nineteen potential deception cues examined, none were related to probing strongly enough to meet the usual social scientific standards of $p < .05$. Some of the behaviors, however, were related to judgments of deceptions. For example, the people who were most often seen as liars tended to smile more, shift their posture more, and pause more while speaking, among other things. And, critically, there was an apparent trend between the (nonsignificant) probing–behavior relationships and the deception judgment–behavior relationships. For twelve of the nineteen behaviors, the direction of effect of the probing–behavior relationship was opposite to that of the deception judgment–behavior relationships. That is, the things that the people who were suspiciously probed did tended to be the things that were done by people who were seen as honest. It should be noted that while a twelve–seven (63%–37%) split departs from the expected fifty-fifty chance level, it does not reach conventional levels for scientific improbability ($p = .0835$). Remember also that none of the behaviors apparently affected by probing were different enough to rule out chance. However, this did not stop Stiff and Miller from speculating that the trend might be real.

They used the trend in behaviors to explain why people who were probed with suspicious questions were more often judged as honest than those subjected to positive, supportive questioning. This account would come to be known as the behavioral adaptation explanation[43] and would become a key prediction of IDT and central to its logic. It was ventured that negative probes made the people being questioned realize that they were under suspicion, and their response to the suspicion was to act more honest. Stiff and Miller also offered their findings as evidence that deception and deception detection needed to be understood as an interactive process, which also became a hallmark of IDT.

IDT took up Stiff and Miller's call to understand deception and deception detection as a dynamic, interactive process.[44] According to IDT, deception and suspected deception are commonplace. The process begins when a sender's expectations, goals, prior knowledge, behavioral repertoire, and skill set combine to produce a truth or a lie accompanied by initial behavioral displays. Deceptive messages include the core deceptive content plus strategic actions aimed at making the deception believable, and nonstrategic behaviors that betray the lie. In IDT nonstrategic behaviors are synonymous with leakage and deception clues/cues. A sender's initial behavioral displays are judged by a receiver, who also exhibits initial behavioral displays of his or her own and who may or may not be initially suspicious. Based on initial suspicion and an assessment of sender behavior displays, the receiver may adjust his or her behavior and communicate his or her suspicion or lack of suspicion to the sender. Based on receiver behaviors, the sender may adjust his or her behavioral displays strategically, and the receiver may adjust his or her assessment of the sender's honesty based on these adjustments as well as his or her prior assessments. The net result is that the deception may or may not be successful. Senders and receivers actively monitor each other and make behavioral adjustments over time so as to achieve their desired communicative goals. However, both senders and receivers leak indications of deceit and suspicion, which leads to a dynamic series of moves and countermoves.[45]

IDT involves eighteen propositions, most of which contain multiple parts.[46]

These propositions constitute the logical structure of IDT and elaborate on the deceptive process summarized above by listing relevant variables. At its core, IDT presumes that communication contexts differ in their degree of inter-activity. Face-to-face communication is maximally interactive, and other types of communication are less interactive, depending on five dimensions: access to social cues, the immediacy of the communication, feelings of relational en-gagement, conversational demands, and spontaneity. Face-to-face communi-cation provides the most access to social cues, is the most immediate, entails the most relational engagement, creates the most conversational demands, and requires the most spontaneity. IDT's first proposition specifies that these five interactivity dimensions affect how communicators think and act.[47] The sec-ond proposition is that the relationship between the sender and the receiver makes some unspecified difference during deception.

Proposition three states that deceivers engage in more strategic impression-management behaviors than honest senders, but they also display more arousal cues, negative affect, diminished affect, noninvolvement, and other unspeci-fied deception cues.[48] That is, deceivers are both more and less strategic than truth tellers.

Proposition four states that in initial displays more interactive contexts lead to greater strategic activity and fewer nonstrategic deception cues. Proposition five holds that in initial displays more interactive contexts entail greater expec-tations for honesty and more positive relational feelings between the sender and the receiver. Proposition six further specifies that deceivers are more wor-ried about getting caught in their lies in interactive contexts and with relation-ally close others and that detection anxiety results in greater strategic efforts to appear honest. The seventh proposition maintains that goals and motivation af-fect strategic and nonstrategic behaviors. Self-benefiting lies lead to more stra-tegic and nonstrategic behaviors than do lies for the sake of others. Receiver behaviors are also affected by goals, including any intent to detect deception.

Proposition eight says that the better a receiver knows the sender, and the closer the relationship between the two, the more a receiver will be apprehen-sive regarding detecting deception on the part of the sender. Nevertheless, the better a receiver knows the sender, and the closer the relationship between the two, the greater the receiver's strategic activity and the more the receiver will show nonstrategic leakage behavior indicative of suspicion.

Proposition nine offers the circular assertion that the more skilled a sender, the more honest he or she appears.

Proposition ten specifies that a receiver's judgment of sender honesty increases the more the receiver is truth-biased, the more interactive the context, and the more skilled the sender. Unexpected communication patterns, however, lower sender believability.

Proposition eleven deals with accuracy. Deception detection accuracy by a receiver is reduced by receiver truth-bias, context interactivity, and sender skill. Accuracy is enhanced by knowledge of the sender, receiver detection skill, and unexpected sender communication behaviors.

The twelfth proposition says that receivers communicate their suspicion to senders through strategic and nonstrategic behavior. Senders, in turn, recognize receiver suspicion when it exists (proposition thirteen). Sender recognition of receiver suspicion is especially strong when receivers act in unexpected ways, when receivers signal outright disbelief, and when receivers ask for more information. The recognition of receiver suspicion, then, leads to increases in sender strategic and nonstrategic behaviors (proposition fourteen).

Proposition fifteen states that deception and suspicion displays change over time, while proposition sixteen holds that interaction adaption patterns tend to be reciprocated by senders and receivers.

The seventeenth proposition states that receiver deception detection accuracy, receiver bias, and receiver judgments of honesty after the interaction is over depend on what the receiver was thinking (i.e., were they suspicious, were they truth-biased), the receiver's skill in detecting lies, and the sender's behavior at the end of the interaction.

On the sender's side, proposition eighteen holds that whether or not senders think their deception was successful depends on what they think (i.e., how much suspicion they perceived) and the behaviors of the receiver at the end of the interaction.

As evidenced by the eighteen propositions outlined above, IDT puts forth numerous variables but provides little in the way of unambiguous, concrete prediction. For example, in a number of places, strategic and nonstrategic behaviors are said to increase, decrease, or simply change. But no detail is provided about the specific behaviors involved. According to IDT, leakage and deception cues are said to exist, but unlike in prior theories, what those behaviors might involve or look like is less well articulated. IDT is specific, however, in the assertion that the degree of interactivity alters the nature of deception and deception detection. This idea that mere extent of communicative interactivity is fundamentally a game-changer is IDT's most directly testable and potentially falsifiable claim.

Research from the IDT perspective has been plentiful and well funded. US taxpayers have invested literally tens of millions of dollars into IDT. This research, however, is largely limited to Judee Burgoon and her students. More recent research by the IDT researchers has increasingly involved the use of cutting-edge technology and deception in computer-mediated contexts.

ALDERT VRIJ, COGNITIVE LOAD, AND PROMPTING CUES WITH QUESTIONING

If judged on the metric of sheer numbers of published academic journal articles, the hottest new thing in deception research in the past decade is surely the work of Aldert Vrij and his many colleagues (such as Pär Anders Granhag, Ronald Fisher, Samantha Mann, and Sharon Leal) from (mostly European) criminal and legal psychology. The work of Vrij and his group tends to be applied, and it tends to focus on deception in legal and criminal applications.

Vrij and Granhag summarize their view and contrast it with some of the theories previously described:

A turning point in our thinking about lie detection came in 2003. In that year, Bella DePaulo and her colleagues published a meta-analysis of deception research that demonstrated that nonverbal and verbal cues to deception are typically faint and unreliable. It made us realise that a new direction in deception research was required aimed at eliciting and enhancing cues to deceit. We will argue that interviewers play a vital role in achieving this. Hereby we distinguish ourselves from other researchers who ignore the role of the interviewer and instead are trying to find exceptional lie-catchers ("wizards"), train people to focus on specific cues, or believe that cues to deceit are more pronounced under certain circumstances (e.g., high-stakes).[49]

And

Accepting DePaulo et al.'s conclusion that cues to deceit are faint and unreliable implies that the only way to improve lie detection is by eliciting and enhancing such cues. We argue that interviewers can achieve this by using appropriate, theoretically sound interview techniques that exploit liars' and truth tellers' different psychological states. We have developed such interview techniques and they take into account that lying is often mentally more taxing than truth telling, exploit the fact that liars prepare themselves for interviews, and take into account the different strategies truth tellers and liars use during interrogations. We have demonstrated that our techniques work.[50]

Thus, the core idea is that deception detection accuracy can be improved by eschewing passive observation of cues but instead prompting cues through strategic questioning. The problem, as Vrij and Granhag see it, is a lack of cues that distinguish truths from lies. But, rather than abandoning cues or the psychological mediating processes that give rise to cues, they see making cues stronger as the *only* solution to achieving improved deception detection.

Vrij and colleagues are highly critical of Ekman's wizards, micro facial expressions, arousal-based lie detection (including the polygraph and vocal stress analysis), and accusatory questioning such as the Behavioral Analysis Interview (BAI) developed and taught by Reid and Associates. They are also critical of lie detection experiments involving short video clips and passive observation and suggest less focus on outcome measures such as percentage-correct deception detection accuracy and greater emphasis on showing differences in cues depending on honesty–deceit. Much of their research involves students who are instructed to lie after perpetrating mock crimes. Although they emphasize interaction between interviewer and interviewee, they ignore the research from my own home academic field of human communication, and the focus is more on psychological processes than interaction. People would never know about most of the research on interactive deception detection research from reading the work in legal-criminal psychology, because it isn't cited.

Arousal and emotions are dismissed as mediating psychological processes. In their place, cognitive effort and strategic planning to avoid detection are embraced as key psychological mediators. Vrij and Granhag note that "a consistent finding in deception research is that liars prepare themselves when anticipating an interview."[51] Regarding cognitive load, they further contend that "there is overwhelming evidence that lying is cognitively more difficult than telling the truth."[52] This difference is then exploited by adding additional load to a potential liar; they assert: "Investigators can exploit the differences in cognitive load that liars and truth tellers experience. If lying requires more cognitive resources than truth telling, liars will have fewer cognitive resources left over. If cognitive demand is further raised, which could be achieved by making additional requests, liars may not be as good as truth tellers in coping with these additional requests."[53] Examples of instilling additional load include requiring interviewees to provide a narrative in reverse chronological order, asking unanticipated questions, and instructing communicators to maintain eye contact.

Besides instilling cognitive load, the legal psychology approach encourages a nonaccusatory, information-gathering approach to interviewing and the strategic use of evidence approach.

SUMMARY

This chapter provides a chronicle of prior theories of deception and deception detection. Ekman's original leakage theory, Ekman's updated perspective, four-factor theory, Bella DePaulo's self-presentation perspective, Interpersonal Deception Theory, and Aldert Vrij's cognitive load approach were each reviewed. I see much communality among Ekman, four-factor theory, IDT, and Vrij. In the next chapter, I offer the catchall idea of cue theories as a way to show the commonalities in the logic behind prominent deception theories and to show how theory has shaped research priorities and design. I offer a critical evaluation of these prior theories in specific, and cue theories in general. I hope it is obvious after this chapter why a new theory is so desperately needed.

5

Critiquing the Rivals

THE PREVIOUS CHAPTER DESCRIBES SEVERAL prior theories of deception. In this chapter, I evaluate those theories. I also offer here the idea of *cue theories* as a meta-theoretical umbrella that captures the core logic underlying most deception theory and research in the social sciences.

CRITERIA

Since this chapter involves assessing the viability of several theories, I briefly address here my criteria for assessing the quality of theory. Good theories have many desirable qualities that contribute to their theoretical merit. A good theory, for example, must be coherent. That is, all the parts of the theory must fit within a common logic, and all parts of a theory must be logically consistent with one another. A good theory must also be unambiguous. It needs to be clear what a theory predicts and why. Wishy-washiness and fence-sitting are not virtues when it comes to theory. Instead, theoretical ambiguity leads to confusion and a lack of falsifiability. A good theory is also efficient and will explain a lot with relatively few principles. The more ground covered with the fewest moving parts, the better.[1] Good theory needs to be generative. A theory points researchers in new directions and leads to new findings that people would not have otherwise considered.

Most of all, good theory needs to lead to new predictions that turn out to be right. That is, theories need to provide valid knowledge, prediction, and explanation. A theory's predictions need to be testable and verifiable. When tested against data, empirical findings must be consistent with the theory. Supportive results need to replicate. Theories that offer explanations, no matter how assertive, coherent, elegant, efficient, creative, and unambiguous, that turn out to be empirically false are myths. Correspondence with evidence is the bottom line for scientific theories. Research findings must not contradict the theory, and if research findings repeatedly contradict the theory, the theory must be modified or discarded, and new, more empirically adequate theories must be sought.

The word "verisimilitude" captures well the most important consideration in evaluating a theory. The trick, of course, is distinguishing verisimilitude from "truthiness." The author-researchers behind all the major competing theoretical perspectives in the academic study of deception claim empirical support for their ideas. Authors have ready answers for apparent failures, and they are often quick to point out the empirical deficiencies of their rivals. What is a reader to think? Debates over theories can seem like scientific he-said-she-said. There is a risk of research consumers concluding that everything is just a matter of opinion, that all theories are "just theories" in the sense that they are mere conjecture, and that all approaches are equal in scientific merit (or lack thereof).

Consistency with data is the primary goal of my theory-building endeavors, and it is the primary criterion I use to judge the adequacy of rival theories. The main questions I ask in evaluating each theory are: (a) are the data consistent with the theory's predictions, and (b) do the findings contradict the logic of the theory? As we learned in chapters 2 and 3, there are vast quantities of data from prior research, and those data provide a reasonably coherent empirical picture. It is my contention that many of the theories reviewed in the previous chapter do a poor job of explaining the existing empirical findings and that a very different set of empirical findings would be expected based on the logic and predictions of the various theories.

There is one criterion for evaluating theory that I purposely avoid. I am not going to ask, "Is it even a theory in the first place?" Personally, I prefer a strict and narrow definition of theory. My preferred definition of theory might be something like "a unifying, logically coherent set of interrelated conjectures that makes novel predictions and explains some phenomenon or phenomena." Other scientists and scholars use the term much more loosely. As a consequence, some "theories" are theories under some definitions of theory but not others. It has been my observation that a great many academic arguments are just disagreements about how something is defined, and such arguments often lead nowhere. So I leave it to other authors to debate what counts as theory in deception.[2]

CRITIQUING THE RIVALS

It is time to explain what problems need to be overcome and why my new theory is needed. My critique begins by presenting the idea of cue theories as a meta-theoretical approach to understanding deception. Cue theories, I argue, lack verisimilitude and have retarded theoretical advances by trapping new generations of researchers in the same old intellectual ruts.

Cue Theories

I introduce the idea of cue theories as an umbrella term that captures and integrates the basic ideas running through so much of the research on deception detection.[3] I see the divide between cue theories and non-cue theories as perhaps the most fundamental issue in deception theory. I believe that breaking out of cue-theory mind-lock is the best chance for progress. Thinking in terms of cues and the psychological processes that produce cues blinds researchers to useful alternatives and weds them to limiting research designs that have led to repeated dead ends in the past.

The core logic of cue theories goes like this:

1. Truths and lies are psychologically different. How truths and lies are different varies from theory to theory, but examples include emotional states (fear of detection, guilt about lying, duping delight), autonomic nervous system arousal, cognitive load or effort, strategic efforts to appear honest, planning for deception, and willingness to be forthcoming.
2. The psychological states produced by deception, in turn, are behaviorally signaled by observable cues. Thus, the psychological states in number 1 above mediate and explain the relationship between truths–lies and cues.
3. Therefore, deception can be detected (albeit indirectly and probabilistically) through observation of the cues arising from the mediating psychological states associated with deception. This is either possible through passive observation or requires additional prompting. But deception can be detected under certain conditions (e.g., high stakes in Ekman, prompting in Vrij, long naturalist interaction in Burgoon, etc.) through the observation of cues.

Examples of cue theories include Ekman's work, four-factor theory, IDT, and the Vrij approach. The various psychological mediators are different. Ekman focuses primarily on emotion, Vrij focuses mostly on cognitive effort, and IDT talks about strategic and nonstrategic processes. I have no doubt that the advocates of the various cue theories will vehemently object to being lumped together with rival cue theories. The authors of specific cue theories are typically very critical of other cue theories. But all of the theories have the same fundamental logical structure and differ only in the fine print.

Not all deception theories, however, share cue theory logic. DePaulo's self-presentation approach is predicated on honest and deceptive self-presentations being (mostly) psychologically similar. Everyone wants to make a good impression and to be seen positively by others. IMT2 sees the message production processes for truths and deception as the same. And in my own TDT, cues and the psychological processes that produce cues play no role in accurate lie detection.[4] In my view, the motives that guide communication are the same for truths and lies, and the path to improved deception detection is through contextualized communication content and persuasion rather than the observation of cues.

The empirical failure to document cues that reliably distinguish between truths and lies seems, on its face, to deal a fatal empirical blow to cues theories. But, both theoretically and empirically, things are not so simple. DePaulo's famous cue meta-analysis was far from a clean kill.[5] Instead, I believe the academic literature on deception is populated by several undead cue theories, some of which are in advanced states of decomposition (four-factor theory), while others are quite active and ravenous (IDT and especially Vrij).[6] These undead theories cannot be stopped merely with disconfirming scientific evidence. If that were the case, they would be dead and would have stayed dead. They would not attract so much taxpayer funding, and they would not repeatedly survive scientific peer review.

Empirically, one problem is that at the level of the individual study, there are almost always strong cue effects.[7] Because there are almost always significant cue findings at the level of the individual study, and because the "significance" of a specific test in a specific study is unfortunately the conventional currency marking scientific worth, authors of individual studies can almost always claim support for their hypotheses. Review articles summarizing the literature can provide long lists of citations as evidence for a preferred theory. Ultimately, of course, such findings lead precisely nowhere because specific cue findings are ephemeral and don't replicate. For every supportive finding, there are findings suggesting just the opposite. Meta-analysis eventually shows that the emperors and empresses have no clothes. Still, it is difficult to launch decisive empirical arguments against cue theories because their advocates can provide long lists of supportive evidence from individual studies. It comes down to one group of scientists listing evidence for one view while another group cites loads of evidence for the exact opposite position. What is a research consumer to think? The empirical deficiencies of cue approaches require sophisticated understandings of things like overfit models[8] and *p*-hacking[9] that can be lost on the casual bystander or the average researcher. I hope to convince the reader, however, to see past the smoke and mirrors and the he-said-she-said, to the empirical big picture that led me to reject cue theories.

Theoretically, as the philosopher of science Imre Lakatos describes, theories often have a self-defensive logic built in that lets them explain away problematic findings.[10] Perhaps the best example is Ekman's perspective, where the role of stakes and, to a lesser extent, the use of student data provide a convenient data-dismissal mechanism that can vaporize pesky anomalous findings.[11] The circular logic goes like this:

1. Cues are expected only when lies are high-stakes.
2. Because cues were not observed, the deception was not high-enough-stakes.
3. The deception was not high-enough-stakes because no cues were observed.

Or, more generally:

1. Our theory is right.
2. If the data are inconsistent with our theory, that's because you did the research wrong.
3. We know there was a problem with your nonsupportive study because the data didn't support our predictions.

In IDT the vague use of strategic and nonstrategic actions, eschewing percentage-correct accuracy as a bottom line, the degrees of interactivity, and the duration of communication all play protective roles. Vrij's work, too, often avoids easily understood metrics like percentage-correct accuracy. The result is that most cue theories have internal logics and research practices that protect them from the data. These adaptations allow them to survive in an otherwise uninhabitable empirical world.

Before presenting more of my own critique, two strong and historically noteworthy critiques of the deception literature are briefly summarized. In rereading Kraut and McCornack articles for this chapter, I was struck by how ahead of their time each was. I can't help thinking that if Kraut and McCornack had

had greater influence, deception research would be in so much better shape today. They are spot on-target.

KRAUT 1980 CRITIQUE

Here is how Kraut[12] began his argument in 1980: "I will argue that much research on human lie detection has been misguided. Specifically, researchers who have expected high accuracy in perceivers' judgments of deception or valid and easily observable cues to deception have been misled in their expectations by the expressive approach to nonverbal communication and by psychophysiological work on lie detection. The standard assumption of most nonverbal communication research, that nonverbal behavior expresses a person's internal states, has blinded researchers to a priori arguments that no such cues should exist as indicants of deception."[13]

Note that the quotation of Vrij and Granhag in the previous chapter placed the turning point for them at 2003. Kraut was making the case twenty-three years earlier! Kraut pointed out way back in 1980 the now very well-documented findings that accuracy is only slightly-better-than-chance,[14] and that "few behaviors are strongly and consistently associated with deception across studies."[15]

Relevant to TDT and critical of cue theories, Kraut speculated: "The ability to discover deception does not necessarily imply an ability to decipher nonverbal arousal cues, although this may be part of it. Instead, the skills may be in remembering personal information and noting inconsistencies, in interrogating others, in setting traps, or in inferring ulterior motives from other social information. None of these skills are tested in the typical lie detection paradigm."[16] And, "In any case the assumption implicit in much research on naive detection of deception, that there are some easily observable verbal and nonverbal behaviors which are signs of deception per se, is implausible, and the search for these cues to deception may therefore be futile."[17]

Kraut was also critical of individual differences in lie detection that would, a decade later, start to play a critical role in Ekman's a-few-can-catch-a-liar thinking. "These findings, that the same people are not consistently good at judging deception across liars or affects and that people with very different experiences with deception in their professional lives use similar cues and combination rules to judge deception, are inconsistent with any simple notion of stable and general individual differences in detecting deception. Indeed, my conclusion is that most deception judgments (and many other personal perception judgments based on actual behavior) are stimulus driven. What a liar does and the motivational context in which a lie occurs compel most observers to agree about whether he or she is lying."[18]

MCCORNACK 1997 CRITIQUE

Steve McCornack[19] begins his 1997 chapter "The Generation of Deceptive Messages" by distinguishing what he characterized as "hopeful myths" from "extant data." His list of hopeful myths includes the following:[20]

- the encoding of deceptive messages entails active, strategic, and detailed cognitive processing;
- the encoding of deceptive messages requires greater cognitive load than the encoding of truthful messages;
- the encoding of deceptive messages is more physiologically arousing than the encoding of truthful messages;
- there is an identifiable and consistent set of deception-arousal-based behavioral cues that deceivers "leak" when encoding deceptive messages;
- human beings are innately capable of deception detection, and
- deceptive messages have specifiable characteristics that render them distinct from truthful messages.

The first two hopeful myths contrast sharply with the reasoning of Aldert Vrij and colleagues, while the last few apply most directly to IDT. These myths, McCornack argues, are reified through nonecological research design and selective interpretation of data. But they are, according to McCornack, myths, and not science. Each myth rests on unsound reasoning, and each was undercut by data that existed back in 1997.

McCornack argued that deception occurs fairly often in normal conversation and is often enacted casually. Most deception is not especially effortful, arousing, or strategic.[21] He is especially critical of the idea that deception is more cognitively effortful than honesty. His arguments are both theoretical and empirical, and they are too detailed to repeat here.[22] The short version involves an important and useful distinction between bald-faced lies, bald-faced truths, packaged deception, and packaged truths. The idea is that research tends to study the differences between bald-faced truths and bald-faced lies, whereas normal conversation typically entails packaged truths and packaged deception. Given the conversational situations in which deception naturally occurs, packaged deception is enacted precisely because it is easier than trying to package the truth in a palatable manner. In the typical mock-crime experiment, for example, honest senders are asked about recent events fresh in memory where the truth is completely unproblematic and easy to recall. Liars, on the other hand, need to make stuff up. This leads to a comparison between bald-faced truths and bald-faced lies. But, McCornack argues, people don't lie when the truth is unproblematic. And, McCornack argues, most deception is not blatant fabrication, but instead a subtle shading of the truth—maybe just leaving out a critical detail in an otherwise truthful statement. Further, says McCornack, when people do outright lie, they are often not making things up, but instead pulling from true memories.

Try this little thought experiment. Out loud, quickly and spontaneously, answer the following question: What did you do two weeks ago, Thursday night? Now, follow-up questions: How easy was an honest response? If you were to lie, might you say what you typically do on weekday evenings? Which involves more cognitive effort: recalling a specific evening a few weeks ago or recalling a typical evening? According to McCornack, what is cognitively easy is what is more accessible in memory, and what is easiest to bring to mind may not be "honest."

EVALUATING EKMAN ET AL.

Paul Ekman's theoretical contributions have been incredibly influential in how deception theory and research have progressed over the past forty or so years. The ideas of leakage, deception clues, lie stakes, and wizards are deeply ingrained in the social scientific lore of deception and, to a lesser extent, in popular culture. Ideas like the Othello error have real utility. But, as a scientific theory, data in general have not been kind to the Ekman approach. If the bottom line is reliable, replicable theory–data match, then I think we must consider the theory sufficiently falsified. To summarize: bits and pieces have merit (e.g., Othello error, leakage), the verdict is still out on other parts (e.g., wizards), but too many key elements conflict with too many data for the whole to stand as a coherent, scientifically sound theory.

The cue meta-analyses reviewed in chapter 3 are not especially supportive of the existence of deception clues, especially those linked with emotions. There is less independent evaluation of microexpressions, and at least one experiment failed to identify any evidence for full microexpressions in a sample of emotional deceptions.[23] Evidence was reported for partial microexpressions, but they were infrequent and did not differ in frequency between genuine and deceptive emotional displays. More generally, in the journal *Nature*, Weinberger offers a nice summary of scientific controversy regarding facial leakage as it applies to the TSA's SPOT program.[24] The upshot is that Ekman's ideas are, at best, regarded as scientifically controversial.

Evidence has generally not supported the key Ekman contention that high-stakes lies exhibit more deception clues or are more detectable than low-stakes lies. Meta-analysis shows that cues are no more predictive of deception under high sender motivation than otherwise.[25] Even Frank and Ekman report that threatening punishment did not affect displayed emotions in facial measures or any other outcome in their experiment.[26] Finally, meta-analysis finds no differences in deception detection accuracy as a function of stakes (motivated lies, 53.9% accuracy compared to 53.4% for no motivation).[27] However, consistent with DePaulo's motivational impairment effect,[28] motivated lies are slightly less believable (believed 53.4%) than lies absent motivation, which are believed 57.2% of the time.[29]

Research has also not found support for differences in deception detection accuracy based on occupation or experience. Meta-analysis has failed to substantiate reliable differences between student and nonstudent populations, including law enforcement, the intelligence community, and other professional populations. In my own data, I have failed to find reliable differences between professionals and students in passive lie detection,[30] and I sometimes found that experts do worse than students.[31] Meta-analysis also finds too little variance in accuracy to support much in the way of individual differences in detection accuracy.[32]

IDT

IDT scores poorly on every metric of theory assessment except two. If theory is judged based on the number of published articles and the number of US tax dollars invested in research, then IDT has been remarkably successful. People who value such metrics above all else will greatly appreciate IDT work. I have only half-jokingly told students in graduate methods classes that there are now four types of validity: internal validity, external validity, construct validity, and grant validity.[33] IDT research excels on the fourth type.

If the criteria for evaluating theory are clarity of specification, logical consistency and coherence, the scientific quality of the research generated, and consistency of the theory with data, then IDT is arguably the worst social scientific theory I know. IDT has been widely criticized in the academic literature.[34] I could write a whole chapter on the problems I have with IDT and still not have enough space. There are plenty of other things to cover in this chapter, so I will try to prioritize but still make my point.

In terms of lack of specificity, ambiguity, and coherence, let us consider the following quotes from Buller and Burgoon as they lay out their first proposition and some hypotheses that might follow from the proposition:

Proposition 1: Sender and receiver cognitions and behaviors vary systematically as deceptive communication contexts vary in (a) access to social cues, (b) immediacy, (c) relational engagement, (d) conversational demands, and (e) spontaneity.

Sample hypotheses derivable from this proposition are that (a) receiver truth-biases decrease as communication contexts move from high interactivity (e.g., face-to-face) to low interactivity (e.g., electronically mediated communication), and (b) sender detection fear and (c) deception displays differ between dialogic (e.g., face-to-face) and monologic (e.g., videotaped presentation) contexts.[35]

On one level, it is undoubtedly true that people have different thoughts and different behaviors in different social situations and that the nature of social cues, conversational demands, and relationship status no doubt affect how people think and feel. On the other hand, this is so vague and imprecise as to be scientifically pointless. Buller and Burgoon offer the sample hypothesis that receiver's truth-bias might decrease as interactivity decreases. But the exact opposite hypothesis is equally consistent with proposition one: receiver's truth-bias might decrease as interactivity increases. Proposition one does not specify the direction of effect. We can also derive absolutely ludicrous hypotheses from proposition one. Evidence that increased conversational demands are negatively correlated with the frequency and valence of thoughts about goldfish would be consistent with and support proposition one. Proposition one is also consistent with the observation that nose-picking decreases (or increases) with access to social cues. Proposition one does not specify types of thoughts or behaviors, so systematic variance in any thought or behavior is consistent with the theory.

Consider the conditions under which proposition one might actually be false. Disconfirming evidence would logically be possible only in two completely implausible situations: (a) thoughts and behaviors are constants and do not vary, or (b) variability in thoughts and behaviors is completely random and unaffected by social context.

In the places where IDT does actually make meaningful predictions about deception, it performs even more poorly than other deception theories. At its core IDT presumes that interactive, face-to-face deception is different from mediated deception, and that variables such as access to social cues and conversational demands affect outcomes such as deception detection. Proposition eleven, for example, predicts that accuracy is inversely related to interactivity. Yet we know from meta-analysis that mere interaction makes little difference with respect to accuracy, and neither does communication medium.[36] Interaction can make a big difference, but IDT does not tell us where to look for it, nor has IDT been able to produce large effects for interaction. When interaction does make a difference, the direction of the effect is opposite to that predicted by IDT. Interactivity can improve accuracy.[37]

Proposition three states: "Compared with truth tellers, deceivers (a) engage in greater strategic activity designed to manage information, behavior, and image, and (b) display more nonstrategic arousal cues, negative and dampened affect, noninvolvement, and performance decrements."[38]

Proposition three makes IDT a cue theory, and thus the general concerns about cue theories apply to IDT. Like other propositions, this too makes IDT's predictions hard to pin down, because liars do strategic things that make them look more honest and nonstrategic things that make them look deceptive at the same time. Specific activities and cues are not identified.

Proposition four qualifies the predictions of proposition three by specifying that (at least initially) as interactivity increases, liars do even more strategic activities and fewer nonstrategic things like leakage and deception cues. If this is true, then liars but not honest senders should be more believable as interactivity increases. It is the case that senders are believed with greater frequency in interactive situations (65.3% vs. 54.5% truth-bias),[39] but it is not clear that this stems from dishonest sender behavior. Meta-analysis shows that the magnitude of cue effects does not vary by interactivity,[40] and even IDT research suggests that the trend holds for honest communications too.[41]

Proposition seven contrasts with Bella DePaulo's motivational impairment effect. The motivational impairment effect holds that people who are more motivated to lie successfully are less successful at lying. IDT predicts and claims to find the opposite: motivation improves lie success.[42] Meta-analysis reports that across forty-two tests of this issue, motivation decreases believability, a finding consistent with DePaulo's work and inconsistent with IDT.[43]

Proposition eleven predicts, among other things, that accuracy is lower as interactivity increases. Again, this prediction has not held up in meta-analysis. Proposition eleven also predicts that detection accuracy and truth-bias are inversely related. As we will later see, TDT and IDT make very different predictions about the relationship between truth-bias and accuracy. In TDT, truth-bias makes us more, not less, likely to be right.

In one of the most obviously false hypotheses in IDT research, the Interpersonal Deception IV experiment actually predicted "H1: Receivers perceive deceit when it is present."[44] Meta-analysis and the literature reviewed in chapter 3 show vast quantities of data inconsistent with this IDT prediction. But, for IDT to function as specified, both senders and receivers need to maintain vigilance, both need to recognize deceit and suspicion in others, and both need to adapt and counter-respond to the other in a game of cat-and-mouse. In this sense IDT and TDT are polar opposites. In IDT, receivers are suspicious souls, quick to pounce at any sign of deceit, but also prone to leaking their suspicions to liars, who strategically react on the fly with more-honest-looking behavioral displays. In TDT, receivers are more often than not accepting of what others say, and the thought of deception only rarely even enters conscious awareness. In IDT, truth-bias is lazy, flawed thinking that lowers accuracy.[45] In TDT, truth-bias is adaptive, it fosters communication and cooperation, and it usually leads to correct beliefs.

Empirical tests of IDT are also problematic.[46] Consider, for example, the Interpersonal Deception V experiment.[47] The first hypothesis was "Deception accuracy differs across deception types."[48] The article reports significant effects for a dependent variable other than accuracy. On the basis of this, it is concluded that "results strongly confirmed Hypothesis 1."[49] The second hypothesis predicts that suspicion will lower accuracy. There were no effects for suspicion on any of the dependent variables, accuracy or otherwise. However, they report a significant effect for suspicion within a subset of subjects that would not be significant with conventional tests.[50] This gets interpreted as "qualified support." The discussion starts by asserting: "A guiding premise of interpersonal deception theory is that the act of communicating face-to-face alters deception relative to noninteractive contexts. The current results document several ways in which it does so."[51] Yet the study they discuss here did not even test context interactivity. All data were collected face-to-face. There is just no correspondence between the claims made, the actual design of the experiment, and the actual results found. Statistics are tortured to obtain statistical significance and dubious but impressive-looking effect sizes,[52] and when that is insufficient, things are just made up. IDT is truthiness on steroids.

IDT's strength is its focus on interaction. Interaction is critically important in deception detection, and IDT was way ahead of the times in prioritizing interaction. I fully agree that interaction is of critical importance, and I think research over the past several years has really proven that. But the big breakthroughs have come not out of IDT research, but from programs of research that reject IDT logic, methods, and findings. IDT is absolutely right in the general sense that interaction is critical and that a dynamic process orientation is needed. I agree fully that a communication perspective is not only needed but well suited to overcoming psychology-centric cue theories. But I think IDT gets all the details wrong. It does not prioritize the right variables and ignores critical considerations. It muddles understanding more than it clarifies. And, bottom line, it is contradicted by the data in too many instances.

VRIJ AND THE LEGAL PSYCHOLOGY WORK REVISITED

Vrij and colleagues represent the latest version of cue theory. Much like IDT researchers and perhaps even more so, they have been highly successful in getting a huge number of papers into print in recent years. In sheer quantity of peer-reviewed journal articles, Vrij et al. are unrivaled. The substantive yield, however, is not commensurate with the volume of publication.

Vrij often cites the DePaulo cue meta-analysis as evidence against arousal-based deception cues but then embraces cognitive load as a basis for cues.[53] My reading of the results of the DePaulo cue meta-analyses is that cues linked with cognitive load fare worse than arousal cues. It seems to me that the arguments rest on a selective use of evidence, where helpful evidence is embraced and contrary evidence is ignored. It also seems to me that if liars are really more likely to plan their stories than are honest people, then we might expect less cognitive load in a planned and rehearsed lie than in a spontaneous truth.

I find McCornack's criticism of Vrij's position that lying is typically more cognitively difficult than honesty compelling. Since the logic of instilling additional load as a cue-prompting strategy requires that lying is naturally more cognitively demanding, I just don't accept the premise of Vrij's argument. If the premise is false, the argument is unsound.

At the time I wrote the first draft of this chapter, cognitive load induction studies did not report levels of accuracy notably better than passive approaches. One study compared asking honest and deceptive mock-crime suspects to recall events in either chronological or reverse order.[54] Reverse order interviews (58%) yielded significantly higher accuracy than control interviews (46%), but the 58% accuracy obtained in the reverse-order condition is consistent with the slightly-better-than-chance levels observed in passive studies. A second study reported accuracy of 53.5% with a maintain-eye-contact instruction, compared with accuracy of 52.3% in controls.[55] A third study had adults assess honest and deceptive children who were asked anticipated and unanticipated questions.[56] Accuracy for unanticipated questions was 58.7%, compared with 56.5% in controls. Whereas inducing load produced higher accuracy than controls in each of these studies, accuracy was still well within the range typical of passive lie detection. Thus, there is little evidence that actively inducing cognitive load produces any real bottom-line improvement. Unfortunately, most cognitive load experiments report only cue differences and not accuracy, making the effectiveness of the approach difficult to compare to other approaches.[57]

Although it is not specific to the work in legal psychology per se, I caution researchers to be aware of an issue I call *exploitation of aberrant controls*. We know that absent any special intervention, accuracy is usually better than chance (about 54%). An apparent trend I have noticed is that accuracy in control groups is often poor compared to the across-study average. Experiments are reported touting some approach or phenomenon that improves accuracy. The experiments show that the new approach is statistically superior to a control group. But, when the results are examined closely, it's not so much that the approach produced much improvement over the status quo; instead the statistical difference is the result (at least in part) of the control being usually low. To the extent that aberrant controls reflect a trend, some skepticism may be warranted. Aberrant control findings are prevalent in the legal psychology work on deception, which to me suggests questionable research practices or publication bias.[58]

Pragmatically, I think the application of Vrij's approach is very likely to encourage a version of the Othello error. Truthful people can have honest difficulty in remembering things or have other things on their minds. In such cases, adding additional load and looking for load cues will lead to systematic errors. Similarly, people may not want to be forthcoming for reasons other than being guilty of some offense. Further, research on imagined interactions shows very clearly that honest people plan and rehearse what to say too.[59] Planning is not limited to liars. Adding cognitive load and looking for load cues may make honest people, especially those who are below average in intelligence, look guilty.

The concern about adding load and false positives is a much greater risk outside the lab then in controlled research settings. In the lab, all lies are about the same thing (usually a mock crime); all honest accounts are about the same, recent, easy-to-remember truth; and all subjects (usually college students) are presumably above-average in intelligence and practice memory tasks (college exams) regularly. The inducing-load logic makes some sense in the lab, where the task difficulty is controlled and where the variance in cognitive ability is limited. But the same logic that might make adding load work as a deception detection tool in the lab suggests that adding load should impair an honest person trying to be honest about a difficult-to-remember truth. That same logic also suggests that the approach will impair honest but cognitively less gifted individuals. Instilling load should backfire when honest memories are not fresh and easy to recall or when individuals vary in preexisting cognitive ability. Therefore, I have grave concerns about the utility of the instilling-load approach in practice and think it is highly vulnerable to false positives in the field.[60]

Vrij and colleagues are highly critical of accusatory approaches to questioning and assert the superiority of nonaccusatory questioning. The evidence seems much less clear-cut to me. In the original probing-effect research, asking skeptical questions actually made senders look more honest.[61] Vrij's own research reports no significant differences in accuracy between information-gathering, accusatory, and BAI questioning styles.[62] And, in my own research, I too find no differences in accuracy between accusatory and nonaccusatory questioning.[63] Thus, Vrij's objections seem counterfactual and unresponsive to actual findings.

Beyond Vrij's cognitive approach in particular, I have concerns about deception research in the area of legal and criminal psychology more generally. The group of researchers operating in that space strikes me, as an outsider, as very cliquish and provincial. Researchers coauthor and review one another's work. They seem to have what I call a "publication circle" going. In publication circles, people alternate authorship, citations, and positive reviews with the goal of everyone maximizing publications and citations. It's basically enforced mutual back-scratching. New meta-analysis shows that aberrant controls have become widespread in the legal and criminal psychology literature.[64] Findings that don't follow the party line can't be published in legal and criminal psychology journals because of peer review practices. As a consequence, evidence of strong publication-bias is mounting.[65]

I do, however, much admire the work of Pär Anders Granhag. His work on logical consistency in statements is quite good and influenced TDT.[66] The strategic use of evidence (SUE) strategy is a major advance, and I think it is very compatible with the TDT approach.[67] I suspect I disagree with Granhag a bit on the mechanisms involved, but there is no doubt that SUE is effective. I also think Granhag's new work on the Scharff technique is very interesting.[68] Hanns Scharff was a highly effective German interrogator during World War Two. In an upcoming chapter I provide more detail on his approach to interrogation.

SUMMARY: DECEPTION THEORIES AS CULTS

I close this chapter with a metaphor of prior theories of deception as cults. When I did a Google search on the word "cult," the following definitions came up:[69]

- a system of religious veneration and devotion directed toward a particular figure or object;
- a relatively small group of people having religious beliefs or practices regarded by others as strange or sinister;
- a misplaced or excessive admiration for a particular person or thing.

I think all three apply. Various camps of deception researchers have leaders who are revered by followers (e.g., Ekman, Burgoon, Vrij). The members of the various groups are very devoted to the system of beliefs that form the tenets of the various theories, and they see disagreement by outsiders over core issues as heresy. Each of the groups is relatively small in number, and each group sees the doctrines of rival theories as strange, sinister, and threatening. And, at least from my point of view, I think the admiration that the followers of the various theories have for their theories is both excessive and misplaced. Each of the rivals falls short in verisimilitude.

The rest of the book describes the scientific evidence pertaining to truth-default theory in detail. I hope this chapter has made a strong and valid case for why a new theory is needed. I further hope that TDT overcomes the problems and limitations of its rivals.

This ends part one. The ending of this chapter marks a transition from previous research and rival theories to the TDT view of deception and deception detection. Chapters 7 and 8 make the transition by moving beyond intent and lies, discussing issues in defining deception and deception as information manipulation. By chapter 9, the transition will be complete, and the focus will be squarely on TDT. But first, an overview of TDT is provided in chapter 6.

PART II

Truth-Default Theory

6

Truth-Default Theory Summarized

THIS CHAPTER PROVIDES AN OUTLINE of Truth-Default Theory (TDT).[1] After a brief introduction, key concepts and terms are defined. My goal is to provide a basic glossary for the ideas that populate TDT. Next, each of TDT's modules is listed and very briefly summarized. After the annotated modules, the propositions that constitute the key predictions and logical structure of the theory are listed. The propositions weave together TDT's modules, showing how they fit together to create the larger theoretical picture.

Each of the modules, all the propositions, and all of my research providing evidence for TDT will be more fully described in chapters 9 through 14. This chapter is an executive summary and an overview of the logic and structure. Outlining the ideas before I get to the detail will assist readers in seeing the bigger picture and the flow of the logic as the book progresses. Readers who find the lists tiresome or tedious can just skip ahead to chapter 7, which returns to the voice and style of the previous chapters. I encourage readers to come back and reread this chapter after reading through chapter 14. The structure and style of this chapter may then be more appreciated. Chapter 15 provides a retrospective rather than a summary.

Because this chapter diverts in style from the rest of book by providing what amounts to a series of lists, an explanation is needed. The point of this book is to provide needed integration. Most of the bullet points in this chapter require a paragraph, a page, or even more of explanation to really unpack. The rest of the book does this. But what is also needed is a succinct way to bring it all together in one place. TDT has a flow and a logic that easily get lost among the details and explication. Seeing the theory in outline, I believe, is the best way to provide the integration and flow I want to convey. It also helps, I think, to be clear about the terminology up front.

INTRODUCING TDT

At the core of TDT is the idea of the truth-default. When we humans communicate with other humans, we tend to operate on a default presumption that what the other person says is honest. This presumption of honesty is highly adaptive. The truth-default enables efficient communication, and this presumption of honesty makes sense because most communication is honest most of the time. However, the presumption of honesty makes humans vulnerable to occasional deceit. A key insight of TDT is that this trade-off is more than worth it. What we gain in terms of efficient communication and social functioning is far more valuable than the cost of being deceived on occasion. Further, there are times and situations when people abandon their presumption of honesty. TDT describes when people are expected to suspect a lie, the conditions under which people conclude that a lie has been told, and the conditions under which people make lie judgments correctly and incorrectly.

TDT Core Concepts and Definitions

The following terms describe the main constructs that populate TDT. Brief definitions are provided for each term.

- *Deception* is intentionally, knowingly, or purposefully misleading another person.[2]
- A *lie* is a subtype of deception that involves outright falsehood, which is consciously known to be false by the teller and is not signaled as false to the message recipient.[3]
- *Honest communication* lacks deceptive purpose, intent, or awareness. Honest communication need not be fully accurate or true, or involve full disclosure of known information.
- The *truth–lie base-rate* refers to the proportion of any set of messages that are honest and deceptive. It is the relative prevalence of deception and nondeception in some defined environment or collection of communicative acts.
- *Truth-bias* is the tendency to believe that another person's communication is honest independent of actual honesty.
- The *truth-default* involves a passive presumption of honesty due to a failure to actively consider the possibility of deceit at all or as a fallback cognitive state after a failure to obtain sufficient affirmative evidence for deception.
- *Honesty judgment* involves the belief state that a communication is

honest. Honesty judgments can be passive (truth-default), stemming from a failure to consider the possibility of deceit; a reversion to truth-default stemming from a failure meet the threshold for a deception judgment; or active decisions based on exculpatory evidence.

- *Deception judgment* is an inference that a communication is deceptive or a lie. Unlike honesty judgments, most deception judgments are active and have an evidentiary or reasoned basis.
- *Demeanor* refers to a constellation of intercorrelated behaviors or cues, which function as a gestalt, relating to how people present themselves, the image they convey to others, and how they are perceived by others.
- *Honest demeanor*, a subtype of demeanor, is the tendency for a person to be seen as honest independent of actual honesty. People vary in the extent to which they have an honest demeanor.
- *Suspicion* is a state of suspended judgment and uncertainty regarding the honesty or deceptive nature of a communication. It is an intermediate cognitive state between the passive truth-default and a firm judgment of deceit.
- *Communication content* refers to the substance of what is said and can be contrasted with demeanor, which also involves how something is said.
- *Communication context* refers to the situation in which the communication occurs, the situation(s) relevant to understanding the communication content, and to the communication event as a whole. Understanding communication content often requires knowledge of context, and communication content presented without its context can be misleading or uninformative.
- *Transparency* refers to the extent to which the honest and/or deceptive nature of some communication is apparent to others.
- *Diagnostically useful information* refers to the extent to which information can be used to arrive at a correct inference about the honest and/or deceptive nature of some communication.
- *Coherence* involves the logical consistency of communication content.
- *Correspondence* involves the consistency between communication content and external evidence or knowledge.
- *Deception detection accuracy* refers to correctly distinguishing between honest and deceptive communication.

TDT MODULES

TDT is a modular theory. The modules are various minitheories, models, effects, and hypotheses that can stand alone. They can be understood without reference to larger theory. Empirical support or disconfirmation for one module does not imply support or disconfirmation of another module. The modules discussed in the following chapters are:

- **A Few Prolific Liars** (or "outliars"; chapter 9)—The prevalence of lying is not normally or evenly distributed across the population. Instead, most people lie infrequently. Most people are honest most of time. There are a few people, however, who lie often. Most lies are told by a few prolific liars.
- **Deception Motives** (chapter 10)—People lie for a reason, but the motives behind truthful and deceptive communication are the same. When the truth is consistent with a person's goals, he or she will almost always communicate honestly. Deception becomes probable when the truth makes honest communication difficult or inefficient.
- **The Projected Motive Model** (chapter 10)—People know that others lie for a reason and are more likely to suspect deception when they think a person has a reason to lie.
- **The Veracity Effect** (chapter 12)—The honesty (i.e., veracity) of communication predicts whether the message will be judged correctly. Specifically, honest messages produce higher accuracy than lies. The veracity effect results from truth-bias.
- **The Park–Levine Probability Model** (chapter 12)—Because honest messages yield higher accuracy than lies (i.e., the veracity effect), the proportion of truths and lies (base-rates) affects accuracy. When people are truth-biased, as the proportion of honest messages increases, so does average detection accuracy. This relationship is linear and is predicted as the accuracy for truths times the proportion of messages that are true plus the accuracy for lies times the proportion of messages that are lies.
- **A Few Transparent Liars** (chapter 13)—The reason that accuracy in deception detection is above chance in most deception detection experiments is that some small proportion of the population are really bad liars who usually give themselves away. The reason accuracy is not higher is that most people are pretty good liars.
- **Sender Honest Demeanor** (chapter 13)—There are large individual

differences in believability. Some people come off as honest. Other people are doubted more often. These differences in how honest different people seem to be are a function of a combination of eleven different behaviors and impressions that function together to create the BQ (believability quotient). Honest demeanor has little to do with actual honesty, and this explains poor accuracy in deception detection experiments.

- **How People Really Detect Lies** (chapter 14)—Outside the deception lab, in everyday life, most lies are detected after the fact, based on either confessions or the discovery of some evidence showing that what was said was false. Few lies are detected in real time based only on the passive observation of sender nonverbal behavior.
- **Content in Context** (chapter 14)—Understanding communication requires listening to what is said and taking that in context. Knowing about the context in which the communication occurs can help detect lies.
- **Diagnostic Utility** (chapter 14)—Some aspects of communication are more useful than others in detecting deception, and some aspects of communication can be misleading. Diagnostic utility involves prompting and using useful information while avoiding useless and misleading behaviors.
- **Correspondence and Coherence** (chapter 14)—Correspondence and coherence are two types of consistency information that may be used in deception detection. Correspondence has to do with comparing what is said to known facts and evidence. It is fact-checking. Coherence involves the logical consistency of communication. Generally speaking, correspondence is more useful than coherence in deception detection.
- **Question Effects** (chapter 14)—Question effects involve asking the right questions to yield diagnostically useful information that improves deception detection accuracy.
- **Expert Questioning** (chapter 14)—Expertise in deception detection is highly context dependent and involves knowing how to prompt diagnostically useful information rather than passively observing deception cues.

TDT Propositions

The TDT propositions provide a string of assertions, predictions, and conjectures that weave the constructs and modules together to describe and explain human deception and deception detection and to provide coherence. That is, the propositional structure shows how the various modules fit together. The propositions also provide specific, testable, and falsifiable predictions. The propositions are numbered one to fourteen and reflect the logical flow of TDT.

- **Proposition one**. Most communication by most people is honest most of the time. While deception can and does occur, in comparison to honest messages, deception is relatively infrequent, and outright lies are more infrequent still. In fact, deception must be infrequent to be effective.
- **Proposition two**. The prevalence of deception is not normally distributed across the population. Most lies are told by a few prolific liars.
- **Proposition three**. Most people believe most of what is said by most other people most of the time. That is, most people can be said to be truth-biased most of the time. Truth-bias results from, in part, a default cognitive state. The truth-default state is pervasive, but it is not an inescapable cognitive state. Truth-bias and the truth-default are adaptive both for the individual and for the species. They enable efficient communication.
- **Proposition four**. Because of proposition one, the presumption of honesty specified in proposition three is usually correct. Truth-bias, however, makes people vulnerable to occasional deception.
- **Proposition five**. Deception is purposive. Absent psychopathology, people lie for a reason. Deception, however, is usually not the ultimate goal, but instead a means to some other ends. That is, deception is typically tactical. Specifically, most people are honest unless the truth thwarts some desired goal or goals. The motives or desired goals achieved through communication are the same for honest and deceptive communications, and deception is reserved for situations where honesty would be ineffectual, inefficient, and/or counterproductive in goal attainment.
- **Proposition six**. People understand that others' deception is usually purposive and are more likely to consider a message as potentially or actually deceptive under conditions where the truth may be inconsistent with a communicator's desired outcomes. That is, people project motive states on others, and this affects suspicion and judgments of honesty and deceit.
- **Proposition seven**. The truth-default state requires a trigger event to abandon it. Trigger events include but are not limited to: (a) a pro-

jected motive for deception, (b) behavioral displays associated with dishonest demeanor, (c) a lack of coherence in message content, (d) a lack of correspondence between communication content and some knowledge of reality, or (e) information from a third party warning of potential deception.

- **Proposition eight.** If a trigger or set of triggers is sufficiently potent, a threshold is crossed, suspicion is generated, the truth-default is at least temporarily abandoned, the communication is scrutinized, and evidence is cognitively retrieved and/or sought to assess honesty– deceit.

- **Proposition nine.** Based on information of a variety of types, an evidentiary threshold may be crossed, and a message may be actively judged to be deceptive. The information used to assess honesty and deceit includes but is not limited to: (a) contextualized communication content and motive, (b) sender demeanor, (c) information from third parties, (d) communication coherence, and (e) correspondence information. If the evidentiary threshold for a lie judgment is not crossed, an individual may continue to harbor suspicion or revert to the truth-default. If exculpatory evidence emerges, active judgments of honesty are made.

- **Proposition ten.** Triggers and deception judgments need not occur at the time of the deception. Many deceptions are suspected and detected well after the fact.

- **Proposition eleven.** With the exception of a few transparent liars, deception is not accurately detected, at the time in which it occurs, through the passive observation of cues or sender demeanor. Honest-looking and deceptive-looking communication performances are largely independent of actual honesty and deceit for most people and hence usually do not provide diagnostically useful information. Consequently, demeanor-based deception detection is, on average, only slightly better than chance due to a few transparent liars, but typically not much above chance due to the fallible nature of demeanor-based judgments.

- **Proposition twelve.** In contrast, deception is most accurately detected through either (a) subsequent confession by the deceiver or (b) comparison of the contextualized communication content to some external evidence or preexisting knowledge.

- **Proposition thirteen.** Both confessions and diagnostically informative communication content can be produced by effective context-sensitive questioning of a potentially deceptive sender. Ill-conceived questioning, however, can backfire and produce below-chance accuracy.

- **Proposition fourteen**. Expertise in deception detection rests on knowing how to prompt diagnostically useful information, rather than on skill in the passive observation of sender behavior.

CHAPTER SUMMARY

This chapter provides a rough sketch of Truth-Default Theory (TDT). The truth-default is that people tend to believe others' communication, and in conversation (or mediated communication) questions of honesty and deception often do not come to mind, except in specific and relatively unusual situations.

TDT departs from prior theories of deception and deception detection in several critical ways. The very idea of the truth-default distinguishes TDT from theories that presume that people typically scrutinize others' communication for veracity. TDT is unique in seeing deception as infrequent relative to honesty and in specifying that most deception is perpetrated by a few prolific liars. The idea that truth-bias is functional and adaptive, and not the result of flawed thinking, also distinguishes TDT from some rival theories.

Key testable predictions of TDT specify the conditions under which the truth-default holds and when it is abandoned in favor of scrutinizing communication for veracity. Factors such as third-party prompting, projected motives, and the logical consistency of communication content, among others, are advanced as triggers that can kick people out of truth-default.

The final set of predictions specifies conditions under which people accurately detect lies. Unlike many prior theories, TDT holds that observing nonverbal deception cues hinders accurate deception detection. Instead, TDT advocates as best paths to improved accuracy a reliance on contextualized communication content and persuading liars to honestly confess their lies.

7

Defining Deception
(Beyond BFLs and Conscious Intent)

SOMETIMES PEOPLE TELL OUTRIGHT LIES. People sometimes say things that they very well know are false with the intent and for the purpose of duping others. But outright lies are not the only ways people go about deceiving others. In fact, outright lies probably account for only a small proportion of deceptive messages.

Chapters 7 and 8 set the stage for TDT by addressing some issues that have been skirted so far but are essential to understanding deception and TDT's place in deception theory. This chapter explores one fundamental question in considerable detail: What is deception? Chapter 8 addresses the closely related issue of the various forms deceptive messages can take. Two theories by my good friend and colleague Steve McCornack (information manipulation theory, IMT, and information manipulation theory 2, IMT2) addressing deceptive message form, function, and production are presented in chapter 8. Together, the next two chapters move our understanding of deception beyond both conscious intent and outright lies.

This chapter is subtitled "Beyond BFLs and Conscious Intent." Steve McCornack's ideas of bald-faced lies (BFLs) and bald-faced truths (BFTs) were briefly mentioned in chapter 5 as a critique of prior theory. Almost all deception research compares outright lies (BFLs) to unproblematic, unpackaged, easy truths. Deception, however, is not limited to BFLs, and, if IMT2 is correct, BFLs are not even the deceptive message of choice in most deception-prompting situations. BFLs constitute only a small and nonrepresentative minority of deceptive messages.

Further, and especially relevant to this chapter, most theorists and researchers define deception as an intentional act. In contrast to the conscious intent requirement, IMT, IMT2, and TDT take a more functional approach to defining deception. Steve McCornack and I certainly don't preclude intent, but we tend to think that if someone was "deceived," then there was deception. Our theories let us talk about messages that function to deceive without knowing the intention states of the person who is doing the deceiving. In short, this chapter and the next outline a theoretical stance that moves beyond BFL and conscious intent.

The relegation of deceptive intent to a lesser role marks a departure for TDT (and companion theories IMT and IMT2) from the theories of deception reviewed in the previous chapters. Because TDT defines deception differently than its rivals, it makes sense to spend some time working through various issues in defining deception and discussing the theoretical implications of various definitions.

In this chapter attention is turned to conceptual issues in defining honesty, deception, and lying. My approach to defining these terms is explained. It might be surprising that a whole chapter is dedicated to defining deception. It is my opinion, however, that defining deception is not as straightforward as it might at first seem, and that a new approach to deception and deception detection is well served by reconsidering what we mean by deception. Good theory, I believe, requires a solid, well-thought-out conceptual foundation. I have been thinking about how to define deception for almost three decades, and this chapter describes that thinking.

DEFINING DECEPTION

In chapter 6, the following definitions of deception, lying, and honest communication were provided without explanation:

- *Deception* is intentionally, knowingly, or purposefully misleading another person.
- A *lie* (or bald-faced lie, BFL for short) is a subtype of deception that involves outright falsehood, which is consciously known to be false by the teller, and is not signaled as false to the message recipient.
- *Honest communication* lacks deceptive purpose, intent, or awareness. Honest communication need not be fully accurate or true, or involve full disclosure.

Before discussing my definitions,[1] let's take a look at definitions of deception by Ekman, Burgoon, and Vrij for comparison:

One person intends to mislead another, doing so deliberately, without prior notification of this purpose, and without having been explicitly asked to do so by the target.[2]

Deception is defined as a message knowingly transmitted by a sender to foster a false belief or conclusion by the receiver. . . . More specifically, deception occurs when communicators control the information contained in their messages to convey a meaning that departs from the truth as they know it.[3]

A successful or unsuccessful deliberate attempt, without forewarning, to create in another a belief which the communicator considers to be untrue.[4]

As you can see, the wording is a little different, but there is a general consensus among Ekman, Burgoon, and Vrij on what constitutes deception. Like the three examples just provided, most definitions of deception these days define it as an intentional or knowing attempt to mislead another person.

It follows from these definitions that speaking the literal truth and being honest are not the same things. Along the same lines, deception and falsehoods are not synonymous. Deception is not a matter of the truth or falsity of what is said but an issue of deceptive intent. An "honest mistake," that is, saying something that one incorrectly believes to be true, is false but it is not considered as deception. Further, saying something known to be false is not deceptive if it is said in such a way that the hearer should know it is false. Sarcasm is an obvious example. If I say "Nice job!" after you make an obvious mistake, you know not to take me literally. None of these cases involve intent to mislead. However, saying something that is literally true in a sarcastic way so that the listener infers something false can be deceptive. In short, what is literally true can be deceptive and saying something false need not be deceptive. What makes something deceptive is, according to most definitions, the conscious intent to mislead.

Also, according to prevailing definitions, what matters is the intent, not what is achieved. Lies that fool no one still count as deception. Focus is placed almost entirely on the intention state of the would-be deceiver. If a sender is trying to deceive, then it's deception according to most definitions. The Vrij definition above makes this most explicit.

Some cases of deception are clear-cut. When someone says something that is clearly false, it is clear that the person speaking the falsehood knows that it is false and intends to deceive the target person, and if the target is indeed

misled by the statement, we have a successful bald-faced lie (BFL). The deceptive nature of such lies is uncontroversial and unequivocal. In such cases, the
peculiarities of particular definitions matter not. Successful BFLs are deception according to all academic and nonacademic definitions alike. In the next
chapter, I present some research showing that just about everyone everywhere
sees BFLs as deception. But, evidence will also be presented showing that BFLs
are only one type of deception, and not an especially common type. BFLs are
deception, but most deception is not achieved through BFLs.

BEYOND BFLS AND INTENT

BFLs populate much of the experimental work on deception and deception detection. But deception is not always so simple and clear-cut, especially outside
the lab. I have several situations in mind that muddy the conceptual waters
and pose challenges for the deceptive-intent approach to defining deception.
The considerations discussed here led me, after much thought, to the definitions I provide in this book that move beyond mere intent and outright lies.

I engage these issues with a little more tentativeness than I approach many
issues in the book. I do not believe that one definition is necessarily right and
the rest are wrong. Definitions are not like theories that can be tested against
data and falsified. I am certainly not after a normative definition here. That is,
I am not seeking to define deception in a way that is consistent with common
everyday usage of the term among English speakers. I am not approaching the
task of defining deception as if I am creating an entry in a dictionary. Instead,
I see the issues discussed here as considerations that make some definitions
more or less useful for various theoretical, empirical, and practical purposes.
I seek a definition that works well for the scope of this book, that fits within
the logic of TDT, and that makes the most sense to me as a theoretician seeking a precise understanding of my topic.[5]

My method here is to offer some thought experiments and then provide
commentary. Let's start. What if you say something to a friend, you did not set
out to mislead them, but you realize soon after you spoke that they misunderstood you and were misled by your words? Let us further presume that this
misunderstanding is not trivial to the other person. The misunderstanding
may cause that person some harm, and an accurate understanding is in his
or her best interests. But, even though you know they were misled because of
something you said and you know this might have some undesirable consequences for them, for whatever reason you don't set the record straight. You
don't correct their misunderstanding. Did you deceive them?

I think the answer is yes. If you know you misled someone and don't correct that, that is deception even if there was no deceptive forethought, intent to do so, or at-the-time recognition. Some readers might disagree or think that this is splitting conceptual hairs. But read on. If Steve McCornack's IMT2, described in the next chapter, is right, we sometimes start talking (i.e., the speech production systems are moving forward creating speech) before we consciously know what we are going say. That is, we are producing on the fly. We are composing our words and forming our ideas as we go. Consequently, misleading statements that work to our benefit can come out of our mouths without prior conscious intent, planning, or forethought of deception. Of course, some lies are deliberate, planned, consciously intended and the like. But I don't want to be limited only to deception involving prior intent. As a consequence of considerations like these, I have long favored a definition of deception involving intent *or* awareness, such as: "*Deception involves knowingly or intentionally misleading another person.*"[6]

The word "knowingly" in my 2010 definition was meant to include even after-the-fact awareness that someone was misled under the scope of deceit and thereby moves beyond the conscious-intent requirement.[7]

FUNCTIONAL DEFINITIONS

I have also long preferred definitions of deception in terms of its effect on people rather than how it is accomplished. In my view, what makes deceptive actions deceptive is that someone is deceived (excuse the circularity), not the specifics of how that deception is accomplished. From my perspective it matters not for the purpose of defining deception whether a person is misled by a false statement, a mixture of true and false information, a mere omission of a relevant detail, an equivocal message, an evasive shift in the direction of conversion, etc. Consequently, the words "misleading" or "misled" are critical to my definitions of deception. When I first began to study deception, it was not unusual for scholars to try to provide a list of the various ways deception might be accomplished. Various categories of deceptive messages were offered. Such lists typically included falsification and omission but missed many other forms of deceptive messages. As we will see in the next chapter, deceptive messages just don't fit neatly into a manageable set of mutually exclusive types. Trying to define deception by listing all the ways it can be accomplished is misguided.

My preference for a functional definition of deception is not universally shared. I have a friend who claims to eschew deception almost completely, and he is quite proud of his honesty, seeing it as a virtue marking moral rectitude. In discussing this virtue with him, I learned that he holds a very narrow definition of deception. Only BFLs, he says, count as dishonest. Strategic omission or ambiguity, he claims, is not dishonesty—only outright intentional falsehoods matter. As I watched him communicate with others, I saw him mislead people from time to time, but never with BFLs. He would omit a detail or be vague, or subtly change the subject. Being a skilled communicator, he didn't need to lie outright to mislead. From my point of view, the outcome was the same: people were deceived. But his narrow definition of deception as strictly limited to BFLs lets him hold the belief that he is an honest person who fastidiously avoids deception. I once thought his view was idiosyncratic, but I have since met others with the same view.

If we view deception primarily from an ethical-moral point of view in which deception is viewed as a bad thing and the goal is to be a good person who does not do bad things, then a narrow definition of deception is psychologically useful. Such views let people see themselves as good, moral people while still being able to function in a social world. But I don't think such a limited definition of deception provides any comfort to those who are deceived by messages that mislead without being BFLs. All this aside, I think there is much more to deception than just the ethical-moral question of good–bad, right–wrong. Don't get me wrong; I think ethics and integrity are very important considerations, but that's not the focus of this book or TDT. In line with the meta-theoretical stance of my former professor Gerald Miller, I see questions of definition and questions of value as different sorts of questions that require different sorts of answers.[8]

SELF-DECEPTION

Another issue that clouds things is self-deception. If deception is defined as a knowing or intentional act, self-deception is precluded, and so is other-deception that stems from self-deception. If I am self-deluded, my communication reflects my delusions, and you are misled by me into believing that my delusions are true because of my communication, is this deception? If we define deception as knowingly or intentionally misleading another, then the answer is no. Delusional messages are not deceptive. The sender consciously believes the message to be true, so self-deception is excluded by definition, and the communication is classified as sincere and honest even though it is false and misleading to the audience.

This issue has come to the forefront of political news coverage with the presidency of Donald J. Trump. The *Washington Post* has a running tally of Trump's false and misleading statements. As I write this, Trump's average stands at 8.3 falsehoods per day, with a one-day high of 125 on September 7, 2018.[9] Can we say that Trump is lying?

The more I have thought about this, the more uncomfortable I am with excluding all other-deception that involves self-deception. The turning point in my thinking was reading a book by Robert Trivers.[10] As a theoretical evolutionary biologist, Trivers was puzzled by self-deception. Wouldn't accurate perception better enable survival?[11] Trivers's solution to the puzzle is that self-deception is adaptive because it makes us better at other-deception. The idea is, the more sincere I am, the better I can fool you.

I don't know that I fully accept Trivers's ideas. But I don't want to rule out subconsciously motivated deception. To me, intention implies conscious awareness. Using the word "knowing" in definitions definitely involves conscious awareness. But I think actions can have function and purpose without conscious awareness. So, I added "or purposefully" to my definition of deception as a nod to the kind of deception Trivers was thinking about.

Daniel Kahneman popularized the ideas of "system one" and "system two" thinking.[12] For people who have not read *Thinking, Fast and Slow*, system one is fast, automatic, and subconscious, while system two is conscious, deliberate, and calculating. Much work on deception presumes that deception is a system two activity. If Trivers and McCornack are right, however, deception can also be the output of system one processes.

Here is a really good example. Let's consider Mrs. Keech and the Seekers from the social scientific classic *When Prophecy Fails*.[13] Basically, the Seekers were a cult that predicted the end of the world. As we all know, the world did not end in the 1950s. The Seekers' prophecy proved objectively false. In the immediate aftermath of the failed prediction, one of the leaders, Mrs. Keech, received a spiritual message that she shared with the group. The faith of the group had been so pure that God called off the mass destruction. The Seekers, as you can imagine, rejoiced. They weren't a loser cult holding objectively false beliefs that had just been unequivocally proven wrong. Instead, they were the saviors of the planet (or at least the Great Lakes states)!

For the purpose of discussion, let's presume that the Seekers' system of beliefs really was fantasy, that disaster was not actually averted that December night in 1954, and that the messages Mrs. Keech received were fiction of some sort or another. Fiction or not, however, it is clear from the story's telling that Mrs. Keech's messages were accepted with enthusiasm by the Seekers. My question is, Was Mrs. Keech's salvation message (and other spiritual messages for that matter) deceptive?

From the standpoint of most definitions of deception, we can't be sure about the deceptiveness of Mrs. Keech's messages, even though we can be reasonably certain about ground truth. According to intent-based definitions, the deceptiveness of the messages hinges on whether Mrs. Keech was a conscious fraud or a sincere but delusional true-believer. Those who believe that it was all an act will see the messages as deceptive. Those who think Mrs. Keech was sincere but delusional will see the messages as false but, by definition, not deceptive. The thing is, if we accept an intent-based definition of deception, we can never know the deceptiveness of the message, because we don't know what was inside Mrs. Keech's head. Maybe she was a conscious fraud. Maybe she was just crazy.

I find this ambiguity deeply unsatisfying. One really troubling implication of deceptive-intent definitions of deception is that outside the lab, it is often the case that we just can't ever know if something is deceptive, because we can't mind-read. Deception researchers often speak about the issue of knowing "ground truth." That is, to know that a statement is false, we have to know what is true. In a criminal context, for example, if a suspect claims innocence, we have to know factual guilt or innocence to establish ground truth. But, from a definition point of view, when we adopt deceptive intent as the critical issue, knowing ground truth is not sufficient to settle the issue. It is the communicator's understanding of the truth that is at issue. Consider the implications for an eyewitness account. The issue is not what actually happened but what the witness thought he or she saw.

This is a tough issue, but I think the messages were deceptive regardless of Mrs. Keech's intent. The messages functioned deceptively. People were misled. The communication had deceptive purpose. They served Mrs. Keech and the group well. By including "or purposefully" in my definition, I get to count examples such as this as deceptive even if we don't know her intent. We don't have to get inside senders' heads. I prioritize ground truth and deceptive impact and function over deceptive intent.

THEORY OF MIND

At this point in the discussion, it is worth mentioning that intent and awareness play a different role in my thinking about deception than in the various cue theories discussed in chapters 4 and 5. In the logic that undergirds cue theories, the leakage, clues, and cues that give away liars are byproducts of psychological differences between liars and honest people. Those psychological differences that produce cues might not exist without the awareness that one is deceiving and without the intent to deceive. A person needs to know that he or she is lying if he or she is to fear detection, experience guilt, or enjoy duping delight. A person who does not know that would not necessarily be expected to experience heightened arousal as a result of lying, or to exert more cognitive effort, or to engage extra strategic efforts to appear believable. This is precisely why Trivers argues that self-deception enhances other-deception. Without intent and conscious knowledge, the logic of cue theories falters. Thus, cue thinking ties theorists and researchers to intent-based definitions.

But TDT (and IMT and IMT2) are not cue theories, so the byproducts of intent and awareness that might bring about leakage and cues are not needed for theoretical coherence. Nevertheless, intent and awareness play a different, albeit critical, role. Human and primate deception involves a cognitive ability that is sometimes called *theory of mind*.[14] It involves thinking about thinking, in both self and others. It involves understanding mental states such as intentions and beliefs, the realization that both the self and other people have mental states such as intentions and beliefs, and the insight that our own intentions and beliefs might be different from others' intentions and beliefs. Theory of mind lets us, among other things, take the perspective of others. Theory of mind allows me to understand that what my wife may want for a gift is not the same as what I want for myself. I understand that what she wants and what I want may not always align.

Human deception typically involves theory of mind. In order to effectively deceive someone, we need to understand that others don't automatically know what we know and that we can do and say things that affect others' belief states. Consider deception by omission. I'll give a personal example here. About the time I started working on this chapter, I was in the process of being recruited by another university. A university (UAB) contacted me, persuaded me to apply, invited me for an interview, and made me an attractive job offer that I accepted a week before writing this sentence. As I write this, I have not yet told my current employer, and I do not plan to do so until it is near the time to resign. If my current employer is likely to find out about my new job before I want to disclose it, it makes sense for me to disclose my new job before it is discovered. If I don't and they find out, I look deceptive. Nothing is gained from hiding known information, and there are potential costs. However, it is probably in my best interest to postpone my current employer's knowing about my departure, so that I am not treated differently in the meantime. This will postpone much awkwardness. The point of this story is that for omission to work deceptively, the deceiver (me) must have some idea what the target person (people at my current university) already know and don't know, and have ideas about how the target person(s) might find about. People need to mentally represent others' thoughts for deception to function.

My example implied a very conscious consideration of others' mental states, but I do not think theory-of-mind cognition is of necessity in conscious awareness. We have much knowledge about others' knowledge states, but we don't keep that information active in working memory all the time. I don't require constant active effort and intent to keep from blurting out my secret.

Theory of mind is also critical from the target person's perspective. If deception requires inferring others' mental states, so too does deception detection. As we will see in later chapters, people are more likely to infer that someone is lying in situations where the person has a motive to lie. My projected motive module of TDT is a special case of theory of mind.

The lack of conscious awareness has interesting implications on the target person's end too. If TDT is right, people do not actively and consciously monitor others for signs of dishonesty. We believe others as a passive default state. But trigger events can kick us out of our default and into conscious consideration of honesty.

Theory of mind raises a very important point about deception. It matters what the target person knows and what a sender thinks the target person knows. Most people won't lie if they think the truth is already out of the bag. If you lie but the target knows the truth, any advantage gained by deception is not realized, and your own credibility is reduced. It is all downside. Regarding omission, as I said previously, there is no reason to withhold information that is already known. This was part of the Scharff technique (named after the WWII Nazi interrogator) of interrogation. If detainees were fooled into thinking the information was already known, they need not hide the information: "Scharff began by asking a prisoner a question he already knew the answer to, informing the prisoner that he already knew everything about him, but his superiors had given instruction that the prisoner himself had to say it. Scharff continued asking questions that he would then provide the answers for, each time hoping to convince his captive that there was nothing he did not already know. When Scharff eventually got to the piece of information he did not have, prisoners would frequently give the answer, assuming Scharff already had it in his files anyway, often saying so as they provided the information."[15]

Not only can people be tricked into revealing sensitive information that they believe is already known, but bluffing about what is known can be used as lie deterrence. Because there is little deceptive value in lying about something known, leading a sender to believe you already know the truth (or that you can and will find out) can prevent a lie. Alternatively, target persons can use known information as a lie detection tool if they don't let senders know what they know. This is done by asking someone a question whose answer you already know. If the person contradicts what you know, this suggests the possibility that he or she is lying.[16]

This last possibility reminds me of a story involving my wife and two of her graduate students. My wife teaches her students the importance of reading original work and of not second-hand citing. Second-hand citing is relying on some third party's description of work, but citing the original work as if it had been read. Back to the story, my wife had read the first student's thesis draft and asked the student about some suspicious citations. The student replied that she had read the original work, having found it in the university library. My wife knew for a fact that the library's only copy had been checked out (because she had been the one who checked it out). Just to be sure, she asked the student some details about the book in question. It was clear that the student had not read the work in question, although the student tried to bluff her way through it. The bluff was unsuccessful, but my wife never told the student that she knew the student was lying. My wife didn't trust the student after that, and eventually the student found a new (and more gullible) advisor. The student was more effective in bluffing her new advisor, but had more difficulty bluffing her way through the life of a young professor.

Not long after that experience, my wife was talking with another of her students. She asked about some citations in the student's thesis as she had with the first student. This student too said that she had read the original. It had been hard to find. The library's only copy was checked out, so she had to go through interlibrary loan. The student went on to talk about details of the book with my wife. To this day, this second student is one of my wife's favorites. Unlike the first student, she passed the secret integrity test.

A final example of the importance of theory of mind comes from research on the development of deception and theory of mind in children. In an experiment I find especially informative, three-year-old and five-year-old children selected among desirable and less desirable stickers while interacting with either a good puppet or a bad puppet.[17] Children were asked which sticker they wanted. Good Puppet would take a sticker other than the one the child had indicated, while Bad Puppet would always take the sticker that the child said he or she wanted. Several trials ensued. Three-year-olds were repeatedly frustrated by Bad Puppet and often became quite upset. But, when asked which sticker they wanted, they would point to the desired sticker, only to be thwarted once again as Bad Puppet took their preferred sticker. The experiment went very differently for most of the five-year-olds. After figuring out that the Bad Puppet really would take the desired sticker, when asked to their preference, the older children simply lied. They "picked" a disfavored sticker, which was snatched up by Bad Puppet, leaving the actually favored sticker for the clever child. Thus, as we can see from these examples, intent, perceptions of others' intent, and the broader issue of theory of mind are critical to how deception functions.[18]

CONVENTIONALLY AND TRANSPARENTLY FALSE STATEMENTS

The next situation to consider is that of conventionally or transparently false statements. Maybe the best example of a conventionally false statement is when (presuming Americans in the United States) a person, in passing, casually asks, "How are you?" and the reply is "Fine." This exchange is highly routinized and conventional. So is "What's up?"—"Nothing much." I don't consider "fine" or "nothing much" deceptive even if the factually accurate answerer is not fine or something really is up. People in the language community understand, or at least should understand, that when we ask routinized, conventional questions in greetings, we get a routinized, conventional answer in return. I once had a socially awkward colleague who used to answer honestly to such questions. A passing "How are you?" in a hallway yielded an extensive and graphic reply about current digestive problems. The answer was honest, but "Fine" would have been a much better answer. Had we not heard about the digestive problems, we would not have felt deprived or deceived. (Almost) no one really thinks "fine" means everyone is currently wonderful and good. It's just what we say, and we all know it.

It's not always clear, however, just what is conventional and what is common knowledge that members of a community should have. I, for example, enjoy online gaming. If I am playing *World of Warcraft*, and I encounter a female character in the game, I don't presume that the person playing that character is female. And if I find out that a female character is played by a male, I would not necessarily feel deceived. It's role-playing. I don't presume that the actors in movies have the personalities of the people they play. I don't feel deceived that James Bond or Spider-Man are not real or that the actors who play them don't really have their powers or abilities. It's the movies. We know it's fiction.[19] Similarly, I don't see role-playing as deception. The whole point of role-playing is to play a role.

For a while I was playing a female character in an online game similar to *World of Warcraft*. During that time, I met another female character online, and we adventured together in the game world a few nights a week over a few months. Not that it really mattered to me either way, but I guessed with reasonable confidence that this other person was really female. But we never really chatted about things outside the game world except for things like "be right back, taking the dog out" or "early night, got to work in the morning." Nevertheless, I thought she probably knew I was male, just as I had pieced together that she was an adult female who lived in Colorado. One night I said something that made clear that I was male playing a female character. I could tell she felt shocked and deceived. I did not think I was deceptive. I never claimed to really be female, and it was just a role-playing game. But is this an example of deception?

Situations like these led to a discussion with a colleague, Joe Walther, who studies computer-mediated communication and who was interested in information on online dating sites. If a female who actually weighs 129 pounds lists her weight as 120, is she lying? Joe mostly saw the question as issues of deceptive intent and ground truth. Do people actually know their current weight? Weight can fluctuate. Then there is liberal rounding. Still, I wondered about convention. What if everyone knocks off five to fifteen pounds, and everyone knows that everyone does this? If I know that 120 really means 130, it's not deception, I argued. Might this be similar to how-are-you-I'm-fine? We actually did a series of experiments to try and sort it out.[20] Unfortunately, the results were not entirely clear; they did suggest that a little self-deception might be at play but also that reports of weight might also be knowingly adjusted downward. We never really got at the issue of how statements of body weight are heard and understood in the online dating community.

A related issue is transparently false statements. As a general rule, I don't think that obviously false statements are deceptive. People should know better, and the tellers of such tales ought not expect to be believed and taken literally. For example, if I say, "I just looked out the window, it is a clear night, and I can see all three of Earth's moons," you wouldn't believe that the Earth had three moons, would you?

But things are murky here too. The title of my theory is truth-default theory, after all, and sometimes people do believe some pretty unbelievable things.[21] I gave some examples in chapter 1. Here is another humorous yet informative example.

Several years ago, when I was a professor of communication at Michigan State University, there were the beginnings of a strong push by the university administration to encourage faculty to get external grants. In the beginning the pressure was mostly incentive based. To publicize and encourage grant-getting and to try and create a culture change, the college started naming a researcher of the month.[22] Large posters were made and visibly posted each month naming the awardee, and describing the funded research project. Much to my initial horror, I was named September's researcher of the month for my deception research funded by the National Science Foundation. Professor September with a photo shoot and all. Yikes! But my initial consternation gave way to much amusement and even appreciation when I saw the poster. It was truly a gem.

The right column accurately described the research, the grant, and my work on truth-bias. The left column offered the following biographical sketch, complete with what appeared to be me on the cover of *Rolling Stone* magazine.

Tim Levine gained his BS in Psychology from Northern Arizona University while leading the Lumberjacks to their first Big Sky Conference basketball title ever, scoring 34 points in the decisive double-overtime victory over the University of Montana. Picked 19th overall by the Knicks in the NBA draft, Tim chose his MA over the big money and hot lights of pro sports. While earning his Masters in Communication at West Virginia University, Tim was approached by a young coal miner from Seattle named Chris Cornell, who heard Tim jamming on the bass with a Morgantown band in the Wharf District pub. Cornell immediately invited Tim on tour with his band, a then-little-known quartet called Soundgarden. Thus, Tim's MA was delayed for ten years, seven international tours, and five full-length CDs.

The early 90's found Tim pursuing his PhD at MSU. His thesis, entitled Pinnochio: an in-depth study of deception in 19th-century Italy, is still required reading for all CIA interrogators. One of Tim's breakthrough discoveries is elucidated on pages 943–944. . . . Observations of a carbon-based arboreal subject engaged in purposeful prevarication showed unmistakable increase in length of the proboscis, at times 300 microns, depending upon the magnitude of the deception. —Bart Moore (2007).

Despite the obviously outlandish content and the fact that the poster was about deception research, more than one person approached me and said something like "Wow, I didn't know you were in Soundgarden," or, "I can't believe you turned down a chance to play in the NBA." Amusement aside, this was more evidence that I was on the right theoretical path with TDT. But with particular respect to transparent falsehoods, even the most outlandish things can fool some people. The implications for defining deception are intriguing.[23]

FAILED DECEPTIVE ATTEMPTS

The last of my little thought experiments regarding defining deception asks if deception has to be successful to be deception. I think most people who accept intent-based approaches to defining deception see deceptive intent as sufficient. If a person was trying to deceive someone else, that is still deception, even if the lie fails and no one was deceived. It's the thought that counts, so to speak. In my view, however, someone must actually be misled for deception to exist. I prefer to call failed attempts at deception "attempted deception," to distinguish them from successful deception.

CONCLUSION

To sum up this discussion, I see useful distinctions between conscious intentional deceptions, deceptive attempts, messages perceived as deceptive, and messages that are functionally deceptive. Intentional deception is meant to deceive, and it achieves this end. The target person is misled by design. In deceptive attempts, someone tries to deceive another person, and there is deceptive intent, but the target is not actually misled. This situation may be thought of as failed deception. In perceived deception, the target person attributes deception to a communication regardless of the actual intent or infers intent that was not there. Finally, messages that are functionally deceptive mislead others regardless of the actual or perceived intent. Functionally deceptive messages lead to the same outcome as deception, without getting into the message source's head regarding their intention states.

An important implication is that message features like the truth and falsity of specific content, message intent, and message function or impact need to be distinguished because these things do not map perfectly onto one another. So, someone can say something that is objectively false, omit information, change the subject, and so forth, in a manner that is either intended to deceive or not. The objective truth or falsity of messages may or may not actually function as deception, and such messages may or may not be perceived as deception. In short, speaker intent, purpose, and message consequence in combination define deception, not the objective qualities of messages or information dimensions (discussed in the next chapter). Further, mere speaker intent is neither sufficient nor necessary in and of itself to define deception.

8

Information Manipulation
(Beyond BFLs and Conscious Intent, Part 2)

THIS CHAPTER TURNS OUR ATTENTION to the various ways people deceive others with words. As noted in the previous chapter, most deception research focuses on what Steve McCornack calls bald-faced truths (BFTs) and bald-faced lies (BFLs).[1] But there are many ways to deceive besides the outright lie, and many honest messages are not BFTs. This chapter makes a distinction between lies and the broader issue of deception. To this end, two theories (information manipulation theory [IMT] and information manipulation theory 2 [IMT2]) are reviewed. Both move the discussion well beyond BFTs and BFLs.

IMT and IMT2 are theories that complement TDT. But the overlap is minimal, and the focus is different. TDT covers areas of traditional concern in deception research, such as deception detection. IMT is about how people deceive with words, and why it is that words can be used to deceive. IMT also provides a useful descriptive framework for thinking about variation in messages that function to deceive. IMT2, in contrast, is a theory of deceptive message production. That is, IMT2 is a theory that tries to explain how it is that people verbalize deceptive messages.

Both IMT and IMT2 are the creations of my good friend and colleague Steve McCornack. IMT2 is new and a major extension of the original IMT. Although these theories are wholly Steve's, I played a role in testing the original IMT, and our collaborative research on IMT is covered in this chapter. IMT is described, and several of Steve and my old studies testing IMT are enumerated. Next, IMT2 is summarized, and its implication for deception theory is explained.

INFORMATION MANIPULATION THEORY (IMT)

Steve McCornack developed IMT as his doctoral dissertation at the University of Illinois under the guidance of Barbara O'Keefe and published an article-length theoretical statement in *Communication Monographs* in 1992, along with a companion article testing key predictions.[2] IMT adapted ideas from the philosopher of language Herbert Paul Grice to deception. A similar application of Grice to deception was also made about the same time in the context of perjury law,[3] and the Polish linguist Dariusz Galasinski independently had an idea remarkably similar to IMT.[4] Interpersonal deception theory (IDT) describes dimensions of information management that parallel IMT dimensions, but the IDT versions are not tied to Grice, and according to IDT authors, any similarity is purely coincidental.[5]

Before sketching IMT, a brief primer on Grice's idea of *implicature* is needed.[6] Grice was concerned with the disconnection between formal logic and everyday communication. He observed that people often don't say what they mean but are nevertheless understood. His idea of implicature is a catchall label to capture the idea of implying, meaning, or suggesting something that is not said outright, explicitly, and directly. Grice's conversational implicatures share some similarities with Edward T. Hall's idea of high-context communication in *Beyond Culture*.[7] The meaning is not in the literal understanding of words and requires understanding of the situation or context of the utterance.[8]

For example, I was recently on a college search committee where several professors and I were discussing the suitability of several potential job candidates. One of my colleagues said of one of the applicants who was, on paper, especially well qualified, "I know his work. He has lots of publications." I interpreted this to mean (i.e., what was implicated was) that although the person published much research and might look good on paper, the candidate's research was of low quality. What Grice's ideas are about is explaining the "logic" we use to implicate things to others and that we use to decode what others implicate to us. How is it that (A) "he publishes with high frequency" can be both be meant as and understood as (B) "his work is not very good"? How do we get from A to B?

In order to make sense of implicatures, Grice thought, we need to accept adherence to a cooperation principle (CP) and its maxims. People mean something when they are talking, and they generally want those to whom the talk is directed to understand what is meant. Specifically, Grice's CP holds: "Make your contribution such as it is required, at the stage at which it occurs, by the accepted purpose or direction of the talk exchange in which you are engaged."[9]

The CP has four maxims, or subrules.[10]

- Quantity: Make your contribution sufficiently informative, but don't provide too much information.

- Quality: Make your contribution true. Don't say false things or things that you don't know.
- Relevance: Stay on topic and make what you say relevant to the conversation.
- Manner: Be clear, and avoid unneeded ambiguity.

As long as people follow the maxims fully, understanding is straightforward. Anyone who knows the language can understand what is meant by a statement that is informative, accurate, relevant, and unambiguous. But, of course, people don't always follow the maxims. Sometimes people don't follow them at all, but sometime violations are just on the surface and the maxims are followed on a deeper level. It was the surface violations that involve deeper adherence that most interested Grice. Grice lists several ways in which people can violate one or more of the maxims. People can opt out of the maxims, making it explicit that they are not cooperating. This is the conversational equivalent of a "no comment." The maxims may clash in such a way that fulfilling one violates another. Most interestingly for Grice, people may flout a maxim by blatantly violating it (think sarcasm). Finally, Grice mentions in passing that people can "quietly and unostentatiously" violate a maxim, and in doing so they are likely to mislead others.[11]

Conversational implicatures, according to Grice, occur when a speaker says one thing, means another, and nevertheless expects to be understood correctly. The listener presumes that the speaker is following the CP; the speaker actually means what is implicated, not what is said; and the speaker thinks that the listener should be able to figure it out. Figuring it out follows the logic that if the speaker is following the CP, the speaker does not mean what was said, and probably means this other thing, that which was implicated.

Back to my colleague and his statement about the sheer amount of publishing seemed to flout quantity. If he had read the work, surely he had an opinion of it. If that opinion was positive, he would say so. He would have said something like: "I know their work. They do cool stuff." But, he didn't know what others thought of the candidate, and he didn't want to be on record with a negative evaluation, so he said too little, which still communicated his opinion, just off the record.[12]

Shifting from Grice to IMT's origination, McCornack was generally interested in deception in romantic relationships. He had already published McCornack and Park's model of relational deception, and he was interested in moving beyond deception detection in the direction of deceptive message design. His method involved a series of steps. He first asked a set of research subjects to describe a situation in which they had deceived a dating partner. He basically collected numerous stories of relational deception. Stories that were sufficiently detailed were rewritten to be hypothetical and reworded to maintain anonymity. These situations were then given to and evaluated by a second set of research subjects for deception potential. Situations were selected that were neither too high (everyone lied) nor too low (everyone was honest). Next, a third set of subjects was asked to imagine themselves in one of the situations that had deception potential, and those subjects were asked to write out what they might say if they were in such a situation.

"Committed Chris" was one of the situations he used that will give the reader an idea of the message creation task:

> You have known Chris for over two years and have been dating for over a year. Because of the length of the relationship, you feel very close to Chris. Recently, however, your feelings have begun to change. Chris is extremely jealous, and the two of you have recently been arguing about almost anything. Chris is in the phase where s/he wants to have a serious committed relationship, but you feel like you want to date others. Recently you have been dating someone else, unbeknownst to Chris. This other relationship has been a lot of fun, and has recently become more intense both sexually and emotionally.
>
> One night when you and Chris are out, Chris is acting really cold. Suddenly, Chris looks at you and says "Lately you've been acting really distant. Is there anything wrong?"[13]

Quick, what would you say?
Here are some possible replies . . .

- "No, nothing's wrong."
- "I don't know."
- "I have a lot of things on my mind. Sorry."
- "I was just distracted. Want another drink, or should we go somewhere else?"
- "Chris, why are you always so jealous! You are the one who is acting cold. Don't go projecting things onto me. What's wrong with you? Why do you have to be like this?"
- "I'm not happy with how we fight all the time these days."
- "Yeah, my feelings for you are changing. I know you want a commitment, but I'm sorry, I'm not ready for that. Maybe we should start dating other people."
- "We need to talk. I have been putting it off because I didn't want to

hurt you. I know you want a commitment, but you are too jealous, and we fight too much. Plus, I met this other person, and it is getting serious. Sorry I didn't tell you sooner. . . . I know I should have. We had a good thing, but it's just not working."

- "Yes, I am seeing some else, and I like them more than you. Bye."

The first message option above is a BFL. The last is a BFT. The "We need to talk . . ." message is a packaged truth. As you can see, there are many possible deceptive responses that fall in between BFLs and BFTs.

Steve had almost three hundred subjects complete the what-would-you-say task in response to Committed Chris or one of the other deception-prompting situations. In examining the resulting messages, Steve came to several key insights and conclusions. First, there was a striking amount of variability in the ways in which people responded to the various situations. People said very different things in response to the same situation. Second, although there were examples of BFLs and BFTs (that is, some people told the complete truth without concern for self-presentation or the other person's feelings, and some people just outright lied), neither was especially prevalent. BFLs and BFTs were unusual and infrequent. Third, in contrast to BFLs and BFTs, most people shaded and manipulated the truth in various subtle and original ways. Fourth, the variation in messages that were deceptive seemed to correspond to violations of one or more of Grice's maxims. That is, most deceptive messages involved some combination of omitted information (quantity violation), false information (quality violation), a lack of clarity functioning to obscure information (manner violation), and/or irrelevant information, providing a diversion of attention (relevance violation). Finally, existing taxonomies of deception types (e.g., omissions, half-truths, exaggerations, etc.) failed to capture the variations in deceptive messages. In fact, the messages just did not seem to fall into some manageable set of mutually exclusive "types" or categories.

These observations led to the key idea behind IMT. *Messages that are deceptive are covert violations of one or more of Grice's maxims.* People are misled because they tacitly assume that the deceiver is behaving cooperatively; that is, communicators are trying to be understood and following the CP and its maxims.

For the most part, when we communicate, we have to assume that the people we are communicating with are following the CP and its maxims. Otherwise, we just can't make sense of communication. The catch is that by presuming that others are cooperative, we open ourselves up to being duped by those who feign good-faith cooperative interaction. We get fooled because the violations are *covert*.

Think about the implications of this for a moment. Consider reading this book. Understanding that what I am writing requires that I want to be understood and that you think not only that I want to be understood but that there is a good chance of your understanding what I write. If you think that I just make stuff up willy-nilly, that I leave out important points and include superfluous information at random, that my writing is nebulous and impenetrable, and that what I am writing often has nothing to do with the point of the book, is there really any point in reading it in the first place? I think not. If we can't presume some degree of cooperation, communication loses all functionality. If we have to second-guess every sentence, we can't learn anything. We bog down quickly in uncertainty.

This is where IMT and TDT converge. Presuming speakers follow the CP (at least on some level) and the idea of the truth-default are very similar. And the reason for adherence to the CP and its maxims and the reason for the truth-default are the same: they are required for effective and efficient communication and cooperation. We need something like a CP or a truth-default in order to communicate because the alternative leads to communicative solipsism. The implication of the CP and the truth-default is the same too; these make us vulnerable to deceit.

One of the primary contributions of IMT is that it provides a coherent and theoretically grounded way to talk about variation in deceptive messages. Most deception involves covert violations of one or more of four maxims.[14] Deception by withholding information (i.e., omission) covertly violates quantity. Deception with false information is a covert violation of quality. Covert violations of relevance are deception by evasion. Finally, covert violations of manner are deceptive equivocation. But most deceptive messages are not "pure types" reflecting violations of just one maxim. Rather, most deceptive messages can be thought of as reflecting a point in four-dimensional space with the four maxims forming four dimensions.

IMT STUDY ONE: THE FIRST IMT STUDY

Steve and my first study of IMT[15] simply involved having new subjects read one of the deception-provoking situations and an exemplar message and having the subjects evaluate the message in terms of its honesty or deceptiveness. The prediction was that messages that violated the maxims would be rated as more dishonest than a baseline honest control message that was fully disclosive, factually true, relevant, and clear. We had over a thousand subjects read and rate one of many situation-message combinations. We used two different situations and two different message examples for each of the maxim viola-

TABLE 8.1. INITIAL TEST OF IMT

Message Condition	Honesty Rating
Base-line honest	5.47
Quality (false)	1.74
Relevance (evasive)	2.93
Manner (equivocal)	3.43
Quantity (omission)	4.20

Note: Possible values range from 1 to 7, with higher scores indicating more honest. All scores are significantly different at p < .0001.

tions (quality, quantity, relation, manner, no violation) taken from the research described previously. Subjects rated the honesty of the message on seven-point scales where one was completely deceptive and seven was maximally honest. The results are in table 8.1.

The data were consistent with the main prediction of IMT. Messages violating the various maxims were judged as more dishonest than a control honest message not violating one of the maxims. Further, the effects were huge, with the experimental variation in message example accounting for 47% of the variance honest ratings (that is equivalent to a d of 1.88!). But, even the objectively honest messages were not rated as completely honest. Presumably coming clean involved revealing prior deception. Further, while everyone rated false messages as very deceptive, violations of quantity and manner were rated as kind of deceptive, near the midpoint of the scale range. They were rated as more deceptive than the honest message by more than a full scale point, but more honest than an outright lie by a similar margin.

IMT STUDY TWO: REPLICATION AND INCLUSION OF A DICHOTOMOUS ASSESSMENT

To try and sort things out, in 2001 I replicated our 1992 results with a twist.[16] I had subjects read Committed Chris and rate one of five message examples, just like our original 1992 experiment. The twist was I also asked subjects to make a dichotomous, forced-choice, honest–deceptive evaluation too. The results are in table 8.2.

As in the original, larger 1992 study, all the violations were rated as less honest than the honest baseline control, replicating basic support for IMT. This was true both for scaled honesty and the forced-choice evaluation. And

TABLE 8.2. REPLICATION OF INITIAL IMT FINDINGS

Message Condition	1992	2001	% Honest
Base-line honest	5.47	5.82	98%
Quality (false)	1.74	2.29	13%
Relevance (evasive)	2.93	2.55	11%
Manner (equivocal)	3.43	3.82	51%
Quantity (omission)	4.20	3.34	47%

Note: Possible values range from 1 to 7, with higher scores indicating more honest.

the pattern of the means was similar, although this time quantity was rated as more deceptive than in the previous study. On the truth–deception pick-one question, there was near-unanimity that the honest message was honest. People rated it only 5.8 out of 7 in scaled honesty, but when forced to choose, they rated it as honest, not deception. There was also near-perfect agreement on quality and relevance. Just under 90% of the people said those were deceptive.[17] However, there was a near fifty-fifty split on manner and quantity violations. About half of the people said honest, half said deceptive.

Close examination of the scaled honesty rating gives a clue to what's going on. Although the averages for quantity and manner were quite similar, the distributions of scores were not. Honest ratings of manner were normally distributed around the mean, near the center of the honesty scale. Most people rated the manner violations as neither fully honest nor fully deceptive. They saw them as in-between. The distribution of quantity violations, however, was bimodal. A sizable group of people (just under half) rated omissions as very deceptive. Another sizable group of people rated them on the honest side of the scale midpoint. No one gave it a seven—perfectly honest, but lots of people used four and five. The conclusion I draw from this is that there is a great deal of convergence in how people see outright lies, evasion, and equivocation. But there are large individual differences in how omission is seen. Some people see it as deceptive as evasion or an outright lie. Other people see it more like equivocation, somewhere between honesty and outright deceit.

IMT STUDY THREE: EFFECTS OF DECEPTION SEVERITY

I have two more IMT studies to tell you about before summing up and moving on to IMT2. It seemed to me in thinking about IMT results that how people

rate different violation types isn't just about how the deception was being accomplished (i.e., the type of violation) but also about the nature of the deception, specifically what the deception is hiding. My thinking was that the differences between the violation types might expand or contract depending on
the severity of the consequences of the deception. If the consequences of the
deception were really bad, the type of violation might make less difference.

To test this line of thinking, my students Kelli Asada and Lisa Massi and I
designed some new situations and messages.[18] Continuing the relational deception theme, we told approximately two hundred subjects about a hypothetical dating relationship between Chris and Sam. Chris and Sam do not always
practice safe sex. Some of our subjects were told that Sam had an STD in the
past from a prior relationship, but that it was treated, completely cured, non-
contagious, basically just prior history.[19] The rest of the subjects learned that
Sam is HIV-positive.[20] This was back in the days before drug treatments were
highly effective; HIV was considered fatal. Sam either outright lied (BFL quality
violation) to Chris saying, depending on the condition, that he was tested and
is HIV-negative or denied ever having an STD of any kind, or Sam just does
not tell Chris (quantity violation). Thus, subjects rated an omission or a falsification about a not-such-a-big deal or a really serious big bad deception.

The differences between quality and quantity violations observed in our
prior experiments went away under high deception severity. When the issue
was having unsafe sex with an HIV-positive partner, it didn't matter much
whether the deception was an outright lie or an oh-I-forgot-to-tell-you deception. Either way, the behavior was rated as highly deceptive (averages greater
than six on a seven-point scale). When the issue was a less consequential matter of a prior-but-cured STD, the outright lie was rated as highly deceptive,
but mere omission dropped to mid-range, not-honest-but-not-totally-deceptive,
similar to what quality violations had produced in other studies.

IMT STUDY FOUR: RELATIONSHIP AMONG IMT DIMENSIONS

The final IMT study reviewed here looked at the interrelationships among perception of maxim violations.[21] IMT studies typically involve ratings of quality,
quantity, relevance, and manner in addition to ratings of honesty. So, subjects
read a situation and a message in response to the situation and then rate the
message on scales to assess the truth or falsity of the message, the amount of
information revealed, clarity, relevance, and honesty–deceptiveness. One IMT
replication by other researchers found that messages exemplifying one type of
violation were also rated as violations of the other violations as well, and this
was thought to be a problem.[22]

I did a study to try and sort this out. I reanalyzed two large IMTs data sets, each involving around a thousand subjects.[23] In both data sets, ratings of the various dimensions were highly intercorrelated. The correlations ranged from $r = .51$ to $.85$. Using a statistical analysis called confirmatory factor analysis, I found that a second-order unidimensional model fit both data sets. What this means is that the maxims and maxim violations are not stand-alone, independent sorts of ideas. They have a common force guiding how they function. This is evidence that something like the CP is playing a causal role behind the scenes. This idea that the dimensions are intertwined and are different variations or aspects of the CP is very much consistent with IMT. It would be a problem for IMT if it were otherwise.

This also suggests that people who don't know Grice's ideas or IMT don't really make clear distinctions between violations of various sorts. Once it's pointed out, recognizing violations of various sorts is very useful in spotting potential deception. Having worked on IMT research and taught IMT ideas, I am now very sensitive to answers that don't answer the question actually asked and subtly try to answer a different, not-asked question. I often notice vague, ambiguous statements open to multiple interpretations. People who seem to be saying too little or too much catch my attention. I don't interpret such things as deception, but instead as what Ekman calls "hot spots"—things that might (or might not) signal deceit. Knowing Grice and IMT gives me labels for these things. Having words to describe observations can help sharpen those observations and provide structure to my thinking, helping me make sense of what is observed. What the findings of IMT study 4 suggest is that absent awareness of the theory behind IMT, everyday people don't make these kind of distinctions. Various violations reflect degrees of deceptiveness, but there is little nuance to the perception beyond mere deceptiveness. Rather than posing a problem for IMT, this observation, I think, points to IMT's utility. IMT is not a folk theory of how communication is perceived. Instead, it adds insight that we would not have without the theory.

Another nice thing about IMT's approach is that the CP provides coherence to the maxims. Grice and CP provide an overarching structure that keeps the various maxims from just being an arbitrary list. This is a big advantage over various typologies of deception types. The problem with most observation-based category schemes is that any two different researchers looking at the same set of messages will invariably come up with different ways to classify the messages into types. The fact is that there are usually lots of different ways any finite set of messages can be classified. Of course, different researchers think their own categories are right and that others are misguided. Theory-based approaches provide a way out of arbitrariness. If we look at IDT's five dimensions of information management and ask why these five and not some other set, there is not a clear answer other than the opinion of IDT authors. But, for IMT, the basis for selecting quality, quantity, relevance, and manner is clear. It has to be those four. The theory would not make sense if it were any other way.

IMT2

For McCornack, the original IMT was just a starting point—a small part of a much larger theoretical ambition. Ever self-critical, McCornack has said many times that the original IMT is not even a theory.[24] In his view IMT is theoretical, but not a theory in a strict sense of theory. More importantly for Steve, the original IMT did not do what he really wanted to accomplish. Steve was after a theory of deceptive message production. How is it that people say deceptive things? When do people answer honestly? When will people simply omit a critical piece of information? When do people outright lie? What determines the options, and how exactly does this work? The original IMT is silent on such questions. IMT tells us why people are misled by messages, and it provides a theoretically based descriptive framework capturing the various forms deceptive messages can take. But it is not a theory of message production.

Around the time that Buller and Burgoon published IDT in 1996, Steve was becoming increasingly frustrated with deception theory and research. The practice of social scientific scholarship on deception had become very contentious as different groups of researchers struggled, often behind the scenes, to further their own perspectives and undermine the competition. Between 1997 and 2014, Steve took a long break from deception to focus on writing some amazing and successful communication textbooks.[25] So, although his 1997 article really set the stage for IMT2, IMT2 was not completed and published until 2014. IMT2, just recently completed as of this writing, was published in a special issue of *Journal of Language and Social Psychology* that also contains the article-length summary of TDT and our joint statement on our vision for deception theory.[26]

Steve begins his explication of IMT2 by observing that most deception research, whether the focus is on leakage and cues, detection accuracy, or deceptive message production, presumes that people produce one of two types of messages: BFTs and BFLs. As mentioned earlier in this chapter, the original 1992 IMT research showed unequivocally that BFTs and BFLs don't describe the kinds of discourse people actually generate in deception-provoking situations like Committed Chris.

McCornack is critical of what he sees as the prevailing model of deceptive discourse production that is top-down, linear, and step-by-step sequential. In the prevailing model to which McCornack objects, the sender faces a difficult situation where information in the sender's head, if disclosed, creates problems for the sender. The sender then sizes up the choices: BFL or BFT. The truth is assessed to be problematic, so a decision is made to lie. Now that the sender has the intention to lie established, they start to construct a lie from scratch. The sender makes something up. This process involves cognitive high load because the sender has to come up with something plausible, and it is scary because he or she might get caught. This is all very arousing. Finally, once a convincing lie is mentally composed, the final step is to engage speech production and actually speak the lie. In contrast, if BFT was selected, then the sender simply calls up memory, which is presumed to be easily accessible, downloads memory into speech production, and out comes an honest message absent the load, emotion, and arousal of a BFL. This prevailing model, McCornack argues, runs afoul of what is known in areas such as speech production, cognitive neuroscience, linguistics, and communication.

In contrast to the prevailing view, IMT2 takes an opportunistic problem-solving approach to message production. There is a starting place, a desired end state, and a problem space in between that must be traversed. Solving a problem is guided by a principle of least effort. People opportunistically start down the easiest path that seems to work, adjusting course as they go. People begin to speak while still in the process of planning, omitting information that might be problematic or dropping in a falsehood on the fly as needed when obstacles are met. As McCornack explains:

> The prevailing model of deceptive discourse production presumes a top-down, linear-sequential, stepwise process: people decide a priori to lie, cognitively construct a deceptive message, and then present this message as verbal and nonverbal behavior. In contrast, an opportunistic problem-solving model of deception suggests that we often begin speaking before any intent to deceive exists, and before such discourse actually becomes deceptive. While we are speaking (and streaming activated, relevant, truthful information from memory to speech production), we often opt "on the fly" to delete relevant information or include false information that then renders our discourse—mid-utterance—functionally deceptive. Why? Because, while we are speaking, we continue to calculate initial-state/end-state discrepancies. And as new truthful information is acti-

vated in memory and marked as relevant for disclosure, if this information widens (rather than narrows) these discrepancies, we'll respond by deleting or distorting it.[27]

IMT2 does not presume that problems are attacked all at once, but instead that our brains break up problems into parts that are processed in different modules in parallel. Rather than producing messages as intact units that are downloaded for speech output, the process involves cyclical processing of microbursts of mental activity, most of which go on outside conscious awareness. Further, how solutions are addressed is guided largely by memory and past experience. Problems are seldom solved with a "Eureka!" moment novel solution that pops into our heads out of the blue. We usually don't need to make things up from scratch. Reapplying what worked previously is much more efficient. Putting this and more together, McCornack et al. describe the central premise of IMT2 as:

> Deceptive and truthful discourse both are output from a speech production system involving parallel-distributed-processing guided by efficiency, memory, and means-ends reasoning; and this production process involves a rapid-fire series of cognitive cycles (involving distinct modules united by a conscious workspace), and modification of incrementally-constructed discourse during the turn-at-talk in response to dynamic current-state/end-state discrepancies.[28]

The formal structure of IMT2 is presented as three sets of theoretical propositions: intentional states, cognitive load, and information manipulation. The IMT2 propositions[29] are as follows:

Intentional States (IS)

IS1: Deceptive intent and conscious awareness of it both arise only after initial state/ end state gaps are perceived as irreconcilable through truth.

IS2: Deceptive intent may arise, exist, and decay at any temporal point during the production of deceptive discourse.

Cognitive Load (CL)

CL1: The comparative cognitive load associated with the production of truthful versus deceptive discourse is based on the gap between activated information units in memory, the functional demands of the initial state, and the desired end state, that is, the difficulty of reasoning through perceived problem spaces.

CL2: Communicators disclose information units in their discourse that constitute the most-efficient communicative paths through perceived problem spaces.

CL3: Deceptive discourse that proves successful in efficiently reconciling problematic initial-state/end-state discrepancies is repeated recurrently when similar states arise.

Information Manipulation (IM)

IM1: Communicators produce "BFL" quality and quantity violations when the most salient, activated information units within memory are perceived as untenable to disclose.

IM2: Quantity violations are the most frequent form of deceptive discourse.

IM3: Relation violations are the least frequent form of deceptive discourse.

IM4: Manner violations will occur less frequently than quantity or quality violations, but more frequently than relation violations.

IM5: Within deceptive discourse, disclosed information units that violate quality derive from truthful information units that previously have been stored in long-term memory- and that are activated within working memory by initial-state conditions.

IM6: When the activated units of truthful information in memory are judged as untenable to disclose, but no alternative, associated information units are activated from which speakers can construct quality violations, discourse production falters.

The intentional-state propositions hold that deceptive intent is the result of a contextual problem-solving process where deception is deemed the most efficient solution and that deceptive intent may, but need not, precede deceptive speech production. These propositions, of course, are very germane to our previous discussion of intent in defining deception. For the purposes here, the most interesting thing about these propositions is that deceptive intent is treated as an empirical issue rather than as a given that is true by definition. If IMT2 is correct about the timing of intent, most commonly accepted definitions of deception need to be rethought.

The cognitive load propositions directly challenge Vrij's and the four-factor theory's contention that deception is more cognitively effortful than honesty. As Steve puts it: "High cognitive load is not intrinsic to deceptive discourse production. Instead, both truthful and deceptive discourse production may generate high or low cognitive load, depending on the information activated within memory and the contextual degrees of freedom constraining potential problem solutions. . . . Rather than an a priori decision to lie or tell the truth being the determinant of consequent cognitive load, the projected cognitive load of potential problem solutions should determine whether one pursues a discourse path that ends up being truthful or deceptive."[30]

From the perspective of IMT2, deception is often enacted precisely because it provides an easy and efficient path through some problem space. That is, according to McCornack, prior deception theories get the causal direction wrong. Load determines deception; deception doesn't cause load. Further, deceptive practices that are most likely to be used have proven successful in the past, making them easy and low effort.

The information manipulation propositions form the core of IMT2 and reflect a degree of precision absent in most other deception theories. Propositions IM2 to IM4 specify the relative frequency of various ways to deceptively manipulate information. According to IMT2, the most frequent approach to deception is simple omission. Compared to omission (quantity violations), BFLs (quality violations) are rare. But manner violations are more unusual still, and relevance violations are the least frequent of all. This frequency gradient follows from the idea that people do what's most efficient. It is easy to covertly violate quantity. If some specific information bit is problematic, it's easy to just edit it out, or just not bring it up in the first place. When mere omission can't remain covert, like when you are put on the spot by a direct question, then quality violations typically provide the easiest solution. Manner and relevance are the least frequent because their use is limited to situations where they can remain covert.

For example, if we are asked a direct question, it is hard to violate relevance without that being obvious. If we are not put on the spot, then mere omission is easier than active evasion.

Proposition IM5 says that when people do outright lie, the content tends to come from memory that is already activated by the nature of the situation and the direction of the conversation. That is, "lies are built from truth."[31] As a consequence, IMT2 holds that honest messages and lies involve fundamentally the same speech production process.

Proposition IM6 is especially intriguing from the perspective of this book and TDT. The issue is raised about what happens when the truth can't be said but there is nothing in memory to form a lie. The answer is that message production falters. As McCornack explains:

At least three factors should intersect to create the potential for production disruption: the possession and activation of truthful information untenable for disclosure, the asking of questions that place demands on speakers for specific and detailed information, and the failure (through memory search and retrieval processes) to find associated false information that quickly can be deployed to construct a quality violation responsive to these questions. The practical implication of this is profound: within certain contexts, deception—or more precisely, the possession of problematic information—should be detectable. The key to such detection is asking the right questions.

Following the faltering of speech production, speakers may simply "default" to confession of truth. Because the truth already will be activated within working memory—but they cannot find plausible alternative information from which to build a problem solution—speakers may spontaneously decide that the simplest, most efficient path for resolving the situation (despite the high projected costs associated with disclosure) is to dump all salient truthful mental contents. Thus, it is not just that the right questions may allow for "deception detection"; the right questions may trigger confessions.[32]

As we shall see in chapter 14, IMT2 provides a nice account of the conditions under which deception detection is improved. The differences from Vrij's cognitive approach are striking. Deception is not necessarily more cognitively effortful than the truth. The trick is not adding load, but cutting off covert quantity, manner, and relevance violations with careful questions, and then, once BFTs and BFLs are the only options, options for credible lies can be cut off.

IMT2 has several important implications beyond deception detection. As mentioned previously, it offers a damning critique of the cognitive load approach. I hope my reader will excuse another long quote and the redundancy of the point, but Steve makes his case persuasively and eloquently, and the point bears repeating:

No valid scientific reason exists for presuming that the production of deceptive discourse is intrinsically more difficult than the production of truthful discourse. This is especially the case with regard to the most common form of deception used in conversations: Quantity violations. Such violations borrow on similar production mechanisms to everyday truth telling; hence, they should not evoke escalation in load above and beyond truth.

Deception should evoke greater load than truth telling when four conditions obtain: the form of deception being produced is a BFL, the truthful information one possesses is contextually unproblematic, the truthful information is easily accessible within memory (i.e., involves data that recently were uploaded to working memory), and any false information that might be used to construct the BFL must be retrieved from long-term memory. In such cases, the generation of a BFL should involve more cognitive effort than the generation of a BFT.

Here is the catch. In such situations as above, people do not produce BFLs; unless they are sociopathic, recreational liars. That is, when the truth is not difficult to disclose (because it is easily accessible to conscious mind and contextually palatable), people disclose it. When do people lie? When they judge the truthful information as being so problematic that it cannot be disclosed. And why do they lie? Because it is less load-intensive to construct a message based on situationally appropriate, false information than it is trying to package the problematic truthful information into face-maintaining linguistic form.[33]

A second implication of IMT2 is that there seems to be a tacit assumption in thinking about deception, fostered by the priority placed on deceptive intent in most definitions, that the point of deception is to deceive. IMT2 (and TDT, as discussed in later chapters) views deception more tactically. Deception is a means to an end, almost never an end in itself. In IMT2 what people want is some desired end state, and people communicatively work through problem spaces to achieve those ends. Deception sometimes provides an efficient path.

I think a third and related implication is especially interesting. If we ask who lies, IMT2's answer is "people who have things to hide." Basically, people who do bad things have things to lie about. But most of us are simply not in situations where deception is needed very often, and hence honesty is the efficient way through most conversations.

This is relevant to one of the things I noticed in my expert interrogation experiment described in chapter 14. The expert interrogators spend a lot of time trying to get at the interviewee's character. In most deception experiments (but not several of mine), interviewees are randomly assigned to truth or lie. If IMT2 and TDT are right, however, honesty and deception are not random. People deceive when the truth is problematic for them. As Steve says, people deceive when their activated memories contain information that is untenable to disclose. Thus, the interrogators' strategy of assessing character makes perfect sense from the point of view of IMT2 and TDT. People who have poor characters have things to hide and need to lie. People who act with integrity need not deceive. So, assessing general integrity should be informative. But this strategy would have no utility at all in the mock-crime experiments that dominate the legal and criminal psychology literature, where random assignment and instructed lies rule. Maybe the performance of experts in those experiments tells us more about the experiments than the experts.

CONCLUSION

This wraps up chapter 8, in which IMT and IMT2 are summarized. As promised in the chapter title, we have now moved beyond conscious deceptive intent and bald-faced lies to a more nuanced and ecological understanding of deceptive communication. The next chapter begins an in-depth look at TDT propositions and research.

9

Prevalence

It's time to delve into TDT! Chapters 9 through 14 cover each of the TDT propositions and modules. My research relevant to each is reviewed in a series of fifty-five numbered experiments.

First up is the issue of lie prevalence, TDT's first two propositions, and the Few Prolific Liars module. We investigate the question, How often do people lie? After our discussion of prevalence, we will move on to when and why people lie. But that is the next chapter.

Let's start off with a quiz question. True or False: *Most adults in America lie less frequently than average?* Does this seem too easy? Are you wondering if it is a trick question? Are you thinking that surely the answer must be false, but I would not be asking if the answer were so obvious? In any case, it is a true statement. In TDT study one reported in this chapter, 75% percent of people surveyed were below average. If you missed the quiz question, don't feel bad. Most people get it wrong. As we will see, this surprising fact follows from the logic of TDT. Read on for the details and explanation.

PREVALENCE OF DECEPTION

My research on the prevalence of deception was, in no small part, inspired by an essay by University of Pennsylvania psychologist Paul Rozin.[1] Rozin argued that psychology research, in the effort to be scientific, tends to jump prematurely into experimental work and statistical hypothesis testing, skipping necessary descriptive research. The main risk in this is that absent a thorough understanding of the phenomenon under study, experiments and hypothesis tests may reflect presumptions about the nature of the phenomenon that don't actually comport with nature. Social scientists who think that doing science requires experiments, hypotheses, and significance tests should take a look at biology, which often involves highly descriptive, nonexperimental research, and where hypothesis testing is often eschewed. To see what I mean, search for biologist Frans De Waal online. But biology is science. In fact, I would argue that the two most important discoveries/advances in the life sciences, evolution and DNA, bear little resemblance to the experimental hypothesis testing in the social sciences.

Upon initial reading of the Rozin paper, I was struck by the implications of his critique for the social scientific study of deception. It fit like a glove. As noted in previous chapters, most deception research has been built on a shaky foundation of presumptions that Steve McCornack[2] called hopeful myths. A solid conceptual and descriptive understanding of deception as a social activity is needed. While there have been important descriptive studies of deception in the published literature, these are relatively few.[3] Worse still, the implications of these more descriptive and naturalistic studies have, more often than not, been ignored in both theory and experimental research. I thought to myself that I had better establish a sound descriptive foundation and a rich naturalistic understanding of the phenomena of deception upon which to build TDT.

There is also a key theoretical motive for looking at prevalence. In fact, the whole logical structure of TDT actually hinges on the issue of prevalence. Thus, it is no accident that the first two TDT propositions are about prevalence. It is a fundamental consideration because the truth-default state has very different implications depending on whether deception is a low-prevalence occurrence, a ubiquitous, high-frequency activity, or whether the chances of deception are the flip-of-a-coin sort of thing that exists in almost all random-assignment deception detection experiments. TDT is unique among deception theories in focusing on the truth–lie base-rate. It is critical from the TDT perspective to get a feel for base-rates outside the lab, because base-rates matter so much according to TDT. Claims that the truth-default is adaptive make sense only if deception is infrequent.

Reaching definite conclusions about the exact prevalence of deception may be impossible. There is just no way to randomly sample communication across people and situations,[4] and even if that were possible, we could not establish ground truth or deceptive intent in such a way as to accurately classify communication as honest or deceptive. Fortunately, there are imperfect ways to try and estimate the prevalence of deception.

Efforts toward estimating the prevalence of deception can be sorted into three research strategies: self-report surveys, the diary method, and experiments. With surveys, we can just ask people something like "How many times have you lied in the past twenty-four hours?" The chief advantage of surveys is that we can get a large and representative sample of people. But the limitations are obvious. The validity of survey methods rests on people's ability to be able to answer the questions (do people know how often they lie?) and their willingness to provide honest answers (people might lie about lying?). Further, we are sampling people, not units of communication, so we are only indirectly assessing the issue at hand.

The second option is to have people keep a diary and log their lies. Diaries overcome the problem of imperfect memory, but there are still concerns about lazy subjects and honesty of reporting. Still, diaries are probably better than surveys in these regards. Diary methods are labor intensive and typically involve much smaller and less representative samples, so diary studies are not a panacea. They nevertheless provide informative data.

The third option of experiments largely overcomes the problems with surveys and diaries but adds a new and maybe even more important limitation. We can experimentally put people in a situation where they might have a motive to deceive and then see what they do. The limitation, however, is that the findings are situation specific. Experiments tell us what happens in a specific controlled situation, not how often people are in that situation. Think of it this way. Even the biggest liars lie only when there is opportunity to lie. The frequency of deception is a joint function of being in a situation where the truth is problematic and the probability of deception given that situation. Experiments just tell us about the latter and thus are likely to radically overestimate dishonesty. Despite the imperfections of the various methods, however, it might be possible to triangulate across methods to achieve at least an approximate estimation of the prevalence of deception in everyday life.

Before getting into the research, there are two TDT modules that are relevant to when and how often people lie, the Few Prolific Liars module and the Deception Motives module. Recall from chapter 6:

The Few Prolific Liars module: The prevalence of lying is not normally or evenly distributed across the population. Instead, more people lie infrequently. Most people are honest most of time. There are a few people, however, who lie often. Most lies are told by a few prolific liars.

And

The Deception Motives module: People lie for a reason, but the motives behind truthful and deceptive communication are the same. When the truth is consistent with a person's goals, he or she will almost always communicate honestly. Deception becomes probable when the truth makes honest communication difficult or inefficient.

In combination, the point of these two modules is that deception is not random, and it varies across both people and situations. As the name of the Few Prolific Liars module implies, there are a few people who lie with great frequency, but most people lie infrequently. That is, there are substantial individual differences in honesty and deceptiveness. But there is also a critical situation component. Absent psychopathology, people deceive only when the truth is problematic. And, as McCornack pointed out, these two factors are not independent.[5] Different people may be more or less likely to place themselves in situations where deception is required, and, over time, people who are frequently in deception-provoking situations may, as a result, be more prone to lie, get better at lying with practice and become less inhibited about dissembling.

TDT's specific predictions with regard to the prevalence of deception are contained in the first two propositions. Proposition one holds that, relative to honest communication, deception is infrequent.

TDT Proposition One: Most communication by most people is honest most of the time. While deception can and does occur, in comparison to honest messages, deception is relatively infrequent, and outright lies are more infrequent still. In fact, deception must be infrequent to be effective.

Proposition two specifies individual differences in how often people lie.

TDT Proposition Two: The prevalence of deception is not normally distributed across the population. Most lies are told by a few prolific liars.

In stark contrast to these two propositions, a casual reading of the deception literature might make it seem that TDT's prediction of infrequent deception is pretty far-fetched or even outright false. A selection of quotes from various authors over the years follows. It is easy to get the impression that deception is pervasive, frequent, and ubiquitous. Here are a few representative quotations:

Deception is a pervasive, and some would argue a necessary, phenomenon in human communication.[6]

Okay now, I don't want to alarm anybody in this room, but it has just come to my attention that the person to your right is a liar. Also, the person to your left is a liar. Also, the person sitting in your very seat is a liar. We are all liars. . . . On a given day, studies show that you may be lied to anywhere from 10 to 200 times.[7]

In practice, however, communicators frequently decide that honesty is not the best policy. Job applicants overstate their qualifications to make a favorable impression, spouses lie to minimize relational conflict, students claim purchased term papers as their own work, politicians misrepresent their actions to the media, and public officials conceal their true motives to representatives of foreign governments. In short, deception and suspected deception arise in at least one quarter of all conversation.[8]

The one-hundred and thirty respondents recorded a total of 870 statements or replies to others; of those 870 responses, 61.5 percent were verbal expressions which controlled information. [Only] 38.5 percent of the actor's conversational statements were classified as complete disclosure, "what I felt to be a completely honest statement." . . . Every respondent controlled information at least once in every encounter. . . . On the other hand, numerous respondents [had] no complete disclosures during the course of the conversation.[9]

60% of the participants lied during the 10-min conversation, and did so an average of almost three times.[10]

Participants discussed paintings they liked and disliked with artists. . . . There were no conditions under which the artists received totally honest feedback about the paintings they cared about. As predicted, participants stonewalled, amassed misleading evidence, and conveyed positive evaluations by implications. They also told some outright lies.[11]

Research from social psychology suggests that as many as one third of these typical daily interactions involve some form of deception.[12]

In 2 diary studies of lying, 77 college students reported telling 2 lies a day, and 70 community members told 1.[13]

These quotes suggest that lies and deception are an everyday occurrence and imply that we are all frequent liars.

But there is also evidence that maybe things are not so bad for honesty after all. There was a story on the evening news last night that caught my attention.[14] According to the report, a growing number of businesses have customers pay on an honor system. If most people were dishonest, such businesses would quickly go under. But, according to the report, 95% of people paid at honor boxes that were secretively monitored.

The authors of the Turner et al. study of information control quoted above actually came to a conclusion different from what their above quote might suggest:

> The most obvious and compelling implication of this study is that our own definition of honesty as "complete disclosure" of all relevant information may be quite inaccurate when placed in the kinds of social situations we have explored. For rather than using this common sense and rather folklorish definition, our respondents instead seemed to see honesty more as fidelity to the maintenance of some on-going relationship, and consequently maneuvered information in such a way as not to jeopardize that relationship. Seen in this way, selectively controlling information, rather than being regarded as deceptive, . . . was interpreted as the right thing to do.[15]

And

> Our respondents also seemed to know the difference between honesty and frankness. If honesty is frankness, it becomes an extremely easy virtue to attain, for it turns extreme rudeness into moral superiority.[16]

BELLA DEPAULO'S EVERYDAY LIES STUDY

The most influential source for claims about the frequency of lying is a diary study by Bella DePaulo and her colleagues.[17] That study is frequently cited as showing that people lie between one and two times per day, or that people lie in one of every three to one in five social interactions. From these findings, it is usually inferred that lying is therefore an everyday activity for most people.

Because the everyday lie diary study has been so influential, and because its findings are often interpreted as directly refuting TDT proposition one, it makes sense to take a close look at the study and its findings. My criticism is directed not at the study or its authors—it was a very important study, I am a big fan of Bella DePaulo's research, and her findings have influenced my thinking in many ways—but instead at how the results have been interpreted over the years by those citing it as evidence for frequent lying.

There were two sets of subjects, seventy-seven undergraduate students (61% female) and seventy adults (mostly white, married, and employed, approximately evenly split between men and women). The participants each kept a communication diary for seven days. They were asked to record and report on all interactions lasting at least ten minutes and all interactions, regardless of duration, that included a lie.[18] They also rated the interactions and lies on a number of scales and were also asked things like what the lies were about and who they were talking to. The amount of information collected was extensive.[19]

The college student sample reported telling an average of 1.96 lies per day. One participant reported telling no lies at all over the seven days, while, on the other extreme, the most frequent liar reported 6.6 lies per day. The median was lower than the mean at 1.6 lies per day. The number of lies per social interaction was 0.31 (just under one in three, but see footnote 18).

The adults reported telling fewer lies overall than the college students. The average for adults was 0.97 lies per day, half that of the college students. Six of seventy (just under 10%) adults reported no lies at all over all seven days. The greatest number of reported lies was 10.3 per day. The median number of lies per day was 0.64, showing that more than 50% of the sample reported less than one lie per day. That is, a majority of people reported days on which they told no lies at all. The number of lies per social interaction was 0.2 (one in five).

The depiction of one to two lies per day is an accurate description of the *averages* in the two samples. However, it is not clear that the average is a good way to describe the results. TDT proposition two predicts a highly skewed distribution, and the arithmetic mean (commonly thought of as "the average") is not a preferred measure of central tendency with highly skewed distributions. The mean tends to be pulled in the direction of extreme scores, and the difference between the mean and median in the diary data suggests this was the case, especially in the adult sample. The majority of people told fewer lies than the "average person." The "average adult" told nearly one lie per day, but a majority of the adults told fewer lies than that!

As previously noted in footnote 18, the number of lies per social interaction is surely an overestimate, because honest interactions were counted only if they lasted at least ten minutes, and interactions containing lies were counted regardless of duration. Thus, it is an apples-to-oranges comparison. How many things does the average person say on an average day? Presumably, people say many things in a day. If just one or two of those are lies, then the lies are a very small proportion of what is said. I'm not sure if we are talking one in fifty, one in a hundred, or one in a thousand, but it's not one-in-three!

DePaulo's everyday lie diary studies have subsequently been replicated at least twice.[20] Both replications report fewer lies per day than reported in the original study. Estimates were as low as 0.59 lies per day.

TDT Study One: The Prevalence of Lying in America

We traded the level of detail offered by a diary for the representative sampling offered by a survey.[21] We contracted with a market research firm to include a question about how often people had lied in one of their nationwide panels. We obtained a nationally (US) representative sample (stratified random sampling) of subjects projectable across sex, region of country, age (adults over eighteen only), race, and income. We asked our research subjects the open-ended question, How many times have you lied in the past twenty-four hours? We asked respondents to break down the lies between face-to-face and mediated (writing, phone, internet, etc.) communication and to whom the lie was told (family, friends, work, acquaintances, and strangers). This was done in conjunction with market research, and our question on lying was placed between questions on cat-litter products and water softeners.

In terms of the average number of lies reported, our results were very much in line with the conclusion that people lie once or twice a day. The average was 1.65 lies per day, and the margin of error was plus or minus 0.28 lies per day. The standard deviation was 4.45, the mode and median were 0.0,[22] and the number of lies reported ranged from 0 to 134.

Consistent with TDT proposition two, the distribution was very much skewed. A majority of people, about 60%, reported telling no lies at all.[23] Eighty percent of subjects who did lie (32% of the total sample) told between one and five lies, while 20% of liars (8% of the total sample) told six lies or more. Almost one quarter of all reported lies were told by the top 1% (that's just ten out of the one thousand people surveyed!), and one half of all the lies were perpetrated by only 5% of the sample. A few prolific liars, indeed!

The results are visually presented in figures 9.1, 9.2, and 9.3. Figure 9.1 shows that a majority of those surveyed did not lie, and that among those who did lie, there is a frequency curve showing that the frequency drops, fast at first, but then leveling out, as the number of lies told increases. Figures 9.2 and 9.3 show that the prevalence curve holds across face-to-face and mediated lies, and regardless of to whom the lie was told.[24]

These data provide initial support for TDT propositions one and two. Consistent with proposition one, most people did not report many lies. Consistent with proposition two, the distribution of lying is highly skewed, with most lies being told by a few prolific liars. Both of these findings form the Few Prolific Liars module of TDT.

The strength of the evidence provided by study one is in the sampling. Our

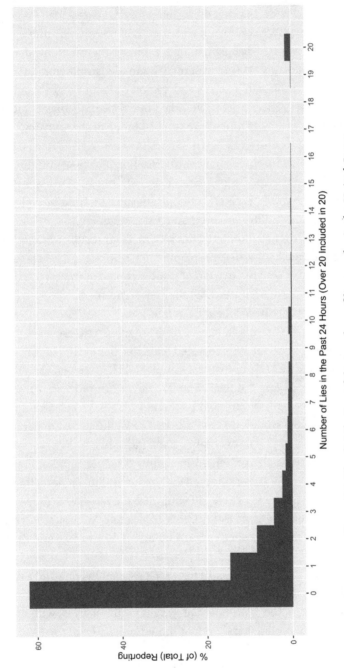

Figure 9.1. The distribution of the numbers of lies per day in the United States.

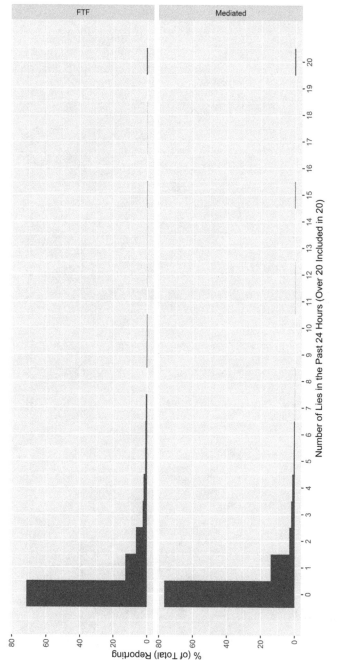

Figure 9.2. The distribution of the numbers of lies per day in the United States separated by face-to-face and mediated communication.

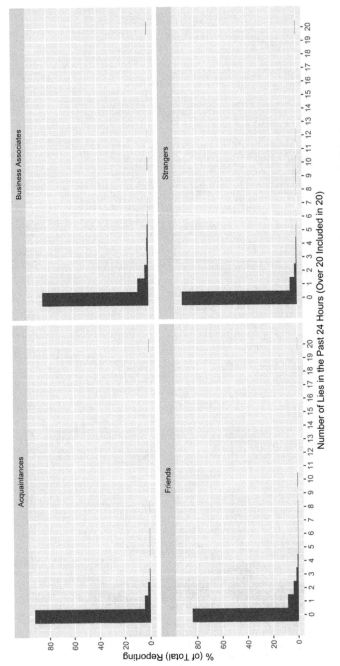

Figure 9.3. The distribution of the numbers of lies per day in the United States separated by target person.

sample was much larger and more representative than the samples used in prior work. The big, obvious concern is, of course, the accuracy of reporting. Because the findings involve self-report survey data, we have to worry about social desirability and under-reporting. But how worried should we be? Common sense tells us that people may lie on surveys, right? But what if TDT proposition one is right? If most people are mostly honest, this would apply to completing surveys too.

I am not very worried about social desirability and under-reporting for several reasons. Our research method used standard protections like anonymity, but this is not the only reason for my confidence. Compared to diary methods, which are usually considered more reliable, actually more lies were reported. If our survey method was especially subject to bias, we would expect the opposite. I have even more confidence now, because as shown over the next few pages, our findings have now been replicated several times, both by my colleagues and me and by others, and not just in the United States.[25] One of those studies included an experimental validation.[26] But, even beyond all that, even if there was some bias, it probably would not meaningfully change the conclusions. It does not matter for TDT if the average number of lies per day is 1.65, 1.99, or even 2.75. What's important is that (a) lies are infrequent relative to truths, and (b) the distribution of lying is highly skewed.

Consider this: How many unreported lies would it take to change the conclusion that lies are infrequent relative to truths? That depends on how much people communicate in a day, but the answer is surely a large number. Surveys aren't biased that much. Further, there is no reason to think that if social desirability bias exists, it would change the shape of distribution of lies. In short, the average lies per day really isn't the issue for TDT, and what is at issue (the shape of the distribution) is not so susceptible to the bias possible in self-reported data. Still, as with all my claims regarding the empirical merit of TDT propositions, I sought to replicate and validate the initial findings. A firm empirical foundation requires much more data.

TDT Study Two: Diary Studies Reexamined

Study two is not a replication per se, but a reanalysis of results from previously published data collected by other researchers.[27] We obtained the original raw student data for the DePaulo diary study and a 2008 two-study replication by George and Robb. Consistent with TDT proposition two and our own survey data, there were substantial skews in the distributions in the number of lies reported in all three diary study sets. Most people did not lie much, and most lies were told by a few prolific liars. Triangulation with diary data was achieved.

TDT Study Three: A Replication with College Students

Our next study sought to replicate our nationwide survey findings with college student data.[28] Recall that the original DePaulo diary studies found that students reported lying more often than the adult sample. Further, in our nationwide survey data, we found that age was negatively associated with the frequency of lying. Younger people lie more. So, we anticipated that there would be more lies in college student data than in the representative sample. Nevertheless, we anticipated the few-prolific-liars skew would again be evident as it was in studies one and two.

We surveyed 229 students at two public universities in Michigan. As we expected, significantly more lies were reported (mean number of lies in the past twenty-four hours = 2.34, median = 1.00, mode = 0.00). In the student data, 29% reported telling no lies in the past twenty-four hours. Despite the increased numbers of lies, the skew in the distribution was similar to our previous findings.

TDT Study Four: Teens Lie a Lot

I wanted to see if the trend of younger people lying more than older adults would continue with an even younger sample. My guess was that teens would, relatively speaking, lie a lot. But I also thought that the same skewed distribution where most people lie relatively infrequently but a few people tell lots of lies would still hold. Just as in the previous study with college students, I expected the mean to shift but that the distribution would hold its shape.

A serendipitous opportunity presented itself when, out of the blue, two high school students from New York, Frankie Carey and Doug Messer, sent me an email. They were in a program where students did research projects with a university-professor mentor-supervisor. They were interested in deception and asked if I would help them. I thought it was a great idea, and I said yes.

We did a few projects together, but one involved surveying their fellow students at their high school about lie frequency.[29] We had fifty-eight teens (aged fourteen to seventeen) complete our survey. The high school students reported telling an average of 4.1 lies in the past twenty-four hours (median = 3.0, mode = 2.0, range 0.0 to 17.0). This was significantly more than what was reported in study one with the adult sample or study three with the college student sample. Despite the increase in lying frequency, however, once again the few-prolific-liars–skewed distribution was observed.

TDT Study Five: The Prevalence of Lying in the UK

Another opportunity presented itself shortly after the publication of our initial studies. The Science Museum of London conducted a survey of 3,042 people in the United Kingdom, asking about the frequency of lying.[30] My coauthor and friend Kim Serota contacted the museum, and they kindly shared their data with us. Responses were weighted to allow the findings to be projectable to the UK population according to their Office for National Statistics. We discarded data from respondents under the age of eighteen to comply with our universities' human subjects requirements and to make the sample align with our own study one. Our reanalysis and findings are based on 2,980 adults.

Unlike our studies, the UK study asked separate questions about white lies and big lies. For white lies, the average was 1.66, with the median and the mode being 1.0. For big lies, the average was 0.41, with a median and mode of 0.0. Seventy-five percent of people reported at least one white lie, while only 21% of people reported a big lie. When we combined white lies and big lies, the average was 2.08 lies per day (median = 1, mode = 1). The frequency of white lies and big lies is graphed in figure 9.4.

Importantly, we checked to see if the distribution of lies in the UK data had the few-prolific-liars skew. It did. When we graphed the power functions fitting the UK data and plotted it against our original US data, the findings were nearly identical, as can be seen in figure 9.5.

AMSTERDAM REPLICATIONS

I place much value on replication. To the extent that a knowledge claim has scientific merit, it should consistently be consistent with the data. Too many findings in the social sciences, and especially in deception research, are hard to reproduce consistently. In such cases, it's hard to know what to think. When a hypothesis gets "mixed support," what should we make of that? Is the hypothesis partly right and partly wrong? Does it hold only under some unknown conditions? Is the hypothesis true and the nonsupportive findings flawed, or is the hypothesis false and the original supporting evidence faulty?

The problem of replication is compounded, because in deception research, as in many areas of social science, theories tend to be tested by the authors of the theory, who clearly have a vested interest in the theory being supported. While some unscrupulous researchers may actively engage in questionable research practices to artificially enhance findings, unconscious biases are also possible and probably pose a bigger risk. Confirmation bias (seeking out and interpreting data consistent with one's own views)[31] is well-documented and certainly applies to social scientists, who, after all, are people too.

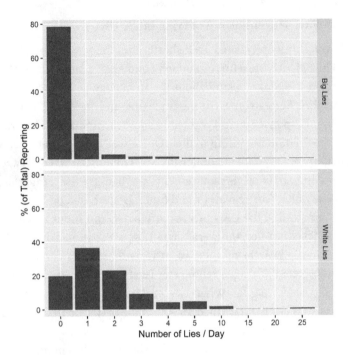

Figure 9.4. The distribution of big lies and small lies in the UK.

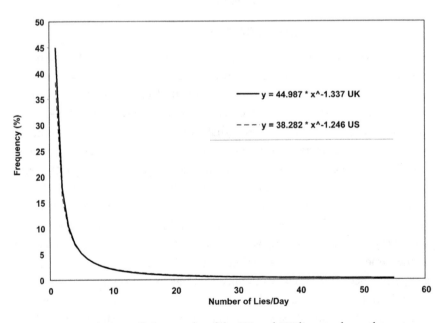

Figure 9.5. Curve fitting results of the US and UK lie prevalence data.

So, while I try to replicate my own findings, I appreciate when others test my ideas. If my ideas are good and my findings sound, others should find results similar to my own. For this reason, I was especially pleased to read a recent series of studies testing the prevalence of lying in Amsterdam.[32]

In a first study, over 500 college students at the University of Amsterdam were surveyed. A Dutch-translated version of our original survey was used. The average number of lies per day was 2.04 (slightly less than 2.34 in the college student data in TDT study 3), with 41% reporting no lies in the past twenty-four hours (compared to 29% in our college student study). Importantly, as in our studies, the data were highly skewed, with most people lying infrequently but a few people lying a lot. In the Amsterdam data, 5% of the respondents told 40% of the lies.

Especially important, the Amsterdam authors did a follow-up laboratory experiment where subjects were given the opportunity to cheat on some experimental tasks for a cash prize. The number of lies reported by individuals in the survey was substantially predictive of subsequent cheating in the lab. This validates the survey data and adds confidence to the conclusions beyond mere replication of survey findings.[33]

SUMMARY AND CONCLUSIONS

TDT departs from most other theories of deception regarding the prevalence of deception. According to TDT, lying is infrequent relative to the truth. Lying is not normally distributed across the population but is instead highly skewed, with most lies coming from a few prolific liars. And, according to TDT, the frequency of lying matters in deception detection.

This chapter discusses TDT predictions regarding the prevalence of lying and reviews evidence relevant to these TDT predictions. Unlike most TDT research, which tends to be experimental, the evidence reviewed in this chapter was mostly based on survey data. Results were reported from a large representative sample of adults in the US (TDT study one), a large representative sample of adults in the UK (TDT study five), college students in Michigan (TDT study three), college students in Amsterdam (Halvey, Shalvi, and Verschuere), high school students in New York (TDT study four), and a reanalysis of previous data from well-known and often-cited diary data (TDT study two). Since I originally wrote this chapter, I have further replicated the findings in data from Japan and Korea. The results of all the studies align neatly with TDT propositions one and two. Most people are honest most of the time, and most lies are told by a few prolific liars.

Confidence in the validity of these conclusions is enhanced by several considerations. First, confidence is heightened by the sheer number of replications and the unanimity of the findings. All the studies triangulate on the same conclusions. Beyond just number of replications, confidence is bolstered by the generality of the findings across different samples of respondents (high school students, college students and non-student adults from multiple countries), different methodologies, and different researchers. Confidence is also enhanced by the experimental validation in the Amsterdam research. The evidence for the first two propositions is scientifically sound, robust, and fully consistent with TDT.

In TDT prevalence matters for two big, important reasons, one more theoretical and the other more practical. Theoretically, the core ideas are that people have a truth-default and that the presumption of truth is adaptive. This requires lying to be infrequent. If lying and deception were pervasive, and if being deceived is undesirable, then pervasive deception would make truth-default and truth-bias dysfunctional. We would all be frequent victims of deception and continued truth-bias would ensure ongoing frequent deceit. Alternatively, if as TDT holds, lying and deception are relatively infrequent, then truth-bias and the truth-default make much more sense. Believing is adaptive because most people and most communication is honest.

Pragmatically, since TDT presumes that people are usually truth-biased, the base-rates of honesty and deception affect deception detection accuracy. How this works is covered in chapter twelve, but here is a quick preview. In most deception detection experiments, truth–lie base-rates are fixed by the researchers. But, we might ask, given that truth–lie base-rates affect the results, do the base-rates in deception detection experiments mirror the base-rates outside the lab that people encounter in everyday life? The results of the research summarized in this chapter show clearly that lying is much more prevalent in deception detection experiments (where it typically occurs in 50% of all communication) than it is in everyday life, where lying is infrequent and mostly restricted to a few prolific liars. The practical implications are that maybe accuracy is better than lie detection experiments suggest, and maybe truth-bias actually improves accuracy in the low-prevalence environments that exist outside the lab.

One point of clarification is that although TDT specifies individual differences in the frequency of lying such that most lies are told by a few prolific liars, it does not follow from TDT that lying is purely an individual difference variable impervious to situational variability. As we will see in the next chapter, according to TDT (and IMT2), the telling of any particular lie or deceptive message is largely situational, in that most people lie only when the truth is a problem. Lying would be a stable individual difference only to the extent that prolific liars are chronically in situations where lying is necessary.

There have been some early findings on who the prolific liars are. Our survey data suggested some demographic differences besides age in lying prevalence. The effect sizes for those differences, however, were pretty small, and I don't think those findings especially informative.[34] The Amsterdam studies found that lying was correlated with psychopathy. The association was not especially strong, but it was stronger than the demographic predictors.

While I see some utility in thinking about prolific liars as a discrete type of person different from the majority of the population, who lie less frequently, I see deception and honesty as a person-in-situation phenomenon. For me, the question is not so much "Who lies?" as "When and why do people lie?" When and why people lie is addressed in the next chapter on the deception motives module and TDT proposition five. TDT studies six through nine are also summarized in the next chapter.

10

Deception Motives

THE PREVIOUS CHAPTER FOCUSED ON TDT's claims that deception and lying are infrequent relative to honest communication and that most lies are told by a few prolific liars. But even people who don't lie very often might lie sometimes. Similarly, people who lie relatively often might be honest. This chapter considers the questions of when and why people lie.

An important idea in TDT is that deception is not random. People typically lie for a reason. It follows that lying and deception are to some extent predictable. It further follows that there are times when we need to be on guard for deception, and times in which there is little need to worry about deception. The trick is distinguishing between these two types of situations.

This chapter is all about deception motives. By deception motives, I simply mean the reasons why people engage in deception. The initial focus of this chapter is on TDT's deception motive module, TDT proposition five, and my empirical research findings relevant to deception motives. TDT's deception motive module and TDT proposition five pretty much say the same thing.

Deception Motives module: People lie for a reason, but the motives behind truthful and deceptive communication are the same. When the truth is consistent with a person's goals, he or she will almost always communicate honesty. Deception becomes probable when the truth makes honest communication difficult or inefficient.

TDT proposition five: Deception is purposive. Absent psychopathology, people lie for a reason. Deception, however, is usually not the ultimate goal, but instead a means to some other ends. That is, deception is typically tactical. Specifically, most people are honest unless the truth thwarts some desired goal or goals. The motives or desired goals achieved through communication are the same for honest and deceptive communications, and deception is reserved for situations where honesty would be ineffectual, inefficient, and/or counterproductive in goal attainment.

INSPIRATION

My thinking on when and why people lie was influenced by the work of two individuals, Sissela Bok and Steve McCornack. Steve has been introduced in previous chapters. Sissela Bok is a philosopher and ethicist,[1] well known in deception research for her book *Lying: Moral Choice in Public and Private Life*.[2] Her book is my top recommended reading for those interested in the moral and ethical aspects of lying and deception.

Bok's analysis of the ethics of lying tries to answer the question: When, if ever, is lying morally justified? Her analysis rests on what she calls the *principle of veracity*. The principle of veracity holds that lying requires a justification, while honesty does not. Truth and deception are not ethical equals. Ethically speaking, she says, we need good reasons to lie. Absent a good reason to the contrary, the default mode of ethical communication should be honesty. She is initially open to the idea that there may be situations in which telling a lie can be an ethical choice over not lying, but she believes such situations require careful consideration. This is not the case for normal honest communication. Much of her book is devoted to examining situations where lying might be argued to be morally justified. She concludes that these situations are likely few and far between and that honesty is typically the better moral choice.

My thinking takes her principle of veracity out of the context of ethics and into the everyday communication practices of normal people. I wondered, What if people generally operated on something like the principle of veracity? Maybe honesty is a default mode of communication, and deception requires justification. When I am thinking about justification, I am not thinking only (or even mostly) of the careful ethical analysis provided by Bok (although people can do that). Instead I have in mind a more simple type of justification, like when deception solves a problem or helps achieve a goal. The analogy is not perfect, because honest communication is goal directed too, but much along the lines of Bok's principle of veracity, I propose that people are honest unless honesty interferes with conversational goals and desired outcomes. Rather than deception being just a moral choice, it might be a practical one. Deception need not even be a conscious choice. But deception almost always serves a purpose.

When honesty works fine for us, virtually everyone is honest. People do not lie when the truth works for them. When the truth makes honesty inconsistent with goals, however, then people may or may not be deceptive. Deception becomes increasingly probable as the truth becomes a stronger impediment to desired outcomes. Some people take the path of deception, and some people are honest even though honesty comes with a cost. But deception is practiced only in situations where honesty is a problem. So I believe that most people usually act in accordance with the principle of veracity.

This application of Bok's ideas fits very nicely with Steve McCornack's view of deception as problem-solving. Here is an excerpt from a larger quote by McCornack from chapter 8: "When the truth is not difficult to disclose (because it is easily accessible to the conscious mind and contextually palatable), people disclose it. When do people lie? When they judge the truthful information as being so problematic that it cannot be disclosed."[3]

This seems to me a clear case of idea convergence. According to McCornack, people are honest when they can be and when the truth is not problematic. People are deceptive when honesty interferes with desired goal states and when deception also provides the easier path to the goals. This is a practical speech production version of Bok's veracity principle, and both are very much consistent with the logic of TDT.

KEY TDT CLAIMS

TDT makes several claims regarding when and why people deceive others. Those claims were summarized in the Deception Motives module and TDT proposition five. The module and proposition can be broken down into a series of five basic claims. Let's make these explicit and take a close look at each.

1. People lie for a reason. That is, deception is purposive. It is therefore not random.

Most, if not all, communication is goal directed. Deception is no exception. The basic functions of communication include being informative and sharing information; influencing the affect, cognition, and behaviors of others; entertainment; and building, maintaining, or ending social, personal, and professional relationships. People say what they do to achieve goals in line with these general functions of communication. If we look closely at what people say and the situations people are in, it becomes clear that what people say is not random. Instead, communication can be understood as working toward one or more communication functions. This is the case for almost all communication, including both deceptive and honest messages.

2. Deception is usually not the ultimate goal but instead is a means to some other end or ends. That is, deception is typically tactical.

People do not deceive others because deception is a desired end in itself. Rather, deception is usually a means to some end. So, when I say "deception motives," I do not mean to imply that deception is the goal. I see deception as a way to *achieve* goals. Maybe an example will help.

Remember the Peskin experiment described in chapter 7, with the children interacting with a good puppet and a bad puppet?[4] The problem the children faced is that the bad puppet would take the desired sticker. What the children wanted was their favored stickers. Lying by telling the bad puppet that they preferred an unpreferred sticker was a simple and efficient means to achieve the desired outcome. The point wasn't deception per se. The goal was to obtain something that they wanted. When the desired sticker could be obtained in other ways, as in when the children were interacting with the good puppet, the children didn't lie.

Thus, I think of deception as tactical. It is a part of a bigger picture. It is a move we sometimes make when the truth gets in our way.

3. The motives behind truthful and deceptive communication are the same.

I have a concern about titling this chapter and module "deception motives." The term "deception motives" might incorrectly imply that the motives for deception are distinct or different from the motives guiding honest communication. This is not the case. It is not what is desired that motivates deception but the fit between what is desired and the truth.

People, for example, usually want to avoid punishment for wrongdoing. People who have done nothing wrong will honestly say, "I didn't do that bad thing." The truth works well for the innocent. Guilty people often deny wrongdoing too, but since they are guilty, their claims of innocence are false. In this example, both honest people and liars say the same sorts of things for the same reasons. They want to be seen as good people, they don't want others to think they did a bad thing, and they want to avoid punishment.

The same reasoning applies to more socially acceptable lies. Consider receiving a gift. It is polite to express gratitude. The gratitude may be actually felt when the gift is appreciated or may be absent when the gift was unwanted or unappreciated. Either way, the motives for expressing gratitude are often the same. We want to be polite and to be seen as polite. We want to maintain a positive social image and not hurt the gift-giver's feelings. Deception is motivated by the match between the situation and the goal. It is not unique to particular goals or desired end states.

As a final example, let's consider the kids in Peskin's experiment again. The kids want the cool stickers. When dealing with Good Puppet, the kids can get what they want by being honest. With Bad Puppet, deception is required to get the desired sticker. In both cases, the goal is to get the cool stickers. Sometimes deception is needed, sometimes it's not, but the goal is the same either way.

4. When the truth is consistent with a person's goals, the person will almost always communicate honesty.

If TDT and IMT2 are correct, people will almost always be honest when honesty is sufficient for goal attainment. That is, when the truth works just fine, people are honest. For the most part, innocent people will not lie and falsely confess guilt.[5] If you like a gift, you generally won't tell the gift-giver that it sucks. The kids in Peskin's experiment never lied to Good Puppet.

I guess by now some readers are finding my repeated hedging irritating. My writing contains frequent use of words like "usually," "typically," and "almost always." No doubt some readers would prefer stronger, more decisive claims. But I use such wording intentionally, because I am talking about trends and not universals, and I have some exceptions in mind that can happen but are infrequent and unusual.

I say people are "almost always" honest when honesty is sufficient for their goals because this may not apply to pathological liars. When I say "pathological liars," I mean people who meet several criteria.[6] They are not delusional or psychiatrically detached from reality, they lie habitually and chronically, they lie without apparent reason and even when the truth would suit them better, and they lie without regard for the potential negative consequences for lying. I have known two pathological liars in my life, and this firsthand experience leads me to believe that they exist. I also believe them to be exceptionally rare. Pathological liars are a clear exception to TDT's view of deception motives. But other TDT propositions and modules have interesting implications for those who interact with pathological liars. Concepts like the truth-default (next chapter) and projected motives (later in this chapter) suggest that dealing with pathological liars is likely an extremely difficult, baffling, confusing, and unpleasant experience. The truth-default has no utility when dealing with a pathological liar, and projecting motives becomes impossible. The resulting uncertainty makes interaction with a pathological liar a troubling and disturbing experience. This has certainly been my experience with the pathological liars I have (to my misfortune) known. I hope you never meet one. If you have, you have my sympathy.

False confessions are a very different issue from pathological lying. Like pathological lying, false confessions may seem inconsistent with my view of deception motives, but unlike pathological lying, I don't see them as an exception. False confessions are usually motivated and follow the principles that people lie for a reason and don't lie when the truth works. There are at least four kinds of false confessions, and they reflect very different motives. But each type is motivated, and all are understandable from the TDT perspective.

The general public may not know this, but police frequently get numerous false confessions to high-profile crimes. These confessions seem to be motived by some kind of weird publicity or fame seeking or perhaps the desire to be infamous. The goal is fame or infamy and the truth is problematic due to actual innocence, so some people lie and confess to crimes they didn't commit. I understand from connections in law enforcement that this sort of deception is often easy to detect. The confessor is too eager to confess, and they typically do not know critical crime facts that have not been made public. Police will often not disclose critical details for this very reason. I think of these cases (please excuse my lack of political correctness) as crazy false confessions. They seem crazy to most of us, but they are not anomalous for TDT, because they are motivated by a problematic truth.

A second type of false confession is rational. My guess is these are very common in plea bargaining in the US legal system. In such cases people are forced into a lose-lose decision: falsely plead guilty and receive some lesser negative consequence or maintain one's innocence at the risk of a more severe negative consequence. Pleading guilty can be the rational choice for an innocent person who believes the evidence is contrived but persuasive (e.g., a judge is likely to believe the police over the accused), if the accused simply cannot afford the legal costs of fighting the bogus charges, or when the certain costs of a guilty plea are tolerable but the uncertain costs of a failed innocence claim are much worse.

Third, false confessions can also be obtained by coercive interrogation practices. In this case, the goal of the confessor is to make the interrogation end, and the truth does not seem to work. Such confessions may not seem rationale to most of us who think about long-term consequences, but if the interrogation is sufficiently aversive, the immediate priority of cessation may take precedence. Further, younger people and mentally disabled people may place more priority on immediate over longer term outcomes and may therefore be especially likely to false confess under pressure to do so. In any case, there is usually a rationality to coerced false confessions and they follow the rules of motived lying.

A final type of false confession stemming from interrogation practices involves planting false memories or persuading an innocent person of his or her own guilt. Sometimes, for example, drinking alcohol in excess can lead to memory loss. The initial honest response to what we did while drunk is that we just don't recall. In such situations, people might be especially susceptible to the implanting of false memories, especially with prolonged interrogations where the honest answer is not effective in ending the interrogation and where false evidence ploys are used.[7]

5. Deception becomes probable when the truth makes honest communication difficult or inefficient.

This last point may be the most important and brings us full circle to the idea that lying is not random. Absent psychopathology, people deceive when the truth thwarts a person's goals. When the truth is a problem, not everyone will be deceptive, but if the truth presents no obstacle, almost everyone will be honest. Thus, deception is not random and occurs in particular and predictable situations.

TDT EXPERIMENT SIX: SELECTING TRUTHS AND LIES

My student Rachel Kim and I, along with Lauren Hamel (who was working on my team at the time), did a series of experiments testing TDT proposition five in a variety of ways.[8] Our first deception motive experiment was a "message selection" experiment. In message selection experiments, research subjects are provided with hypothetical or recalled situations and fixed message choices. They are asked to imagine themselves in (or to recall) the situation described and then asked to pick from a set of prewritten messages what they might say. The situations are experimentally varied, and the goal of research is to see how changes in the situation affect the message choices.

We came up with six base situations where the truth might or might not be made problematic. The situations covered things like what to say to a person who gives a gift, inquires about a woman looking fat, opinions of a movie, or questions about whether a promised favor was done. In each case, we made two versions—one where the truth worked just fine, and the other where the truth was problematic in the situation. Our predictions were, of course, that when the truth was not problematic, honesty would be nearly universal. In situations where the truth was made problematic, however, lying would be prevalent. In both cases, the motives for telling the truth and honesty were the same; only how the goals might be accomplished was altered.

Here is an example of one of the situations from our experiment. Imagine that . . .

You're having dinner at a friend's house. You love the food. They say, "I hope you like the food. I spent all afternoon cooking. How do you like it?"

How would you answer? Please pick one of the following replies:

(a) "I think the dinner is fantastic. This is one of the best home-cooked meals I have ever had."

or

(b) It was kind of you to invite me over and put so much effort into preparing the food, but it is not one of my favorites."

In this version of the situation, message (a) is honest and message (b) is dishonest.

Then we altered the situation by changing just one key word. We provided the exact same two message choices. Imagine that . . .

You're having dinner at a friend's house. You <u>hate</u> *the food. They say, "I hope you like the food. I spent all afternoon cooking. How do you like it?"*

How would you answer? Please pick one of the following replies:

(a) "I think the dinner is fantastic. This is one of the best home-cooked meals I have ever had."

or

(b) "It was kind of you to invite me over and put so much effort into preparing the food, but it is not one of my favorites."

In the first situation we predicted that virtually everyone picks message (a). The truth (you liked the food) is compatible with goals (e.g., protect friend's feelings, be polite). Since the truth works just fine, people are honest. There is no reason to lie and say the food was disliked. In the second situation, where the food was disliked, however, the truth is a problem. The choice is between a packaged truth (thanks, but it was not my favorite) or BFL (yum yum, it was so delicious). We expected many more lies in the second situation than in the first situation.

We used six different base situations and had two versions for each. For each situation, there was an honest message response and a deceptive message response. The responses were the same for both versions of the situation, but in one version the truth was unproblematic and in the other the truth was awkward.

One situation did not work well, but for the other five, subjects picked the honest response 100% of the time when the honest response was not problematic, and no subject ever picked the dishonest message option when the deception worked against the goal of the situation. In contrast, when the situations were flipped and the honest message was problematic and the deceptive option offered a solution, deceptive messages were selected 72% of the time, with deception responses being selected anywhere from 53% to 94%, depending on the situation.[9] Thus, the results were very much in line with our predictions and TDT proposition five.

TDT EXPERIMENT SEVEN: GENERATING TRUTHS AND LIES

Selection methodology like that used in experiment six is often criticized in my field of human communication. In actual conversations, people clearly do not choose from among preset message options. Critics of selection methods often prefer a generation method. Subjects are given situations, and, instead of selecting from prewritten message options, they are asked to write out what they would say. The written responses can then be coded into the same categories of messages reflected in the selection choices.

We thought that our prediction would hold regardless of method, but we needed to show that. So we replicated TDT experiment six using the same situation variations but just asked our new subjects to write out what they would say. We then coded all the written messages as either honest or deceptive. All the messages were independently coded by two of the authors, and coding agreement was 99.7%. Because we were worried about researcher bias and wanted to be sure the coding was valid, we also used two additional coders who didn't know our hypotheses. We recruited a professor familiar with deception research and a person with no training at all in social science. Agreement with our coding was 100% for the professor and 97% for the nonexpert coder. This gave us much confidence that messages coded as honest were really honest and that the messages we thought were deceptive were clearly deceptive.

Once again, for the five situations that worked in study six, when the truth worked just fine, people were 100% honest. Not a single person generated a message coded as deceptive in any of the versions where the truth was nonproblematic. But things were much different in the versions where the truth was inconvenient. Messages were coded as deceptive 76% of the time, with the five situations ranging from 58% to 91%.[10] Thus, regardless of whether the method involved selection or generation, the data came out as expected.

TDT EXPERIMENT EIGHT:
INTRODUCING THE NSF CHEATING EXPERIMENTS

Up until now the evidence for the prevalence and deception motive predictions all relied on various types of self-report methods. As the label implies, self-reports involve asking research participants to respond to open- or closed-ended questions about their feelings, thoughts, or behaviors. Self-reports are widely used in social science research, and they can yield useful data. The utility of self-reports, however, is typically limited by two considerations. The validity of self-reports usually depends on the extent to which respondents can answer accurately and the extent to which the subjects are willing to answer honestly. In the prevalence studies reported in the previous chapter, the main concern is with the second of these requirements. How do we know that research subjects aren't lying about how much they lie? But the first concern might be an issue too. Do people even know how often they lie? That is, even if we presume honest answers to the survey questions, how accurate is the recall?

There is a similar concern with the two previous deception motive studies (TDT experiments six and seven) just described. In particular, I am skeptical of inferring a one-to-one correspondence between what I might call projected communication, recalled communication, and actual communication. That is, presuming honest, well-intentioned research subjects who take their task seriously, I think that what people think they might say in some imagined situation may be different from what they would recall having said in some remembered situation. Both of these might be different from what would actually come out of their mouths when we objectively look at what they actually say when they are actually in that situation. Projected communication, recalled communication, and actual communication behavior can be very different.[11] But they are not necessarily different. The trouble is, we often just don't know.

My preferred research strategy for dealing with concerns such as these is through multimethod triangulation. My thinking is that if we can study the same question different ways, and if the findings from different methods converge on the same conclusion, then we can be confident in the conclusion. Alternatively, if different methods lead to different results, then we need to figure out what it is about the different methods that is causing the differences.

This was the logic behind TDT experiment eight. Experiments six and seven showed clear convergence among selection and generation methods, but both involved self-reports of projected communication. Experiment eight tested TDT proposition five and the deception motives module by observing actual observed communication of people in situations where the truth was and was not problematic.

I developed the cheating experiments like that used in experiment eight to get "real lies" that I knew were really lies. Most deception experiments involve what I call *instructed lies* (or *sanctioned lies*). In deception experiments using instructed lies, research subjects are randomly assigned to honest or deceptive conditions, and those who are supposed to be deceptive are told to lie about something, while honest subjects are instructed to be honest. For example, in the first deception detection experiment way back in 1941,[12] senders were asked questions of a factual and autobiographical nature. Immediately after each question was asked, a card was flashed to the sender instructing the sender to either lie or tell the truth. As a second example, in a classic Ekman and Friesen deception detection experiment,[13] senders (female nursing students) watched pleasant and unpleasant film clips. They were subsequently asked about the films, and they were instructed to lie about the unpleasant nature of the unpleasant films while being honest about the pleasant films.[14] The mock crime research common in modern deception research in legal and criminal psychology also uses instructed lies. Some subjects, usually based on random assignment, are instructed to steal something (or perpetuate some other make-believe crime) and then lie to proclaim their innocence. Honest participants, in contrast, do some control activity and are instructed to honestly maintain their innocence regarding the staged wrongdoing.

Instructed lie experiments make me uneasy. Are instructed lies even deception? Are instructed liars really trying to dupe someone, or are they just trying to be good subjects and follow instructions? If instructed lies are really lies, do they work in the same way and have the same outcomes as spontaneous, non-instructed lies? This, I suggest, is an issue of *ecological validity*, and different theories of deception see different features of ecology as especially important. In TDT motives to lie play a central role, so why people are lying (or honest) matters for my understanding of deceptive communication.

The basic idea of ecological validity in research design is that all social behaviors exist within a social context, and the context matters.[15] That is, we must consider the ecology in which people are a part. We want the behaviors and processes we study to reflect the processes and behaviors of interest, and thus we worry that if the ecology of the research lab is different from the ecology of deception outside the research setting, then maybe the findings are limited to the ecology of the lab.

One way different theories of deception differ is in which aspects of the ecology are considered important. For example, it is not surprising that mock crimes are used more in legal and criminal psychology than in other deception research. If what the lies are about matters, and the concern is legal or criminal situations, then maybe lies should be about guilt or innocence of some crime. Mock crimes are used to simulate truth and lies in real crime situations. But if real guilt or innocence (and all that comes with a life of crime or a life as a law-abiding citizen) is critical, then maybe having college students play-act crimes is very different from real crime and real criminals. So, what aspects of a crime situation are most important?

As mentioned earlier, lie stakes play a critical role in Ekman's thinking and research. In Ekman's theory, leakage and deception clues stem from the emotional stakes linked with deception. What is important is whether the liars fear detection and experience guilt. From the Ekman perspective, therefore, an ecologically valid experiment would need to simulate the emotional experiences of liars in nonresearch settings. Detected liars should expect punishment.

IDT, in contrast, places the emphasis elsewhere. IDT researchers object to short snippets of videotaped behavior, instead insisting that long streams of real interaction are required if data are to be ecologically valid.[16] Deception cues stemming from strategic and nonstrategic affect and cognition presumably require longer segments of communication behavior before becoming observable.

Because TDT is not a cue theory, stakes, communication duration, or mere interactivity are not especially important from the TDT standpoint. The research reviewed in chapter 3 bears this out. Stakes, communication duration, and mere interactivity make little difference in deception detection. In TDT, in contrast, what matters are things like individual differences in sender lie prevalence (previous chapter), sender transparency and demeanor (chapter 13), receiver understanding of context and receiver ability to solicit honest confessions (chapter 14), and, most important for the current chapter, sender motivation. Thus, for TDT, a key aspect of ecological validity is that the motives for deception in the lab are similar to the motives that guide deception outside the lab. The cheating experiments achieve this.

There are only a few experiments looking at differences between instructed and noninstructed lies.[17] Although cue theories predict that instruction to lie (compared to noninstructed lies) should affect the prevalence of deception cues (deception cues are expected to be more prominent in unsanctioned deception),[18] research has not borne this out.[19] Instruction to lie does, however, appear to affect confession rates.[20] Subjects who are instructed to lie confess less under questioning. This suggests that subjects' main goal may be to be good subjects and follow instructions. Because confession seeking (and not observation of cues) is a path to effective detection in TDT, using noninstructed lies is important for empirical as well as theoretical reasons.

The issue of *ground truth* is even more important than ecological concerns in the validity of deception research design. In order to know if some communication might be deceptive, we need to know the truth. Outside the lab it is often impossible to be certain about the truthfulness of some communication. But if we are going to compare truths and lies, we must know what the truth is. This is the issue of ground truth.[21] So, when I wrote earlier that "I developed the cheating experiments like that used in experiment eight to get 'real lies' that I knew were really lies," by "real lies" I meant noninstructed lies; "that I knew were really lies" referred to my knowing ground truth.

TDT experiment eight used a version of my cheating experiment.[22] Briefly, the method goes like this: Subjects come to my lab for a study about "teamwork." They are paired with a partner who they think is another subject but who is actually working for me. Together the subject and the partner play a trivia game for a cash prize of five or ten dollars per right answer. Between the third and the fourth questions, the experimenter is called out of the room for some contrived reason, and the answers are left in a closed folder in easy reach of the subject. The partner suggests cheating, but it is up to the subject whether or not to cheat. After a few minutes, the experimenter returns and completes the trivia game. Next, the subject is interviewed about the experiment and asked, among other things, if they cheated. Honest answers are noncheaters who deny cheating, and cheaters who confess to cheating. Lies are if a noncheater falsely confesses, or a cheater falsely denies cheating.

The prediction in experiment eight was that subjects who did not cheat would answer honestly to the cheating question (because the truth works well for them), but cheaters are more prone to lie. And this was just what we found. We ran 126 subjects through this version of the cheating experiment. Of these 126, ninety-six (76%) chose not to cheat. When asked, all of them were honest about not cheating. In fact, of the more than five hundred subjects we have run through various versions of the cheating experiments, we have never had a spontaneous false confession. In contrast, of the thirty subjects who did cheat in experiment eight, 40% were honest and confessed, while 60% lied about cheating.[23] Thus, experiment eight replicated experiments six and seven with actual behavior. Together, TDT experiments six through eight provide clear evidence with a variety of different methods for TDT proposition five and the deception motives module.

CLASSIFYING DECEPTION MOTIVES

If people lie for particular reasons, what might those reasons be? Or, put differently, in what sort of circumstances does the truth become problematic, therefore creating an incentive to deceive? Several studies and authors have sought to classify deception motives. One early list of deception motivations included (a) to save face, (b) to manage relationships, (c) to exploit, (d) to avoid tension/conflict, and (e) to control situations.[24] Ekman provided a more extensive list of why children lie: (a) to avoid punishment, (b) to get something, (c) to protect friends, (d) to protect themselves, (e) to win admiration, (f) to avoid social awkwardness, (g) to avoid embarrassment, (h) to maintain privacy, and (i) for power over authority.[25] Alternatively, others have categorized motives for deception in terms of locus of primary benefit, that is, whether the lie benefits the self, another person, or the relationship.[26] These various approaches have been combined, resulting in two-dimensional typologies, with one dimension being reward categories representing different social motivations (e.g., to save face) and the other being target categories pertaining to who would benefit from the potential reward (e.g., self or other).[27]

TDT STUDY NINE: TOWARD A PAN-CULTURAL LIST OF DECEPTION MOTIVES

Given the prominence of motives in TDT, I wanted to take a look at the range of motives that guide human deceptive communication. So, TDT study nine took a broad look at why people lie.[28] I put together a multicultural team and collected some informative data.

Our method was pretty simple. We created an open-ended questionnaire asking subjects to recall an instance of lying or deception, from the perspective of either the liar or the target of the deception. That is, we asked some subjects to describe a situation in which they had been lied to and some subjects to describe a situation where they had lied to someone. Sometimes we used the word "lie," and other times we asked about "deception." We collected data in Egypt, Guatemala, Pakistan, Saudi Arabia, and the United States. In all, we collected 409 accounts of deception. After translations (when the language was other than English), my research team and I read through the accounts and came up with a list of deception motives that captured both the prior literature and the accounts in our new data. Once we had a list we were happy with, we went back through the data and sorted the various accounts into our deception motive categories. We did the sorting task independently and then cross-checked for agreement to ensure objectivity.[29]

The list we came up with follows. People lied to cover up wrongdoing or to gain some type of advantage or benefit. People lied to protect others and out of concern for politeness. People lied to look good in the eyes of others. People lied to be funny or to be mean.

1. *Personal transgression.* A lie to cover up a misdeed. Examples include lying to hide relational infidelity and making false excuses for why one was late to work.

2. *Economic advantage.* A lie motivated by monetary gain. Examples include knowingly selling defective products, seeking loans under false pretenses, and con-artist schemes.

3. *Nonmonetary personal advantage.* A lie to seek some desirable outcome for the self other than economic advantage. Examples include bogus excuses to get class notes for a missed class or to get a coworker to do a disliked task.

4. *Social/polite.* Lies told to conform to a social rule or to avoid rudeness. An example is saying that one liked a gift that was not liked.

5. *Altruistic lies* (other than social/polite). A lie told to protect another person, or another person's advantage. An example is a father hiding a health problem from a child to avoid upsetting her.

6. *Self-impression management.* Lies motivated by the desire to appear more favorably to others. An example is exaggerating accomplishments to impress a romantic interest.

7. *Malicious.* Lies to cause harm to others. Common examples include spreading false rumors about another person to harm their reputation or to sabotage a relationship.

8. *Humor/joke.* Deception to be funny or prank another.

9. *Pathological lies.* Lies without apparent motive or purpose, lies borne out of delusion, or lies told with blatant disregard for reality and detection consequences.

10. *Avoidance.* Lies told to avoid another person. An example includes fabricating an excuse to avoid attending an event with a friend.

A surprising category was what we called *avoidance lies.* In avoidance lies people want to avoid another person or to decline an invitation and lied about the reason. For example, there was an event last night related to work that I should have attended. When asked, I expressed my regrets, claiming a previous engagement. That wasn't true. I just didn't want to go. Perhaps that could have been considered a politeness motive, or a face-saving/impression management motive, but avoidance motives were so common (almost 15% of all accounts fell into this category) that we made them their own category.

Generally, self-serving lies were more common than polite or altruistic lies. Seeking some advantage for personal gain (30%), covering up a transgression (22%), and avoidance lies (15%) were more common than the other types.

Self-impression management motives accounted for 8% of the described deception, and politeness, altruism, maliciousness, jokes, and pathological lies were each evident in 5% or fewer of the deception accounts.

There was a great deal of similarity across the different countries. With the exception of pathological lies (the least frequent type of deception reported), all of the motives were reported in a majority of countries where data were collected, and most of the motives were evident in all of countries. Thus, the motives seem general across a wide variety of deceptions in a variety of very different human cultures.

There were a few notable differences between countries. The worst lies were disproportionally from the data collected in Pakistan. There, 17% of the lies were considered malicious. Purely malicious lying occurred in less than 4% of the cases in the other countries. Pakistan also stood out in the prevalence of economically motivated deception. Forty-three percent of the deception accounts in Pakistan involved some sort of fraud, scam, or rip-off to separate people from their money. In fact, our decision to separate out economic gain from other types of self-advantage motives was based on the Pakistan data so that we might capture this difference.

Other notable cultural differences were observed in the data from Guatemala. There were more humor-joke lies (12%) there than elsewhere (5% or below everywhere else). Hiding transgression (30%, especially romantic in nature) was also unusually prevalent in the Guatemalan lies relative to the rest.

PROJECTED MOTIVES

As we have seen in this chapter so far, deception motives play an important part in TDT. Lying, I believe, is not random. Most people do not lie often. When people do lie, they do so for a reason. People are likely to lie in situations where the truth conflicts with some goal or desired state of affairs. Otherwise, people are almost always honest.

To the extent that it is the match between the reality of the situation and the goals a communicator has prioritized that makes deception likely or not, understanding the nature of this match should be useful in anticipating when people will be deceptive and when deception is improbable. Two critical implications follow from this. First, it should be possible to improve lie detection by factoring in the presence or absence of a deception motive, and second, people may, at least tacitly, factor in situational considerations related to motives when assessing others' communication. These considerations now lead us to think about deception motives from a message receiver's perspective and consider projecting deception motives onto others.

Two lines of prior social-scientific research on topics other than deception show the importance of perceived or projected motives in forming impressions of others' honesty. First, in classic persuasion research, it has long been known that communicators are more credible when they argue against their own apparent interests.[30] For example, a store clerk who pushes the most expensive brand or model will come off as less sincere than a clerk who endorses a less expensive product. The clerk pushing the more expensive item may be seen as having his or her own interests (especially if the clerk works on commission) or the employer's interest in mind. That is, the employee may have an ulterior motive (economic profit) and is seen as less trustworthy. In contrast, the clerk who tells you that the less expensive item is just as good and is a better buy than the more expensive alternative does not seem to be communicating in self-interest. The only reason to say such things is because they are true. Thus, people very much do project motives onto others, and the motives one person projects onto another shape perceptions of honesty and integrity.

Second, projecting motives can be understood as a subcategory of a larger category of social cognition called *attributions*. Attributions are perceived causes or reasons for behavior. That is, attributions are the academic label for the idea that people think about why other people do what they do. There is a long and extensive history of theory and research on attributions in social psychology.

In Bertram Malle's theory of attributions,[31] people explain intentional and unintentional behaviors differently. When behavior is unintended, people look for causes (e.g., it is because of a person's own nature or because of the environment), but when a behavior is intentional, people look for reasons. Since deception is usually considered intentional, it follows that people presume that others have reasons for being deceptive. While attribution theories look at how people infer causes and reasons from behavior, I'm suggesting the reverse is also true; people can and do anticipate behavior from knowledge of reasons. Consistent with this claim, attribution research shows that knowledge of ulterior motives produces suspicion.[32]

This leads us to the Projected Motive Model and TDT proposition six:

The Projected Motive Model: People know that others lie for a reason and are more likely to suspect deception when they think a person has a reason to lie.

TDT Proposition Six: People understand that others' deception is usually purposive and are more likely to consider a message as potentially or actually deceptive under conditions where the truth may be inconsistent with a communicator's desired outcomes. That is, people project motive states on others, and this affects suspicion and judgments of honesty and deceit.

The projected motive thinking plays a critical role in TDT. Projecting a motive for deception is one of the trigger events that can lead people to abandon the truth-default and actively consider the possibility of deception. That is, if there are no obvious motives for another to be deceptive, people need not worry about deception because deception happens only when people have a reason to lie. But in situations where deception might be motivated, then the truth-default loses its utility, and people are well served by being on guard for possible deception.

Motives and projected motives, however, are irrelevant or useless in most deception detection experiments. In experiments using instructed lies, the reason for lying is experimental instruction to do so, and instructions are usually determined at random. People watching and judging instructed truths and lies cannot meaningfully use motive information because the sender's decision to lie is random and because, from the message receiver's point of view, situational factors that might motivate deception are constant across honest and deceptive senders. The part of the ecology that motivates deception in nonresearch settings is taken out of the equation in most deception detection experiments.

As an analogy, most deception detection experiments are like a murder mystery where either none of the suspects have a motive or all the suspects have the same motive. Solving the crime without the help of motive information to differentiate between suspects and nonsuspects makes the task of solving the mystery more difficult. In real-life murders, of course, most murderers have a motive to lie about their crime and most people who have not murdered someone have no reason to lie about murder. Consequently, understanding motive is usually helpful in solving and prosecuting the crime.

If researchers only care about lie detection based on behavioral cues, controlling motive might make good sense. Good research design controls variation in factors considered extraneous. But if our interest is a more general understanding of deception and lie detection, then instructed lie research may be distorting the picture. That is, if people do, as TDT claims, lie for a reason, and if people do, as TDT says they do, project motives when evaluating the honesty of others, then the ecology of instructed lies differs in critical ways from naturally occurring deception and deception detection situations. The next three experiments were designed to make this point and provide initial evidence for TDT proposition six and the Projected Motive Model.

TDT EXPERIMENTS TEN, ELEVEN, AND TWELVE: PROJECTED MOTIVES

Rachel Kim, Pete Blair, and I did a series of experiments testing TDT proposition six and the idea of projected motives.[33] The truths and lies came from
the first version of the cheating experiment. The second version of the cheating experiment was described in TDT experiment eight, but all the cheating
experiments are variations on the same basic design.[34]

When Rachel Kim and I began the first version of the cheating experiment,
we were surprised by a couple things. We were surprised by how few people
cheated. Of the first forty subjects we ran through the experiment, only seven
cheated, and we had to run thirteen subjects before we got our first cheater. We
were also surprised by the number of confessions. Of those first seven cheaters,
five of them confessed. So, after all the time it took to run the first forty subjects, we had only two lies on tape that we could use in later detection experiments. Most of our subjects didn't cheat, and of those who did, many did not
lie about it. We had expected more cheating liars. Eventually we got more lies
on tape, but we got off to a slow start because our subjects were more honest
than we had initially expected.[35] This predated our work on lie prevalence. In
retrospect, we should not have been so surprised, but we did not have a completed TDT back then to shape our thinking.

Once I observed that honest confessions occurred, I added a variation. We
ran a few additional subjects. Like most subjects, these new ones didn't cheat,
and when interviewed they honestly denied cheating. Then, I asked each of
them if they would please redo their interview, lie, and falsely admit to cheating. Seven participants agreed.

Thus, with the addition of these instructed false confessions, we had four
types of interviews. We had all combinations of subjects who were honest or
lying about being guilty or innocent. In the language of experimental design,
we could experimentally cross veracity with guilt–innocence to create a two-
by-two factorial design. That is, we had people who honestly confessed cheating, people who honestly denied cheating, people who denied cheating but
were lying, and the false confessors who lied about cheating when they actually had not cheated.[36]

When we show new subjects these four sets of interviews, what will they
make of them? Deniers have a possible motive for deception. Maybe they
cheated, maybe they didn't, but either way we can expect them to deny cheating. But there is no obvious reason why people would confess if they had not
cheated (and, in fact, if not instructed to false confess, they would not have
done so otherwise; our subjects never false confessed in the cheating experi-

ments without explicit instructions to do so, not even once). So, confession should be believed because there is no apparent motive for lying. This was our hypothesis in experiments ten through twelve. People believe confessions more than denials. As a consequence, accuracy would be very high for true confessions, very low for false confessions, and in the middle for denials. Accuracy should be higher for true denials than false denials (this is the veracity effect, covered in chapter 12), but the difference between truths and lies is expected to be much smaller for denials than confessions. That is, we predicted the highest accuracy for true confessions, a big drop, then true denials, followed by false denials, then a big drop, and the lowest accuracy for false confessions.

In TDT experiment 10, we showed 127 students twenty-seven videotaped interviews from the cheating experiments containing true and false confessions and denials. Subjects judged each interview as honest or deceptive regarding whether or not the person interviewed had actually cheated. We calculated truth-bias (percentage judged as honest) and accuracy (percentage judged correctly).

The results were just as we expected. Confessions were believed over 90% of the time. In contrast, denials were believed 52% of the time. This, of course, is a big difference.[37] In terms of accuracy, true confessions were judged correctly 95% of the time, true denials 56%, false denials 53%, and false confessions yielded only 12% accuracy.

TDT experiment eleven replicated these results with a slight variation. Experiment ten used a "repeated measures" design. That is, all the subjects saw all four types of honest and deceptive truths and lies. Although there are advantages to repeated measures designs,[38] they have disadvantages, like potential order effects, contrast effects, hypothesis guessing, etc. Such concerns can be controlled with an "independent groups" design in which subjects are randomly assigned to different experimental conditions. In the language of experimental design, the experimental variables are crossed, but subjects are nested with condition. So, to ensure that our results were not an artifact of the repeated measures approach, we recruited sixty-eight new subjects and randomly assigned them to see just the confessions or just the denials.

The results were similar to experiment ten and, again, just as we expected. Confessions were believed 81% of the time, compared to 56% for denials. In terms of accuracy, true confessions were judged correctly 87% of the time, true denials 56%, false denials 47%, and false confessions had only a 26% accuracy. The results were not quite as strong, but the order held, and the predictions passed statistical standards.[39]

In experiment twelve we went back to the repeated measures design used in experiment ten, but instead of recruiting college students, we showed the tapes to thirty-one professional investigators (a mix of police, mostly detectives, and fraud investigators working for banks). We wanted to show that our predictions would hold for people other than college students. The "the findings are limited by the use of college students as research subjects" refrain is the most overused criticism and lament in social science. Sometimes the use of college students does make a difference, but more often than not, it really doesn't. The only way to know is to check. Generally, I prefer to rule out potential criticism and concerns, even when I think them farfetched or trivial.

Besides ruling out a knee-jerk criticism and documenting generality across samples of research participants, I had another more substantive motivation for a replication of this particular prediction with professional investigators. Again and again I had heard researchers and practitioners alike say that police were a cynical bunch prone to lie-bias.[40] I had a different interpretation. Prior research and thinking had often confounded deception and guilt. When comparing guilty liars to innocent honest folk, police and other lie detection professionals are less truth-biased than college students.[41] I thought the bias might go the other way for confessions. That is, police might be more cynical about denials but more accepting of confessions. Experiment twelve offered an opportunity to disentangle deception and guilt.

The results of experiment twelve were surprising. The investigators believed confessions (82%) much more than denials (59%), supporting the main hypothesis and replicating the experiments with college students. The professional investigators were not lie-biased. In fact, they did much better on true denials (40%) than false denials (22%). What was surprising was how much worse they were at the denials than were the students. Accuracy was only 31%! They were wrong more than two-thirds of the time in sorting out honest from deceptive denials. And they were not lie-biased. They believed 78% of the liars denying wrongdoing.

The findings of study twelve were strange indeed, and inexplicable by any theory in existence at the time. I now know they were not a fluke, because I have since replicated these results.[42] The explanation is stuff for chapter 14, but to give a glimpse ahead, the idea is that the results had to do with the wording of the questions in the interviews. There are some questions that can make innocent people seem guilty and guilty people look innocent in comparison, thereby producing below-chance accuracy. Professionals may be more susceptible to this inadvertent misdirection. The important lesson is that answers are shaped by the questions asked, but people tend to infer that answers reflect the person answering.

TABLE 10.1. TRUTH-BIAS AND ACCURACY RESULTS OF TDT EXPERIMENTS TEN, ELEVEN, AND TWELVE

Experiment	CONFESSIONS		DENIALS	
	Truths	Lies	Truths	Lies
Truth-Bias (percentage believed)				
Experiment 10	95%	88%	56%	47%
Experiment 11	87%	74%	62%	51%
Experiment 12	86%	77%	40%	78%
Accuracy (percentage correct)				
Experiment 10	95%	12%	56%	53%
Experiment 11	87%	26%	62%	49%
Experiment 12	86%	23%	40%	22%

Anyway, the results of TDT experiments ten through twelve are summarized in table 10.1. The findings of all three experiments are very much consistent with the idea that people project motives for deception, and people are more likely to believe others when there is no apparent reason for the person to lie.

CHARLIE BOND ALSO TESTS THE OVERLOOKED OBVIOUS

Unknown to me at the time I was collecting the data for the projected motive experiments, psychologist Charlie Bond independently came up with pretty much the same idea. He tested the idea a little differently and published his results under the title "Overlooking the Obvious: Incentive to Lie."[43] As we did, he tested his idea with three experiments. His work took longer to get into print than ours, but both sets of studies tell the same story. Deception motives determine deceptive communication, and awareness of others' motives is very useful in detecting deception.

In the Bond experiments, some subjects were given either an incentive to lie or an incentive for honesty. Subjects could choose to be honest or not, but if they didn't choose the incentivized action, they had to do a boring activity for fifteen minutes. The incentive was avoiding the boring task. The incentive proved powerful. All subjects chose the incentive. When they could avoid the undesirable task with honesty, they were honest. When the unpleasant task was avoidable with a lie, they lied. Another group of subjects watched video-tapes of the first group of incentivized subjects. The second group got to see the first group's communications and the offer of incentives. Knowing the incentive structure let the second group of subjects correctly assess the actual honesty of the first group with nearly perfect (99%) accuracy. Accuracy dropped slightly, to 97%, in the second and third experiments, but the upshot was the same. Understanding the incentives and motives is obviously useful in predicting behavior, and people use knowledge of motives and incentives to interpret others' actions.

SUMMARY AND CONCLUSIONS

This chapter is about deception motives. Lying is not random. People lie when the truth is inconsistent with their goals. When the truth is not a problem, people are honest. This makes deception somewhat predictable. This also means that understanding the context in which deception occurs is important, because there are situations when we really don't need to worry about deception and other situations in which we need to be on guard for deception.

A series of experiments using a variety of methods provided evidence consistent with key TDT claims regarding motives. People communicate honestly unless they have a reason not to. Research also looked at the motives that lead to deception, and a list of motives was derived. Finally, a series of experiments showed that people use contextual information regarding motivation when assessing others' honesty and that the availability and use of motive-related information can improve deception detection accuracy.

The next chapter continues the change here in focus from senders and truthful and deceptive messages to the receivers of those messages. Chapter eleven takes a close look at truth-bias and TDT's namesake, the idea of a truth-default. In doing so, we will finally get at the core of TDT.

11

Truth-Bias and Truth-Default

HERE WE DISCUSS TDT'S NAMESAKE idea, the truth-default, and the closely related (but conceptually distinct) variable, truth-bias. It was the empirical observation of truth-bias that started me down the path that eventually led to TDT. In fact, early versions of the theory in academic talks I gave from 2006 to 2010 were called TBT (Truth-Bias Theory) rather than TDT. However, TDT is a much better name for my idea.

Professor Torsten Reimer of Purdue University suggested the label "truth-default" in a conversation a few years back. He told me that he thought "truth-default" better captured my ideas than "truth-bias." Torsten's concern with "truth-bias" as a label was that people were likely to get caught up on the word "bias." Biases, after all, are bad things, to be avoided. But I was no longer thinking of truth-bias as either a bias or a bad thing.

Back in the 1990s, I thought of truth-bias as distorted and lazy thinking. Over time, however, I came to see truth-bias and the truth-default as adaptive and not necessarily as biased in the usual sense of the word. Torsten's points were that the label "truth-bias" no longer fit my ideas well and that an alternative word or phrase might better capture the main idea. Calling the theory "truth-bias theory" would mislead readers because of the connotation carried by the word "bias." "Truth-default," Torsten suggested, captured my thinking much better. He was right.

As I carefully thought about it, I came to see many advantages in taking Torsten's advice. I think he was right about people getting stuck on the word "bias." There are plenty of examples of that happening in the published literature on deception.[1] But more than that, as I thought it through, I came to see big theoretical and empirical payoffs in distinguishing between a truth-default and truth-bias. They are not the same thing. The truth-default is one cause of truth-bias, but people can still be truth-biased even if they are not operating from a truth-default. That is, the truth-default is sufficient for truth-bias but not necessary for truth-bias. Believing another person's communication can be an unconscious default, or it can be actively based on exculpatory evidence. Thus, truth-bias can be active or passive, but the truth-default is, by definition, always passive.

TDT's perspective on truth-bias and the truth-default is captured succinctly in proposition three.

> **TDT Proposition Three:** Most people believe most of what is said by most other people most of the time. That is, most people can be said to be truth-biased most of the time. Truth-bias results, in part, from a default cognitive state. The truth-default state is pervasive, but it is not an inescapable cognitive state. Truth-bias and the truth-default are adaptive both for the individual and the species. They enable efficient communication.

TDT proposition three sets forth five specific subclaims:

- People are typically truth-biased.
- People have a cognitive default state set to believing others—the truth-default.
- The truth-default state is a primary causal mechanism leading to truth-bias.
- The truth-default can be "switched off" as specified in subsequent propositions.
- Truth-bias and truth-default are adaptive—that is, they are usually good things. They evolved because they serve us well. Specifically, they are necessary for efficient and effective communication.

The five subclaims are unpacked in this chapter. It is worth emphasizing up front that it is this last point about truth-default and truth-bias being adaptive that really distinguishes TDT from most other approaches to human deception. While most prior theoretical perspectives acknowledge the empirical existence of truth-bias, truth-bias in pre-TDT theory is typically viewed as an error or bias reflecting flawed judgment. Truth-bias is often depicted as a distorted perceptual state that is maladaptive and interferes with deception detection accuracy.[2] What is new and different in TDT is the claim that both the truth-default and the truth-bias that results are functional and adaptive and improve accuracy in most non-research settings.

I see a parallel in the contrast between TDT and rival deception theories (especially IDT) and the contrast between the Gigerenzer and the Kahneman-Tversky approaches to judgmental heuristics under uncertainty.[3] Cognitive heuristics are relatively mindless decision rules that people use to make intuitive judgments under conditions of uncertainty. For example, imagine you are at the grocery store shopping for shredded cheese. There is a more expensive name brand and a less expensive store brand. You have not tried either, so you don't know whether the price trade-off reflects quality. There is no way at the time to make a fully informed decision, so there is uncertainty regarding the best choice. You could just adopt a simple decision rule such as "go with the name brand" or "pick the lowest price." Using a simple decision rule avoids getting bogged down in weighing the pros and cons of an uncertain decision. Kahneman's research finds that the use of simple decision rules like these can lead people to biased, less-than-statistically-optimal choices. The take-home message is that heuristics make us dumb, biased, and wrong. Gigerenzer, in contrast, offers a very different point of view. In a nutshell, he says people use heuristics in situations where uncertainty is inescapable and that heuristics evolved precisely because they lead to the best decisions in the situations where they are used. According to Gigerenzer, heuristics make us smart and efficient decision-makers. This difference is much like the different views of truth-bias in deception theory. Like Kahneman's view of heuristics, most deception theory sees truth-bias as flawed thinking, while TDT, analogous to Gigerenzer's view of heuristics, sees truth-bias as functional and adaptive and as having evolved precisely because it was functional and adaptive. As I mention in the acknowledgments for the book, I am a big fan of Gigerenzer's work. He has deeply influenced my thinking, and I see TDT as very much in line with his work on bounded rationality, heuristics, and the adaptive toolbox.[4]

The scientific evidence for the functional and adaptive nature of the truth-default and truth-bias is explained further in the next chapter, where the focus shifts to two important outcomes of truth-bias, the "veracity effect" and base-rate effects. When these ideas and findings are considered in conjunction with the findings on prevalence of deception reviewed in chapter 9, the adaptive and functional nature of truth-bias will become clear. In this chapter, the focus is on conceptualizing and documenting the existence of truth-bias and the truth-default.

TRUTH-BIAS

Truth-bias is the tendency to believe that another person's communication is honest, independent of its actual honesty. The term was coined by Steve

McCornack.[5] Steve scored truth-bias as the proportion of messages judged as honest in some defined setting.[6] So, if a subject in a deception detection experiment viewed and judged ten interviews, and if the subject judged six out of ten interviewers to be honest, the truth-bias score is 0.6 (6 ÷ 10), or 60%. Scored in this way, truth-bias scores can range from zero (100% of messages judged as deceptive) to 1.00 (100% of communication rated as honest). Values above the 0.50 midpoint are seen as "truth-biased." The more a result is above 0.50 and the closer the value is to 1.00, the greater the extent of truth-bias.

Scores on truth-bias can, of course, fall below 0.50. Steve and I called this possibility "lie-bias" in a 1990 article.[7] There are two points I want to make about lie-bias. First, we think about truth-bias and lie-bias as the same variable—just different ranges of values on the same continuum ranging from 100% attribution of honesty to judging 100% of communication as deceptive. Second, I regret using the term "lie-bias." It has caught on. The problem is that people are seldom lie-biased, and when lie-bias is observed, it tends to be ephemeral. Don't get me wrong. Lie-bias can and does happen. But it tends not to happen, and it is hard to make it happen experimentally in a way that replicates. Some researchers claim that police officers are typically lie-biased. But a close look at the research shows that a more correct description is that police tend to be less truth-biased than college students, but they are still truth-biased.[8] By naming something, the impression is created that that which is named is real. These days, I see lie-bias as an ephemeral anomaly.[9] Research tends to show more or less truth-bias, rather than an actual lie-bias. My bad.

I define truth-bias as "independent" of actual honesty because it is scored the same way regardless of the relative proportion of truthful and deceptive messages judged. So, if all ten interviews were actually truthful, but only six were judged as honest, truth-bias would still be 0.6. The same would be true if the messages were all lies. Not all researchers score truth-bias this way,[10] but I want to be clear about how I conceive of and score truth-bias.

I also want to reiterate that truth-bias is only a "bias" in relation to the arbitrary 0.50 standard marking the fifty-fifty point on the scale. Even in deception detection experiments where messages are a fifty-fifty split between truths and lies, this is still an arbitrary standard. We'll look at this much more in the next chapter, but please keep in mind that the word "bias" is merely a label for a score obtained in research, and that one should not make the easy move from the finding that people judge more than 50% of messages as honest in deception detection experiments to the conclusion that people are biased in the direction of truth outside the lab relative to the actual prevalence of deception in everyday interaction.

TDT EXPERIMENT THIRTEEN: LOVERS JUST AREN'T LEERY

This experiment may be lucky number thirteen as presented in this book, but in chronology it is number one.[11] That's right, we are about to talk about my first-ever deception experiment. This is the research that started it all for me. I mentioned some of the background in the first chapter. I was about halfway through my PhD program, Steve McCornack had just arrived as a new professor, and I was assigned as his research assistant. We titled our first paper "When Lovers Become Leery," but looking back, that title was misleading. The most important implication of our findings was that lovers just aren't leery, even when they should be.

As mentioned in chapters one and three, Steve's prior work had looked at how the closeness of the relationship between the sender and the judge affected deception detection accuracy. Steve had studied college dating couples and found that the closer the relationship, the more confident the subjects were in their ability to read their partners, the more they believed their partners (i.e., the greater the truth-bias), and (albeit indirectly) the lower the accuracy.[12] This finding was surprising because at the time many researchers thought that knowing a person would increase accuracy.

Steve reasoned that if truth-bias blinds us to the lies of those close to us, suspicion might counteract that. More precisely, he thought (and we hypothesized) that a little suspicion might be a good thing for accuracy. Absent suspicion, truth-bias would prevail, and truth-bias would lower accuracy.[13] Too much suspicion, too, was predicted to hinder accuracy. While truth-bias might blind us to others' lies, we predicted that high suspicion would lead to lie-bias, and honesty-blindness. But maybe there was a sweet spot in the middle. What if there was enough suspicion to abandon truth-bias but not so much as to create a lie-bias? Maybe with just the right amount of suspicion, there would be little bias in either direction. Accuracy would soar. Thus, we hypothesized a nonlinear relationship between suspicion and accuracy such that moderate suspicion would produce higher accuracy than either low or high suspicion.

We recruited 107 heterosexual college dating couples to our lab. The couples were separated, and one was randomly assigned to be the sender, the other the judge. The sender was asked to honestly answer twelve edgy (from a Machiavellian personality scale) attitude-belief questions. They were then videotaped discussing their answers to these twelve questions, one at a time. For half of the questions (assigned at random), they discussed how they had actually answered the question. For the other half, they lied about how they had answered the question and why.

In a different room, the judges received one of three different sets of instructions (determined at random) designed to instill low, moderate, or high levels of suspicion regarding the partner's answers. For senders in the low-suspicion condition, we never even mentioned lying or deception. Judges were asked a question about whether their partner was lying or telling the truth, but this question was imbedded in a set of filler questions disguising the true purpose of the experiment.[14] We told them (honestly) that we just could not tell them what the experiment was about, but from reading the questions, it appeared the research was interested in how well people know their partners (and debriefing confirmed that this is what most of the low- and moderate-suspicion subjects thought). In the moderate-suspicion condition, there was brief mention of the possibility that the partner might be lying. In the high-suspicion condition, subjects were directly and explicitly told that the experiment was about lie detection, that the partner would be lying about some of their answers, and that it was their job as a subject in the experiment to identify the lies.

We showed the twelve videotaped segments, one at a time, to the partner-judge, who answered a series of questions about each tape, including a question about whether the sender's response was an honest reflection of the actual answer or whether the sender was lying. Truth-bias (simple percentage rated as honest) and accuracy (simple percentage correct) were scored. The results are shown in table 11.1.

Looking at the first row of values in table 11.1, we can see that the results for accuracy are very much in line with our hypotheses. While overall accuracy was in line with the slightly-better-than-chance accuracy typical of the larger literature reviewed in chapter 3, accuracy was improved in the moderate-suspicion condition (65%) relative to the low- (53%) and high-suspicion (57%) conditions. Contrary to what we thought at the time, in hindsight these were not the important findings.

Check out the truth-bias scores in the second row of table 11.1. Generally, suspicion reduced truth-bias. This makes good sense, right? It could not really be otherwise unless we just did a poor job of varying suspicion. What's important here, however, is not so much the strong effect of suspicion on truth-bias but the power of truth-bias in the face of suspicion. When subjects didn't know they were in a deception detection experiment and were no more suspicious than they would be in any other lab experiment, they circled "honest" on four out five (80%) of the interviews (and hence judged messages as lies on only one out of five responses). But even under high suspicion, truth-bias still prevailed. It was lower, for sure, but judges still picked "honest" two-to-one over "lie."

TABLE 11.1. RESULTS OF TDT EXPERIMENTS THIRTEEN AND FOURTEEN

Outcome Variable	SUSPICION			Across Conditions
	Low	Moderate	High	
TDT experiment 13: College dating couples				
Detection Accuracy	53.2%	64.6%	57.2%	58.2%
Truth-Bias	80.3%	72.0%	64.2%	72.2%
TDT experiment 14: Unacquainted college students				
Detection Accuracy	55.7%	55.7%	48.1%	53.1%
Truth-Bias	78.0%	75.7%	58.7%	70.7%

The big news of experiment thirteen is the robust nature of truth-bias! Even in a lab experiment where subjects are suspicious to begin with, even when they know the experiment is about deception, and even when they are told to expect lies, our subjects were still truth-biased. Truths and lies were equally prevalent, but truth judgments occurred twice as often as lie judgments. Wow!

The results show the power of truth-bias. But what really drove the power of truth-bias home does not show up in the tabled results. Since the experiment used dating couples and because the study was about deception, Steve and I had some real ethical concerns. We were worried about participation in our experiment damaging our subjects' relationships.[15] Consequently, we adapted an extensive debriefing protocol explaining the experiment and making sure there was no relational damage or fallout. I did many of those debriefings.

Steve and I learned during the debriefing that our concern regarding relationship harm was misplaced. While I was happy that there weren't adverse reactions from the subjects and that they were not upset by their participation in the experiment, I was quite shocked by the outright denial of the nature of the experiment by some subjects. Several subjects refused to believe that the experiment was about deception, explaining that their partner just does not lie to them, experiment or not. These participants were given their research credits, politely thanked, and sent on their merry way. But they left a lasting impression on me. My take-home message from the 1990 suspicion experiment was the robust, pervasive nature of truth-bias. It was these results and these experiences debriefing subjects that planted the first seed for TDT in my mind. Truth-bias was a strong and important finding. Although I did not foresee where it would lead me, I wanted to understand it better.

TDT EXPERIMENT FOURTEEN:
RACHEL KIM AND SUSPICION REDUX

We now warp ahead two decades. I was a tenured full professor at my alma mater (Michigan State University) with my own research team, and Rachel Kim (former undergraduate student of mine at University of Hawaii) was my PhD student and my valued lab assistant. For her preliminary research paper, Rachel did a replication and extension of Steve's and my suspicion experiment.[16] There are several differences between experiments thirteen and fourteen, but two are important here.[17] Rachel's version used strangers rather than dating couples, and the truths and lies came from our NSF cheating tapes rather than truths and lies about personality-related attitudes, beliefs, and values. The results of experiment fourteen are provided in the bottom half of table 11.1.

The accuracy findings didn't replicate the earlier findings neatly. Accuracy was overall about five points lower, and the pattern was different. Whereas moderate suspicion was clearly the highest in the 1990 study, in the 2011 version, low and moderate suspicion produced about the same accuracy, and the high-suspicion condition was the stand-out, with only 48% correct. But let's focus on the truth-bias findings.

While the accuracy results were different, the truth-bias results were quite similar. Just as was the case in the first experiment, suspicion reduced truth-bias but did not eliminate it. Both experiments show a linear decrease in truth-bias as a function of increased suspicion,[18] but even under high suspicion, judges pick honest more often than lie. Truth-bias is robust.

WANT MORE DATA?

Experiments thirteen and fourteen document the robust nature of truth-bias. The importance of experiment thirteen for the current discussion is largely historical, and experiment fourteen shows that the conclusions about truth-bias are not unique to the nature of the subjects (dating couples or strangers), the type of lies (attitudes-beliefs or covering transgressions), or the times (late 1980s or early 2000s). These experiments make the point about the power of truth-bias nicely because both show truth-bias even under suspicion. But when specific studies are selected as examples, a critical reader might wonder how representative the results really are. To preempt any concern regarding cherry-picking results, table 11.2 provides observed truth-bias scores in my research over the past twenty-five years. As you can see, subjects in my experiments are always truth-biased.

TABLE 11.2. TRUTH-BIAS IN MY RESEARCH

Experiment	Truth-bias	Experiment	Truth-bias
TDT experiment 10	72%	TDT experiment 29	54%
TDT experiment 11	68%	TDT experiment 30	56%
TDT experiment 12	70%	TDT experiment 31	66%
TDT experiment 13	72%	TDT experiment 32	61%
TDT experiment 14	71%	TDT experiment 28	69%
TDT experiment 15	58%	TDT experiment 39–44[1]	54%
TDT experiment 16	88%	TDT experiment 45	70%
TDT experiment 17	68%	TDT experiment 46	67%
TDT experiment 18	66%	TDT experiment 47	60%
TDT experiment 19	64%	TDT experiment 48	53%
TDT experiment 20	65%	Group experiment[2]	66%
TDT experiment 21	63%	LSS2010 background questioning[3]	59%
TDT experiment 24	63%		
TDT experiment 25	62%	LSS2010 direct question	60%
TDT experiment 26	56%	LSS2010B[4]	61%
TDT experiment 28	56%	Probing experiment 1[5]	72%
		Probing experiment 3	56%

[1] Control conditions only, averaged across studies.

[2] Ernest S. Park, Timothy R. Levine, Chad M. Harms, and Merissa H. Ferrara, "Group and Individual Accuracy in Deception Detection," *Communication Research Reports* 19, no. 2 (2002): 99–106, https://doi.org/10.1080/08824090209384837.

[3] Timothy R. Levine, Allison Shaw, Hillary C. Shulman, "Increasing Deception Detection Accuracy with Strategic Questioning," *Human Communication Research* 36, no. 2 (April 2010): 216–31, https://doi.org/10.1111/j.1468-2958.2010.01374.x.

[4] Timothy R. Levine, Allison Shaw, Hillary C. Shulman, "Assessing Deception Detection Accuracy with Dichotomous Truth–Lie Judgments and Continuous Scaling: Are People Really More Accurate When Honesty Is Scaled?" *Communication Research Reports* 27, no. 2 (2010): 112–122, https://doi.org/10.1080/08824090903526638.

[5] Timothy R. Levine and Steven A. McCornack, "Behavioral Adaptation, Confidence, and Heuristic-Based Explanations of the Probing Effect," *Human Communication Research* 27, no. 4 (October 2001): 471–502, https://doi.org/10.1111/j.1468-2958.2001.tb00790.x.

MODERATORS OF TRUTH-BIAS

While truth-bias is very robust in existence, as we saw with suspicion, it does vary systematically in degree. Look at table 11.2 again. Subjects are always truth-biased (honesty judgments are over the 50% threshold), but they are not always truth-biased to the same extent. Values range from as high as 88% to as low 53%. Clearly, sometimes people are more truth-biased than at other times. Below are some of the more important variables known to impact the extent to which people are truth-biased.

- *Experimentally primed suspicion*—The more suspicious, the lower the truth-bias (as shown in TDT experiments thirteen and fourteen). As can be seen in table 11.1, primed suspicion can make almost a 0.20 difference in truth-bias.
- *Closeness of relationship*—Truth-bias increases as the relationship between communicators becomes closer.[19]
- *Face-to-face interaction*—Truth-bias is higher when communicating face-to-face than otherwise. Within various media, truth-bias is higher when there is audio than when there is video only. Truth-bias averages 0.55 with no interaction, 0.65 with direct face-to-face interaction, 0.52 with video only, 0.56 with audio-visual, and 0.63 with audio only.[20]
- *Mere question asking*—In a finding called "the probing effect," senders who are answering a heard question are seen as more honest than when the same answer is judged, just absent the question. The size of the difference is a little less than 0.10.[21]
- *Students vs. experts*—Student judges are more truth-biased than experts (like police). The difference, however, is fairly small: 0.56 for students down to 0.52 for experts.[22]
- *Sender demeanor*—Some senders are much more believable than others regardless of actual honesty. Demeanor seems to be the strongest of the moderators, creating differences larger than 0.30 (from 0.36 for insincere demeanor to 0.69 for sincere senders).[23] I cover demeanor findings in detail in chapter 13.

In each case, the general conclusion is that human judges are truth-biased, but truth-bias is more or less pronounced under some conditions. Further, the six variables listed above affect truth-bias much more than they impact accuracy.[24]

THE TRUTH-DEFAULT

The truth-default involves a passive presumption of honesty. People typically presume without conscious reflection that others' communication is honest. My thesis is that the possibility that a message might be deception does not even come to mind unless suspicion, skepticism, or doubt is actively triggered.

The truth-default state has three parts: truth, default, and state. By a default, I mean a passive starting place. You don't have to do or think anything. For example, as I type this sentence, I have the default font in my word-processing software set to twelve-point black Calibri. I can actively change the font to make it bold, or italic, or larger, or smaller, or some color other than black. If I do nothing and just start typing, black twelve-point Calibri print shows up on my screen. This default usually works well for me, and I don't change it unless I need to. Further, I don't even need to think about the font most of the time. I can focus on what I am trying to say, sentence structure, word choice, and the like. As I type this, I wouldn't be thinking about the font at all if I weren't offering it as an analogy.

TDT holds that when communicating with others, the default cognitive state is belief. This is the truth part. If we don't change the default, we presume that what we hear (or see or read) is honest and truthful.

By state, I mean the particular condition at a particular time. Since the truth-default is a cognitive state, it is a particular state of mind at a particular time. States exist "at the moment," and states can change. Putting this all together, the truth-default is a default state of mind where we accept or believe others' communication.

We believe other people unless we actively decide not to. Changing or temporarily turning off the truth-default state requires some sort of *trigger*.[25] A trigger is anything that catches our attention and gets us to consciously consider the veracity of some communication. We will talk about some specific triggers later when we lay out TDT proposition seven, but for now it is sufficient to say that some triggers, once pulled, can switch off the truth-default autopilot and get us thinking about whether some communication might be deceptive.

Once active consideration of the possibility of deception is triggered, three additional cognitive states become possible: a belief that some communication is deceptive, an active assessment that the communication is honest, or an intermediary state of suspended belief and uncertainty. We start with the initial presumption of honesty—the truth-default. If we are kicked out of the truth-default by some trigger event, either we can become suspicious and uncertain about honesty, or if there is good reason to do so, we go straight to the belief that the communication is in fact deception. If there is a suspicion-uncertainty state, we will not stay in that state indefinitely. The suspicion state will end in one of three ways. We might make an active determination of deception. Or, if exculpatory evidence is discovered, we will make an active determination of honesty. However, lacking evidence one way or the other, we will eventually revert to a passive truth-default.[26] The idea is akin to the sleeper effect in persuasion research in which a low credible source, over time, can become more influential as people forget the source but remember the message.[27]

Putting this all together, there are four cognitive outcomes related to inferences about the honesty and deceitfulness of others' communication. The most common situation is that the question of deception never occurs to us. The truth-default stays in place, and we passively presume the communication was honest. Second, something can spark suspicion, and we actively consider the possibility of deception but consciously decide that the person was honest and that the suspicion was unfounded. Third, we can become suspicious but never really find out one way or another. Over time, the suspicion will fade, and we will unconsciously revert to the truth-default. Finally, a trigger event can kick us out of the truth-default, and we can decide that we were deceived (or at least that the other was trying to deceive us).

The we-judge-something-is-deception outcome can play out before the message is even received, immediately upon receipt, or (most commonly) well after the fact. We can, of course, go into situations expecting deception. Or, the suspicion or assessment of dishonesty can occur as the message is received. This typically happens when there is something in the content or presentation that does not seem right. Perhaps the message contradicts prior knowledge or seems too implausible. Maybe the person is acting oddly. Finally, assessment of dishonesty can occur well after the fact when new information comes to light showing that a previously believed message was deceptive. The reverse is also possible; new information can lead us to change our minds and conclude that a message once thought deceptive was actually honest. Inferences about honesty and deception need not be final, and trigger events can happen before, while, or after the communication takes place.

The idea of the truth-default is consistent with Harvard social psychologist Dan Gilbert's Spinozan model of belief, in which incoming information is believed unless subsequently and actively disbelieved.[28] Gilbert was interested in how people mentally represent true and false information. A mental representation simply means thinking about or understanding something and holding that thought in mind. In line with the fifteenth-century Dutch philosopher Baruch Spinoza, Gilbert's idea is that the belief that some information is true is a default that comes automatically with comprehension. To understand something, we must, at least momentarily, accept it. People can unbelieve, but unbelieving comes later and is conscious and controllable; initial belief is automatic. Gilbert and his colleagues published six experiments showing that if people are distracted from evaluating information, they tend to mistake truth for fiction more than mistaking fiction for truth.[29]

The truth-default is also consistent with Grice's logic of conversation (discussed in chapter 8), wherein people generally presume communication is fundamentally cooperative. That is, people typically make sense of what others say based on the premise that others are trying to be understood. We must do this to make sense of what others say, because what is literally said and what is meant are not always the same.

The TDT perspective is that we humans evolved to have a truth-default. The reason we evolved this way is that the truth-default is adaptive. The truth-default works well for us both as individuals and as a species.

Humans are, at our very core, social beings. Our survival as individuals and our success as a species depend on in-group cooperation. Cooperation requires efficient communication. The truth-default enables efficient communication. It is a prerequisite. Without the truth-default, communication falters. It lets us form friendships, lasting spousal relationships, and cooperative work groups. It lets us maintain family ties, engage in commerce, and pass on useful knowledge. Efficient communication serves us well, and this is why the truth-default evolved.

As I said, we humans are social down to our cores. I can't emphasize this enough. Social interaction with other humans is our nature. We are born with an amazing ability to pick up language and to learn to communicate with other humans. Our whole lives are spent interacting with others. Nothing is as important to us as our social ties with other humans. Without others, we can't survive. Even if you are a competent hermit-survivalist who can hunt, gather and grow your own food, and make your own weapons, clothes, and shelter, you didn't learn those skills on your own. You learned things from others. We humans not only cooperate but also pass down knowledge. Cooperation and passing along knowledge are central to the human condition.

Try this thought experiment. Consider for a moment the alternative to a truth-default. What would life be like? Absent a basic and deep presumption of honesty and validity of communication, cooperating with and learning from others would be perilous and uncertain. We'd constantly be second-guessing everything. Why cooperate if you have no reason to expect cooperation in return? What is the point of learning if what is learned might be disinformation?

The very fact that you are reading my book would make little sense if you had to second-guess every word and idea.

I'm currently reading *Liars and Outliers* by Bruce Schneier.[30] The subtitle is *Enabling the Trust That Society Needs to Thrive.* The ideas Schneier talks about are very much in line with TDT, although TDT is more narrowly focused on communication and deception, and Schneier's focus is more macro and at the level of society. The basic logic is the same. Society requires trust to function well. The erosion of trust leads to chaos and anarchy. Schneier calls people who play well with others, who follow the rules, and who are trustworthy "cooperators." Most people are cooperators. But where there is trust, there are those who exploit others. Schneier calls such noncooperative people "defectors." Society creates and enforces rules to punish defectors and keep the harm they do to a minimum. The fewer defectors, the more trust. The deeper the trust, the more gained from violating trust, and the greater the incentive to defect. Societies get to an equilibrium state, with some proportion of cooperators and defectors. The fewer the defectors, the better for society.

Just as society requires trust to function, so too does communication require the presumption of honesty, the truth-default. Without a truth-default, communication would lose efficiency and, ultimately, utility. Most people are honest, so the truth-default works well for most people most of the time. Communication works. But the presumption of honesty enables successful exploitation by deception and deceivers. Society makes and enforces rules to discourage deception, thereby facilitating efficient communication. This makes deception much less prevalent than honesty, but it does not prevent deception altogether.

The truth-default makes us vulnerable to deception. The truth-default and the risk of deception involve a trade-off. But the trade-off is a good one. This is where TDT departs from almost all evolutionary thinking about deception. I have heard and read the argument many times that since humans evolved to deceive, we must have evolved the ability to detect deception. Evolution, it is argued, necessitates a coevolutionary arms race between the ability to deceive and the ability to detect. While I don't doubt basic evolution and the idea that humans have evolved, I do not think that accepting evolution requires accepting a coevolutionary struggle between the ability to deceive and the ability to detect deception in real time.

There are at least four reasons why I don't buy the coevolutionary arms-race argument. First and foremost, TDT sees the tradeoff between the truth-default and the risk of deception as a great deal for us. What we get in exchange for being vulnerable to an occasional lie is efficient communication and social coordination. The benefits are huge, and the costs are trivial in comparison. Sure, we get deceived once in a while. That is just the cost of doing business. It's like going through security at an airport. We get much benefit out of smooth and efficient travel. We could evolve a security screening system where every passenger is strip-searched, every bag is triple checked, and every passenger is fully interrogated every time. No doubt we would be safer. But that would bog down the system, and most times the harm caused by being deceived isn't fatal. Most deception is not as serious as a terrorist with a bomb boarding a plane. Being deceived once in a while is not going to prevent us from passing on our genes or seriously threaten the survival of the species. Efficient communication, on the other hand, has huge implications for our survival. The trade-off just isn't much of a trade-off. The risk simply doesn't justify a coevolutionary struggle.

Second, evolving the cognitive ability to detect lies in real time is not the only evolutionary solution for dealing with the risk of deception. By analogy, there is no need to evolve resistance to a new disease if we can invent a vaccine. This is what we humans have done. We have created cultures, religions, and socialization that seek to prevent deception. Parents everywhere teach their children not to lie. Every major world religion has prohibitions against deception. Prevention is not 100% effective. There are the few prolific liars out there. Prevention reduces the prevalence and risk of deception to make the truth-default payoff stronger. It's more efficient to prevent deception than to evolve brains well suited to real-time deception detection. Evolution favors the more efficient solution.

Third, social interactions in social species are often not one-offs. People talk among themselves about other people. This reduces the need for real-time deception detection and creates further deterrence against dishonest behaviors. As we will see in chapter 14, many if not most lies are discovered well after the fact. As we have seen already, most lies are told by a few prolific liars. It's the prolific liars we need to worry most about. So, once a prolific liar has been identified, we can know to be on guard when dealing with him or her. Better yet, maybe we can just avoid that person. We can also warn others; the word gets out. What I am suggesting here is that the truth-default means we will get burned by deception once in a while. But we can learn and not repeat past mistakes, and we can pass that information along. Once a prolific liar is outed, his or her ability to deceive is reduced. Also, prolific liars may be shunned and shamed, enhancing deterrence. This also reduces the need for coevolution.

Fourth, empirically, we are not good real-time lie detectors. This was the take-home message from chapter 3. If there was a coevolutionary struggle mandated by evolution, this would not be the case. We would expect much better performance in lie detection experiments. Research findings are much more in line with a truth-default view than the arms-race speculation.

The bottom line is that as long as the prevalence of deception is low and the harm caused isn't catastrophic, a truth-default makes good sense. But how can we research a cognitive default? It is, after all, passive and operates outside conscious awareness. Even thinking about it makes it go away. We know people are typically truth-biased, but documenting truth-bias does not provide convincing evidence for the truth-default because they are not the same thing.

The truth-default offers one explanation for the empirical observation of truth-bias, but the concepts are not interchangeable. Truth-bias need not reflect a cognitive default, especially as measured in deception detection experiments. The results in table 11.2 and other prior deception research involved prompted active assessment of honesty. In fact, if TDT is correct, truth-bias rates (i.e., the proportion of messages believed) would be much higher in research if the possibility of deception was not primed by the research setting and measurement instruments. Knowing that one is in a deception detection experiment and requiring truth-deception assessments as part of the research protocol should create an active assessment of honesty and deceit that often may not occur in communication outside the deception lab. Prompted judgments are antithetical to the very idea of the truth-default.

TDT EXPERIMENTS FIFTEEN AND SIXTEEN: DAVID CLARE AND EVIDENCE FOR THE TRUTH-DEFAULT

In experiment fourteen, I introduced Rachel Kim, my student, research assistant, and lab coordinator. David Clare started his graduate work about the time Rachel moved on, and David took Rachel's place as my lab assistant. David did both his master's degree and his PhD under my direction. As of this writing, Dr. Clare is a data scientist working in Washington, DC. We collaborated on many experiments. For his preliminary research paper, David set out to provide direct evidence for the truth-default.[31] Well, sort of.

I think David and I were interested in experiments fifteen and sixteen for different (but related) reasons. Documenting the truth-default state was my main interest. I see these experiments through the lens of TDT. I think David was more interested in the methodological issue of prompted truth–lie judgments as related to ecological validity. He was also (or at least became) very interested in the issues addressed in TDT propositions seven through nine, discussed at the close of this chapter.

The last chapter examined ecological validity in relation to deception motives and the instructed lies that populate most experiments. Prompting truth–

lie judgments also raises ecological concerns by explicitly asking research subjects whether a source is lying. If there really is a truth-default, questions of honesty and deception typically do not come to mind during normal communication situations. The very act of asking about deception therefore makes the task in the lab very different from many non-research settings.

TDT propositions seven through nine talk about trigger events and the conditions under which people infer that others are lying. David was very interested in when people believe others and when people don't. David and I designed two experiments to try to get at the twin questions of (1) whether the very act of prompting deception judgments affects assessments of honesty and deception, and (2) absent prompting, whether issues of honesty and deception even come to mind.

We predicted, of course, that prompting deception judgments by asking explicit truth–lie questions would reduce truth-bias in comparison to no prompting. We also predicted evidence for the passive truth-default. That is, we predicted that thoughts of honesty and deception might not come to mind without prompting. We thought that thoughts about honesty and deception might sometimes come to mind even absent experimental prompting or priming, but we just didn't know how often. The idea of a truth-default requires that we don't constantly monitor communication for deception. But would thoughts of honesty and deception come to mind one-third of the time or only one in ten times?

Experiments fifteen and sixteen had very similar (and complex) designs. In both experiments, subjects were in both prompted veracity judgment and unprompted veracity conditions. In the prompted condition, subjects were explicitly asked whether they thought the communication was honest or deceptive. Subjects were instructed to circle either "truth" or "lie" after each in a series of messages. In the unprompted condition, we just asked subjects to list open-ended what they were thinking. Then we coded the thoughts for anything related to truth, lies, honesty, or deception. Half the subjects did the prompted first, then the unprompted. The other half did the unprompted, then the prompted.

In both experiments, the communication was a get-to-know-you interview where the interviewee told truths and lies about autobiographical information. Besides prompting, the lack thereof, and order (prompting first or second), the other variables in the experiments were plausibility of content and actual honesty. All subjects were exposed to plausible and implausible truths and lies. There were seventy-two participants in experiment fifteen and sixty-eight participants in experiment sixteen. The difference between the two experiments (besides just that different subjects participated) was that experiment fifteen involved watching videotapes, and experiment sixteen involved live face-to-face interaction between the subject and a confederate.

In experiment fifteen, prompted judgments yielded typical levels of truth-bias (58% of messages judged as truthful). Regarding the unprompted thoughts, when the unprompted thoughts were first, thoughts related to honesty or deception occurred in response to only 4.23% of the messages. That is, more than 95% of the time, the thoughts people listed had nothing to do with truths and lies, honesty, or deception. Things were very different, however, for the people who did the prompted explicit truth–lie judgments first. Those subjects mentioned something related to veracity on 39.58% of the messages.

The results of experiment sixteen were even more extreme. Even with prompted judgments, there was massive truth-bias: 88.43% of the prompted judgments were honest. When unprompted assessments were first, fewer than 1% of the messages (0.57%) generated listed thoughts related to honesty or deception. There were more veracity-related thoughts when the prompted task was first, but most of the time nothing related to honesty or deception was mentioned (average = 8.46%).

These results are stunning. The truth-default looks stronger than even I expected. In pretty much every prior deception detection experiment, subjects made truth-deception determinations because they were asked to. When asked, people think about it and circle "honest" more often than "deception" or "lie." But without prior prompting, when asked the open-ended "What are your thoughts about the person's answer?" participants' thoughts (or at least the thoughts that they listed) usually had nothing at all to do with honesty or deception. Questions of honesty, veracity, lying, and deception didn't come to mind. Unprompted consideration of anything related to honesty or deceit came to mind less than 5% and 1% of the time in experiments fifteen and sixteen respectively.

From my point of view, the results of experiments fifteen and sixteen pretty much seal the deal for the idea of the truth-default. Before TDT, no one ever thought to do this sort of study. It is an obvious experiment to do, yet no one did it. Once the experiments were done and the results were in, there seemed to be absolutely compelling evidence for a truth-default. That veracity-related thoughts were listed only 5% and 1% of the time absent prompting is perfectly in line with TDT. This held even with implausible truths and lies! Wow!

The results also align with David's concerns regarding the ecological validity of typical deception experiments. There seems little doubt that directly asking subjects about honesty and deception prompts thoughts that do not otherwise occur to the subjects.

Although we will get into this more in the final chapter, David's experiments also move us much closer to solving the previously noted mystery of deception accuracy in research not about deception. Certainly a key difference between research about deception detection and deception in research that is not about deception is that in deception research, subjects are asked about deception, bringing the question of deception to mind. So simple.

BREAKING OUT OF THE TRUTH-DEFAULT: SUSPICION AND LIE JUDGMENTS

Experiments fifteen and sixteen show that a truth-default state can exist. The results also show that absent prompting, the truth-default is pervasive. Prompting made a big difference. People can and do abandon the truth-default when prompted. In the lab, prompting is accomplished by research instructions and questions asking subjects to assess whether someone is honest. TDT holds that prompting happens outside the lab too. Trigger events can lead people to temporarily abandon the truth-default and actively assess others' honesty. TDT proposition seven lists five triggers.

> **TDT Proposition Seven**: The truth-default state requires a trigger event to abandon it. Trigger events include but are not limited to (a) a projected motive for deception, (b) behavioral displays associated with dishonest demeanor, (c) a lack of coherence in message content, (d) a lack of correspondence between communication content and some knowledge of reality, or (e) information from a third party warning of potential deception.

We have discussed projected motives and will later address in detail sender demeanor, coherence, correspondence, and third-party information, all of which, according to TDT, can trigger suspicion. Surely these are not the only things that can trigger suspicion. My goal is not to provide an exhaustive or comprehensive list but instead to prioritize by offering a short list of triggers that fit well within the logic of TDT.

> **TDT Proposition Eight**: If a trigger or set of triggers is sufficiently potent, a threshold is crossed, suspicion is generated, the truth-default is at least temporarily abandoned, the communication is scrutinized, and evidence is cognitively retrieved and/or sought to assess honesty–deceit.

I define suspicion as a state of suspended judgment and uncertainty regarding the honesty or deceptive nature of a communication. It is an intermediate cognitive state between the passive truth-default and a firm judgment of deceit. Proposition eight sets up the first of two thresholds. The first threshold is when the truth-default state gives way to suspicion. The second threshold is established in proposition nine.

> **TDT Proposition Nine**: Based on information of a variety of types, an evidentiary threshold may be crossed, and a message may be actively judged to be deceptive. The information used to assess honesty and deceit includes but is not limited to (a) communication context and motive, (b) sender demeanor, (c) information from third parties, (d) communication coherence, and (e) correspondence information. If the evidentiary threshold for a lie judgment is not crossed, an individual may continue to harbor suspicion or revert to the truth-default. If exculpatory evidence emerges, active judgments of honesty are made.

Propositions seven and nine offer similar lists. The difference is in intensity. It takes more to see a message as deception than to trigger the suspicion that a message might be deceptive.

I debated whether to explicitly list message plausibility in propositions seven and nine. Plausibility is among the strongest cues related to assessments of honesty and deception, and it is among the most valid.[32] However, I'm not sure mere implausibility is sufficient as an initial trigger. In experiments fifteen and sixteen, once prompted by the explicit requirement to assess honesty, implausible information was more likely to be judged as dishonest (regardless of actual honesty) than plausible messages. However, absent prompting, plausibility made little difference. This might suggest including plausibility in proposition nine but not proposition seven. Although I didn't formally include plausibility in proposition nine, I'm OK with adding it. Or perhaps plausibility could be included within correspondence information, because implausible statements lack correspondence with what is typical or normal.

Toward the end of chapter seven I tell the amusing story of being named September's researcher of the month, and of the poster with the fake biographical information. Even though the content was far-fetched (I was a star basketball player selected in the NBA draft and a member of a famous rock bank), many people were duped. This account exemplifies the impotency of plausibility as an initial trigger.

IS THE TRUTH-DEFAULT JUST AN IN-GROUP THING?

The logic behind the truth-default makes the most sense in the context of in-group interaction. Our in-groups are people with whom we share some common identity or group membership. In-groups might include people of the same ethnicity, the same political affiliations, the same religious beliefs, people we work with, family, and the like. Members of our in-groups are the people with whom we cooperate and most frequently interact. As work on intergroup conflict and prejudice shows, members of out-groups can be seen as threats and viewed with suspicion.[33]

Contemplating the application of the truth-default in intergroup interaction is challenging for TDT. It exposes an ambiguity. Here are my current, albeit tentative, best guesses. I would expect that as a general rule both truth-bias and the truth-default would be stronger and more persistent in in-group inter-action than in intergroup interaction. I would not think that the mere fact that someone is a member of an out-group would be sufficient to dissolve truth-bias and the truth-default, unless there was intense hostility or conflict be-tween groups. I would nevertheless expect the thresholds for suspicion and at-tributions of deceit to be lower for communication by out-groups or out-group members than for in-groups. That is, I expect TDT to hold for both in-group and intergroup interaction, but I expect trigger sensitivity to be higher in in-tergroup communication relative to in-group interaction.[34]

CHAPTER SUMMARY

This chapter is all about the two most central ideas in my thinking about de-ception: truth-bias and the truth-default. Truth-bias is the tendency to believe others regardless of whether or not they are honest. Truth-bias is definitely a tried-and-true finding in deception research. It was the realization of just how strong truth-bias is, and the curiosity about why this is the case, that sent me down the path toward TDT.

Back in the old days, twenty to thirty years ago, when I first started to re-search truth-bias, I thought of it as a product of flawed and lazy thinking. Bias loomed large in my understanding of truth-bias. But gradually my thinking began to change. This change is further described in the next chapter, when we get to the veracity effect and base-rates. For now, it is sufficient to say that I believe that truth-bias is good for us. Truth-bias and the truth-default let us communicate efficiently with other humans. They are essential for social functioning.

The truth-default state is the idea that we often passively believe others' communication, and the thought of deception does not come to mind un-less suspicion is triggered. TDT experiments fifteen and sixteen showed that this was case. Nevertheless, trigger events can kick us out of the truth-default state, and this chapter describes the conditions under which suspicion and lie judgments happen.

The next chapter follows up by discussing the two big implications of truth-bias for deception detection research. These I call the veracity effect and base-rates. Chapters 9 (prevalence of deception), 11 (truth-bias and truth-default), and 12 (veracity effects and base-rates) combine to form the core of TDT. Together, the ideas and research findings described in these three chapters make the case for why the truth-default and truth-bias are functional and adaptive. So, let's get on to chapter 12 to wrap up this part of TDT.

12

The Veracity Effect and Truth–Lie Base-Rates

As the chapter's title says, we now move on to the veracity effect and truth–lie base-rates, which are the main implications of truth-bias and the truth-default for deception detection. The veracity effect and base-rate findings follow directly from and are caused by truth-bias and the truth-default.

Alternatively, I could have titled this chapter "How Hee Sun Park Changed Deception Research, Part One." It was Steve McCornack and our early studies together that got me transfixed by truth-bias in the first place, but it was Hee Sun who got me to see why truth-bias is not a bias. Hee Sun originated the ideas in this chapter. I helped her refine them, test them, write them up, and publish them. But the veracity effect and base-rate predictions were her ideas, ideas that forever changed the way I understand deception detection. It is not an understatement to describe her impact on the social science of deception as transformative and revolutionary.

Although Hee Sun is an exceptionally accomplished researcher and thinker, I am older, male, and better known for deception research. There might be a tendency for some to presume that I was the main driver in our collaborative work. Here is an example from a few years ago that has stuck with me. I know a very senior and accomplished communication professor who is a big fan of TDT experiment eighteen. In a conversation we once had, I mentioned that the idea was Hee Sun's. This professor told me in so many words: "No way. Everyone knows you are the brains, and Hee Sun is just riding your coattails." For the record, I am not being modest. The ideas in this chapter originated with Hee Sun Park. She planted them in my head. Maybe I would have had them anyway and come to the same conclusions on my own in time, but that is counterfactual.

Today, Dr. Hee Sun Park is a professor in the Media School at Korea Uni-

versity in Seoul, South Korea. South Korea is her home country, and KU is the
top private university in the country. She has published more than a hundred
journal articles to date. Her main specialties are cross- and intercultural communication (particularly expressions of apology and gratitude) and the statistical analysis of data. Coming up as a new professor, she won several presti-
gious early career awards from different professional associations. She recently
became a fellow of the International Communication Association. The point
here is that she is not some intellectual lightweight. She is among the most
accomplished communication professors of her generation.

This story begins with a young Hee Sun Park finishing up her undergraduate degree in communication at Michigan State University, where she took
a class from Steve McCornack. She came to America as a college student to
better learn English, and she discovered communication as a topic of study.
Like me and so many others, she didn't even know communication was an
academic field before taking classes in it. Like me, she got hooked. She discovered that communication was the academic field that best captured her interests. So she decided to go to graduate school in communication and learn
more. She was born to be in academics, and understanding social interaction
was and still is her calling.

Hee Sun went to Steve's office hours to discuss graduate school. Steve rec-
ommended University of Hawaii, where I was at the time. My colleagues and
I had created a top-notch master's degree program there. Hee Sun applied to
Hawaii and elsewhere. She got in most places to which she applied, but Hawaii did not initially offer her full-ride funding, while another program did.
Nevertheless, she chose Hawaii over the program offering guaranteed funding, because she thought she'd get a better education there (based largely on
Steve's advice). I met her when she showed up one day in Hawaii, ready to
start graduate school. She ended up working her way into funding at Hawaii
as well as winning consecutive top student awards both her years there. It did
not take long for those of us with an eye for academic talent to spot her. To
this day, I can't say that I have taught a better student.

Her first year in graduate school, I was teaching a seminar in deception, and
she enrolled in my class. I assigned, among other readings, the Leery Lover
study described in the previous chapter (TDT experiment thirteen), which Steve
and I had published a few years earlier. The class read the assigned articles,
and we discussed them. First-year graduate student Hee Sun Park explained
to the class that the logic behind our hypotheses was flawed and our interpretation of findings was wrongheaded.

So here is a new student saying that two of her professors (Steve and I) had our logic wrong and that a paper that made it through the peer-review process at the top journal in our field was critically flawed. She claimed to see something obvious that Steve and I and the journal editor (Judee Burgoon) and the three reviewers had missed. Wow! Really? What are the odds that a first-year master's student understood something about deception that Judee, Steve, I, and the rest of the deception researchers at the time had missed?

I've now been a professor for a long time. There have not been a lot of students who have directly challenged me on a point of logic and interpretation of results in my own work. Fewer still are the students who had whatever it takes to confront me, not only on my own work but on one of the papers I thought to be among my better works. Even fewer students turned out to be right. The number might be zero if not for Hee Sun Park.

Here's the thing, though. Hee Sun was the type of student who read all the assigned readings multiple times. She was known to go through the references of assigned works and read referenced work to trace back ideas or chase down loose ends. When she took a firm position on an idea, she had thought about it good and hard, and she had done her homework.

Honestly, it took me a while to understand Hee Sun's argument. I was stuck in a mental rut of the conventional thinking at the time. I hate when that happens. My thinking was clouded by how deception researchers thought at the time and how things were done in the published research of the time. Hee Sun didn't have that indoctrination into the status quo, and she was (and is still) an exceptionally good critical thinker able to think outside the box. But even though I was initially skeptical of her argument, I took her criticism seriously and reanalyzed our data to check out her point. When I did that, the results were just what she predicted.

I took her argument from that day in class and gave it the label "the veracity effect." I reanalyzed the data from Steve's and my prior experiments, designed a new study, wrote them all up, and published the package as an article in the same journal as our original Leery Lover experiments, thereby setting the record straight.[1] That paper has become my second-most cited article and my most cited paper on the topic of deception (currently with more than three hundred Google Scholar citations). This was all because Hee Sun Park took me on, didn't back down, and opened my eyes to a different way of thinking about deception detection research findings.

I was not the only professor at the University of Hawaii that Hee Sun challenged. She polarized the faculty. Several of us thought she was everything an ideal graduate student should be. She was exceptionally hardworking, smart, insatiably curious, and an original but disciplined thinker, and she loved to debate ideas. Today she calls debating ideas "ping-pong." Ping-pong is verbally batting ideas back and forth. She engages her own students in ping-pong. When I play intellectual ping-pong with Hee Sun Park, I know to bring my A-game. It's a great way to test ideas. Most of the ideas in this book have been ping-pong tested by Hee Sun Park (as well as Steve McCornack, Pete Blair, Kim Serota, Tom Hove, René Weber, Torsten Reimer, and Frank Boster, my intellectual ping-pong buddies).

Back to Hee Sun's story. One good thing about her willingness to argue her thoughts is that she quickly gained the respect of those who value that sort of thing. Oh, by the way, she changed the trajectory of deception research. Once the veracity effect is understood, research findings are interpreted differently. Nevertheless, other faculty thought Hee Sun was disrespectful and face threatening. No doubt this perception was all the worse because she was an Asian woman who did not act in accordance with the stereotype of the demure Asian woman. As a consequence, she also took many lumps from those who didn't appreciate being challenged. Not every professor is open-minded, and not everyone is secure enough to appreciate smart, thoughtful criticism. Hee Sun even had her newly earned funding pulled for a while, until supportive faculty intervened on her behalf.

Anyway, that's the story behind the veracity effect. It would not be Hee Sun's only contribution to deception research. Many might even say it's not her most important insight. The story of how Hee Sun changed deception research part two is told in chapter 14. I will say that her insights impressed the hell out of me! But now I should explain her insight that led to the veracity effect.

THE VERACITY EFFECT

In the original Leery Lovers experiment, Steve's and my reasoning was based on the misguided idea that truth-bias and lie-bias would lower accuracy. We predicted low accuracy when suspicion was low, because absent suspicion, people would be truth-biased. Truth-bias, we presumed, would impair accuracy. As suspicion increased, we reasoned, truth-bias would decline, and accuracy would improve, but only to a point. There would be a sweet spot of not-too-much and not-too-little suspicion. Too much suspicion would create lie-bias, and accuracy would again decline. Thus, we predicted higher accuracy for moderate suspicion than for either low or high suspicion.

Our results fit our prediction nicely (see the top row in table 11.1). Accuracy was highest under moderate suspicion. Our nonlinear inverted U prediction showed up just as we anticipated. So, we inferred that since the results came out just as we had predicted, our thinking that gave rise to our hypothesis was right.

In terms of logic, we predicted that if A (our argument), then B (our findings). We found B. We inferred that since B was obtained, A was correct. Researchers do this all the time. If the data come out as predicted, it is inferred that the data came out that way because the reasoning that led to the hypothesis is correct. But that is affirming the consequence, a common logical fallacy. Logically, B, of course, can happen for reasons other than A. Affirming the consequence wasn't Hee Sun's criticism, but falling for it did make me more confident in our original thinking than I should have been.

Even prior to Hee Sun's criticism, there was a warning sign in the data. I don't know if this is what tipped her off. Remember from the last chapter that even in the high-suspicion condition, there was no evidence of pervasive lie-bias. In our original argument, lie-bias produced the downturn from moderate to high suspicion. We found the downturn, just as we expected. But if people weren't lie-biased, why did the downturn occur? We speculated about the reasons for the downturn in the original paper, but that speculation explained away the small part of the results that didn't fit our thinking rather than instigate a full-scale questioning of our original thinking. In hindsight, there is an important lesson here about the dangers of confirmation bias and affirming the consequence. Confirmation bias is the tendency to interpret evidence in such a way that it falls in line with our own preconceptions.

I would like to think that I am both older and wiser now, but confirmation bias is insidious. It is easy to see flaws in others' thinking, and so much harder to see the holes in one's own thinking. This is why we need to stay vigilant for our own intellectual blind spots. It is also why good ping-pong partners with diverse knowledge bases are so valuable. I rely on smart people like Hee Sun Park and my other intellectual ping-pong buddies to point out the self-serving blind spots in my own thinking.

What Hee Sun pointed out was that our reasoning was based on a false premise. Our reasoning rested on the idea that truth-bias and lie-bias would lower accuracy. She said this was wrongheaded given the way our experiment (and most other experiments) was designed. You see, we (like most deception detection experimenters then and now) had exposed the subjects to an equal number of truths and lies. We also calculated accuracy by averaging across truths and lies. In the Leery Lover experiment, all subjects saw and evaluated twelve video segments: six truths and six lies. When there is an equal number of truths and lies, Hee Sun argued, neither truth-bias nor lie-bias should affect accuracy (presuming accuracy is scored as the number of correct judgments divided by the total number of judgments). She rightly said that truth-bias would make people better at getting the honest messages right. At the same time, truth-bias makes people miss more lies. The gains and losses would balance out when averaging across equal numbers of truths and lies. So, neither suspicion nor truth-bias should affect total accuracy when there is an equal number of truths and lies. Suspicion should make people better at lies and worse at truths and have no effect when averaging across truths and lies if truths and lies are equally weighted. To really start to understand what is going on, Hee Sun said, we would need to score accuracy for truths and lies separately. Do that, she said, and you will see.

Initially I didn't really get her point. But after class I went back to my office and set about rescoring the data to look at accuracy for truths and lies separately. As you probably guessed, she was, of course, right.

TDT STUDIES THIRTEEN AND FOURTEEN REVISITED

In the previous chapter, I presented the Leery Lovers suspicion experiment and Rachel Kim's replication. The results are provided in table 11.1. Both studies show that suspicion reduced but did not eliminate truth-bias. Both studies also found the slightly-better-than-chance accuracy typical of the literature. But accuracy was higher in some conditions than others. In TDT experiment thirteen (Leery Lovers), accuracy was higher under moderate suspicion (65%) than under low (53%) or high (57%) suspicion. In TDT experiment fourteen (Rachel's replication), accuracy was better under low (56%) and moderate (56%) suspicion than high suspicion (48%).

Table 12.1 shows what the results of those experiments look like when accuracy for truths and accuracy for lies are scored separately. These are the same data as reported in table 11.1, just scored differently. The first two rows are what I saw when I reanalyzed the data the way Hee Sun suggested.

In the Leery Lovers experiment, when Steve and I scored accuracy across truths and lies, overall accuracy across suspicion conditions rounded to 58%. When broken down by truths and lies, accuracy for truths was 82% and accuracy for lies was 34%. Total accuracy is the average of truth accuracy and lie accuracy (34 + 82 = 116; 116 ÷ 2 = 58). With an equal number of truths and lies, this is always the case.

When looking at table 12.1, probably the most noticeable thing is that accuracies look pretty good for truths but pretty dismal for lies. Truth accuracy is always above 50%, sometimes by quite a bit. Accuracy on lies is always below 50%, sometimes by quite a bit.

TABLE 12.1. RESULTS OF TDT EXPERIMENTS THIRTEEN AND FOURTEEN REVISITED

Outcome Variable	SUSPICION			Across Conditions
	Low	Moderate	High	
TDT experiment 13: College dating couples				
Truth accuracy	84.3%	87.9%	73.5%	81.8%
Lie accuracy	22.5%	37.4%	43.1%	34.3%
TDT experiment 14: Unacquainted college students				
Truth accuracy	84.0%	81.3%	56.8%	73.8%
Lie accuracy	27.3%	30.0%	39.4%	32.3%

So, when the communication was honest, subjects were usually correct. When the messages were lies, subjects were usually incorrect. One of the things that Hee Sun argued is that whether people are accurate or not depends to a huge extent on simply whether a truth or a lie is being assessed. As long as someone is truth-biased (and we know from the last chapter that people usually are truth-biased), people are more likely to be right about truths than lies. That is, the veracity of the message (whether or not it is honest) is a strong determinant of the correctness of a judgment about the veracity of the message. This is the veracity effect.

The Veracity Effect—The honesty (i.e., veracity) of communication predicts whether the message will be judged correctly. Specifically, honest messages produce higher accuracy than lies. The veracity effect results from truth-bias.

Both TDT experiments thirteen and fourteen show strong veracity effects. Subjects did much better on the truths than on the lies. In experiment thirteen, it was 82% for truths to 34% correct for lies. In experiment fourteen, the split was 74% for truths to 32% for lies. Further, the veracity effect is biggest when suspicion is low. Truths are in the eighties, and lies are in the twenties. As suspicion increases, truth-bias goes down, and the gap between truth accuracy and lie accuracy gets smaller. The veracity effect gets smaller. But it does not go away. This was true in both experiments.

This was another of Hee Sun's insights. Truth-bias and suspicion affect accuracy for truths and accuracy for lies in opposite ways that cancel out when we average across truths and lies. Unless accuracy for truths and lies is scored separately, what's going on is obscured. In table 11.1 with overall accuracy averaged across truths and lies, it looks as if experiments thirteen and fourteen tell different stories about how suspicion affects accuracy. In Table 12.1, with truth and lie accuracy scored separately, we can see that both experiments actually tell the same story. Clarity is achieved.

TERMINOLOGY

"Accuracy," as the term is typically and traditionally used in most (but not all) deception detection research, refers to the raw percentage correct for truth–lie discriminations. For example, in the Leery Lover study, research subjects saw and rated twelve messages. Judges made a dichotomous, forced-choice truth or lie judgment for each. Accuracy was scored as the number of judgments each subject got correct divided by twelve. It is a percentage-correct score, just like scoring a true-false test. It is important to remember that accuracy (defined and scored in this way) is an average across truths and lies.

We could also calculate percentage correct separately for just the truths and just the lies (as is done in tables 12.1 and 12.2). I call these scores *truth accuracy* and *lie accuracy*. So, we can talk about truth-bias (the percentage of total judgments that are truth/honest judgments), truth accuracy (the percentage of truthful messages correctly judged as honest), lie accuracy (the percentage of lies that are correctly judged as lies), and overall accuracy (or accuracy for short, which is the percentage of all messages that are judged correctly). Overall accuracy is the weighted average of truth accuracy and lie accuracy. The weighting is equal when truths and lies are equally prevalent or probable. The veracity effect takes place when truth accuracy and lie accuracy are different. Truth accuracy is typically larger than lie accuracy, and overall accuracy is halfway between the two.

Some researchers prefer sensitivity and bias measures from signal detection math. But, I prefer accuracy, truth-bias, truth-accuracy, and lie-accuracy. Averages are easier to understand and are accessible to a much wider audience. I can safely presume that everyone reading this book understands a simple average, but not everyone knows signal detection math. I further doubt that many of the researchers who claim to prefer signal detection metrics really understand it. I think this because if I report accuracy, truth-bias, truth-accuracy, and lie-accuracy, then those who know signal detection have all they need to calculate signal detection metrics. The conversions are a simple matter for those in the know, but most signal detection advocates I have encountered don't seem to realize this. But the real reason for my preference is more theoretical. I'll come back to the reasons for my preference once the main ideas of this chapter are fully developed.

WHY, WHEN, AND SO WHAT?

Table 12.2 summarizes the evidence for the veracity effect in my experiments over the years. In every deception detection experiment I have ever done, accuracy for truths has been greater than accuracy for lies. Further, the stronger the truth-bias, the stronger the veracity effect. When I correlate the truth-bias observed in each prior study with the size of the veracity effect (accuracy of truths minus accuracy of lies), the correlation for the twenty-five experiments in Table 12.2 is a whopping $r = .96$. This nearly perfect correlation is graphed in figure 12.1 to make the point visually.[2]

Before moving on to base-rates, there are five important points I want to (re)emphasize regarding the veracity effect. These involve why the veracity effect happens, when and how often it happens, and why it is such a game changer for understanding deception detection. Once the veracity effect and its implications are fully understood, the findings and conclusions from chapter 3 are seen differently. Sweeping claims about chance-level or slightly-better-than-chance accuracy must be qualified as applying only to an unusual and arbitrary research-induced situation that departs from most everyday communication experiences described in chapter 9.

1. Truth-bias causes the veracity effect. Look at figure 12.1 again. The horizontal axis of the graph plots the percentage of messages judged as honest in each of my experiments. A truth-bias score of fifty corresponds to neither truth-bias nor lie-bias. That is, at fifty, truth and lie judgments are equally prevalent (i.e., fifty-fifty). None of the plotted results found a lie-bias. If they had, lie-bias would show up as a truth-bias score below fifty. If we extrapolate from the line formed by the pattern of plotted results, we notice that if there is no truth-bias (i.e., truth-bias = exactly fifty), then the corresponding value of the veracity effect on the vertical axis is zero. That's right, if there is no truth-bias, there is no veracity effect. On the other end of the diagonal (upper right of the graph), if truth-bias was one hundred (all messages judged as honest), the veracity effect would be one hundred too. If research participants judged every message as honest, then they would get 100% of the honest messages right and 0% of the lies right. The veracity effect (the difference between accuracy for truths and accuracy for lies) would be 100% (100%-0% = 100%).

TABLE 12.2. "THE VERACITY EFFECT" IN MY RESEARCH

Experiment	Truth-Bias	Truth Accuracy	Lie Accuracy
TDT experiment 10	72%	75%	32%
TDT experiment 11	68%	74%	38%
TDT experiment 12	70%	63%	23%
TDT experiment 13	72%	82%	34%
TDT experiment 14	71%	74%	32%
TDT experiment 15	58%	68%	51%
TDT experiment 16	88%	96%	17%
TDT experiment 17	68%	69%	38%
TDT experiment 18	66%	67%	34%
TDT experiment 20	65%	72%	44%
TDT experiment 24	63%	65%	39%
TDT experiment 25	62%	66%	43%
TDT experiment 26	56%	65%	56%
TDT experiment 28	69%	77%	39%
TDT experiment 39 - 44[1]	54%	63%	52%
TDT experiment 45	70%	72%	52%
TDT experiment 46	67%	88%	55%
TDT experiment 47	60%	87%	68%
TDT experiment 48	53%	78%	73%
Group experiment[2]	66%	67%	37%
LSS2010 background questions[3]	59%	53%	35%
LSS2010 direct question	60%	77%	58%
LSS2010B[4]	61%	69%	46%
Probing experiment 1[5]	72%	75%	31%
Probing experiment 3	56%	57%	44%

[1] Control conditions only, averaged across studies.

[2] Ernest S. Park, Timothy R. Levine, Chad M. Harms, and Merissa H. Ferrara, "Group and Individual Accuracy in Deception Detection," *Communication Research Reports* 19, no. 2 (2002): 99–106, https://doi.org/10.1080/08824090209384837.

[3] Timothy R. Levine, Allison Shaw, Hillary C. Shulman, "Increasing Deception Detection Accuracy with Strategic Questioning," *Human Communication Research* 36, no. 2 (April 2010): 216–31, https://doi.org/10.1111/j.1468-2958.2010.01374.x.

[4] Timothy R. Levine, Allison Shaw, Hillary C. Shulman, "Assessing Deception Detection Accuracy with Dichotomous Truth–Lie Judgments and Continuous Scaling: Are People Really More Accurate When Honesty Is Scaled?" *Communication Research Reports* 27, no. 2 (2010): 112–22, https://doi.org/10.1080/08824090903526638.

[5] Timothy R. Levine and Steven A. McCornack, "Behavioral Adaptation, Confidence, and Heuristic-Based Explanations of the Probing Effect," *Human Communication Research* 27, no. 4 (October 2001): 471–502, https://doi.org/10.1111/j.1468-2958.2001.tb00790.x.

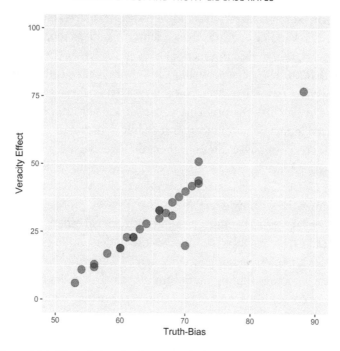

Figure 12.1. The relationship between truth-bias and the veracity effect.

It has to be this way. The more the truth-bias, the better the performance on truths, and the lower the performance on lies, and the
larger the difference between truth accuracy and lie accuracy.

2. Because truth-bias is incredibly robust, so too is the veracity effect. If
there were no truth-bias, the veracity effect would go away. If there
were lie-bias, then the veracity effect would flip sign, and accuracy
for lies would be higher than accuracy for truths. But, as TDT proposition three (chapter 11) tells us, most people believe others' communication most of the time. Truth-bias is pervasive. Where there
is truth-bias, there is the veracity effect. As a consequence, accuracy
for truths is typically higher than accuracy for lies. Recall from chapter 3 that this is just what meta-analysis has found.

3. Any variable that affects truth-bias will also affect the veracity effect.
Several variables impacting the extent of truth-bias were discussed
in the previous chapter. Applying those variables here, the veracity
effect will be stronger with senders with an honest demeanor,
people who know each other, when people interact face-to-face, and
for people who vicariously observe interaction involving questions
and answers. The veracity effect is weaker with experts, when judges

are primed to be suspicious, and when senders have less honest demeanors. Variables such as these (demeanor, suspicion, relational
closeness, face-to-face interaction) have much larger effects on truth-
bias than truth–lie discrimination and consequently impact the veracity effect more than overall accuracy. That is, these variables increase or decrease the probability that some communication is
believed independent of whether it should be believed. This means
that there are many studies out there that are looking for findings in
the wrong place by focusing on overall accuracy rather than the veracity effect. This also undercuts rival theories like IDT that do not
recognize the veracity effect and how it plays out in research, especially in face-to-face communication with known others.[3]

4. Critically, the veracity effect changes the understanding of the
   well-documented and often-mentioned 54% "slightly-better-than-
   chance" accuracy finding. Recall from chapters 1 and 3 that the average accuracy in deception detection experiments is just under
   54%. Hopefully, it is now clear that "54%" makes a very misleading soundbite. Now that the veracity effect has been explained, we
   can add the critical nuance that is needed to understand what the
   54% does and does not mean. What it does mean is that people are
   54% correct at truth–lie discrimination in tasks involving an equal
   number of truths and lies. It does not mean that people are better
   than chance at detecting lies per se. Because of the veracity effect,
   people are typically worse than fifty-fifty at correctly calling out a
   lie. Because it matters a great deal whether a truth or a lie is being
   assessed, the average across truths and lies (i.e., overall accuracy)
   does not apply to truth accuracy or lie accuracy scored separately.
   The 54% is overall accuracy, and this is often not clear when that
   figure is tossed out as a soundbite. Overall accuracy corresponds
   with lie accuracy only when truth-bias is zero, and truth-bias is almost never zero.

5. There is another thing to consider about the 54% accuracy soundbite truth–lie in *tasks involving an equal number of truths and lies*. I
   call the ratio of truths to lies in a lie detection task the *truth–lie base-
   rate*, or just base-rate for short. The 54% average accuracy comes
   from studies with fifty-fifty base-rates (equal numbers of truths and
   lies), and the 54% average applies only to the fifty-fifty base-rate environment. If the base-rate changes, so does overall accuracy. As we
   will see shortly, overall accuracy changes very predictably as a result

of changes in the base-rate. For now, I just want to reiterate a few related points about 54% accuracy and base-rates. Fifty-fifty base-rates are ubiquitous in deception research. Fifty-fifty base-rates are researcher imposed for the sake of "balance" and do not reflect or model the base-rates outside research settings (see chapter 9). As I said before, 54% does not generalize beyond the artificial, research-imposed, fifty-fifty base-rate. Therefore, 54% is a product of the lab, not communication outside lab constraints, and if we are interested in deception detection accuracy outside the lab, we had better understand how base-rates impact accuracy.

BASE-RATES

I have thought about this a lot, and I still find it stunning that my coauthors and I are the only deception researchers who study base-rates and that TDT is the only deception theory to prioritize base-rates as an important variable. If my claims are true that (a) accuracy findings from studies with fifty-fifty truth–lie base-rates do not generalize beyond fifty-fifty base-rates, and (b) fifty-fifty base-rates are highly unusual outside the lab, then it follows that (c) findings from the lab hold only in the artificial lab settings, and (d) the 54% accuracy soundbite is very misleading. One would think that this is important to know. Instead, most research continues to be done the way it has always been done, and 54% accuracy is tossed out as an undisputed fact that applies to all human deception detection.

The main impact of the veracity effect paper was that it drew attention to the difference between truth accuracy and lie accuracy. After its publication, more and more studies started reporting truth accuracy and lie accuracy in addition to overall accuracy. That, I think, is a good thing.

Here's the thing, though. I would probably not have ever bothered to do base-rate experiments if I did not know about and understand the veracity effect. Base-rate effects follow directly from the veracity effect. Truth-bias causes the veracity effect, and the veracity effect causes base-rate effects. Without making these links, it is easy to miss the importance of base-rates.

The dearth of research on base-rates by people outside my small circle of coauthors highlights one of the important but underappreciated aspects of good theory: It points us to the important variables. Absent good theory, we are liable to look for the wrong things in the wrong places and to overlook that which seems obvious once pointed out. Good theory needs to be generative. It points us in a direction that, lacking the theory, we would not have thought to go. TDT's concerns with lie prevalence and truth-bias/truth-default coupled with Hee Sun's insights into the veracity effect lead us right to the importance of base-rates. The reason my team studies base-rates while other labs don't is that my team understands deception through the lens of TDT and not one of the cue theories. As we will soon see with the Park–Levine model, TDT makes some very precise and very accurate predictions about how base-rates affect accuracy.

Obviously, base-rates vary drastically in different situations. Sometimes, base-rates are extreme. If we are thinking about terrorists with bombs at airport security screening checkpoints, the ratio of terrorists to non-terrorists is minuscule. These days I travel through the Atlanta airport a lot. Atlanta Hartsfield-Jackson Airport claims a quarter million passengers per day.[4] That's more than 90 million per year. No planes flying out of Atlanta have blown up recently, so I infer that none of those 90 million passengers had a bomb with the intent to down a plane. But, one day, some terrorist with a bomb might try to slip through. The task of stopping them is the cliché needle-in-the-haystack.

On the other extreme, my friend and coauthor Pete Blair works with police on improving interviewing-interrogation skills and has access to real video-taped interrogations of suspects. In one tape, a murder suspect is being interviewed about a neighbor who was fatally stabbed multiple times. The suspect denies any knowledge of the crime and claims to have been asleep the whole time. This guy came to be a suspect because the police followed a trail of bloody footprints to his door, and inside his apartment found half-washed bloody clothes and a bloody knife, among other incriminating evidence. What are the chances the suspect is lying about his lack of knowledge about the crime?

My wife, dressed in gym clothes, just told me she is going to work out. To give you a little more information, she left on foot, the gym is a short walk, she is serious about her workouts, and we work out at the same gym, so there is a good chance I will see her there later, after I write a few more paragraphs. A little earlier today I heard an interview with US presidential candidate Donald J. Trump. He told the reporter that he doesn't talk about himself very much. This caught my ear because, among other things, he spent most of the interview talking about himself. Listening to a politician being interviewed by an aggressive journalist asking tough questions is different from talking to your spouse about the day's plans. Getting pitched by a salesperson is different from getting advice from your doctor. As we have learned, lies are usually less likely than truths, because most people are mostly honest most of the time. But there are those people who lie much more than the rest of us, and there are those situations where lies are more likely than difficult truths. One of TDT's insights is that situations are not all the same. Situations and people differ in truth–lie base-rates, and these differences matter a great deal.

According to the logic of TDT, sometimes people are sensitive to base-rates, and sometimes people are not. For example, TDT proposition six and the Projected Motive Model specify that people project others' motivational states and adjust their expectations accordingly. In the last chapter, a variety of other trigger events were listed. To the extent that a trigger event reflects the actual probability of deception, people are to some extent sensitive to changes in base-rates. If there isn't a sufficiently powerful trigger, the truth-default state will make people insensitive to base-rates. People in the truth-default state believe others regardless of the base-rate.

To be theoretically precise here, according to TDT there are two factors that determine sensitivity to base-rates. First, people are insensitive to base-rates in the absence of a trigger event due to the truth-default state. That is, people in the truth-default state are invariably insensitive to base-rates. They believe regardless. Second, even if there is a trigger, and the possibility of deception is actively considered, people will still be insensitive to base-rates if there is little or no contingency or association between the presence of triggers and the presence of deception. People are sensitive to base-rates only when triggers are both present and informative about the actual base-rates.

One particular situation where people should be insensitive to base-rates is in everyday conversation. TDT experiments fifteen and sixteen (from the last chapter) showed that absent experimental priming to consider honesty, the truth-default state was nearly universal, and the idea that some communication might be deceptive just did not come to mind. In situations like this, people are completely oblivious to truth–lie base-rates.

Another particular place where people should be insensitive to base-rates is in typical deception detection experiments. In the type of experiments that produce the 54% average accuracy results, triggers prompt active consideration of honesty–deceit, but the triggers are not useful for correctly distinguishing truths and lies. In most experiments, deception motives, situations, and prompted suspicion are held constant across truths and lies. People are not in the truth-default state because they know they are in a deception detection experiment, but the truths and lies all occur in the same situation (e.g., did they commit a mock crime? did they cheat?), and suspicion is constant across truths and lies.

TDT EXPERIMENT SEVENTEEN: THE FIRST BASE-RATE EXPERIMENT

To review, truth-bias and the veracity effect mean that truth accuracy is higher than lie accuracy. So, if subjects in deception detection experiments were shown only honest messages, they would get higher accuracy then if we showed them only lies. In the Leery Lover data in Tables 11.1 and 12.1, people were 82%

correct on just truths, 34% correct on just lies, and 58% correct with a fifty-fifty truth–lie mix. But, in that experiment, all subjects saw an equal number of truths and lies.

In TDT experiment seventeen, we experimentally varied the proportions of truths and lies.[5] Subjects (177 students at the University of Hawaii) watched and judged twelve videotaped interviews and were randomly assigned to one of three conditions. One-third of the subjects were in a 75% honest condition (nine truths and three lies), one-third were in a fifty-fifty condition (six truths and six lies), and the remaining one-third were exposed to 75% lies (three truths and nine lies). Each subject judged each of the twelve segments as either a truth or a lie, and we scored the judgments for overall accuracy. We predicted that accuracy would be highest with 75% truths, lowest with 75% lies, and in between with 50% truths and lies.

We found a nice big effect for our base-rate induction. The statistical test was highly significant ($p < .0001$), and the effect size was a substantial $r = .46$. Accuracy was 59.5%, 51.9%, and 39.8% for 75%, 50%, and 25% honest base-rates, and all three averages were significantly different from one another.

Two other findings should be mentioned for comparison to later experiments. First, the base-rate induction did not affect truth-bias. That is, subjects were insensitive to base-rates. Showing subjects more truths made them right more often, but it did not make them guess truth more often. Second, we did a test for linearity in accuracy results. That is, we tested the extent to which 59.5%, 51.9%, and 39.8% form a straight line. The linear decomposition accounted for 98% of the variance in the omnibus effects. What this means is that a straight line fit the results very well. These two findings show up in all seven base-rate experiments (TDT experiments seventeen through twenty-three) I have done to date. Base-rate effects are linear in every experiment, and subjects are always insensitive to base-rates in these experiments.

THE PARK–LEVINE PROBABILITY MODEL

Due to time (and relevance) constraints, we now skip ahead a few years in Hee Sun's story. After getting her master's at the University of Hawaii, Hee Sun moved on to the University of California, Santa Barbara (UCSB). Not long after that, I accepted a faculty position at Michigan State University, where I stayed for twelve years. While at UCSB, and against faculty advice, Hee Sun started taking classes in math and mathematical statistics. She was told that math has little to do with communication. All she needed was the pull-down menus in the statistical software and to know where to look on the printouts. That is all many quantitative communication researchers want to know about statistics. But Hee Sun didn't (and still doesn't) see it that way. So while maintaining a full load of doctoral classes in communication and teaching a full graduate assistant load of classes, she also was taking a second full load in math and statistics. Among the first payoffs was the Park–Levine Probability Model. As it turns out, math can inform communication theory and research. Math is the language of science whether social scientists want to admit it or not.

In the beginning of a basic probability class in math (it may well have been basic, but the prerequisites for enrollment were four years of college-level calculus plus advanced linear algebra), Hee Sun and the other students were learning some theorems related to conditional probabilities. Ever the integrative thinker, Hee Sun thought something like "Oh! This would apply to the veracity effect and overall accuracy at different base-rates." She called me and explained it; I did a little reading in basic probability to get up to speed, and we set out writing it up for a communication audience. We sent the paper off to a top journal in the field, and our paper was accepted.[6] The paper laid out and explained what has come to be known as the *Park–Levine Probability Model*, which is another module in TDT dealing specifically with accuracy and base-rates.

The Park–Levine Probability Model—Because honest messages yield higher accuracy than lies (i.e., the veracity effect), the proportion of truths and lies (base-rates) affects accuracy. As long as people are truth-biased, as the proportion of messages that is honest increases, so does average detection accuracy. This relationship is linear and predicted to be the accuracy for truths times the proportion of messages that are true plus the accuracy for lies times the proportion of messages that are lies.

The Park–Levine Probability Model is a formula for predicting overall accuracy in deception detection experiments at different base-rates. As previously mentioned, overall accuracy is the proportion of truth–lie discriminations that are correct, truth-accuracy is the proportion of truthful messages correctly judged as truthful, and lie accuracy is the proportion of lies correctly judged as lies. P(T) is the proportion of messages that are truthful and P(L) is the proportion that are lies. P(T) and P(L) sum to 100% and reflect the truth–lie base-rate. The Park–Levine formula is:

Overall Accuracy = [Truth Accuracy × P(T)] + [Lie Accuracy × P(L)]

So, using the numbers from the Leery Lover experiment in tables 11.1 and 12.1, we have:

.58 = (.82)(.5) + (.34)(.5)

TABLE 12.3. USING THE PARK–LEVINE MODEL TO FORECAST ACCURACY AT DIFFERENT BASE-RATES USING THE LEERY LOVER RESULTS FROM TDT EXPERIMENT THIRTEEN

Base-Rate	Calculation	Predicted Overall Accuracy
100% honest	(.82)(1.00) + (.34)(.00)	82%
90% honest	(.82)(.90) + (.34)(.10)	77%
75% honest	(.82)(.75) + (.34)(.25)	70%
50-50	(.82)(.50) + (.34)(.50)	58%
75% lies	(.82)(.25) + (.34)(.75)	46%
90% lies	(.82)(.10) + (.34)(.90)	39%
100% lies	(.82)(.00) + (.34)(1.00)	34%

Overall accuracy was 58%, or .58, truth accuracy was .82, lie accuracy was .34, and P(T) and P(L) were both .5, since the experiment used the ubiquitous fifty-fifty base-rate. But what if the base-rate were different? Six different projections are provided in table 12.3 to demonstrate how the Park–Levine formula works. As you can see, the more the base-rate tips toward more truths than lies, the higher the overall accuracy. The greater the proportion of lies, the lower the accuracy. But just how accurate are these projections?

Here are a few things about the Park–Levine predictions. If we plotted the predicted overall accuracy in Table 12.3, we could see that all the values fall perfectly on a straight line. Park–Levine predicts that accuracy is a linear function of truth–lie base-rates. Further, the steepness of the slope is a function of truth-bias. If there were no truth-bias, the line would be flat. The larger the truth-bias, the steeper the slope. In the Leery Lover projections in Table 12.3, subjects were quite truth-biased, so the veracity effect was concomitantly strong and the slope of the base-rate effects relatively steep.

TDT EXPERIMENT EIGHTEEN: ACCURACY IS A PREDICTABLE LINEAR FUNCTION OF BASE-RATES

Moving ahead in the story again, Hee Sun completed her PhD at UCSB and got a job as a new tenure-track Assistant Professor at Michigan State University. About the same time, Rachel Kim had finished her MA at the University of Hawaii. She had been an undergraduate student of mine at Hawaii at the same time Hee Sun was an MA student there. I successfully recruited Rachel to MSU to work on her PhD under my direction, and Rachel became my lab supervisor. Also about this time, we secured funding from the National Science

Foundation to start creating the cheating tapes introduced in chapter ten and TDT experiment eight. The cheating tapes provided us a good way to give the Park–Levine formula a serious test. We wanted to find out just how good the Park–Levine formula is at projecting accuracy across base-rates.

At this point, let me introduce the twin ideas of confirmatory research and risky (vs safe) tests. The vast majority of quantitative social and health science research today uses a family of inferential statistical techniques called null hypothesis significance tests (NHST), or just significance testing for short. With NHST, research predictions are tested against a nil-null hypothesis of no difference or no effect. When researchers say a finding is "significant" or "$p < .05$," what this means statistically is that the obtained finding is less than 5% likely, presuming that there were no effect at all.[7] The logic is, if we can statistically show that the straw man hypothesis of no effect whatsoever is improbable, then there is probably some difference between the experimental groups or some non-zero statistical relationship between the variables. With NHST, simply not-zero translates into proof that a research hypothesis is right.

It is my opinion that the sort of statistical evidence that NHST provides is pretty weak and far from risky. The bar to pass for supporting a hypothesis is just ruling out zero. Any finding where zero is unlikely is significant and counts as support. That is not a very high bar. If the research involves a large enough sample size, support is pretty much guaranteed, because, in social science, pretty much everything is related to everything else at least a little bit.

Think of it this way. The null hypothesis is a "point prediction." It is exactly zero. In NHST, the research hypothesis expresses a wide range of values, everything that is other than zero. If zero is ruled out as statistically improbable given the data, then the research hypothesis is supported.

Confirmatory tests work in a way that is opposite from the logic of NHST. In confirmatory research, the research hypothesis makes a point prediction. If the data are such that the predicted value is within the margin of error of the observed finding, the research prediction is sustained. The hypothesis is said to be consistent with the data. All values, zero or otherwise, outside the margin of error are inconsistent with data. In this way, confirmatory tests require much more precise predictions and are much more risky than NHST. In NHST predictions can be wrong and still supported so as long as the findings are anything but zero. In risky, confirmatory tests, the bar is set much higher. The predictions are precise, and if the predictions are wrong, the data are much less likely to provide spurious support. I always wanted to have predictions precise enough for point predictions and a risky confirmatory test. TDT experiment eighteen and the Park–Levine formula gave me the chance.

Here is what we did.[8] We had the first set of NSF cheating tapes where

Rachel was the confederate, Mikayla Hughes was the interviewer, and I was the experimenter. The set of tapes we were working with contained seven lies (false denials of actual cheating) and fifteen honest interviews (truthful denials). The average duration was about two minutes per interview.

From these tapes, we first created a "control set" using all seven lies and seven randomly selected truths, thus giving us fourteen segments with a typical fifty-fifty base-rate. Next we created a 100% lie set of tapes using all seven lies from the control set with all the truths removed. Once we had the all-lie set, we proceeded to create sets of seven interviews with all possible different base-rates. From the seven lies, we randomly chose one to remove and replaced that with a randomly selected honest interview from the control set. This was repeated without replacement until we had eight sets of interviews ranging from seven to zero lies plus the control set.

Next, we recruited 463 students to be judges in our experiment. Subjects were randomly assigned to one of nine experimental conditions: either the fourteen interview, fifty-fifty base-rate control group or one of the eight base-rate conditions with seven interviews ranging from seven to zero lies. We scored the judgments in the control group for truth accuracy and lie accuracy, and we scored the judgments in the various base-rate groups for overall accuracy and truth-bias.

We predicted that subjects would be least accurate when they viewed 100% lies, they would score highest in the 100% truth group, and that the base-rate groups would show a linear increase in accuracy as the proportion of honest messages was incrementally increased. We also expected insensitivity to base-rates. That is, accuracy would increase, but truth-bias would be flat across base-rates.

In the fifty-fifty control, truth-bias was 66.1%, overall accuracy was 50.7%, truth accuracy was 67.1%, and lie accuracy was 34.3%. Accuracy scores in the eight base-rate conditions were (from 0% honest to 100% honest): 36.4%, 35.6%, 39.2%, 47.5%, 56.0%, 56.6%, 58.8%, and 65.1%. The base-rate effect on accuracy was statistically significant and large, $p < .001$, $r = .49$. The test of linearity was also statistically significant and large, $p < .001$, $r = .47$. The linear decomposition accounted for 95% of the omnibus base-rate effect. The deviation from linearity was not significant. Truth-bias did not vary across base-rate conditions, $r = .00$.

But here is the really cool thing. We took the truth accuracy and lie accuracy from the control group and plugged them into the formula along with the base-rates that we experimentally changed to predict the accuracy in each of the eight experimental groups. We compared the resulting calculations to

TABLE 12.4. TDT EXPERIMENT EIGHTEEN RESULTS:
ACCURACY IS A PREDICTABLE LINEAR FUNCTION OF BASE-RATES

Base-Rate (% honest)	Calculation	Prediction	Actual Result
100%	(.67)(1.00) + (.34)(.00)	.67	.65
86%	(.67)(.86) + (.34)(.14)	.62	.59
71%	(.67)(.71) + (.34)(.29)	.57	.57
57%	(.67)(.57) + (.34)(.43)	.53	.56
50% (control)			.51
43%	(.67)(.43) + (.34)(.57)	.48	.48
29%	(.67)(.29) + (.34)(.71)	.44	.39
14%	(.67)(.14) + (.34)(.86)	.39	.36
0%	(.67)(.00) + (.34)(1.00)	.34	.36

the actual results in each of the conditions with different base-rates. The calculations, predictions, and results are in table 12.4 and graphed in figure 12.2.

The predictions were not perfect, but they were all close. All eight of the actual results came within 5 points of the predictions, and on average, the predictions were off by only 2.5 points. All the predicted values fell within the margins of error around the obtained results.

Based on the predicted values, the formula for the line was:

Accuracy = .34 + .33 (base-rate)

When we use linear regression to fit a line to the actual data, the line was:

Accuracy = .34 + .32 (base-rate) + error

As you can see, both the slope and the y-intercept of the line best fitting the findings closely approximate the line predicted based on the control group results and the base-rate experimental induction. We titled our paper accordingly: "Deception Detection Accuracy Is a Predictable Linear Function of Message Veracity Base-Rates." We published these results in *Communication Monographs* in 2006. In 2007 the article received the Franklin H. Knower Article Award from the Interpersonal Division of the National Communication Association.

TDT experiment eighteen shows several important things. It replicates the linear base-rate effects of TDT experiment seventeen with different research

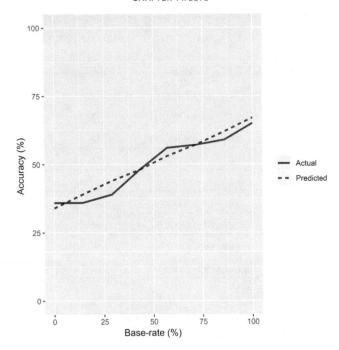

Figure 12.2. Predicted and actually observed accuracy as a function of truth-lie
base-rate in TDT experiment eighteen.

subjects viewing different types of truths and lies and using a wide range of
base-rates. In both studies the effects were linear, the deviation from linearity
was not statistically significant, and subjects were completely insensitive to
base-rates. TDT experiment eighteen added a risky confirmatory test of the
Park–Levine Probability Model, and the model passed beautifully. But most importantly, TDT experiment eighteen shows (a) base-rates matter a great deal,
and (b) truth-bias is adaptive in environments where honesty is more prevalent than deception.

TDT EXPERIMENTS NINETEEN, TWENTY, AND TWENTY-ONE: THE INTERACTIVE BASE-RATE EXPERIMENTS

Before getting into the rest of the base-rate experiments, I want to say a few
words about replication and generality. Throughout the book, I have asserted
the importance of replication many times. Good scientific findings are repro-
ducible, period. The next five experiments (presented in two sets) bring my total number of base-rate experiments to seven. While there is not some magic
number of replications I seek, I am to the point where I am sufficiently con-

fident about how and why base-rates play out in deception detection experiments.

So, why do I go through all the effort to replicate, replicate, replicate? There is more to it than just good scientific practice, although that is part of my motivation. Part of it is just for my own peace of mind. I want to have confidence in my findings and claims. Part of it is persuasion. If I can show that my findings replicate consistently, then others are more likely to accept my claims and evidence.

A big part of my insistence on replication is my personal experience (or more often that of graduate students working under my direction) of failing to replicate others' work. I talked in chapter 2 about deception-cue findings failing to replicate. The problem is bigger than that. A paper recently published in *Science* showed that 60% (almost two-thirds!) of experiments in top psychology journals fail to replicate.[9] Yikes! Psychology is currently in a replication crisis, and no doubt the situation is not much better in other health and social sciences. So insistence on replication is prophylactic. I don't want to be part of the problem, and I want to be a positive scientific role model.

In my view, the replication crisis has two main causes. The first has to do with NHST, questionable research practices, and publication bias. The basic idea is that there are lots of tricks to getting $p < .05$ findings, like doing lots of tests but reporting only the significant ones. This makes the findings look stronger than they really are. Journals are more likely to publish supportive work, and this makes the problem worse. Over the past decade I have become increasingly cynical about research practices. I don't think it is outright fraud or deception, but I think current practice creates an environment where research findings don't replicate. I think there are lots of authors out there playing the just-get-published game, and the net result is findings that are less likely to replicate.

There is a second, much less cynical, reason why many findings don't replicate. Some findings are just temperamental and fragile by nature. The findings are "real," but they hinge on a constellation of factors that are not understood. When the stars align, so to speak, the findings are there. Sometimes the stars align by chance in a study. Other times, researchers have figured out how to align them by trial and error. In either case, an experiment needs to be done exactly the right way. Change a little seemingly trivial detail here or there, and the results are different. That is, some effects are more situationally variable than others.

I have in mind a continuum with fragile (ephemeral) findings on one end and very robust findings on the other end. Robust findings usually come out;

if you change up the research design, no matter. I have very intentionally built my theory on a foundation of robust findings. The more stable my foundation, the better. This is why I replicate, replicate, replicate with intentional variation in research design from study to study. I not only want findings that replicate; I want robust findings that hold up under a variety of conditions. I want to be sure I am building on a solid foundation.

TDT experiments nineteen, twenty, and twenty-one sought to replicate TDT experiments seventeen and eighteen in a face-to-face setting.[10] The previous two experiments involved watching videotaped interviews. Experiments nineteen to twenty-one involved live interaction with truths and lies about autobiographical information. The judges either asked the interview questions or observed the interaction from across the room. Either way, it was all done in real time. Also, the senders and judges were either strangers or previously acquainted. We predicted that in live interaction the same linear base-rate effects would be observed as were previously observed with videotape, and that the linear effects would hold for participants and observers and for friends and strangers alike.

Experiments nineteen through twenty-one were done over a couple years in the communication interaction lab at Michigan State University. Respectively, the subjects were 120, 205, and 243 students at MSU. Scheduling was done such that at least two subjects came to the lab for each session. In experiment nineteen, subjects were scheduled individually and did not know the other participants scheduled at the time. In experiments twenty and twenty-one, subjects were asked to bring a friend. We kept track of who knew each other and who didn't.

Subjects in the experiments were randomly assigned to one of three roles: sender, interviewer, or observer. If there were just two subjects for any given session, there were just senders and interviewers. That was the minimum. If more than two subjects showed, all those not selected as the sender or the interviewer were made observers. The interviewers asked the senders questions, the senders answered (sometimes truthfully, sometimes lying), and the observers looked on. Interviewers and observers judged each of the sender's answers as a truth or lie, and we scored each interviewer and each observer for truth-bias and accuracy.

Senders got their instructions in a different room from the interviewers and observers. Senders first wrote truthful answers to ten autobiographical questions. Examples included a favorite vacation, if the sender had pets, number and ages of siblings, career aspirations, and the like. Once all questions were honestly answered in writing, the sender was randomly instructed to lie when answering anywhere from zero to all ten of the quesstions. They were given an instruction sheet to lie on such and such questions and answer honestly on such and such questions. It was fully randomized as to the number of lies and which question was lied about. If two different senders were randomly assigned to lie three times, they would not be lying in response to the same three questions.

The researcher collected the honest answers to verify that during the interview the sender really lied as instructed. Senders were told to be as believable as possible, and, as an incentive, they could win a cash prize. The more often they were believed, the more money they won. Then senders were brought to the interview room where the interviewer and observer(s) waited.

Interviewers asked the ten questions one at a time, and interviewers and observers judged each response as a truth or a lie. As an incentive, interviewers and observers could earn a cash prize, depending on how many they got right. Higher accuracy paid better. Interviewers and observers were told that senders might be lying on some or all answers, but answers might be truthful too. Any number of truths and lies were possible. After the game, truth-bias and accuracy was scored on the spot, and cash was paid out based on real performance. The subjects in these experiments found the task fun and engaging.

The base-rate induction had significant and large effects in all three experiments, $p < .001$ and $r = .69, .65$ and $.50$. In all three, the linear decomposition was significant, and the deviation from linearity was not significant. The linear base-rate held for interviewers and observers and friends and strangers. Base-rate effects appear robust.

TDT EXPERIMENTS TWENTY-TWO AND TWENTY-THREE: THE KOREAN BASE-RATE REPLICATIONS

In the two most recent replication experiments,[11] we returned to the cheating tapes, but this time we used interviews from the second set of tapes with Lauren Hamel as the interviewer and shorter, twenty-second, segments. By the time we did experiments twenty-two and twenty-three, Hee Sun and I were on the faculty at Korea University in Seoul, and the subjects in the experiments were students at Korea University. The tapes they watched were MSU students denying cheating.

Experiment twenty-two involved 133 subjects who saw and rated eight interviews, of which either 25%, 50% or 75% were honest. Experiment twenty-three had 121 new subjects judge six interviews (different from the interviews used in the previous experiment), which were either 0%, 50%, or 100% honest.

Both experiments found the expected linear base-rate effects. As with all previous studies, the deviations from linearity were again not significant. This was true for both studies individually and when the results were pooled. Once again, subjects were insensitive to base-rates. These data show that the linear base-rate effects extend to an intercultural setting.

IMPLICATIONS OF THE BASE-RATE EXPERIMENTS

TDT experiments seventeen through twenty-three show a remarkably consistent pattern of results. All seven experiments show the same linear pattern. As the proportion of messages becomes increasingly honest, accuracy at distinguishing truths from lies improves proportionally. This happens because of truth-bias and the veracity effect and because, in deception detection experiments, people are insensitive to base-rates.

Although I hope it is now obvious, let me try to succinctly summarize why the base-rate experiments are so important for TDT. Its core claim is that truth-bias and the truth-default are adaptive. The truth-default works well for us as individuals and as a species. In chapter 9, TDT studies one through five on lie prevalence showed that most people are mostly honest most of the time. If we think about those findings as evidence for base-rates outside the lab, what that means is that in everyday communication settings, the truth–lie base-rates are tipped heavily in the direction of mostly honest. Deception is infrequent relative to honest communication.

What TDT base-rate experiments seventeen through twenty-three all show is that accuracy improves substantially as the base-rates move away from the artificial fifty-fifty base-rates of the lab and move closer to everyday life. The 54% accuracy finding from chapter 3 applies to situations where truths and lies are equally probable. But in everyday communication situations, where lying is less frequent than it is in a lab, truth-bias works well for us. The base-rate experiments show this. Reliable linear base-rate effects are a big win for TDT, because TDT is the only deception theory that emphasizes base-rates, the seven experiments all show the hypothesized base-rate effects, and the base-rate effects show the utility of truth-bias outside the lab.

This past summer, I gave a talk at SARMAC (Society for Applied Research in Memory and Cognition) in Victoria, British Columbia. The title of my talk was "Truth-Bias: Who Is Biased, Subjects or Deception Researchers?"[12] In it, I tried to make the points I am making here. Yes, subjects are truth-biased. They think messages are truthful more often than they are in deception detection experiments, with the researcher-imposed fifty-fifty truths and lies. But subjects' responses in experiments match the base-rates outside the lab much better than the researcher-imposed base-rates in the lab. Maybe, I argued, it's not the subjects who are biased. Subjects are put into an artificial environment where lies are much more prevalent than in normal life; then, when subjects respond in ways that more closely mirror real communication situations than in the lab, the researchers conclude that it is the subjects who are biased. Really? I argued that maybe we researchers should be a little more self-critical and a bit more concerned with the ecological validity of research. Maybe we researchers should ask ourselves why we design our experiments to be so unrealistic and why are we so blind to the fact that we are doing so.

Base-rates along with instructed lies (see chapter 10 for that rant) are among my biggest concerns about ecological validity in deception research. The base-rate experiments clearly show that 54% accuracy does not generalize beyond fifty-fifty truths and lies. If we want findings to apply to everyday situations, we need a better understanding of the prevalence of deception in different situations and of how different base-rates impact findings.

After my SARMAC talk, during the Q & A, one researcher asked me a very good question. Unfortunately, I did not answer it very well, and I am afraid I was dismissive. I have been stewing about a better, more thoughtful answer ever since. The question was about the meaning of "accuracy," and it came from a signal-detection perspective. The point of the question was that raw accuracy may be a larger number when the base-rate tips toward more honest messages, but because subjects are insensitive to base-rates, it is misleading to say they are more "accurate." Sure, they get a higher percentage correct, but that is mere capitalization on chance. In terms of the relationship between being correct and chance, the higher percentage correct with more truthful messages is just the same slightly-better-than-chance accuracy we see at the fifty-fifty base-rate.

Here is my do-over. It really comes down to what we mean by "accuracy." There are two distinct views here. In one view, reflected in inter-coder reliability statistics or sensitivity metrics in signal detection, someone is accurate to the extent that they are better than chance. From this perspective, if you always say "heads" when flipping a two-headed coin, you are not accurate. There is no skill needed. You can just play the odds.

The way I am using the term "accuracy" is more naive. It is just whether you are right or not. You make a correct pick, you win. It does not matter if it was skill or luck. It is kind of like different ways of playing billiards. Do you have to call your shot in advance, or are "slops" allowed?

I have been thinking about this a lot, especially the implications for TDT logic. My idea is that the truth-default evolved because it was adaptive. It does not matter that it exploits chance. In fact, that is the point. We evolved the way we did because this way chance works in our favor. Evolving the cognitive ability to beat chance is expensive. Adapting to chance is so much more efficient. But this view rests on a particular meaning of accuracy. No doubt many smart people will object to my use of the word "accuracy."

The final point I want to make about the base-rate experiments is that finding that people are insensitive to base-rate kills interpersonal deception theory (IDT) dead. This is unequivocal falsification. As mentioned in chapters 4 and 5, IDT is predicated on people being sensitive to the truthfulness and deceptiveness of others' communication. Sensitivity to deception starts the cat-and-mouse sequence of target suspicion and sender adaptation. In the TDT view, in contrast, except for the very specific conditions outlined in this chapter and chapter 14, people are oblivious to the veracity of others' communication.

SUMMARY

This chapter describes the veracity effect, the Park–Levine Probability Model, and our research on linear base-rate effects. The veracity effect is the finding that the veracity of the sender's message affects the correctness of the judge's inferences about honesty and deceit. As long as people are truth-biased, truth accuracy is greater than lie accuracy. Accuracy for truths is typically much higher than 50%; accuracy for lies is usually below 50%.

The veracity effect gives rise to base-rate effects. Almost all prior deception research involves an equal number of truths and lies. Research using fifty-fifty base-rates yields the often-cited 54% average accuracy. But changing the ratio of truths and lies in experiments changes accuracy in very predictable ways. The more truths relative to lies, the higher the accuracy.

13

Explaining Slightly-Better-than-Chance Accuracy

THE SLIGHTLY-BETTER-THAN-CHANCE deception detection accuracy findings reviewed in chapter 3 pose a serious challenge for deception theories that speaks to the issue of human accuracy in deception detection. Recall that accuracy findings in standard deception detection experiments have been remarkably consistent and are exceptionally well documented. Viable theory, I believe, needs to adequately account for the various nuances of these findings. It is my contention that prior theories and explanations come up short in this regard. TDT, in contrast, not only makes good sense of prior findings but does so in a way that leads to several new insights about what is going on.

Besides just the intellectual satisfaction of having a coherent explanation for why the findings are the way they are, there is a big practical payoff as well. If we can understand why improved accuracy has been so elusive for so long, then we might be able to leverage this knowledge to uncover alternative approaches that can produce the long-sought-after improvement. This is part of why I think the TDT explanation for accuracy is so compelling. TDT's explanation of poor accuracy in deception detection points to new ways forward.

TDT's approaches to improving accuracy are covered in the next chapter. Here we set the stage by understanding what had been holding accuracy back for so long. Along the way, we will cover some of the most useful information my research has ever produced: uncovering what makes some people so much more believable than others. So, let's unleash our critical thinking skills, embrace our inner detective, and get ready to solve a long-standing mystery.

A PERSISTENT PUZZLE

Toward the end of chapter 1, I briefly described *the mystery of normally distributed slightly-better-than-chance-accuracy*. In chapter 3, I described prior findings

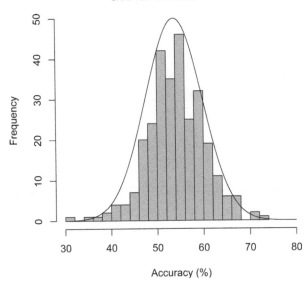

Figure 13.1. Accuracy in deception detection experiments prior to 2006.

on deception detection in detail. By the time of the Bond and DePaulo meta-analysis in 2006,[1] there were almost three hundred findings spanning sixty-five years of research. That's a whole lot of data. All those results painted a consistent yet curious picture of human lie detection.

This chapter explains why the accuracy findings are the way they are. We want an elegant solution where all the facts cohere and make sense. Let's begin by briefly reviewing the crucial facts from chapter 3. Then I will make clear what is so puzzling about these facts.

Figure 1.1 graphed findings from deception detection experiments prior to 2006. That figure is reproduced here for easy reference as figure 13.1. The accuracy obtained in each of 289 separate experiments is plotted on the horizontal axis, and the number of experiments finding each accuracy result is plotted on the vertical axis. The normal curve is superimposed as a reference to aid interpretation.

In meta-analysis, the average accuracy across prior studies was just under 54%.[2] As we saw with lie prevalence, averages can be misleading when findings are not normally distributed. But this is not the case with accuracy. Findings from the individual studies are neatly and normally distributed around the average. Averages from individual studies seldom fall very far from the across-study average of 54%. The standard deviation is only about 6%. Further, the across-study average is both at the center of and at the peak of the distribution of prior findings. What all this means is that all the findings from hundreds of experiments completed over several decades by different labs all converge on a single point just under 54%. The across-study average is nicely descriptive of prior research findings plus or minus some relatively small amount. More than half of prior findings fall between 50% and 60%. More than 97% of prior results fall between 40% and 68%. There were no studies below 30% or above 73%.

Although 54% is only four points above fifty-fifty chance, the 54% is nevertheless highly statistically significant. This is an important fact to keep in mind. Accuracy is not chance! It drives me nuts when I read research describing accuracy as no better than chance. It is an easy simplification to shorten the awkward but factually correct slightly-better-than-chance to just-chance. Statistically speaking, however, there can be no debate. On the social science standard of the null hypothesis significance test at $p < .05$, chance accuracy is thoroughly discredited at $p < .00001$. In terms of effect sizes, the difference is about $d = .4$. Social science rules of thumb call this a difference of moderate size. The main point to remember here is that accuracy is reliably better than chance.

There are at least three key features of the prior results that we need to reconcile if we are to adequately solve the mystery of normally distributed slightly-better-than-chance accuracy.

First, why is accuracy just slightly-better-than-chance, never much more, never much less? If people could not detect lies at all, the findings would be centered around 50% chance. They are not. But if at least some people could detect lies in some situations, one would think that there would be more instances of higher accuracy. There are not. As we saw in chapter 3, prior findings show a pattern where the results constituting the tails of the distribution are exclusively from small-sample studies. The more reliable results based on more data all fall within the narrow 50%–60% range. What kind of social processes might make people so invariably just a little bit better than chance?

Second, why are prior findings so robust, consistent, and persistent? As we saw in chapter 3, there is a curious lack of moderators. Slightly-better-than-chance accuracy holds across media (text, audio only, audio-visual), for both high- and low-stakes lies, for both experts and students, for mediated communication and face-to-face interaction, for both planned and spontaneous lies, etc. Because the findings we want to explain hold across all these potential moderators, any explanation for the findings that rests on one or more of these moderators making the difference must be rejected as false. A viable explanation needs to account for the robust nature of prior findings across moderators like communication media, communication duration, and stakes.

Third, why are the standard errors for accuracy scores invariably so small?[3] The standard errors in deception detection accuracy research are unusually small on social scientific standards. This is an unappreciated fact, but it is a fact all the same, and all the facts need to be accounted for. The small standard error is perhaps the oddest and most perplexing aspect of the puzzle. There just aren't large individual differences in how judges perform in deception detection experiments. In just about every other aspect of social life I can think of, people are different from one another. Whenever I give a test in one of my classes, some students do better than other students. Some students ace the test, others fail, and there are students spread out in between. There is always substantial variation in performance from person to person. Some people are better athletes than others. Some people are more extroverted than others. Some people are more perceptive than others. You name it, in social science individual differences are typically huge. In statistical analyses all this individual variation gets tossed into the error terms. Consequently, error terms in human data are usually big. But not in deception detection findings. Error terms aren't much bigger than mere chance variation.[4] What causes this unusual constancy not just across the findings of studies but also across the individual research subjects within studies?

THE THREE USUAL SUSPECTS

Combing through the literature, there seem to be three usual suspects. The mystery of normally distributed slightly-better-than-chance accuracy has been around since the 1980s[5] and has been the subject of much speculation and conjecture over the years. If one or more of these usual suspects is the culprit, then maybe the mystery has already been solved. But I don't think so, and I'll explain why. Further, ruling out these three usual suspects will help us avoid the same old mind blocks and mental pitfalls that have plagued deception theory over the years, thereby freeing us up to look for new, previously overlooked, suspects.

The first and oldest of the usual suspects is the idea that people simply look for the wrong cues. The research we discussed in chapter 2 on the widespread belief that liars won't look you in the eye, for example, seems to support the idea that people look for the wrong cues. Recall that a lack of eye contact is the worldwide number one folk belief about deception.[6] Yet eye contact has no actual utility in distinguishing truth from lie.[7]

The most obvious problem with the wrong-cues explanation is that it implies that there are right cues. As we saw in chapter 2, the evidence for the existence of a reliable set of diagnostic cues is dubious at best. The claim that cues are weak and inconsistent fits the data better.[8] Further, if the problem was simply that people looked for the wrong cues, then the solution to poor accuracy would be obvious. We could just train people to ignore the wrong cues and pay attention to the right cues. But, as we will see in TDT experiments twenty-four through twenty-six, slightly-better-than-chance accuracy persists despite training. Training lowers truth-bias, but it does not substantially affect truth–lie discrimination enough to break out of the slightly-better-than-chance range.[9]

TDT EXPERIMENTS TWENTY-FOUR, TWENTY-FIVE, AND TWENTY-SIX: CUES-BIASED LIE DETECTION TRAINING LACKS EFFICACY

I call experiments twenty-four and twenty-five the "Bogus Training Experiments."[10] Experiment twenty-six is the Lie to Me experiment, named after the television show.[11] To toot my own horn a bit, these are experiments with important implications. Together these experiments provide evidence allowing us to confidently rule out the wrong-cue explanation.

If it were the case that cues had utility but people just use the wrong cues, then training people to look for the right cues should improve accuracy. To summarize, the research finds that cue training improves accuracy, but only a little bit, from 54% with no training to 58% or 59% with training.[12] Accuracy is in the slightly-better-than-chance range either way.

Training studies typically only compare trained subjects to no-training controls. I thought it would be informative to include the deception detection equivalent of a placebo control. TDT experiments twenty-four and twenty-five randomly assigned subjects to one of three groups. Some subjects got valid training, some were in a no-training control, and some received bogus training. Valid training involved instructing subjects to look for cues that should have utility, while bogus training involved cues unrelated to actual honesty. What I expected was that much of the improvement from no-treatment controls to valid training was placebic. Because cues lack utility, whether the cues are "valid" or not would be moot, but the act of training would sensitize subjects, providing a small boost to accuracy and a reduction in truth-bias.

In TDT experiment twenty-four, 256 students were assigned to one of the three training groups. All subjects watched and judged sixteen messages (eight honest, eight lies). The valid training was based on cue effects from the best available research. The content of bogus training was based on cues that prior research suggested had no utility. When the results came in, subjects getting the bogus training actually did best of all (56%), followed by the no-training control (52%), and the valid training produced the lowest accuracy (48%).[13] Wow!

We changed up the content of the training in TDT experiment twenty-five. Rather than base our training on prior research, we coded the sixteen messages used in experiment twenty-four to see what cues (if any) actually distinguished truths from lies in those particular sixteen messages. The valid training in experiment twenty-five involved cues actually diagnostic in those specific communications. In the bogus training, participants were instructed in cues that did not differentiate those particular truths and lies. Some 158 new subjects were recruited and assigned to one of the three groups. This time the valid training group did the best (58%), followed closely by the bogus-training group (56%), and the no-training control (50%).[14]

Two aspects of the bogus-training findings really drive home the futility of cue-based lie detection. The valid cues that were actually useful had to be obtained from the specific communication being evaluated. Training based on prior research findings actually backfired. This is because cues are ephemeral. What is telling for one person in one situation often does not apply beyond that instance. Second, most of the improvement from training is placebic. Valid training, even when based on cues that applied to the specific situation, did not produce accuracy much better than the bogus-training controls. Accuracy is not poor merely because judges were looking for the wrong cues.

The opportunity for TDT experiment twenty-six came about when a prime time crime drama called *Lie to Me* began airing in 2009.[15] The show was about a nonverbal-behavior expert who solves crimes through observation of body language and micro facial expressions. The ideas presented in the show were based on the work of Paul Ekman covered in chapter 4.

In our experiment we randomly assigned 108 subjects to watch either an episode of *Lie to Me*, an episode of another crime drama about solving crimes with math (*Numb3rs*), or no show at all (control). Then subjects were given a lie detection task involving twelve interviewers from my cheating experiments.[16] Accuracy was 60% for the *Lie to Me* group, 62% in the *Numb3rs* control, and 65% in the no-show control.[17] As in the previous training experiments, learning about facial expressions and body language did not improve lie detection accuracy. Also as in the training experiments, learning about cues did make subjects more cynical. Subjects watching *Lie to Me* were less truth-biased and performed worse on honest interviews than subjects in the other two groups.[18]

And if TDT experiments twenty-four through twenty-six aren't enough to discredit the wrong-cue explanation, the 2011 Hartwig–Bond Brunswik Lens Model–inspired cue meta-analysis put the final nail in the wrong-cue coffin.[19] When the behaviors that actually affect honesty judgments are considered (as opposed to self-reported folk beliefs), people don't rely on the wrong cues. Cue reliance and cue utility are correlated. Clearly, there are many good reasons to discount the wrong-cue explanation of poor accuracy.

THE REMAINING USUAL SUSPECTS

The second usual suspect is weak cues. This view holds that accuracy is poor because cues are only weakly diagnostic. Even if people rely on the "right" cues, they will still not be very accurate because even the most useful cues are just not very useful. The DePaulo[20] and Hartwig–Bond[21] meta-analyses of cues seem to back this up, as do the findings of TDT experiments twenty-four through twenty-six.

But the most recent (2014) Hartwig–Bond meta-analysis challenges the weak-cue idea.[22] Cue effects do indeed appear weak when looking at the evidence for any specific cue across multiple studies and over time. But what the 2014 analysis showed was that this is not the case for multiple cues within specific experiments. Most individual experiments actually find strong cue effects. Cue effects are weak and inconsistent only when aggregated across experiments. If cues are strong within specific experiments, poor accuracy within specific experiments cannot be due to weak cues, because cues aren't weak.

Accuracy experiments show a very different pattern of results than cue studies. Accuracy experiments show slightly-better-than-chance accuracy at the level of the individual subject within experiments, at the level of individual experiments, and across experiments. Cues, in contrast, have substantial effects at the level of the individual subject within experiments, at the level of individual experiments, and appear weak only across experiments. Thus, I think there must be more to it than just weak cues.

The third usual suspect is defective research design. This argument holds that accuracy is poor and cues are weak because of how deception detection experiments are typically designed. There are several variations on this theme. There is the counterfactual assertion that if lie stakes were only higher, then cues would be more diagnostic and accuracy would be higher.[23] Or brief video snippets of truths and lies are blamed.[24] If only the communication duration were longer and more interactive, then cues would be more diagnostic, and accuracy would be higher.

While I am generally sympathetic to concerns over ecological validity in deception research, the defective-research assertions regarding stakes, duration, or interactivity have all been tested and soundly discredited.[25] Things like lie stakes and interactivity do not moderate accuracy conclusions. Further, as with the wrong-cue explanation, the defective-research explanation points to an obvious cure. If the defective method reasoning was correct and we fixed the research designs in the suggested way, accuracy should no longer be slightly-better-than-chance. But that's not what happens. Slightly-better-than-chance accuracy persists.

There is probably more than a kernel of truth in all three explanations. People do look for the wrong things, and, as we will see in the next chapter, changing what people look for can dramatically improve accuracy. Cues are, at best, weak indicators of deception, at least across messages, individuals, and situations. More ecological research designs are surely needed.

Despite these kernels of truth, all three of the usual suspects run afoul of some pesky facts. They don't really tell us why accuracy is so reliably better than chance, but not by much. They don't explain the uniformity in accuracy findings across the full range of non-moderators. They don't explain the small standard errors. So, maybe we need to expand our search and see whether there is evidence pointing to suspects who have been overlooked.

SENDER VARIATION

TDT's solution to the mystery is articulated in three modules and two propositions. As a start at explaining these, let me add one more fact that was tossed out at the end of chapter 3 and is critical here. It might be helpful to flip back to figure 3.2 and review the distinctions between ability, truth-bias, demeanor, and transparency. Anyway, here is the critical point. In deception detection experiments, senders vary a lot more than judges. To give you a feel for this with real data, TDT experiment twenty-seven provides a nice demonstration with some previously unpublished findings.

TDT EXPERIMENT TWENTY-SEVEN:
SENDERS VARY MUCH MORE THAN JUDGES

This experiment used tapes from the second iteration of the NSF cheatings tapes. In the second iteration of the cheating experiment, 113 taped interviews were created during 2006 and 2007. Of the 113 interviewees, 22 subjects cheated and lied about cheating throughout the entire interview. That is, 22 of 113 cheated and maintained their denials throughout the interview, never confessing. I went through still images to find an honest sender matching the sex, ethnicity, and approximate physical attractiveness of each cheating liar. With those, I had a collection of forty-four senders, all of whom denied cheating, including twenty-two honest denials and twenty-two liars falsely denying cheating.

Sixty-three subjects (MSU students) served as judges in experiment twenty-seven. Each judge watched each of the forty-four interviews and judged each

```
        Judges (N = 63, M = .56, SD = .06)
.0
.1
.2
.3  6
.4  3444888
.5  0000333333333355555555555777777779999999
.6  111111111144448
.7  00
.8
.9

        Senders (N = 44, M = .56, SD =.20)

.0
.1  4677
.2  7
.3  16999
.4  2247
.5  034556688999
.6  1167
.7  0033222777
.8  18
.9  12
```

Figure 13.2. Stem-and-leaf plots of judge and sender
accuracy in TDT experiment twenty-seven.

sender as either an honest noncheater or as a cheating liar. I scored each of the sixty-three judges for accuracy (average percentage correct across all forty-four senders), just like usual in deception detection experiments. The only thing unusual so far is the number of senders and judgments. In the TDT detection experiments described previously, judges viewed somewhere between one and twelve senders. This time, judges viewed many more senders and made many more judgments. Sixty-three judges evaluated forty-four senders yielding 2,772 judgments. All these judgments makes the findings nicely stable.

Judge accuracy in experiment twenty-seven was very much in line with slightly-better-than-chance accuracy. Judges were, on average, correct 56% of the time. This was significantly better than chance. I plotted out the accuracy scores for each of the sixty-three judges in the top half of figure 13.2. Figure 13.2 is a "stem-and-leaf plot." Let me tell you how to read and interpret the results. If you are not familiar with them, stem-and-leaf plots are fantastic for visualizing data.

As the name implies, stem-and-leaf plots have stems and leaves. In the case of the plots in figure 13.2, the stems are the vertical column of numbers on the left moving down from .0, .1, .2, . . . to .9. There are two stems, one for judges and one for senders. Different plots have different stems. The leaves are each number to the right of the stem. Each leaf is a score. In the top plot, there are sixty-three leaves, one for each judge. In the lower plot, there are forty-four leaves, one for each sender. You get the score for each judge and each sender by combining the stem with the leaf. For example, moving top-down, the first leaf under Judges is a six. The stem for that six is .3. This corresponds to .36 (36%). Moving top-down and left-right, we see that the scores are, in order from smallest to largest, .36, .43, .44, .44. .44, .48, .48, .48, .50 . . . up to two .70s. Got it?

One of the nice things about stem-and-leaf plots is that you get to see all the data. You see every score. But you can also see the overall pattern of scores. You can look at figure 13.2 as a sideways bar chart. See? There is just one score in the .3s, seven scores in the .4s, a whole bunch in the .5s, several in the .6s, and nothing over .70, where there are two scores. You can zoom in to see individual scores or zoom out to graphically see how the scores are distributed.

Looking at the judge scores, notice how the pattern in the top half of figure 13.2 is remarkably similar to the pattern in figure 13.1. Individual judges in experiment twenty-seven are normally and tightly distributed around the average judge score just as individual experiments are normally and tightly distributed around the across-study average in meta-analysis. In TDT experiment twenty-seven, accuracy ranged from 36% to 70%. In the meta-analytic data in figure 13.1, the range was 30% to 73%. The average in meta-analysis was 54% compared to 56% in experiment twenty-seven. Both have a standard deviation of 6%. In both, a majority (approximately 60% of scores) of scores fall in the 50%–60% range, and the vast majority of scores fall between 44% and 66%. The judges in experiment twenty-seven tell the same story and act the same way as in the results of the nearly three hundred previous deception detection experiments in meta-analysis.

But there is another way to score the data in experiment twenty-seven. Because sixty-three judges rated each sender, I also created sender accuracy scores. For judge accuracy, I averaged across senders. Judge scores tell us what percentage of senders each judge got right. This is how accuracy is usually scored. For sender accuracy, I averaged across judges to get a score for each sender. Sender scores tell us what percentage of judges got each sender right. I plotted those in the bottom half of figure 13.2 so you can visually compare judge and sender scores.

I first did this in a published paper in 2010.[26] I can think of only a few other published examples of scoring senders across judges.[27] Judges are the typical unit of analysis in deception detection experiments, and researchers rely heavy on precedence. Most research is guided by what other research did before. These conventions make research more easily comparable across studies, but they also discourage innovation.

When senders are plotted, the data look very different. Interestingly but not surprisingly, the mean is exactly the same. The average is 56%, just as it was for judges. If you think about it for a moment, you will see it has to be this way. In one case, rows are averaged first, then row averages are averaged to get a grand mean. In the other case, individual columns are averaged, then the column averages are averaged. The data are the same, so the grand mean is the same. Row averages and column averages are centered on the same grand average.

However, the dispersion around the grand average looks much different for senders and judges. There are four senders that more than 80% of judges got wrong (14%, 16%, 17%, and 17%). There are also four senders that more than 80% of judges got right (81%, 88%, 91%, and 92%). Whereas the standard deviation for the judges is a small 6%, the standard deviation for the senders was much larger: 20%.

There is just a lot more "action" going on in the senders than in the judges. Judges all do pretty much the same. Senders, in contrast, are all over the place. There are senders for which judges are just a little bit better than chance. There are also senders that judges systematically do well on, and other senders that judges systematically misjudge. Because there are relatively equal numbers of almost-always-right-about and almost-always-wrong-about senders, these cancel out when scoring judges, and these senders become invisible. We see them only when we score by sender, and only then when we plot the data instead of looking at just the average. When I see data like these, I conclude that I had better look at the senders, not just the judges, and I had better look at variability and distributions, not just averages. Judges and averages are not the most interesting or most informative part of the story.

Here is an important bit of statistical wisdom. In research, we want to uncover how variables are related. For a variable to covary with another variable, both must vary in the first place. That which does not vary cannot covary. Covariance, in turn, is necessary for causation (along with time-ordering and ruling out spurious factors). Much like the wise advice in corruption investigations to follow the money, in science, the secret is to follow the variation. Where there is variation, there is the potential for causation. Understanding causation is what explanation is all about. Because there is much more variation in senders than in judges, it is wise to invest our attention there. This was my thinking, and I continue to believe it sound. As we will soon see, looking at sender variation leads to some important new insights.

Note that turning our attention from judges to senders and from averages to variation points us away from the three usual suspects. The wrong-cues explanation is squarely a judge thing. The defective-design explanation is external to both senders and judges and should affect both. Only weak cues is squarely a sender thing. But weak cues is about sender similarity (senders generally have weak cues), not sender-to-sender variation. We want an explanation that is not just about senders but about why senders differ from each other so much, and why this is important. Weak cues does not account for the huge variation in senders in figure 13.2. Instead, if cues were uniformly weak, senders would be clumped around slightly-better-than-chance, just like judges. They are not.

Recall from the end of chapter 3 that senders vary in two important ways: transparency and demeanor. Sender transparency is the sender equivalent to judge accuracy. A sender who is transparent is one that all judges always get right regardless of their actual honesty. Transparent senders are an open book. Everyone can read them. They are believed when they are honest, but seen as lying when they are lying. Highly transparent liars are bad liars. No one believes their lies. They give themselves away. Highly transparent truth tellers are great when honest. They are correctly believed.

Low transparency does not make for a good liar.[28] People with no transparency are inscrutable. We just can't tell whether they are honest or not. People with negative transparency, if such people exist at all, are those that judges always get wrong. The negative transparency person is believed when lying but invariably disbelieved when honest. Good liars, in contrast, are people who are always believed, both when they are lying and when they are not. That is, good liars are people with honest demeanors. They are the credible ones, not the hard-to-read poker-faced types.

Honestly demeanored people are those who are always believed regardless of their actual honesty. They just come off as honest. Poorly demeanored people provoke suspicion and skepticism in others. They come off as insincere, inauthentic, sketchy, and maybe even creepy.

In TDT experiment twenty-seven, demeanor and transparency are confounded, as they are in most deception detection experiments. The reason is that senders were either honest or lying, but not both. If we have an honest sender who is believed by most judges, is that because he or she has an honest demeanor or is just high-transparency? We can't tell. To disentangle demeanor from transparency, we would need senders to tell multiple truths and multiple lies to multiple judges. If our usually believed honest sender is usually believed both when honest and when lying, then it is demeanor driving the belief. But if he or she is believed only when honest and not when lying, then we have a highly transparent sender. Absent that sort of data, all we know for sure is that senders vary much more than judges. Now, you can probably guess what TDT experiment twenty-eight will look like. Before we get there, let me lay out my thinking about how individual differences in transparency help solve the mystery of slightly-better-than-chance accuracy.

A FEW TRANSPARENT LIARS

The part of the puzzle that I address first is why accuracy is typically better than chance.[29] From the weak-cues perspective, the answer is that cues are only a little bit diagnostic; hence, they yield only a little accuracy. Not zero, just a bit. From the logic of cue theories (see chapter 5), this seems to make sense. In the mediated statistical relationships where honesty–deception leads to cues, and cues lead to judgments, if the direct causal links are small but non-zero, then the indirect link between actual honesty and judgments will be not-zero.[30] We get accuracy just a little better than chance.

But I am not trapped within cue theory logic, and TDT is not a cue theory. TDT focuses instead on individual differences between senders, not generalities (averages) across senders. How might sender variation cause consistent slightly-better-than-chance accuracy?

Sometimes thinking by analogy helps. Deception detection accuracy experiments are much like true-false tests. Senders are like the questions on the test. Liars are false statements, and honest senders are the true statements. The judges are like the test takers. Instead of marking test questions as true or false, judges rate senders as honest or lying. In this analogy, TDT experiment twenty-seven was a true-false with forty-four questions (twenty-two true and twenty-two false) given to sixty-three test takers.

I'm going to round the 54% in deception research up to 55% just to make the example easier. What kind of test always yields an average of 55% plus or minus some small amount? It does not matter who takes the test. Honor students score the same as students on academic probation. For that matter, students at elite private institutions do the same as those who can't even get into college. It doesn't matter if the test takers study or not, or even take the class or not. People always average 55%. There are no individual differences in test takers and no moderators. What in the world is going on?

Do you know the answer to this little brain teaser yet? Imagine a true-false test with one hundred questions. Ninety of the questions are super hard.

True or false: the Xingu is the eighth-longest tributary of the Amazon River?[31] No one knows the answer. Everyone must guess. People have just a fifty-fifty chance on the hard questions, getting, on average, forty-five of them right (90 x 0.5 = 45). The other ten questions, in comparison, are really easy. Nearly everyone gets these right. True or false: 1 + 1 = 3.5? How do people do on this imaginary test? They get forty-five plus or minus chance on the hard questions and ten out of ten on the easy ones. 45 + 10 = 55. Such a test always produces an average score of 55% plus or minus chance, no matter who takes it.

I wondered, What if most people are pretty good liars when they need to be? For the vast majority of senders, you just can't tell. It's chance detecting their lies if you have nothing to go on but their demeanor. But maybe there are a few people who just can't lie convincingly. If these poor liars are put in a situation where they have to lie, everyone call tell that they are lying. Pretty much everyone gets them right. And there are just enough of these bad liars out there to make judges, on average, a little better than chance. If something like 10% of the population were exceptionally transparent liars, we would have a situation analogous to my test with ninety hard and ten easy questions. We'd get slightly-better-than-chance accuracy. We would see little variance in judges. And we'd see the variance in senders.

Anecdotally, we have probably all met people who say they can't lie well. I have definitely seen instances of this on the cheating tapes. There have been a few cheating subjects over the years who seem perfectly composed on the background questions, but when directly asked about cheating, they provide unbelievable denials that fool no one. There was one woman who blushed bright red when she started lying. There was another woman who broke into uncontrollable nervous laughter. There was a third guy who began stammering and conveyed a lack of conviction that could not be missed. When I have used these tapes in experiments or shown them in presentations, almost everyone knows that these unusually transparent liars really cheated despite their feeble denials. Everyone gets those senders right.

If there were just a relatively few transparent senders, then we might expect the pattern of results shown in figure 13.1. Accuracy is better than chance because people get the transparent senders right. Accuracy is not much better than chance because most senders aren't transparent. Things like training, expertise, stakes, and duration don't make much difference because we don't need those to see that the transparent liars are lying, and nontransparent senders are nontransparent regardless. Maybe this is why judges all perform pretty much the same, why we see more variability in senders than in judges, and why judge standard errors are so small. In short, if "a few transparent liars" thinking is right, then the various pieces of the puzzle fit together and make sense. Here is a brief summary of the A Few Transparent Liars module in TDT.

A Few Transparent Liars—The reason that accuracy in deception detection is above chance in most deception detection experiments is that some small proportion of the population are really bad liars who usually give themselves away. The reason accuracy is not higher is that most people are pretty good liars.

From the perspective of a few transparent liars, weak cues isn't quite right. It's more that cues are worthless or misleading for most senders, but cues are super telling for a small minority of people. On average, cues are weak, but that hides the real story of why cues are weak. The real story involves individual differences in cue utility between senders.

But, you might ask, if there are just a few transparent liars, why so much sender variance in figure 13.2? That's the one thing that doesn't yet fit. The answer, I think, is that most of that variance is demeanor, not transparency. We know from meta-analysis that there is much more variance in demeanor than in transparency.[32] The trouble is, demeanor variance and transparency variance were confounded in experiment twenty-seven. We need to unconfound them. That, as it turns out, is easier said than done, but the next TDT experiment gave it a shot.

TDT EXPERIMENT TWENTY-EIGHT:
LOOKING FOR A TRANSPARENT LIAR

To separate out all the sources of variation in deception detection (judge ability, judge truth-bias, sender transparency, and sender demeanor), we need multiple senders who tell multiple truths and lies that are all assessed by multiple judges. I had the opportunity to do this one semester when I taught an undergraduate special topics class on deception. The class met one night per week for two and a half hours, which provided almost enough time, given the thirty or so students who showed up for class on any given night. The experiment provided a great way to exemplify ideas relevant to the class with real data from the class.[33] So, one night we tried it out and spent the class with students trying to lie to and detect the lies of their fellow students. I brought in the results to the next class. The students thought it was really cool, and I got a peek at some hard-to-collect data.

First, each student privately and honestly answered the same ten open-ended autobiographical questions. These questions were previously used in TDT experiments nineteen through twenty-one. One by one, each student came up in front of the class and was asked each of the ten questions. Based on a random assignment different for each sender, each sender had to lie on five of the answers and give honest answers on the other five questions. All the rest of the students judged each answer as honest or not.

Thirty students attended class that night, but given tardiness and early departures, only twenty-seven students judged all the senders. We ran out of time before everyone could be a sender, but twenty-one of the students got to try being senders. Thus, there were twenty-one senders and twenty-seven judges, and all senders were judges for the other senders. It was close to a full round-robin.

Ability and truth-bias were scored for each of the twenty-seven judges. Truth-bias was the percent of answers each judge believed. Ability was the accuracy score for each judge, the percentage of messages each judge got correct. Each of the twenty-one senders was scored for transparency and demeanor. Transparency scores were the percentage correct judges got for each sender. Demeanor was the percentage of the time each sender was believed. For the twenty-one students who were both senders and judges, all four scores were available.

I plotted the results in figure 13.3. There was not as much sender variance as we saw in experiment twenty-seven, but there was still much more sender variance than judge variance. I think that because judges were also senders, they suspected a fifty-fifty base-rate, and that this expectation depressed variation in demeanor. Judges knew better than to believe or disbelieve a large majority of answers for any one sender. However, that is speculation on my part.

Importantly, there was a sender who was unusually transparent. There was one person everyone else got right 84% of the time. This sender was 2.5 standard deviations above the mean on transparency. The mode for this sender was 90%, and even the poorest-performing individual judge obtained 60% when judging this sender. Thus, one individual appeared to be unusually transparent. Perhaps the idea of a few transparent liars has merit.

A few transparent liars nevertheless does not completely solve the mystery. It explains why accuracy is usually just a little better than chance. But what's going on with the non-transparent liars? Senders vary in demeanor as well as transparency, so that is where we turn next.

SENDER DEMEANOR

A person's demeanor is how that person appears to others. Demeanor involves the connection between what a person does (an objective and observable pat-

Judge Truth Bias	Judge Accuracy
M = 56%, SD = 7%	M = 59%, SD = 6%
3	3
3 9	3
4	4 2
4 57	4
5 124444	5 04
5 6666888	5 566667999
6 00001123	6 000001222333
6 5	6 79
7 2	7
7	7 5
8	8
8	8

Sender Demeanor	Sender Transparency
M = 56%, SD = 9%	M = 59%, SD = 10%
3	3
3	3 7
4 344	4
4 5	4 8
5 244444	5 23444
5 589	5 66778
6 123	6 004
6 589	6 79
7	7 004
7	7
8	8 4*
8	8
	* A transparent sender

Figure 13.3. Stem-and-leaf plots of judge and sender accuracy-transparency and believability in experiment twenty-eight.

tern of behavior) and how that person is perceived by others watching him or her. It's about how we present ourselves, what kind of person other people think we are, and the link between the two.

Demeanor is an *individual difference* because we all come off differently. Some people seem shy. Others seem outgoing. Some people seem tense, while others seem more laid-back. Some people come off as aggressive, some creepy, some nerdy, some sophisticated, some just average and unremarkable.

Regardless of the specific type of demeanor conveyed, demeanor has two important characteristics besides just being an individual difference. First, demeanor tends to be a global perception. The specific behaviors that create a person's demeanor come off as a package. They involve a constellation of interrelated behaviors.[34] These constellations of behaviors create a distinct, coherent impression on others. The main idea from gestalt psychology captures this well: Demeanor involves a perceptual whole that is more than the sum of the individual behaviors that create the impression. Second, demeanor involves intersubjectivity in the impressions of an individual formed by others who observe that individual. That is, other people's views of a person's demeanor converge. Thus, *demeanor involves constellations of interrelated behaviors that yield holistic impressions that are consistent across social observers.*

Our interest here is in a particular subtype of demeanor related to credibility, authenticity, and believability. I call this *sender honest demeanor* (or just "demeanor" for short). The idea is that some people just seem more honest than others. There are people whom other people tend to find very honest. Other people typically believe these honestly demeanored individuals. People with less honest demeanors set off warning bells and foster suspicion in others. There are large differences from person to person in honest demeanor. And differences in honest demeanor have little to do with actual honesty. I summarize the sender honest demeanor module in TDT as follows:

> **Sender Honest Demeanor**—There are large individual differences in believability. Some people come off as honest. Other people are doubted more often. These differences in how honest different people seem to be are a function of a combination of eleven different behaviors and impressions that function together. Honest demeanor has little to do with actual honesty, and this explains poor accuracy in deception detection experiments.

The idea that senders differ a lot in believability is not new, and I cannot take credit for its origination. Instead, it is one of those ideas that seem to get reinvented periodically. The famed sociologist Erving Goffman wrote about the general idea of demeanor way back in 1956.[35] Zuckerman and his colleagues used the word "demeanor" to refer to sender individual differences in believability in an insightful but underappreciated 1979 article.[36] They too noted that demeanor had little to do with actual honesty. Frank and Ekman resurrected the idea twenty-five years later under the label "truthfulness generality" without reference to either Goffman or Zuckerman.[37] Somehow the idea got lost again and again as research took off in other directions. I am the first to systematically try to unpack honest demeanor and assert its prominence as a critical explanatory mechanism behind poor accuracy in deception detection experiments.

I clued into demeanor through a confluence of events about eight years ago. Before that I was vaguely familiar with the idea due to my affinity for Goffman's writing and my familiarity with Zuckerman's work. Three things converged about the same time that led me to one of those wonderful epiphanies where I connect the dots. I came to a stunning realization about the mystery of slightly-better-than-chance accuracy.

First, I had recently become familiar with the 2008 Bond–DePaulo meta-analysis findings showing huge sender variation.[38] I was also spending much time watching the NSF cheating experiment videotapes, editing them for various deception detection experiments that I had in the works at the time. Third, new data from those detection experiments using the cheating tapes were rolling in. I'm usually pretty hands-on with my data. I look at the raw data, not just statistical printouts. I often enter my own data into spreadsheets, which might be unusual for grant-funded full professors. As I was entering data, I started seeing unmistakable patterns for particular senders. I cross-checked across different experiments to see whether the patterns held. They did. I watched the tapes yielding the results to further triangulate. I went back and reread Zuckerman. I was pretty sure I was on to something important. I designed a series of experiments to test my thinking. Looking back, these might turn out to be some of the most important experiments of my career. The implications are huge, both in terms of what I set out to accomplish and in terms of some truly stunning unanticipated findings and implications that popped out of the results.

TDT EXPERIMENT 29:
GAMING ACCURACY BY STACKING THE DEMEANOR DECK

When I teach experimental design to my students, I flip the light switch in the classroom on and off as an example. By flipping the switch, I can turn the lights on and off at will. If we didn't know about electricity, lights, and switches, it might seem like magic. I tell my students that if I really understand the causal forces at play in my research, I should be able to turn my phenomena on and off just like a light switch. This is what we want to do in our experiments. We want to turn the effects on and off at will by controlling the causal mechanisms that create the effect.

Applying that concept to this chapter, if I understand slightly-better-than-chance accuracy, then I should be able to control it. In this case, instead of a switch, I have a dial. When I turn the dial down, accuracy plummets. People become much worse than chance. When I crank the dial up, I make accuracy much better than chance. Based on what I saw in the cheating tapes and how subjects responded to particular senders, I thought I could "game" accuracy results. At will, I should be able to produce the typical slightly-better-than-chance accuracy or twist the dial one way or another and produce unprecedentedly low or high accuracy. By doing this, I thought, I could show true mastery over my topic of study, unrivaled by other theorists or researchers. Did I really understand the causal forces behind deception detection accuracy well enough that I could experimentally dial them up or down?

Think of it. For decades accuracy was stuck at 54% plus or minus some random amount. Nobody was able to figure out which dial to turn. Over the years different cue theories pointed to different dials, and lots of dials were tried, but none of them worked. Accuracy remained just above chance. If I had really learned the true cause, then I could experimentally alter the cause. I thought I knew the cause, so I created experiments to turn the metaphorical dial. If accuracy changed in the anticipated ways, maybe I was on to something. Mystery solved?

Before getting to the experiment, let me explain my thinking. Fact number one is that we know for sure that people vary considerably in sender honest demeanor.[39] That is, some people come off as more believable or "honest-seeming" than others. By definition, we know that demeanor is independent of actual honesty. In this way, demeanor in senders should work just like truth-bias and the veracity effect in judges. Truth-bias is the tendency for judges to believe independent of actual honesty. Demeanor is the tendency for senders to be believed independent of actual honesty. In the veracity effect, truth-bias makes judges right about truths but wrong about the lies. When we average accuracy across truths and lies, we get slightly-better-than-chance accuracy. With demeanor, maybe honest and dishonest demeanors average out too. And this is what I was seeing in the data. You too can see it under Senders in figure 13.2.

In figure 13.4, I diagrammed demeanor in relation to actual honesty. People can appear either honest or dishonest, and they can actually be either honest or dishonest. This creates four quadrants reflecting four different types of senders. Moving clockwise from top left, we have honest folks who seem sincere, believable liars, liars with dishonest demeanors, and honest people with dishonest demeanors. In two of the quadrants (top left and bottom right), actual honesty and demeanor are "matched." People are what they seem to be. Judges will be accurate about these matched people. I call these two quadrants demeanor-veracity matched. In the other two quadrants, demeanor and reality are "mismatched." These are the sincere-appearing liars and the suspicion-inducing honest senders. Judges viewing people in these quadrants will be wrong. Accuracy should be well below chance for the mismatched senders.

As we saw in chapter 10, most deception research involves instructed lies

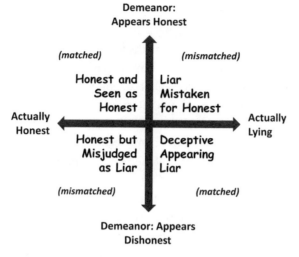

Figure 13.4. Senders matched and mismatched
on demeanor and actual honesty.

and random assignment of senders to honest and lying conditions. In such experiments, honestly demeanored and dishonestly demeanored individuals are equally like to be actually honest or lying because of random assignment.[40] This guarantees an approximately equal number of matched and mismatched senders. Judges are predominantly correct about the matched senders but systematically wrong about the mismatched senders. Look back at the senders in figure 13.2. You'll note that there are sizable groups of senders that most judges do really well on. But there is also a sizable group of senders that trip up most judges. When we score judges and average across senders, those two groups balance out, and this pushes the average down toward chance.

That was my thinking. Now, how to test it? If I am right, there are the four types of senders portrayed in figure 13.4. First, if these four groups exist, I should be able to find examples of them in my cheating tapes. Second, if I show these different groups of senders to judges, then I should be able to produce very different accuracy findings depending on which senders the judges see. I can turn the dial up for accuracy by showing judges just the matched senders. Accuracy should skyrocket. I turn the dial down by showing judges only the mismatched senders. Accuracy should plummet. If I show both matched and mismatched senders, accuracy should be just above chance.

I pretested senders using the same tapes as TDT experiment twenty-seven. There were forty-four senders, twenty-two honest and twenty-two liars. Sixty-four students watched and judged short, twenty-second clips of each sender. I selected the five honest senders who were believed most often, the five honest senders who were the least frequently believed, the five liars who were believed most often, and the five liars who were the least frequently believed. This gave me twenty tapes to work with. I had five of each of the four types with ten honest, ten lies, ten honestly demeanored, and ten dishonestly demeanored. From these, I created two sets of ten interviews, one of matched senders and one of mismatched senders. Each set had five honest and five lying senders. The matched set contained the frequently believed honest senders and least frequently believed liars. The mismatched set, in contrast, contained the infrequently believed honest senders and the frequently believed liars. The prediction, of course, was that viewing matched senders would produce high accuracy, much above the 54% typical of the literature, while viewing mismatched senders would result in unusually poor accuracy.

In experiment twenty-nine, thirty judges were shown all twenty interviews, and matched and mismatched senders were just scored separately. The judges were honor students in a special topics class I was teaching on deception, and the study was done as a class activity. For the matched senders, accuracy was 78.7%. For the mismatched senders, judges were correct only 36.3% of the time. That's more than a forty-point swing! As you might imagine, the effect size was quite large ($d > 4.0$). By the way, if we average the matched and mismatched senders, we get slightly-better-than-chance accuracy (79% + 36% = 115 ÷ 2 = 57.5%). I experimentally changed up the senders, twisted the accuracy dial, and turned up and down accuracy. Score win number one for my demeanor idea.

TDT EXPERIMENTS THIRTY THROUGH THIRTY-THREE: REPLICATING DEMEANOR EFFECTS ACROSS DIFFERENT TYPES OF JUDGES

My logic has another testable component. If it is really the senders that are the cause, then judges should be interchangeable. That is, if some senders are just believable, then everyone should find them believable. But judges should always do well on matched senders and poorly on mismatched senders regardless of who is doing the judging. My logic says that when we change the senders (switch from matched to mismatched), accuracy swings widely, but when we change the judges but not the senders, accuracy is relatively constant. If I could show that this was indeed the case, then we have strong experimental evidence that it is the senders who are causing the changes in accuracy. So, that's what I set out to do.

In TDT experiment thirty, the judges were 113 students. They were pretty similar to the subjects in experiment twenty-nine, but they weren't honor students, and they weren't enrolled in a class on deception. The other change was that the judges were randomly assigned to see either the matched or the mismatched senders. In experiment thirty-one, the subjects were professors rather than students. Kim Serota recruited thirty business professors from nearby Oakland University outside Detroit. We reasoned that the senders were students who denied cheating, and professors might be the most appropriate judges of potential student cheaters. In TDT experiment thirty-two, we took the matched and mismatched interviews around the globe to Korea University in Seoul, South Korea. There we had 182 students at Korea University serve as judges. This let us see if demeanor extends across cultures. This seemed to us a particularly bold test of the interchangeable-judge expectation. Finally, in experiment thirty-three we got thirty-five professionally trained and currently practicing deception detection experts employed by a US security and intelligence agency to watch the matched and mismatched senders.

In experiment twenty-nine with student judges, recall that accuracy for the matched senders was 78.7%. In the four replications that followed with the four different sets of judges, accuracy for matched senders was 77.7%, 78.2%, 70.7%, and 96.3%. Accuracy for the matched senders was lowest for the Korean students and highest for the government agents, but in all cases it was well above the usual slightly-better-than-chance accuracy. For the mismatched senders, the 36.3% accuracy in experiment twenty-nine compared with 41.4%, 40.7%, 33.9% and 34.3% in the different-judges replications. All these were well below chance. The dial worked the same way across different samples of judges.

Interestingly, there was a small group of the government agents who were especially experienced, with more than fifteen years of interrogation experience. These experts were right on every single one of the matched senders. Every one of the ultra-experienced experts got 100% in the matched condition. Ten for ten. But they were only 20.4% correct on the mismatched senders and even worse (14.3%) on the sincere liars. That's right; the sincere liars beat the agents more than 85% of the time. Recall the opening paragraphs in chapter 1 about the CIA agents who wrote the book. It seems the caller in that story was right. The more a judge relies on demeanor, the more demeanor–veracity matching matters.

TDT STUDIES THIRTY-FOUR AND THIRTY-FIVE: UNCOVERING THE BQ

Obviously, the matched and mismatched senders are doing something quite different to cause such large differences in accuracy. Throughout this chapter we have been talking about how senders differ in transparency and demeanor.

But what makes them this way? What are they doing to yield such consistent impressions across judges?

TDT study thirty-four took the first big step to answering the question about what makes some senders so believable and others so much less so. I went back to the same thirty students in my honors deception class who participated in the detection task reported in experiment twenty-nine. Study thirty-four took place the next class period. I put up and explained the results from experiment twenty-nine. We watched each sender again as a class. I showed the students the results for that particular sender. I asked the class why they had thought that particular sender was honest or dishonest. What was it about their answers that yielded such consistent judgments? The class discussed each sender. I took notes. We went through all the senders, watching them all several times. We kept discussing until it was clear the class was out of ideas, we all felt we had pretty much exhausted the topic, and we were confident that we had a good feel for what had guided the initial judgments.

I took my notes and distilled the themes and ideas into a list of eleven behaviors and impressions that together captured the breadth and the essence of the discussion (see the following list). This is what the honest- and dishonest-appearing senders were doing to come off as honest or dishonest.

Sincere (Honest) Demeanor Cues
1. Confidence and composure
2. Pleasant and friendly interaction style
3. Engaged and involved interaction style
4. Gives plausible explanations

Insincere (Dishonest) Demeanor Cues
5. Avoids eye contact
6. Appears hesitant and slow in providing answers
7. Vocal uncertainty (conveys uncertainty in tone of voice)
8. Excessive fidgeting with hands or foot movements
9. Appears tense, nervous, and anxious
10. Portrays an inconsistent demeanor over course of interaction
11. Verbal uncertainty (conveys uncertainty with words)

This was the start of the BQ. What's this BQ? It is short for *believability quotient.*[41] I also call it my demeanor index. People who do these sincere-appearing behaviors while eschewing the insincere-appearing are believed. People who do the insincere behaviors and lack the sincere ones are those who are judged as deceptive. It is the behaviors and impressions on this list that distinguished the honestly demeanored senders from the dishonestly demeanored ones. I put it to you that this list is worth vastly more than what you paid for this book. Coming off to others as a sincere and honest person is more than a little useful (and valuable).

TDT experiment thirty-five sought initial quantitative evidence to validate the BQ. After the subjects in experiment thirty finished judging the senders as honest or lying, we asked them to watch the tapes again. This time they rated each sender for the eleven behaviors and impressions that constitute the BQ.

The ratings of the eleven behaviors and impressions were highly intercorrelated. People who did any one of the honest-appearing behaviors were rated as doing them all. People who did any of the dishonest things were seen as doing them all. And people who were seen as doing the sincere set were seen as not doing the insincere things and vice versa (correlation $r = -.59$). When scored as a single believability index, the resulting score had a high internal consistency reliability approaching .90. I concluded that the eleven behaviors and impressions were not statistically independent. These cues do not travel alone. They travel in a pack, and that is how they function.

The existence of highly interrelated behaviors has groundbreaking and transformative implications. In the past, cues have been understood and studied as isolated behaviors that are independent from one another. In many statistical analyses, for example, having highly intercorrelated behaviors that are not accounted for can drastically skew results, making results misleading. Approaches in the literature like the Brunswik Lens Model falsely assume the independence of cues. Mistakenly trying to understand a gestalt-like impression by looking at isolated fragments is as misguided as trying to understand how a team functions without considering interaction among team members. The implications are clear. We need to see cues as herd animals or team players. Individual brushstrokes do make the masterpiece.

As for the BQ validation part of the results, I scored the eleven ratings as a single index. The sincere and insincere senders differed massively in the BQ ($d = 1.15$). As expected, the senders who were selected in pretesting as appearing more honest had a much higher BQ score than those who pretested as insincere (regardless of actual honesty). Further, when I looked at the statistical relationship between the BQ scores and the honesty ratings from TDT experiment twenty-seven, the correlation was $r = + .60$.

Thus, experiment thirty-five showed that (a) the behaviors and impressions that create demeanor are strongly interwoven and are perceived as a single coherent impression, (b) the action is in the senders, not the judges, and (c) the

BQ is strongly associated with the extent to which any given sender is believed or not. The evidence seems pretty convincing. Nevertheless, as is good scientific practice, I replicated. TDT experiment thirty-six seals the deal, providing the additional evidence that TDT readers should expect.

TDT EXPERIMENT THIRTY-SIX:
A FULL CROSS-VALIDATION OF THE BQ

So far, the demeanor data came from the same relatively small set of twenty senders. To get new senders, we ran 104 more students through the cheating experiment to get 104 new videotaped interviews. Next, I recruited seven paid research assistants to each "code" all 104 interviews. Basically, I trained the research assistants in the BQ and then had them watch and score each of the new interviews. In this way each of the 104 new senders got a score on BQ, which was the average score across the seven research-assistant coders working independently. Next, we needed new judges, so we recruited 157 MSU students from the research subject pool. Watching 104 interviewers was too much to ask, so each judge watched only twenty-six of the senders, judging each as either honest or lying. When all this was done, we had 104 new senders, with each of these senders scored for BQ by seven trained evaluators, and each sender was subsequently judged as honest or not by somewhere between thirty-five to forty-six independent judges.

Now the results. BQ scores were not significantly related with actual honesty, correlation = -.09. But the BQ scores predicted judge honesty rating, correlation $r = .41$. The correlation was especially strong for liars, correlation $r = .86$. These are strong and supportive results. The BQ works.

SERENDIPITY AND THE IMPORTANCE OF THE BQ

A few days ago my friend-colleague-mentor Frank Boster send me a copy of the 1958 article "The Case of the Floppy-eared Rabbits."[42] The article was a case study of two independent scientists who observed the same unexpected finding. One scientist pursued it and made an important new finding, while the other didn't. Frank Boster likes parables, and when floppy-eared rabbits are viewed this way, the lesson is that often the most important findings and breakthroughs are accidental. Science, especially in the soft social sciences, where there is considerable hard-science envy, is often taught as hypothesis testing. So-called post hoc or dustbowl findings are considered poor science. But if the goal is achieving an important new insight rather than following a conventional, idealized caricature of science, the lesson is clear. The wise researcher should embrace the unexpected and follow the data to see where they lead. It seems to me that the BQ provides an excellent example.

My goal in designing the experiments reported in this chapter was very much to solve the mystery of slightly-better-than-chance accuracy. It was a long-standing mystery, and I wanted to be the one to solve it. Along the way I stumbled across the BQ findings. Here was a set of behaviors and impressions that were highly interrelated and that together reliably distinguished between those people who others find believable and those who are less believable.

Let's start a list. Who would benefit from having a high BQ? To whose advantage is it to be seen as sincere? Politicians, certainly. Attorneys. Salespeople. Customer service representatives. Spokespersons of all varieties. Anyone traveling through airport screenings or customs. Teachers. People on first dates. Anyone interacting with the boss at work. Pretty much everyone would be well served by being perceived as sincere.

The real power of the BQ was shown in TDT experiments thirty to thirty-three. Demeanor transcends perceivers. Believable people were believed by students and professors, Americans and Koreans, university students and secret government agents.

The BQ provides a checklist. Do those things, and you will come off as honest and sincere. Practice them. People will find you credible. I didn't set out to create the BQ, but it popped out of the data, and I saw its value at once. It was worth my extra effort to validate it. As I said previously, it is worth much more than the price of this book to learn about it.

THE MYSTERY OF SLIGHTLY-BETTER-THAN-CHANCE ACCURACY SOLVED

The answer to the mystery is summarized succinctly in TDT proposition eleven.

TDT Proposition Eleven. With the exception of a few transparent liars, deception is not accurately detected, at the time in which it occurs, through the passive observation of sender demeanor. Honest-looking and deceptive-looking communication performances are largely independent of actual honesty and deceit for most people and hence usually do not provide diagnostically useful information. Consequently, demeanor-based deception detection is, on average, only slightly-better-than-chance due to a few transparent liars, but typically not much above chance due to the fallible nature of demeanor-based judgments.

Basically, the answer to the mystery lies in the sender variation in transparency and demeanor. There are a few transparent liars that make accuracy systematically better than chance. But because especially transparent senders are a small minority of communicators, they push accuracy up only a little bit. For everyone else, demeanor and actual honesty are unrelated. Sender honest demeanor strongly determines who is believed. Individual differences in honest demeanor are large, creating systematic errors across judges that push accuracy down toward chance. The impact of sender demeanor transcends judges, and this is why there is so little judge variance and so few moderators of demeanor-based lie detection.

LOOKING AHEAD: HOW PEOPLE REALLY DETECT LIES

Slightly-better-than-chance accuracy applies to and results from demeanor-based lie detection. Demeanor-based lie detection has much utility with transparent liars, but they are few and far between. Also, the transparent liars are probably not the ones we need to worry about. This also means that the cue theories described in chapters 5 and 6 apply to only a small segment of the population. Thinking like a cue theorist guarantees only slightly-better-than-chance accuracy.

Fortunately, deception detection experiments documenting slightly-better-than-chance accuracy give subjects a task qualitatively dissimilar to how people detect deception outside the lab. In the next chapter, I introduce TDT experiment thirty-seven and the How People Really Detect Lies module. What we will see is that real-time demeanor-based lie detection bears little resemblance to how real people detect most real lies outside the lab.

If demeanor-based detection causes poor accuracy, the solution to improving accuracy is straightforward. Don't rely on demeanor! By looking at how people really do detect lies we can learn the alternatives to demeanor-based lie detection and slightly-better-than-chance accuracy. The BQ is useful stuff, but so is improved lie detection. Read on. Chapter 14 covers TDT's approaches to improving lie detection.

14

Improving Accuracy

ONCE UPON A TIME, NOT SO LONG AGO, it was a reliable and well-established empirical fact that humans were invariably poor lie detectors. Accuracy rates were statistically better than chance, but unimpressive on the face. Further, these poor accuracy findings had been amazingly persistent. One might wish it otherwise, but beliefs to the contrary were, for a long time, simply counterfactual.

A few years ago, however, things began to change. The once solid accuracy ceiling began to crumble. My lab started to see accuracy rates in the midsixties. Those findings replicated. Then we obtained and replicated findings in the seventies. And it was not just our lab. Others, too, were reporting levels of accuracy that departed substantially from old and reliable slightly-better-than-chance conclusions. One of my most recent series of experiments reported and replicated accuracy over 90%.[1]

This chapter tells the story of how the once-upon-a-time fact of poor accuracy (summarized in chapters 3 and 13) gave way to much higher accuracy results. As an introduction to my new and improved approach to lie detection, I begin with an odd but true story of suspected deception at a deception research conference.

Hee Sun Park and I were attending a boutique legal-criminal psychology conference in the Netherlands. At one session a leading deception researcher spoke. During his talk, the speaker said that he had never said such and such a thing.[2] The claim he disavowed was one that I closely associated with him and his work. I was confident that I did not mishear his denial. He made the claim more than once. Hee Sun heard him say it too. I was confused because I was quite confident in my understanding of his work. I had recently read works authored by him that made the claim that he was now saying he never made. I was worried because I credit that claim to him in my work. I did so earlier in this book. I routinely cite him (as do others) as a leading advocate of that position. Could I have been mis-citing him? That would be awful.

I felt like one of the subjects in the Asch conformity experiment.[3] I knew which line actually matched the standard, but here was someone saying something that seemed objectively false. I wondered, Did I mishear? No, I didn't think so. Had I previously misread? Maybe, but I didn't think so. How very odd. What was going on?

When I got back to my hotel room, I fired up my laptop. I pulled up an article authored by this guy and quickly found the quote I thought I had remembered reading. I was not mistaken. There was the claim in print, as clear as day. I reread it carefully to be sure, and made sure I was taking it in context. The earlier denial was objectively false, just as I had thought when I heard it.

Had we the audience attending the talk just been lied to? Why would someone lie about something so easily fact-checked? Stranger still, this guy continues to make the same original claim in print. His disavowal apparently didn't last long. Very odd indeed.

Before moving on, here is a little fantasy of mine, an imagined interaction existing only in my head until now. I ask this guy, "Did I hear you correctly say blah-blah-blah?" I see if he commits to saying it. If he does, I pull out highlighted text and confront him with his own quote and ask for an explanation. I never did this because it would be hugely face-threatening. Even when I know I am being lied to, I typically don't call the liars out unless I have a good reason. Why be a jerk? But if that interaction had occurred, it likely would have been informative in ways very relevant to the content of this chapter.

Simply knowing that a statement is false is not sufficient to conclude that the statement is a lie. Maybe it was an honest mistake, a misunderstanding, a delusion, or just plain bullshit.[4] Later in the chapter, I'll make the case for a four-step inferential process in evidence-based lie detection that goes well beyond just knowing ground truth. Lie or not, however, the statement certainly would have misled anyone who accepted its literal meaning. But ascertaining whether it is a lie or not, or deceptive or not, isn't where I am going with all this. The point I want to make here with this strange story is how very different this experience was from the task faced by research subjects in the typical deception detection lab experiment yielding slightly-better-than-chance accuracy.

I'm listening to an academic talk. The thought that a speaker might be lying usually does not enter my consciousness in professional research presentations. There is no researcher there asking me to make a truth–lie assessment. What kicks me out of my truth-default is that something is said that contradicts my prior knowledge. Prior knowledge is of little relevance in most lab experiments. So, what do I then do once I am wary? I after-the-fact fact-check the suspicious statement. There is no need for me to judge the statement right away. In contrast, there is no opportunity to fact-check suspected lies in the lab, and truth–lie judgments must be made on the spot. Further, cues and demeanor played no role in my story. In the lab, that's all subjects have to go on. I did not seek to question the guy, but I could have had I been so inclined. I had the opportunity. I don't know how that would have played out, but that sort of thing isn't even an option in most lab experiments.

My odd-occurrence-at-the-psychology-conference story sets up my next story, which occurred more than a decade earlier. Back in chapter 12 when introducing the veracity effect and base-rates, I mentioned that the chapter could have been titled "How Hee Sun Park Changed Deception Research, Part One." Well, here is how Hee Sun Park changed deception research, Part Two. If I had to pick one, I'd say this is even more of a game changer than her veracity effect or base-rate ideas. This is what first put me on the path to eventually breaking the accuracy ceiling.

TDT STUDY THIRTY-SEVEN: HOW PEOPLE REALLY DETECT LIES

The idea for TDT study thirty-seven occurred to Hee Sun Park[5] about the same time that she came up with the Park–Levine Probability Model. She was a doctoral student at the time, maybe halfway through her program of study. One day she told me her latest study idea. She knew it was a little outside the box. She anticipated my usual initial skepticism. Unbeknownst to me, she had already collected pretest data demonstrating her point. That way she could skip the extensive explanation and persuasion and shut me up with some hard evidence. That has been known to work on me.

She made the point to me that I just made with the conference story. She told me, lab experiments have people watch others and make real-time judgments based only on at-the-time observed behaviors (i.e., cues and demeanor). This, she said, bears little resemblance to how people really detect lies outside the lab in real life. She said she could prove it.

For initial evidence, she gave one hundred students at UCSB a short, open-ended survey. She asked them to describe a recent time that they had discovered being lied to. How had they found out? Try this yourself. When was the last time someone lied to you? How did you find out that the lie was a lie? Ask someone else. See what they say.

Lots of prior research (covered in chapter 2) had asked subjects how they could tell when someone was lying to them. Answers usually involved nonverbal cues like gaze aversion. Hee Sun asked the question just a little differently than the prior research. Instead of asking hypothetically or in terms of generalities, she ask for a specific recollection of an instance where the subject had detected a real lie. This subtle difference in the way the question was asked yielded huge differences in the sorts of answers obtained.

Reading the accounts in Hee Sun's pretest data, two things immediately popped out. There was no need for statistics or formal analysis. First, many if not most of the recalled lies were discovered well after the fact. Second, at-the-time behavioral displays (cues and demeanor) had little to do with it. Instead, most of the discovered lies were revealed either through comparing what was said to some external evidence or because the liar later told the truth, revealing the lie for what it was. The recalled lie detection stories were much more similar to my odd convention story than to the task presented in deception detection experiments.

Hee Sun explained to me that it was no wonder people perform poorly at lie detection experiments: that's not how people really detect lies. This became the title of our eventual article "How People Really Detect Lies" (or the "How Lies" study, for short). Typical deception detection experiments are the creation of cue theorists and make good sense from within that perspective. Researchers have been imposing their view of lie detection on subjects without ever considering how people typically discover lies outside the lab.

Hee Sun's pretest was effective in persuading me that her idea was worth pursuing. But her initial data collection was more of a proof-of-concept thing than the stuff of an A-level peer-reviewed journal article. Graduate students can use all the first-authored articles in A-level peer-reviewed journals they can get. It was one heck of an idea that had the potential to turn lie detection research on its head. So I enlisted Steve McCornack and Kelly Morrison and my graduate student at the time, Merissa Ferrara, and together with Hee Sun, we set out to redo Hee Sun's little study in a way that would get her idea into a top-flight journal.

We used Hee Sun's pretest data to create a coding system that we could then apply to new data. We worked to refine Hee Sun's survey questions. Then we administered the refined survey to 202 MSU students. We trained two coders and gave them the data to sort. The data came back just as Hee Sun had predicted.

There was much more nuance to the coding and the results than is needed here. The short version can be summarized in four bullet points.

- At the time verbal and nonverbal behaviors were listed as the sole basis for lie detection only 2% of the time.

- Only 15% of the lies were detected immediately. A majority of lies were uncovered a week or more later.
- Over 80% of detected lies involved some sort of external evidence (information from informants, physical evidence, or prior factual knowledge).
- In more than one-third of the detected lies, the liar confessed to telling the lie. In about 14% of instances, a confession was the only thing that revealed the lie.

These results were absolutely stunning. Literally hundreds of prior experiments were devoted exclusively to a lie detection method that is used only 2% of the time. Sweeping claims about poor lie detection seem to be based on a very thin slice of the lie detection pie.

Our findings have now been replicated twice. Jaume Masip recently replicated the How Lies study in Spain with police officers and civilians.[6] As with the research reviewed in chapter 2, they found that when asked about beliefs, both officers and civilians in Spain believed in the utility of behavior cues in spotting lies. But when asked to recall a successfully detected lie, evidence ruled the day, just as it had in our results.

The second replication is an unpublished study Hee Sun did with her student Austin Lee using data collected in Korea. Confessions were less common in the Korean data, but otherwise results were pretty similar. Fewer than 6% of the lies were detected on the sole basis of cues or demeanor. More than half of the lies were detected using only evidence. Again, the vast majority of lies were detected after the fact.

Hee Sun's idea and TDT study thirty-seven form the How People Really Detect Lies module in TDT.

How People Really Detect Lies—Outside the deception lab, in everyday life, most lies are detected after the fact based on either confessions or the discovery of some evidence showing that what was said was false. Few lies are detected in real time based only on the passive observation of sender nonverbal behavior.

Study thirty-seven as well as the Spanish and Korean replications also provide evidence for TDT propositions ten and twelve. There will be more evidence for proposition twelve as this chapter progresses.

TDT Proposition Ten. Triggers and deception judgments need not occur at the time of the deception. Many deceptions are suspected and detected well after the fact.

TDT Proposition Twelve. Deception is most accurately detected through either (a) subsequent confession by the deceiver or (b) comparison of the contextualized communication content to some external evidence or preexisting knowledge.

CONTENT VS. CUES

If cues are not very useful in lie detection, then perhaps there are better alternatives. Hee Sun's idea about how people really detect lies got me started down a line of thinking that would eventually lead me to break out of slightly-better-than-chance accuracy and produce some much improved accuracy findings. Central to the evolution in my thinking is a distinction between cues and content. By *communication content* I mean the substance of what is said. Communication content is contrasted with cues and demeanor, which involve how something is said and how a person is behaving when they say something. My key insight is that if you want to know if someone is honest or not, your best bet is to listen carefully and critically to what is said (communication content) and don't get distracted or unduly influenced by cues and demeanor. As shown in the last chapter, reliance on cues and demeanor pushes accuracy down toward chance. So, don't go there. On this, I stake out a position almost opposite to Ekman's. Ekman argues that "one reason why most people do so poorly in judging deceit is that they rely too much upon what people say and ignore the discrepancies between the expressive behaviors and what is said."[7] I say people rely too little on what is said and rely too much on expressive behaviors.

UNPACKING COMMUNICATION CONTENT: CORRESPONDENCE AND COHERENCE INFORMATION

Pete Blair, Torsten Reimer, and I wrote a paper focusing on two classic ways communication content might be used to assess truth.[8] We call these correspondence and coherence, and together they form a TDT module by that name.

Correspondence refers to the extent to which what is said (communication content) matches (i.e., corresponds with) some known facts and evidence (i.e., known ground truth). My previous conference example where I fact-checked a claim is an example of using correspondence information. Statements that check out and align with the facts merit belief and acceptance. Statements that fail to correspond with what is known are considered to be objectively false.

Correspondence is basically an evidence-based lie detection. It is much like empirical science. True statements are data consistent. That which does not correspond with the data is deemed false and rejected.

Coherence refers to logical consistency. Another way we could use communication content to detect lies is to listen for contradictions and inconsistencies. Logically, we know that both A and not-A cannot both be true at the same time. The idea is that honest messages do not contradict other honest messages. When people change their stories or make logically inconsistent claims, perhaps they are lying, or at the very least they should not be trusted or believed.

Two European psychologists, Pär Anders Granhag and Leif Strömwall, did a series of intriguing experiments a number of years ago exploring logical consistency as an indicator of deception.[9] They found little evidence that liars are less consistent in their stories than honest people. There are even some cases where liars are actually more consistent. The clear conclusion from their research is that coherence information is not especially useful as a lie detection strategy.

My opinion is that coherence is best used along the lines of what Ekman calls a "hot spot." If a person contradicts an earlier statement, make note, but don't jump to a "gotcha, you're lying" conclusion. Honest people are often not completely coherent in what they say. Everyday talk just doesn't meet the standards of sound logic.

> **Correspondence and Coherence**—Correspondence and coherence are two types of consistency information that may be used in deception detection. Correspondence has to do with comparing what is said to known facts and evidence. It is fact-checking. Coherence involves the logical consistency of communication. Generally speaking, correspondence is more useful than coherence in deception detection.

EVIDENCE-BASED LIE DETECTION

In my opinion, an evidence-based lie approach is the most preferred method of lie detection. Let's be clear, though. It's not perfect. Sometimes evidence gets tainted or biased. Sometimes evidence is just incomplete. Sometimes alternative explanations exist but aren't apparent. Evidence isn't perfect and inferences based on evidence aren't either. But if statements can be fact-checked, fact-checking is the best bet for discovering the truth and assessing honesty. Further, in real-life lie detection, the concern usually isn't merely the recognition of a deceptive attempt. The goal is usually knowing the truth of the matter. Evidence is our best bet for getting to the truth behind deception.

I have encountered much resistance to my view that evidence-based lie detection is preferable to cue-based approaches, especially from psychologists. Some of this is probably due to stubborn adherence to entrenched ways of thinking along the lines of cue theories. I also think sometimes that evidence-based lie detection is dismissed as obvious and therefore uninteresting. There is no fascinating counterintuitive psychology to it. Evidence-based lie detection is the stuff of Sherlock Holmes, not Sigmund Freud. I think some of the resistance also reflects a wish for a lazy shortcut. Doing the detective work to properly fact-check is effortful and time consuming. It would be nice to just read body language or something. I have heard it said that we need nonverbal lie detection because there are times when evidence is unavailable. This is partly true. Relevant evidence is not always obtainable. Even then, however, I still think communication content is more useful than cues. And just because there are times when evidence cannot be used does not justify failing to use evidence when it could be used.

Earlier I said that knowing a statement is false does not mean it is deceptive. Maybe the false statement was an honest mistake. Maybe it was delusional. Maybe it's just bullshit. People often don't say what they mean but are still understood. How can we address the false-does-not-equal-deception-and-vice-versa problem with an evidence-based approach to lie detection? I propose the following four conditions as the inferential process in an evidence-based approach to lie detection.

1. Does the message in question lack correspondence with the evidence? That is, does the message run afoul of the ground truth as suggested by the evidence?
2. Is the message likely to mislead reasonable members of the language community?
3. Can it be reasonably inferred that the sender knows that the message is false, knows the message is misleading, or at least should know that it is false and misleading?
4. Is the truth problematic in some way for the sender, and is the misleading nature of the message functional for the sender? That is, does the message, by virtue of its misleading nature, help to negate a problematic truth for the sender and further the sender's communicative goals?

The first question deals with the truth or falsity of the message. That is the first step in ascertaining ground truth. Next, we want to know if what was said is misleading to listeners. This rules out transparently false statements that fool no one. Third, we consider the likelihood that the sender actually knew that the message was false and/or was misleading. Here we try to rule out an honest mistake, delusion, or ignorance. Finally, we consider motive. We know from chapter 10 that people deceive for a reason. We apply the evidence and critical thinking to all four steps. If the evidence is sound, and if the answer to all four questions is "yes," then it is a good bet the message was deception.

Applying these criteria to the odd statement at the conference show why I am reluctant to infer deception. The statement was clearly false. It would certainly fool many if not most listeners. The speaker should know what is in his own published work. But I don't see anything to be gained by the statement. The false statement does not seem to solve a problem for the speaker. So, the statement was false, it was misleading, but its status as deceptive is still murky.

PLAUSIBILITY, SITUATIONAL FAMILIARITY, AND CONTENT IN CONTEXT

Even in situations where sound evidence is lacking and ground truth is unknown, attention to content allows for the assessment of plausibility. That is, even when we don't have direct evidence upon which to objectively and confidently ascertain ground truth, in most communication situations we have some knowledge about what is typical and usual. We can also project motive. Having an understanding of the context in which the communication is taking place lets us meaningfully evaluate the content of what is said in light of sender motivation and typicality.

TDT EXPERIMENT THIRTY-EIGHT: A FIRST PEEK AT SITUATIONAL FAMILIARITY

This is an experiment I did with Steve McCornack in the early 1990s before I ever met Hee Sun Park or Pete Blair.[10] I was a visiting instructor at Indiana University, and Steve was a young assistant professor at MSU at the time. It took us ten years to publish the results, but that is a story for elsewhere.[11] It took me twenty years to see the real value of the findings. It is only when looking back at the results of experiment thirty-eight knowing what I know now that I realize what I should have seen all along. Having some context matters a lot.

Experiment thirty-eight had 136 judges view videotaped interviews of four senders discussing their opinions on currently controversial issues on campus. Some of the issues were local (e.g., current issues at MSU, where the judges were also students), and some issues were hot topics at a different, out-of-state university (Indiana U.). The senders lied on some issues, giving opinions opposite to their own while providing honest opinions on other issues. Each sender was asked a follow-up probing question about each expressed opinion, but the probing questions (but not the answers) were edited out of half the messages. In sum, judges rated each of several taped interviews as honest or deceptive where the interviewees expressed true or false opinions about issues at a familiar or an unfamiliar campus, and where probing follow-up questions were heard or were not heard.

Hearing the probing questions or not made little difference in accuracy (probes 57%, no-probes 59%), and overall accuracy was 58%. Subjects, however, were much better ascertaining the true opinions of senders on issues at their own school (69%) than on the other-school issues (48%). It seems having some knowledge about what the senders were talking about provided a big boost to accuracy.[12] Our situational familiarity findings have subsequently been independently replicated in a series of studies by Marc-Andre Reinhard and Sigi Sporer.[13]

At the time, Steve and I were much more interested in probing than topic familiarity. We had included familiarity as a proxy for cognitive processing, not as an important factor in its own right. But the 69% accuracy for familiar topics stayed in the back of our heads. It was not until I met Pete Blair and we did our content-in-context experiments (TDT experiments thirty-nine through forty-four) that I realized the full implications.

Now is a good time to introduce Pete Blair. Pete and I met at Michigan State University when he was a PhD student studying criminal justice. Before graduate school Pete had worked for John Reid and Associates[14] as both a trainer and an investigator. He was interested in deception detection, and when he learned about me, he made an appointment and we met. Pete ended up taking statistics and persuasion classes in communication from my mentor Frank Boster. He worked on some of Judee Burgoon's grants. He became friends with many of the communication graduate students at the time. And we got to know each other.

Pete brought a real-world, applied flavor to my research, which previously had been decidedly more academically oriented. Pete thought that Hee Sun's How Lies study (TDT experiment thirty-seven) was awesome. He was also a big fan of my cheating experiments. We began to collaborate on research, mostly after he graduated and became a professor. Over time he has become one of my most valued coauthors. These days, Pete researches active-shooter situations.

Our first project together was the projected-motive experiments described in chapter 10 (see TDT experiments ten, eleven, and twelve). Shortly thereafter, we began working on two ideas that we called content in context and diagnostic utility questioning, each of which became modules in TDT. Content in context is covered first.

Content in Context—Understanding communication requires listening to what is said and taking that in context. Knowing about the context in which the communication occurs can help detect lies.

Content in context is nearly synonymous with situational familiarity. They are different labels for very similar ideas. These days, I prefer "content in context" because I want to emphasize the role of communication content and taking what is said in context. Of course, taking what is said in context requires being familiar with a situation.

TDT EXPERIMENTS THIRTY-NINE THROUGH FORTY-FOUR: CONTENT IN CONTEXT

We are all familiar with the idea of taking a statement out of context. When we only hear words and lack an understanding of the context in which the words were said, some of the meaning gets lost or misunderstood. Taking statements in context minimizes lost meanings and reduces misinterpretation. The basic idea here is that the more statements can be understood in context, the more potentially valuable the communication content becomes in making sense of something that is said. On the flip side, stripping context reduces the utility of content.

Author Edward T. Hall popularized the idea of high- and low-context communication.[15] In low-context communication, statements have a literal meaning and can be understood by anyone who knows the language. If you know what the words mean, you can understand what is said. If I say, "I am going to the gym in a half hour to get some exercise," you know what I mean. High-context communication, in contrast, requires understanding of the context, human relationships, situation, culture, and the like in which the communication is embedded. In other words, high-context communication requires background knowledge to understand what is meant. Hearing or reading just the words is not enough. If Hee Sun yells at me, "Tim, Ami is barking at me," you can probably guess that Ami is a dog. Knowing that this means that she wants me to take Ami out requires more context. When I teach this idea, I use the example of the TV show *South Park*. Getting the humor in *South Park* requires knowing current American pop culture. The humor involved in parody and satire requires an understanding of what is being parodied in order to "get it." That is the context. Hall's thesis was that part of what makes intercultural communication so difficult is that culture provides a context, and when communicating with people from different cultures, we often lack context.

Pete and I thought that accurate lie detection is often a high-context activity. Typical lie detection experiments deny judges the context to understand a sender's statements. This makes content less useful. But, we thought, outside the lab much communication happens in situations where listeners have context. When we are talking to a person we know, for example, we have relational history with that person. In our professional lives, we have occupational experience. As members of a culture, we know the norms and the culture. A little bit of contextual understanding, we thought, might go a long way in improving the usefulness of communication content in lie detection.

We designed a series of six experiments to test our hypothesis that a little context information could dramatically improve accuracy.[16] TDT experiments thirty-nine through forty-four all involved the same basic comparison. Subjects were randomly assigned to a control group or a little-bit-of-context-provided group. In the control condition in each experiment, subjects did a typical deception detection task and were scored for accuracy. In the context-added group, subjects were given a little bit of useful background (context) information.

TDT experiments thirty-nine through forty-four differed from one another in two ways. Experiments thirty-nine, forty, and forty-one used students as judges, while experiments forty-two, forty-three, and forty-four used experienced government agents-interrogators. The experiments also involved one of three different lie detection tasks. Experiments thirty-nine and forty-two involved the cheating-experiment interviews from my NSF cheating tapes. Experiments forty and forty-three involved suspects in a mock crime Pete staged at the Texas State University library. The mock-crime senders all confessed, some falsely, some honestly. Finally, experiments forty-one and forty-four involved interviews of real suspects (some guilty, some innocent) in a bank embezzlement case. In this way, experiments thirty-nine through forty-four involved all of the six possible combinations of judges and tasks. We wanted to show that our point about content in context was robust and not specific to a particular lie detection task or set of judges.

The added contextual information, by necessity, varied from task to task. For the cheating interviews, the useful contextual information was that the cheating questions were difficult and that few people knew more than one or two answers without cheating. That is, interviewees who got more questions correct winning more money were likely to be cheaters. In the mock-crime task, the context information included basic crime data such as a description

TABLE 14.1. RESULTS OF TDT CONTENT-IN-CONTEXT EXPERIMENTS
THIRTY-NINE THROUGH FORTY-FOUR

Experiment	Judges	Task	Accuracy in Control Group	Accuracy when Context Provided
39	students	cheating	61%	77%
40	students	mock crime	33%	80%
41	students	real crime	42%	69%
42	experts	cheating	69%	72%
43	experts	mock crime	34%	81%
44	experts	real crime	68%	75%
Average across experiments 39–44			51%	76%

of the victim, the location of the crime, a list of what was stolen, and information about the weapon used. In the real crime task, the context information included information about the crime that the actual investigators had before the suspects were interviewed.

The results for our six content-in-context experiments are provided in table 14.1. As you can see, performance in the control group varied quite a bit from task to task and from students to expert agents. The range in the controls was from 33% to 69%. Absent context, everyone did poorly on the mock-crime false-confession task (students = 33%, experts = 34%). Everyone did pretty well on the cheating interviews (students = 61%, experts = 69%). The experts did much better on the real crime interviews (68%) than the students (42%).

With the addition of a little bit of context information, however, accuracy was both more uniform and higher. With context provided, accuracy ranged from a low of 69% up to 81%. Averaging across the six experiments, accuracy was 51% in the controls compared to 76% with context. That's a 25% bump![17] Across the three different tasks and the two groups of judges, judges who had some context in which to put the potentially deceptive statements consistently performed better than the slightly-better-than-chance norm in deception detection experiments.

The content in context experiments together with the experiments under the label situation familiarity provide good scientific evidence for two important and robust conclusions. First, having some background knowledge to situate or contextualize what is said leads to detection accuracy rates substantially above the slightly-better-than-chance rate typical of the deception detection lit-

erature. Second, experiments involving lie detection tasks in which communication is evaluated in a way that deprives judges of content in context artificially depress accuracy. Slightly-better-than-chance accuracy findings apply to
experimentally decontextualized communication.

CONTEXT AND MOTIVES

One of the most important aspects of context relates to deception motives.
TDT experiments six, seven, and eight (chapter 10) showed that lying and deception are not random acts. Lies and deception happen when the truth poses
a problem for a communicator. When the truth works in our favor, unless we
are pathological, we are 100% likely to be honest. Not everyone lies when the
truth is problematic, but that is when lies occur. It follows that if we have a
feel for the likelihood of a deception motive, we should be able to improve our
odds substantially over just fifty-fifty or 54%.

Here is an example of the power of context from my cheating experiments.
Across all the versions, we have more than five hundred taped interviews.
Let's round down to an even five hundred, for simplicity. The rates of cheating, lying, and confessions vary from version to version, but saying that about
one-third of subjects cheat, while two-thirds don't cheat, is probably close to
the mark. Of those who do cheat, approximately one-third confess (although
this depends a lot on how they are questioned; rates vary from 20% to 100%).
So, of the 500, let's say 335 don't cheat and honestly deny cheating. Of the 165
who do cheat, 110 lie while 55 honestly confess. We never had a false confession in any version of the cheating experiment. Combining honest denials and
honest confessions, 390 (78%) of interviews are honest, and 110 (22%) are lies.

If we have no context at all, and we just make unbiased guesses, we would
expect 50% accuracy. If we instead base our predictions on the research reviewed in chapter 3, then we would expect a little better than that, about 54%.
These provide points of comparison.

What if we add a little context information? For the first bit of context, let's
say we know, based on a prior cheating experiment, that the majority of subjects in the cheating experiments don't cheat and lie. That is, we know the approximate base-rates. What if we just guess honest 75% of the time? We would
expect to get 75% of the 390 honest senders right (that's 293/390) and 25%
of the 110 lies right (28/110).[18] That gives us 321 correct out of 500, which
is 64%! We have improved fourteen points on chance and ten points on the
meta-analytic average with a bit of informed guessing.

Now let's add in motive. Confessors have no reason to lie, so we believe them
100%. Based on base-rates, we are just going to guess on the denials (as before,

75% honest). For the 335 non-cheating denials, we expect to be right 75% of the time (251/335). For the 110 lying cheaters, we are correct only 25% of the time (28/110). We get all 55 confessions right (55/55). This gives us 334/500, which is 67% right. Not a big improvement, but our informed guesses are now a little better. Further, if we could improve our questioning to increase the honest confession rate, then the bump for motive would be bigger.

Now let's add one final important bit of context. We know the trivia questions are really hard. Most (but not all) noncheaters know only one or two questions. Most (but not all) cheaters get three or more questions right. We adopt a decision rule where a trivia game score of 20% or less is an honest denial, while a score of 30% or more lies. In the cheating experiments, this decision rule produces a correct assessment about 80% of the time. If we use that on the 445 senders who deny cheating, we would expect to get 356/445 correct. Then we add in the 55/55 correctly judged confessions. Now we get 411/500, which is 82%! Not bad for informed guessing.

In the preceding example from the cheating experiments, contextual information regarding base-rates and task difficulty proved relatively more useful than projecting motive. But consider an example that happened just yesterday in my role as a department chair. A professor in my department witnessed two students cheating on an exam, and all three ended up in my office telling their sides of the story. The professor said she was 100% confident that the students were cheating. According to the professor, a book was open on one student's lap while the test was in progress, and the two students were communicating. The students denied cheating, the existence of the open book, etc. Obviously, the professor's account and the students' statements cannot both be true. The question is, are the students lying, is the professor lying, or might there have been a misunderstanding?

My opinion is that it is very unlikely that the professor was lying. This has nothing to do with cues or demeanor. Instead, the professor has nothing to gain from a false accusation. If the students were in fact cheating, the truth works against the interests of the professor. The situation was not pleasant. The easy way out would have been to give the students a warning and leave it at that. Further, this is an experienced professor who is well liked and widely respected by students. In my professional experience, malicious false accusations of student cheating by professors are exceeding rare. When they do happen, the professor is generally a known jerk or crackpot, not a widely liked, popular professor.

Misunderstandings are probably more common, but still unusual. In ambiguous cheating situations, experienced professors usually will express suspicion, not confidence and certainty. Students will often initially deny cheating but often honestly confess cheating under questioning. However, persistent, tearful, sincere-appearing denials are not unusual. Confessions are more likely when there is hard evidence, such as in plagiarism cases. In this situation there was no hard evidence (at least none that the students knew about). I know all this, having been a professor for twenty-five years. I therefore have a pretty good idea about the relative odds of various scenarios.

I think it is possible that there might have been an honest misunderstanding (i.e., the professor misperceived), but I think it was much more likely that the students were cheating and just denied it. I'm not 100% sure about my assessment, but my informed estimation is that if the truth were known for sure, I have a much better than 54% chance of being correct in my assessment. Maybe the probability that I am correct is in the 85% to 95% range?

None of this matters in deception detection experiments with instructed lies and random assignment to truth and lie conditions. The way lie detection is usually researched, lying is literally random, and motive is irrelevant. But, if TDT is right, lying is not random outside the lab. Motives predict dishonest behavior, and understanding the situation in which communication occurs allows us to project motive and the potential for deceptive communication. Projecting motive can improve our odds considerably.

ACTIVE QUESTIONING AND DIAGNOSTIC UTILITY

Besides evidence and content in context, a third factor in improved lie detection is diagnostic questioning. Two relevant modules in TDT are Question Effects and Diagnostic Utility.

> **Question Effects:** Question effects involves asking the right questions to yield diagnostically useful information that improves deception detection accuracy.
>
> **Diagnostic Utility:** Some aspects of communication are more useful than others in detecting deception, and some aspects of communication can be misleading. Diagnostic utility involves prompting and using useful information while avoiding useless and misleading behaviors.

ACTIVE QUESTIONING DOESN'T ALWAYS HELP

I want to be clear. Merely asking questions of a sender makes little difference. It is not merely that questions are asked that is important, but what questions are asked and how they are asked. Further, there is no one, ideal way to question a potential liar. The diagnostic utility of various questioning strategies is highly contextual. Active questioning can be very helpful. Before we move to the evidence that active questioning can improve accuracy, however, I will document my claim that questioning does not necessarily improve detection accuracy. Neither mere interactivity nor the tone of questioning seems to matter much for accuracy.

As we have seen, meta-analysis[19] reports little impact for mere interactivity on deception detection accuracy findings. In the meta-analysis, there were eighty-five experiments involving no interaction at all—just judges evaluating sender statements. Average accuracy in these no-interaction experiments was 53%. There were 189 experiments in which passive observers viewed an interaction between an interviewer and an interviewee. Average accuracy in these observed-interaction studies was 54%. There were also eighteen experiments involving direct interaction between a sender and a judge who questioned the sender. Average accuracy in these interactive questioning experiments was 52%. Clearly, slightly-better-than-chance prevails regardless of mere interactivity.[20] Mere question asking or passive observation of questioned senders has little impact on deception detection accuracy. We get the same old results regardless.

As was briefly mentioned, in the early 1990s Steve McCornack and I were interested in a finding that came to be known as the *probing effect*. The probing effect refers to the empirical finding that probing (questioning) a sender does not impact accuracy but does impact believability. Probed senders are believed at higher rates than senders who are not questioned. As research on the probing effect progressed, it became clear that the probing effect was a small but robust effect that held for honest and deceptive senders, active questioners and passive observers, friends and strangers, and whether or not the judges were primed to be suspicious.[21] The point here is the probing effect applied to perceived honesty, not accuracy, and it provides more evidence that mere interaction matters little for improving lie detection.

In our probing effect experiments, Steve and I also found that tone of questioning mattered little.[22] By "tone," I mean whether the questions are supportive, implying acceptance, or accusatory, expressing skepticism. The mere act of questioning, regardless of tone, affected truth-bias but not accuracy.[23] The supportive or skeptical tone of the questioning didn't matter for either truth-bias or accuracy. This was surprising, because if I didn't know the research findings, I would guess that harsh, accusatory questioning might make a sender look more deceptive or guilty in the eyes of third parties.

In 2007 Aldert Vrij and his colleagues revisited the issue of questioning styles and tone.[24] They compared information gathering, the behavior analysis interview (BAI), and accusatory styles.[25] There were no differences in accuracy. Accuracy was similar across conditions (52% for information gathering, 51% for BAI, and 48% for accusatory).[26]

TDT EXPERIMENT FORTY-FIVE:
A (FAILED?) QUESTIONING STYLE EXPERIMENT

In one version of the cheating experiments, my research team and I tried head-to-head experimental testing of four different question styles.[27] Questioning style should matter, right?

We ran 104 new participants through the cheating game. Postgame, based on random assignment, each sender was interviewed with one of four different sets of questions, each reflecting a different style or strategy. All the questioning started the same way, with three open-ended questions generally asking about the trivia game. In the nonaccusatory questioning, senders were asked what they did when the experimenter was out of the room. This was followed up by "Is there anything you haven't told me?" In the accusatory questioning, the interviewer said, "To get such a high score, you must have cheated, just admit it." That was followed by "Why should I believe you?" The bait question came from the BAI. For the final question, the interviewer asks, "As you know, we have already interviewed your partner. Is there any reason why (s)he would have answered the previous question differently?" It was basically a bluff. The partner was not really interviewed. In the false-evidence questioning, the interviewer said, "As you know, we have already interviewed your partner. (S)he said that you cheated. Just admit it." Again, the partner had not really been interviewed, much less incriminated the interviewee. Once all the tapes were made, we showed the tapes to a sample of 157 student judges, who made truth–lie assessments, and we also coded each interview for BQ (see chapter thirteen).

The results are in table 14.2. There were no statistically significant differences. Questioning style had little impact on accuracy, truth-bias, or sender BQ. Accuracy was high across the board, ranging from a low of 68% to a high of 72%. Truth-bias was also high. There was no evidence that accusatory questioning or false evidence lowered sender credibility.

Confession rates varied quite a bit. Only 20% of the cheaters confessed under nonaccusatory questioning. I find it surprising that even one cheater in that condition confessed. In contrast, 80% of cheaters questioned with the false-evidence ploy confessed. In a later experiment (see TDT experiment fifty-two), false evidence and the bait question together yielded 100% confessions from cheaters with an expert interrogator. So, it looks like question style and strategy might impact confession rates. But since the differences weren't significant, we just can't rule out chance in experiment forty-five.

TABLE 14.2. RESULTS OF TDT EXPERIMENT FORTY-FIVE

Variable	Accusatory	Nonaccusatory	False Evidence	Bait
Number cheating	6 of 26	5 of 26	5 of 26	6 of 26
Number confessing	3 of 6	1 of 5	4 of 5	3 of 6
Percentage of cheaters confessing	50	20	80	50
False confessions	0	0	0	0
Accuracy (excluding confessions)	72.2%	67.5%	70.4%	70.1%
Truth-bias (excluding confessions)	73.2%	64.2%	70.4%	71.4%
BQ score* (excluding confessions)	2.02	1.55	1.87	2.13

* BQ (believability quotient) was scored from –6 to +6 with 0 as the midpoint and positive values indicating higher believability.

Here is my thinking. We know so far that mere question asking and mere interactivity are insufficient for improved accuracy. We know that the tone questioning is not critical either. We also know, however, that sender content, when taken in context, is highly useful. Therefore, maybe the key to effective questioning is to elicit useful communication content.

MY QUEST FOR HIGHER ACCURACY
THROUGH DIAGNOSTIC QUESTIONING

We just reviewed boatloads of negative evidence showing that questioning doesn't matter much. But here's the thing about negative evidence. The failure to find effects shows only that questioning *sometimes* doesn't matter. The nuanced conclusion is that questioning does not matter much in research with certain research designs and certain aspects of questioning. The research does not show that questioning never matters. Catch the difference? When we don't find something, it's possible we are just looking in the wrong place.

Does questioning always matter? Clearly the answer is no. But let me now show you the TDT evidence that questioning *can* matter quite a bit.

Let's look back at the results of TDT experiment forty-five and table 14.2 again. The four questioning styles yield similar levels of accuracy. The standard knee-jerk decontextualized interpretation of the findings is that questioning style doesn't matter much. The findings for the four questioning styles were, after all, not significantly different.[28] But while the four styles did not differ from one another, accuracy was 72.2% overall (including confessions, 70% excluding confessions), with a 95% margin of error of plus or minus 3.4%. This is hugely better than the 54% typical finding. Maybe the correct interpretation is not that questioning makes no difference. Maybe the takeaway is that all four sets of questions made a (albeit relatively equal) big difference!

As I mentioned previously, to date, more than five hundred subjects have been run through various versions of my cheating experiments first introduced in chapter 10, TDT experiment eight. Over time my team changed up the scripts used by the interviewers. Experiment eight was actually the second version. Experiment forty-five was the third version. In all, there have been six versions to date.

Judee Burgoon and I wrote the first two question sets.[29] In the third and subsequent versions, Pete Blair and I tried with each successive version to improve the interview questions in a way that would yield higher accuracy. As we better understood lie detection in the context of the cheating game, we were able to come up with better questions that solicited answers containing more useful content.

The evolution of the questioning scripts is provided in table 14.3. The wording and order of questions are provided along with the TDT experiments that used the materials produced in each version. Table 14.4 lists accuracy results from the various TDT experiments involving the different versions of the cheating interviews. Tables 14.3 and 14.4 list some experiments we have yet to cover. Worry not. We will get there soon.

Looking at table 14.4, here is what we see. The most noticeable thing is how accuracy improved progressively over the versions. With the one exception of experiment forty-nine, students viewing the first set of interviews performed pretty much as expected from the literature. Accuracies of 51%, 53%, 54%, and 55% were obtained. However, various samples of experts did really poorly on these interviews (29%, 31%, 42%). Something is going on that makes experts worse than chance. More on this in a bit.

Accuracy is quite a bit better when using interviews from the second set. Experiments using the second set of interviews yield accuracy ranging from 56% to 72%, with most of the studies finding accuracy of 60-something percent. Experts no longer do worse and might even do slightly better. It is clear that the second set of findings is systematically better than either the TDT experiments using the first set of interviews or the hundreds of non-TDT studies constituting the meta-analyses. By the third time around, accuracy was up to 72%. This was just one experiment, but it was at the upper limit of what was possible given prior research. I was thinking we were on to something. More data were needed to be sure.

TABLE 14.3. QUESTION SETS IN THE CHEATING EXPERIMENTS*

First Question Set (Used in TDT Experiments 10–12, 14, 18, and 49–51)

1. Did you find the trivia questions difficult?

2. Was teamwork much of a factor? If so, please explain.

3. In looking at your score, you did better than other groups. Does this surprise you?

4. How would you explain your success?

5. Did cheating occur when I left the room?

6. Why should I believe you?

Second Question Set (Used in TDT Experiments 8, 22–23, 26–27, 29–35, 39, 42, and 49–51)

1. How much experience have you had working in teams?

2. Have you played trivia games before?

3. How often do you play? [follow-up] Why do you/ don't you play them much?

4. In the current game, did you find the questions difficult? [follow-up] If you were going to scale it on a scale of 1 to 10, what would you say they were in terms of difficulty?

5. Was teamwork much of a factor in your performance?

6. What would you say if I told you that you did better than other groups?

7. How would you explain your performance?

8. Did you cheat when the experimenter left the room?

9. Are you telling me the truth?

10. What would your partner say if I asked them the same question?

Fourth Question Set (Used in TDT Experiments 46–51)

1. Tell me, in as much detail as you can, what happened during the trivia game.

2. How well did you do on the trivia game?

3. Which questions did you and your partner get right?

4. For the answers you got right, explain how you knew the right answer.

5. In detail, what happened when the experimenter left the room?

6. Did any cheating occur?

7. When I interview your partner, what will they say about cheating?

8. Did you and your partner discuss cheating?

9. If someone did cheat, what should happen to them?

Continued on the next page

TABLE 14.3. CONTINUED

Fifth Question Set (Used in TDT Experiments 52 and 53)

1. Tell me, in as much detail as you can, what happened in the trivia game.

2. How well did you do on the trivia game?

3. Which were the ones you got right?

4. How did you know the answers to those questions?

5. The Trivia Master told me he left the room at one point. Can you tell me what happened when the Trivia Master left the room?

6. We have some concern that cheating might have happened while the Trivia Master was out of the room because he left the answers in there. Did any cheating occur?

7. If somebody did cheat, what do you think should happen to them?

8. Under any circumstances would you cut them a break?

9. Obviously, we are going to talk to your partner. When we talk to your partner, what will they say?

[Interviewer excuses self, leaves room "to check on a few things."] [Upon Return . . .]

10. I can't blame you, because the Trivia Master left the room, and they weren't supposed to do that. They weren't supposed to do that, and they definitely weren't supposed to leave the answers. But we know you cheated. I'm not worried about the cheating part. What is important is the data. I don't want to have data in my study that is invalid. I want you to be upfront with me.

11. Are you sure about that? Your partner says you did.

12. Is he lying, or are you lying? One of you must be.

* The third iteration of the cheating experiment used four sets of questions (non-accusatory, accusatory, bait, and false-evidence). These questions were briefly described under TDT experiment forty-five. The full scripts are provided in Timothy R. Levine, Hillary C. Shulman, Christopher J. Carpenter, David C. DeAndrea, and J. Pete Blair, "The Impact of Accusatory, Non-Accusatory, Bait, and False Evidence Questioning on Deception Detection," Communication Research Reports 30, no. 2 (April 2013): 169–74. https://doi.org/10.1080/08824096.2012.76290. No scripts were used in the sixth and final version (see TDT experiments fifty-four and fifty-five).

TDT STUDIES FORTY-SIX THROUGH FORTY-EIGHT: IMPROVED ACCURACY WITH THE FOURTH QUESTION SET

Pete and I wrote the questions listed in table 14.3 under question set four.[30] The questioning starts with requesting an open-ended narrative from the interviewee. Specific questions regarding who got how many questions correct are asked to elicit content-in-context information. The next question asked how the subject knew the correct answer. The idea for this question came from my student Hillary Shulman, who played the trivia master in an ear-

TABLE 14.4. IMPROVING ACCURACY USING DIFFERENT QUESTION SETS IN THE CHEATING INTERVIEWS

Question Set	TDT Experiment	Sample	Accuracy
First	TDT experiment 10 (denials only)	students	54%
	TDT experiment 11 (denials only)	students	55%
	TDT experiment 12 (denials only)	experts	31%
	TDT experiment 14	students	53%
	TDT experiment 18 (control group)	students	51%
	TDT experiment 49	students	39%
	TDT experiment 50	experts	29%
	TDT experiment 51	experts	42%
	Average for question set one		44%
Second	TDT experiment 24	students	56%
	TDT experiment 26 (control group)	students	65%
	TDT experiment 39 (control group)	students	61%
	TDT experiment 42 (control group)	experts	69%
	TDT experiment 49	students	67%
	TDT experiment 50	experts	64%
	TDT experiment 51	experts	72%
	Average for question set two		66%
Third	TDT experiment 45	students	72%
Fourth	TDT experiment 46	students	71%
	TDT experiment 47	students	78%
	TDT experiment 48	experts	75%
	TDT experiment 49	students	72%
	TDT experiment 50	experts	73%
	TDT experiment 51	experts	78%
	Average for question set four		75%
Fifth	TDT experiment 52	experts	100%
	TDT experiment 53	students	79%
	Average for question set five		90%
Sixth	TDT experiment 54	experts	98%
	TDT experiment 55	students	94%
	Average for question set six		96%

lier version. She noticed that cheaters often spontaneously offered up explanations for how information was known. It was as if cheaters provided justifications, while people who actually knew the answers didn't seem to have that need. When asked, it is common for noncheaters not to know how they knew the answer. They often say, "I just knew it." Next, subjects were eventually asked outright if they cheated. This was followed by the bait question we had used previously. Then we asked if they had discussed cheating. Our experience was that noncheaters were more likely to admit thinking about it. Finally, we asked if cheaters should be punished. In retrospect, the final question did not seem to add much.

Armed with these questions, we ran thirty-eight new students through the cheating experiment using the new and improved questions during the interview. Of the thirty-eight, fifteen (about 40%) cheated. Of those fifteen, just over half (eight) confessed under questioning. Once again, there were no false confessions.

David Clare took the seven cheating liars and picked out seven honest noncheaters, matching as best he could on sex, race, and physical attractiveness. This gave us a set of fourteen interviews for use in experiments forty-six, forty-seven, and forty-eight. The point was to see whether we could obtain improved accuracy, and if the accuracy would replicate with different samples of judges.

The judges in study forty-six were thirty-six college students recruited from a standard subject pool. Study forty-seven was populated by twenty students enrolled in a class I was teaching on deception at the time. They had read the content-in-context research for class and had seen many previous versions of the cheating interviews. The judges in study forty-eight were forty-seven elite government agents.

The accuracies obtained by the three sets of judges were 71%, 78%, and 75% in studies forty-six, forty-seven, and forty-eight. All three were well above the usual 54% accuracy. These results were very encouraging. It seemed that questioning can matter quite a bit.

TDT EXPERIMENTS FORTY-NINE, FIFTY, AND FIFTY-ONE: HEAD-TO-HEAD COMPARISONS

The next obvious step was to compare various question sets from the different versions of the cheating experiments head-to-head.[31] I sampled two honest and two cheating liar interviews from the first, second, and fourth versions of the cheating experiments. This gave me twelve interviews, half honest, half deceptive, for use in experiments forty-nine, fifty, and fifty-one. The predictions were, of course, that accuracy would improve from set one to set two

TABLE 14.5. IMPROVING ACCURACY USING DIFFERENT QUESTION
SETS IN EXPERIMENTS FORTY-NINE, FIFTY, AND FIFTY-ONE

Question Set	TDT Experiment	Sample	Accuracy
First	TDT experiment 49	students	39%
	TDT experiment 50	experts	29%
	TDT experiment 51	experts	42%
	average for question set one		37%
Second	TDT experiment 49	students	67%
	TDT experiment 50	experts	64%
	TDT experiment 51	experts	72%
	average for question set two		68%
Fourth	TDT experiment 49	students	72%
	TDT experiment 50	experts	73%
	TDT experiment 51	experts	78%
	average for question set four		74%

and from set two to set four, and that the pattern of improvement would hold across different samples of judges.

The subjects were ninety-three students in experiment forty-nine, 207 law enforcement professionals in experiment fifty, and thirty-nine elite US Customs agents in experiment fifty-one. Experiments forty-nine and fifty used the same twelve interviews, while experiment fifty-one used different interviews culled from the same three sets.

The results are summarized in Table 14.5. Experiments forty-nine, fifty, and fifty-one replicated the accuracy findings of over 70% for question set four. The pattern of improvement over question sets is clear. The findings of studies forty-six through fifty-one lead to two firm conclusions. First, the type of questions asked can make a big difference in accuracy, and second, asking better questions provides one path to improved accuracy in detecting deception.

A BRIEF WORD ABOUT NEGATIVE UTILITY

Check out the low accuracies for the first question set in experiments forty-nine, fifty, and fifty-one. Not only are the accuracies below those obtained in any TDT experiment using any of the other question sets (see table 14.4), they are also significantly lower than both chance and the 54% meta-analysis average. What should we make of that? Should we dismiss the findings as merely aberrant, or might something important be at play?

The below-chance accuracy in the experiments involving question set one does not appear to be a fluke. Below-chance accuracy has been observed in four of the eight experiments using those tapes, and in all three experiments using those tapes in conjunction with expert judges. Below-chance accuracy, in contrast, has never been observed in any TDT experiment using any of the other question sets. In table 14.4, eighteen of eighteen experiments using cheating tapes with questions other than set one produced accuracy that is significantly greater than chance. There is something different about the tapes using the first set of questions.

One feature that separates both TDT and IDT from most other theories of deception is that these are the only two deception theories specifying a mechanism for predicting and explaining below-chance accuracy. If you think about it for a moment, below-chance accuracy is an odd thing. Truth-biased judges, weak cues, focusing on the wrong cues, and individual differences in sender demeanor all tend to push accuracy down toward chance. But these mechanisms should not create negative transparency. Below-chance accuracy requires that honest senders are seen as less honest than liars.

IDT predicts below-chance accuracy when liars but not truth tellers pick up on judge suspicion and strategically adapt their behavior to appear more honest. That does not seem to be what is going on in TDT results, because all iterations of the cheating interviews involve questioning that reveals that both honest and lying senders are under suspicion. In fact, question set one is less accusatory than some of the other question sets where accuracy does not dip below chance. Thus, inconsistent with the IDT mechanism, suspicion-implying questioning does not appear to be the culprit.

TDT's proposition thirteen specifies that poorly conceived questioning can backfire and produce below-chance accuracy.

TDT Proposition 13: Both confessions and diagnostically informative communication content can be produced by effective context-sensitive questioning of a potentially deceptive sender. Ill-conceived questioning, however, can backfire and produce below-chance accuracy.

I suspect that this is what is going on in some of the question set one interviews. Specifically, I think the final question in that set (Why should I believe you?) throws some of the honest noncheaters off. Cheaters know they cheated.

Being under suspicion comes as less of a surprise. Noncheaters, however, have little reason to anticipate skeptical questioning. To compound matters, honest senders have no real way in the cheating experiment to exonerate themselves. When asked why they should be believed, several noncheaters stumbled over the answer and ended up with a perfectly honest but very unconvincing "I don't know." Some cheaters, however, appeared to see the skeptical question coming and answered convincingly but deceptively, "Because I am an honest person." Expert judges who are attuned to demeanor, and especially demeanor shifts, get fooled. They attribute the shift in demeanor and lack of conviction to deception, not its actual cause, which was an unanticipated question that cannot be answered in a way that is both convincing and honest.[32] The upshot is that questioning can make honest people look deceptive. This makes me very skeptical of adding cognitive load through questioning or about asking unanticipated questions in general. The trick is asking questions that are hard for liars but easy for honest folk.

PERSUASION AS LIE DETECTION

TDT proposition twelve lists a subsequent confession by a deceiver as a path to improved lie detection, and TDT proposition thirteen adds that effective context-sensitive questioning can be used to facilitate honest confessions. Combined, these propositions suggest that persuasion is another path to improved lie detection. If you think you might be being lied to, you can persuade the sender to come clean, confess his or her lies, and tell the truth. The results of TDT experiment forty-five were certainly suggestive regarding the power of persuasion as a useful deception detection strategy, and the How Lies study (TDT study thirty-seven) found that liar confessions were a common method of lie detection outside the lab. However, the true power of persuasion as a lie detection method is demonstrated in the final four TDT experiments investigating expert questioning.

EXPERT QUESTIONING

If readers will recall chapter 3, it was mentioned that college students and experts typically perform about the same in deception detection experiments. These conclusions come from two different meta-analyses, both published in 2006.[33] In the first, accuracy involving students was 54%, compared to 55% for police, 51% for detectives, 55% for federal officers, and 54% for customs agents. Neither age nor education nor professional experience was correlated with accuracy. In the second meta-analysis, the average accuracy in 250 studies involving nonexperts was 53.3%, compared to 53.8% in forty-two prior studies involving expert judges. In an additional twenty experiments testing experts and nonexperts head-to-head, the difference was a tiny $d = -0.03$. Thus, both meta-analyses lead to the same conclusion: experts and students don't differ in terms of accuracy. Experts, however, are a bit less truth-biased (52% compared to 56% for nonexperts).[34]

The TDT research reviewed up to this point leads to the same conclusion. Look again at table 14.4. Students do better on question set one, but that reverses on set two, and there is not much difference on set four. In TDT experiments involving the assessment of videotaped interviews, students and experts yield similar results.

The proper inference from these data, however, is not the obvious conclusion that students and experts just aren't different. Instead, the findings show convincingly that students and experts are not much different in the type of tasks that constitute deception detection experiments. When the task involves passively watching videotapes, the evidence for little difference is compelling. But maybe this isn't how expert lie detection really works.

TDT's final module and last proposition are about how expert lie detection really works:

Expert Questioning: Expertise in deception is highly context dependent and involves knowing how to prompt diagnostically useful information rather than passively observing deception cues.

TDT Proposition Fourteen: Expertise in deception detection rests on knowing how to prompt diagnostically useful information rather than on skill in the passive observation of sender behavior.

According to TDT, what makes expert lie detection expert isn't knowing how to read cues and demeanor. Reliance on cues and demeanor pushes accuracy down toward chance for everyone, expert or not. TDT research (TDT experiments twelve, twenty-nine, fifty, and fifty-one) even shows that cues and demeanor can trip up experts, producing below-chance performance. Instead, expertise resides in knowing how to effectively question people so that honest people seem honest, and lies are revealed. Expert questioning increases sender transparency by prompting diagnostically useful answers.

If TDT is right about expert questioning, then for experts to show their expertise, several preconditions must be met. First, the experts need to either script their own questions (with the freedom to deviate from the script) or be free of a script altogether. That is, if expertise lies in knowing what questions to ask and how to ask them, then imposing researcher-scripted questions should be an artificial impediment to expertise. Second, experts must have sufficient context-situation background knowledge. This is because diagnostic questioning is, according to TDT proposition thirteen, context dependent. Third, persuasion and honest-confession solicitation needs to be a viable option. If part of lie detection expertise is the solicitation of honest confessions, then excluding confessions in the evaluation of expert performance is another artificial impediment to expertise. A fair test of expert questioning must let experts do the things that make them expert.

TDT EXPERIMENTS FIFTY-TWO THROUGH FIFTY-FIVE: SMASHING THE ACCURACY CEILING WITH EXPERT QUESTIONING

When Pete and I tried our hand at the fourth edition of the cheating interviews used in TDT experiments forty-six through forty-eight, we each got 86% (twelve out of fourteen) correct.[35] We compared notes. We thought the questioning made ten out of the fourteen interviews pretty clear-cut. It turned out that we were both right on each of those ten interviews that we thought were pretty easy. There were four, however, that we thought were difficult. As it turned out, we both got only two of the four ambiguous ones correct. The thing was, we knew those four were the questionable ones before we scored ourselves. We knew we were guessing. Because they were taped interviews, we couldn't go back and ask more questions and try to reduce the ambiguity. What if we'd had that option? Might we have done even better than 86%?

In a related experience, I was at a conference, and in attendance was an expert who had been an interviewer in an expert deception detection experiment run at a different lab by different researchers. The expert told me that he thought he could have done much better than he did. He did not think the study he had participated in adequately assessed his ability. The research design, he said, thwarted him. He was given scripted questions and told to stay on script. A few times, he said, he went off script and got the sender to confess. In such cases the researchers had scolded him, said that he wasn't following instructions, and that the data had to be tossed. He said he needed the freedom to resolve ambiguities and to persuade liars to be honest. Sticking to the script and excluding confessions meant that the results did not reflect his ability.

Pete and I put our experiences together with the expert's story of being thwarted by the researchers, and we decided to put our expert questioning ideas to the test. TDT experiment fifty-two provided initial proof of concept. We thought that if we could produce some strong preliminary evidence, we could leverage that to get the funding we would need for a larger-scale experiment. We ran thirty-three more subjects through the cheating experiment. This time Pete did the questioning. As a base script, Pete crafted the twelve questions listed in table 14.3, fifth set. However, he was free to improvise as needed. After each interview, he recorded his assessment as to who he thought cheated and who didn't.

Only four of the thirty-three participants (12%) cheated. All four honestly confessed. Even though Pete used a false-evidence ploy (he told them that their partner had said they cheated), there were no false confessions. When we tallied Pete's judgments, he got all thirty-three correct. 100%! Wow!

Both Pete and I were surprised by the results. We both thought he would do well. Based on TDT experiments forty-six through fifty-one and our content-in-context experiments, we knew we could reliably get accuracy levels in the 70s. We were pretty sure we could beat that and hit accuracy in the 80s or maybe even 90%. But, thirty-three of thirty-three exceeded our expectations. Pete, in particular, was aware that he was assigning honesty at an unusually high rate. He thought that he was probably making too many honesty judgments. The cheating base-rates in the prior versions were always higher. He wondered if he was failing to catch some cheaters. He wasn't. The base-rates were just unusual in that run, and yet he still performed to perfection.

For TDT experiment fifty-three, we showed Pete's thirty-three interviews to 136 college students. The students got 79%. Students passively viewing Pete's interviews did not do as well as Pete, but they did pretty darn well.

The most obvious limitation with TDT experiments fifty-two and fifty-three was that we had just one expert (Pete), just thirty-three interviews, and only four cheaters to catch. Going thirty-three for thirty-three is much too long a string to be a statistical fluke. Pete's performance was not just chance. But the generality of the findings was a big question. So, I put together a dream team of deception researchers (Pete Blair, Steve McCornack, Kelly Morrison, and Hee Sun Park), and we applied to the FBI for funding to replicate TDT experiments fifty-two and fifty-three with different experts.

The FBI gave us the funding, but they would not provide their own interrogators, so I used my connections and got experts from a different government agency. We flew in five experts, one at a time, for a couple days each, and gave them the mission of questioning students after the cheating game to ascertain whether cheating occurred or not, and if so, who cheated.

In the final version (to date) of the cheating experiment (TDT experiment fifty-four), the five experts collectively conducted eighty-nine unscripted interviews. At the end of each interview, we asked the experts whether they thought

cheating had occurred, and if yes, who cheated, both the subject and their partner or just the partner.[36]

Cheating happened in forty of eight-nine (45%) of the trivia games. Of
the forty instances of cheating, the partner but not the subject cheated thirteen times, and both the partner and the subject cheated twenty-seven times.
The experts obtained confessions in thirty-four of the forty (85%) sessions involving cheating. The experts correctly identified whether cheating occurred
in eighty-seven of the eighty-nine (98%) interviews. Three of the five experts
were perfect (fourteen of fourteen, sixteen of sixteen, and twenty for twenty),
while the other two had a single error each. On the more specific question of
who cheated, the experts were 96% accurate. Both additional errors involved
the expert thinking that only the partner had cheated when in fact the subject had cheated too.

For TDT experiment fifty-five, we showed a random sample of thirty-six of
the taped interviews from TDT experiment fifty-four to thirty-four students
in my deception class. The students were correct on 94% of the interviews.

There are three especially important aspects of TDT experiments fifty-one
to fifty-five to highlight. First, the expert questioning results show what is
possible but do not provide much insight into what is typical. Here is what I
mean: The point of the research was to see whether higher accuracy could be
obtained by experts if they were free of imposed scripts and where honest and
believed confessions were counted as correct judgments. The results showed
that high accuracy could be obtained. What the results do not show is whether
those high levels of accuracy extend to other experts or to other situations. The
point of the research was testing a generalization, not making a generalization.
I do not claim that experts are invariably good lie detectors, only that they can
be much better than prior research had suggested.

Second, showing the videotaped expert interviews to student samples adds
critical information regarding the causal forces at play. Specifically, however
the experts did it, what they did was make the senders more transparent. They
interviewed the senders in such a way that even untrained passive observers
could tell who was lying. This provides key evidence for the TDT claim that expertise in deception detection rests on knowing how to prompt diagnostically
useful information rather than on skill in reading sender behavior.

Third, the question arises as to what the experts did in order to increase
transparency. I have not formally analyzed the expert interviews yet, but I have
watched them several times and have noticed several things. First, there is
not just a single way to effectively question a sender. Each of the six experts
(including Pete) had their own styles. A couple were hard-nosed, serious, in-

tense, and accusatory. One guy had a style much like that of Columbo (from the 1970s TV series). One had a very friendly and disarming style.

Mostly, they started off conversationally. All tried to get a feel for the type of person they were talking to. They wanted to know the sender's major in school, how good a student he or she was, and the sender's motivation for participating in the research (just for research credit, interested in the monetary incentive, etc.). They all asked about critical information, such as the number of correct answers, who got which questions right, and how they knew the answers they did. They also asked questions about integrity and the sender's views on cheating and lying.

The experts were very good listeners and had a good memory for what had been previously said. They circled back with questions asking the same thing again. They all paid close attention to logical consistency (coherence). But when they caught an inconsistency or noticed a sender reacting to a question, they did not automatically presume guilt. Instead, they asked more focused questions, trying to figure out what was up.

Another thing they all did was try to work what might be called "themes." Themes are lines of persuasion aimed at honest confessions. For example, one common theme was that a sender who claims to be an honest person needs to admit to cheating if he or she did. They talked to the senders about how they would feel about themselves if they cheated. They provided justification for cheating, while stressing the importance of being honest at that moment. If one theme wasn't working, they shifted to another.

RESPONDING TO CRITICISM

Not long after the article version of our expert experiments was published, three psychologists authored an essay disputing our research and conclusions.[37] Vrij, Meissner, and Kassin noted that our findings were inconsistent with the old 54% findings. Rather than interpreting our results as showing evidence that improved accuracy might be possible, they concluded that our findings simply should not be believed. They argued that our methods were flawed. They even asserted that our findings were dangerous because we did not get any false confessions. They said that expert questioning like that in our study causes false confessions and that all experts lack the skill to be good lie detectors or to solicit only honest confessions. In essence, because our findings were different from what they have found in their research, our research just can't be scientific.

According to these critics, our method was invalid because the cheating experiment provided a super-easy lie detection task in which any interviewer or judge could do well. Lying convincingly about cheating, they claimed, was just too hard. That is, high accuracy occurred because of our experimental task. The task, not the experts, prevented cheaters from telling believable lies. The number of questions interviewees got correct, they argued, was too diagnostic.[38] Anyone could do as well as the experts by simply asking two scripted questions: How many did you get right? And how did you know the answers? Further, they asserted, it was easy for honest noncheaters to prove their innocence, and this prevented false confessions. Near-perfect accuracy, they said, was methodological deck-stacking, not the result of expert skill in questioning.

I do not believe that Vrij, Meissner, and Kassin's criticism is either logically sound or good-faith academic argument. Their critique seems to me to be a brazen series of straw man arguments that mischaracterize TDT research. The flaws they point out simply do not exist in our research and thus cannot possibly explain our results.

The idea that detecting lies in the cheating experiments is a simple matter and that anyone can do as well as our experts did by just asking a couple of simple questions is clearly disproven by the research presented in this chapter. Look back at table 14.4. All those findings are from the cheating experiments. If our critics were right, and lie detection in the cheating game is just an easy task, then accuracy would always be as high as it was for the experts in experiments fifty-two and fifty-four. It is not. Twenty-two (out of 22) prior TDT experiments with the cheating tapes refute Vrij, Meissner, and Kassin's assertion. Six prior TDT studies (forty-six through fifty-one) directly asked the two questions that our critics argue are sufficient. Those questions improve accuracy (nine points over the second version and three points over the third), but not enough to explain the experts' performance (which is more than twenty points higher than question set four). But maybe the most extreme disproof of the lying-was-too-hard claim is reviewed in the last chapter. In TDT experiment thirty-three, experts (from the same agency) watched scripted videotaped interviews of mismatched liars. The most experienced experts incorrectly believed the five mismatched liars more than 85% of the time. Clearly, the demeanor experiments show that convincing lies are absolutely possible in the cheating experiments.

Earlier in the chapter, I show how three bits of context information (proportion cheating, confession or denial, and number of questions right) could improve accuracy in the cheating experiments probabilistically to 82%. There are three things to keep in mind. First, using automatic decision rules and probability as I did in the examples guarantees errors in the long run. Eighty-two percent is quite good, but it means settling for being wrong 18% of the time.

Second, the 82% is a best-case scenario based on past trends applied in retrospect. The actual rates in new data will usually be at least a little different. And the more idiosyncratic the new situation, the less useful a decision rule optimized on old data. For example, in the second iteration of the cheating experiment (see TDT experiment eight), the cheating rate was 24%, and the honest confession rate was 40%. In the next version (TDT experiment forty-five), the cheating rate was 21%, and the confession rate was 50%. In the expert studies, however, the rates were different. In TDT experiment fifty-two, the cheating rate was unusually low, at 12% with 100% honest confessions, while in TDT experiment fifty-four the cheating rate was unusually high, at 45% with an 85% confession rate. We know these rates in hindsight, but experts could not know what the rates would turn out to be. Third, even if the rates did hold perfectly to form, simple decision rules still can't explain the experts' performance, because they were statistically better than 82%.

Our critics' claim that false confessions did not happen because noncheaters could prove their innocence is also false. The question set used in the first-run cheating experiment ended with "Why should I believe you?" Our critics contend that this was an easy question for honest senders. That was not the case. In fact, detection experiments with that question set all found poor accuracy (TDT experiments ten, eleven, twelve, fourteen, eighteen, forty-nine, fifty, and fifty-one). Further, two TDT experiments (forty-five and fifty-two) used a false-evidence ploy on honest interviewees. There were no false confessions in those experiments either. The premises of the critics' arguments are just false.

Earlier in this chapter, I suggested that fact-checking is the best way to detect lies and falsehoods. I don't know why the editor and peer reviewers at *Psychology, Crime, & Law* did not fact-check Vrij, Meissner, and Kassin's essay before publication. The premises of their arguments can easily be fact-checked (just as I did the previous paragraphs). Using the correspondence method, we know their claims to be false. Their assertions do not pass fact-checking. Applying the criteria for moving from false to deception listed earlier, we might ask whether their essay would mislead reasonable readers who were not familiar with the TDT program of research. Did Vrij, Meissner, and Kassin know their claims were false? For example, we could see if they cited the work disproving their claims in the past. Or should they have known? For example, if they read the work they were criticizing, they might be expected to have known about the false-evidence question being included. Did our finding create a problematic truth for them, and did their critique serve a purpose by its falsity? Defending TDT experiments fifty-one through fifty-five provides a clear example of how the TDT approach described in this chapter can be applied.

CONCLUSION

This chapter reviews the TDT evidence for improved lie detection. A chief claim of TDT is that cue- and demeanor-based lie detection hover just above chance. Improved lie detection is possible, but improvement requires moving away from cues and demeanor to focus on contextualized communication content, evidence, and persuasion.

This chapter reviews research documenting five paths to improved lie detection:

- Using evidence to establish ground truth and assessing the correspondence between communication content and ground truth.
- Using situational familiarity and contextualized communication content to assess plausibility.
- Using situational familiarity and contextualized communication content to assess motives for deception.
- Strategically questioning senders to elicit diagnostically useful communication content.
- Persuading liars to be honest and tell the truth.

While TDT research shows that all these paths lead to improved lie detection, choosing one path does not preclude taking the others too. There is not just one way to detect lies, and all five methods work well in combination. Watching the experts in TDT experiment fifty-four at work, I came to appreciate that they had a big toolbox and were not tied to any one or two tools.

The upshot of this chapter is that slightly-better-than-chance accuracy is no longer inevitable. The accuracy ceiling has been smashed. Claims that humans can't detect lies have been disproven. TDT provides much-needed guidance as to what works and what does not work under what conditions.

15

The TDT Perspective

THIS IS THE FINAL CHAPTER. I STARTED writing this book four years ago, while living in Michigan. Since then, I moved to Korea for two years, and now I have been at the University of Alabama at Birmingham for more than a year. I hope you have found the content useful, informative, and engaging. I hope you now have a different understanding of deceptive communication.

This last chapter provides highlights from the previous chapters and summarizes the most important take-home messages of the book. Here I sum things up and emphasize my main claims, themes, and ideas. A word of caution, though: This chapter does not provide a quick summary of TDT the theory. That is provided back in chapter 6. Instead, this chapter provides my closing thoughts and summarizes the perspective offered in this book.

THE TRUTH-DEFAULT

The truth-default is the namesake of my theory and is in the subtitle of this book. Both the theory and the book extend beyond the truth-default, but the truth-default is the central idea. It is the starting point for my thinking about deceptive communication.

The idea of the truth-default is that when we communicate with other people, we tend to passively believe what we hear or read. Even though others might be deceiving us, most often that possibility just does not enter our consciousness, at least at the time of the communication. We certainly can be kicked out of our truth-default state. We can consciously wonder if others are really honest. And we certainly can uncover deception. But such things are aberrations that can occur given the right set of conditions, not the business-as-usual of most communication. The truth-default is the rule that usually governs communication. For the most part, we passively presume honesty.

I want to avoid a potential misunderstanding here. It is *not* TDT's stance that all people are in the truth-default state all of the time. The truth-default is neither inescapable nor inevitable. TDT is clear about this. Triggers of various sorts can take us out of our truth-default. There are people we know better than to trust. There are situations in which we know we need to keep our guard up. But sustained vigilance is effortful; and chronic vigilance is bad for our physical health, our psychological well-being, and our social relationships.[1]

According to TDT, the truth-default is supremely adaptive. It works very well for us. We humans are a social species that evolved in families, tribes, and groups. Our survival as individuals and as a species has always required social coordination and cooperation with our fellow humans. Nothing is more important to us than our ability to communicate with others, and the relationships we build and maintain through communication. The truth-default is essential for efficient communication, cooperation, and coordination. If humans second-guessed all communication, it would lose much of its efficiency and utility, and we would either have long ago become extinct or never have evolved into the social species that we are. Thus, while the truth-default is not always on, it is advantageous for us to keep it on unless we have a good reason to temporarily turn it off.

TDT rejects the idea of an evolutionary arms race in humans between the ability to deceive and the ability to detect deception in real time. First, the payoffs from the truth-default in terms of efficient communication vastly outweigh the costs of being deceived once in a while. It's true we get suckered once in a while, but in return we get to interact efficiently with other members of our species. Second, the human solution to the problem of deception is deterrence, not real-time detection. Humans have cultures, religions, and legal-political-regulatory structures to keep deception in check. Third, after-the-fact detection of deceit is more common than at-the-time detection. Maybe someone does fool us. But if that was about something important, we will uncover the deceit in time. The next time, we will either avoid that person or be on guard. And we may warn others too.

TAKING THE BIAS OUT OF TRUTH-BIAS

The tendency to believe others is an old and robust finding in deception research. For as long as truth-bias has been a thing in deception research, truth-bias has been understood as a "bias." Biases have a negative connotation. Truth-bias has long been seen as the result of flawed and lazy cognition. For previous theorists, truth-bias reflected faulty cognition and led to erroneous judgment.

This is not at all how truth-bias is understood in TDT. Sure, truth-bias can lead to probable errors in environments where deception is unusually prevalent. But most of the time deception just isn't very prevalent. The tendency to believe isn't a "bias" outside the deception lab, where deception is less frequent than it is in the deception detection experiments documenting so-called truth-bias. From the TDT perspective, it is the base-rates in the typical deception lab that are biased in the direction of lies, not the research subjects whose judgments align better with everyday reality. In fact, it was the idea that truth-bias might be adaptive and reflective of reality that led Kim Serota and me to our series of TDT studies on lie prevalence.

PREVALENCE: LYING IS NOT SO UBIQUITOUS AFTER ALL

For a long time, deception researchers made claims about the ubiquity of deception. Deception was everywhere. Frequent deception was tossed out as a known fact, providing a rationale for studying deception. Deception was a worthy thing to study, claimed many academic authors, precisely because it was so prevalent.[2]

TDT claims the opposite. Key to TDT is the idea that most communication by most people is mostly honest most of the time. Most deception, in contrast, is enacted by a few prolific liars.

I have not lied today. I did not knowingly deceive anyone yesterday or the day before, either. Take the TDT lie prevalence challenge. Keep a diary for a few days. What's the ratio of truths to lies in your communication? Most readers will find that lies are quite infrequent relative to honest messages. However, this won't be true for everyone. There will be some "outliars."

LYING IS NOT A RANDOM EVENT

The vast majority of studies on the topic of deception involve some version of an instructed-lie research paradigm. Some people are instructed to be honest while others are instructed to lie, based upon random assignment by the researchers. An important insight of TDT is that *outside* the lab, deception is not random. People lie for a reason. Motivation matters. What most of the situations where people actually attempt deception have in common is that in those situations the truth poses a problem for the communicator, and deception offers a convenient solution. When the truth works just fine, everyone but the pathological liar will be honest. People who often find themselves in situations where the truth is a problem are likely very different from most of us, who are seldom threatened by reality in ways that necessitate frequent deception.

MOTIVES AND BASE-RATES

Among the big implications of non-normally distributed deception prevalence and deception motives is that things like truth–lie base-rates and the nature of situations matter a great deal. Lying is not equally probable in all communication situations; therefore, truth-bias and the truth-default are not equally advantageous across individuals and situations. There are times when it is healthy to be on guard for deception. When dealing with someone that has been dishonest in the past, or in situations where there may be motive to lie, the truth-default can be temporarily suspended. Knowing a person's character and knowing incentive structures go much further in lie detection than paying attention to the person's demeanor. Life experience helps us tacitly play the odds. This way, we can be selectively vigilant while getting the advantages provided by the truth-default the rest of the time.

THE IMPORTANCE OF INDIVIDUAL DIFFERENCES: PREVALENCE, TRANSPARENCY, DEMEANOR

Individual differences play a much larger role in TDT than in most other deception theories. Importantly too, TDT does not presume that these critical individual differences are normally distributed. By not only addressing which individual differences are most important but also specifying how those differences are distributed across populations, TDT offers a level of specificity and precision that rival theories lack.

Besides in their individual proclivity to lie, people vary in their ability to lie convincingly. TDT holds that there exists a minority of people who just can't lie in a way that would deceive anyone. I call these people the few transparent liars. They are the opposite of inscrutable. Transparent liars keep deception detection rates above chance because everyone gets them correct. The transparent liars also provide anecdotal and statistical support for the ideas that cues to deception exist. In TDT thinking, reliable cues do exist, but only in the small minority of the population that are highly transparent.

Besides in transparency, communicators also vary in sender honest demeanor. Some people just come off as more honest than others do, completely independent of their actual honesty. Unlike lie prevalence and transparency, however, the distribution of demeanor exhibits more person-to-person variability and is less skewed. Looking at what honestly demeanored senders do to be so believable led me to the BQ (believability quotient) described at the end of chapter 13.

SAYING NO TO CUE THEORIES

TDT turns attention away from many key ideas that populate rival theories of deception. Foremost among these is the idea of cues. The idea behind cues is that there are specific behaviors that we can observe that (albeit probabilistically) distinguish honest communication from deception. In folk beliefs about deception, a lack of eye contact serves as a cue to deception. In older theorizing about deception, any behavior linked with anxiety, such as fidgeting with the hands or high vocal pitch, is a deception cue. In current legal-criminal psychology, the number and type of details are cues garnering much interest.

Many prior theories of deception exemplify what I call "cue theories." According to the various cue theories, being honest and telling lies are psychologically different. Maybe lies are more cognitively effortful, or more arousing, or associated with specific emotional states such as guilt or fear of detection. Maybe liars are more strategic because they are more invested in being perceived as honest, or maybe liars are less forthcoming because they don't want to get trapped in their lies. In cue-theory logic, these different psychological states, whether just one or some combination of them, are signaled behaviorally. Spotting these behavioral signals (i.e., cues) provides the mechanism for lie detection in cue theories.

TDT takes a view opposite that of cue theories. In TDT, cues are ephemeral and unreliable indicators of deception. Reliance on cues and demeanor pushes accuracy down toward chance. Only the few transparent liars save cues from being completely worthless. Improved lie detection, according to TDT, stems from attention to communication content, not cues.

Details provide a good example of the difference between TDT logic and cue-theory thinking. When details are viewed as a cue, it does not matter what the detail is. We just count the number of details provided in a statement. The fewer the details, the more likely the statement is deceptive. In TDT thinking, in contrast, the number of details is unimportant, except that, as with all cues, if you count details as a method of lie detection, you will push your accuracy down toward chance. Surely the number of details in a statement rests on things like the recentness of a recalled event, individual differences in memory, and a host of other situationally variable factors besides whether or not the communication is honest or deceptive.[3] If you asked about my last sip of coffee, for example, all I might (honestly) say is that it is no longer hot (providing just one detail). That detail, if believed, tells you about the current state of my coffee. That I provide just one detail does not help you know whether I was lying about the temperature of my coffee. In TDT what matters is the content of the details and whether they are accurate when fact-checked. If we can't fact-check, are the details plausible? In my coffee example, good follow-up questions might involve asking how much time had passed since I poured my coffee and whether I was engaged in some activity that might have prevented me from getting up for a warm-up.

Recently, the idea of verifiable details has emerged as a cue.[4] The idea is that the type of details matters. In this case, the cue-theory logic is that liars are strategic and avoid providing details that might be fact-checked. Therefore, if the details in a statement can't, in theory, be checked, maybe the statement is deceptive, but if the details can be checked, the person is probably honest. My friend Steve McCornack would likely counter that, at least in spoken communication, since we produce what we say on the fly considering verifiability would likely bog down speech production, and this would be true for honest people too since everyone has an interest in being believed.

The TDT approach is to actually fact-check verifiable details. In my opinion, some people might be strategic, others less so, but if we want to know the truth, let's check what facts we can. TDT's position is clear: verifiable details that check out are probably true, and those that don't merit skepticism. There is no need to presume that liars use some particular strategy or even that liars think strategically. People think all kinds of things. We shouldn't impose high-level strategic thinking where it might not belong. Much life experience tells me that even smart people often don't think many moves ahead.

I have a similar skepticism about the cat-and-mouse depiction offered by interpersonal deception theory (IDT). IDT, too, presumes that liars are quite strategic. In IDT both senders and their conversational partners closely monitor each other for cues indicative of suspicion and deception. Liars are adept at spotting suspicion cues and adapt on the fly to act more honestly. Deception and deception detection are depicted as a strategic game of moves and counter-moves. In TDT, in contrast, most communicators operate within the truth-default, and consequently most communicators are oblivious to suspicion and deceit most of the time. Thoughts about suspicion and deception just don't enter consciousness. Even absent the truth-default, people just don't have the meta-communicative skill to act so strategically. In TDT when people do detect lies, it is typically well after the fact and based on either evidence or the sender confessing the truth.

SAYING NO TO STAKES, LOAD, MEDIA AFFORDANCES, AND MERE INTERACTIVITY

Because cues don't really matter much in TDT except to distract and misdirect us, a host of other things that have long been seen as critical in lie detection are moot in TDT. In the TDT view, lie stakes, cognitive load, media, and mere interactivity are all largely irrelevant. Studying such factors in lie detection is a waste of time, because there is not much there to find. Theories that prioritize such things should be considered falsified or misguided, the stuff of mythology not empirical science.

Ever since Ekman's first writing on deception, the idea of lie stakes has held a prominent place in deception theory. Stakes have to do with the amount of ill-gotten gain from successful deception and the degree of negative consequences stemming from a failed lie. The idea is that the greater the stakes, the greater the psychological difference between truth and lie, and the greater the likelihood that telltale cues will manifest as a consequence. Unfortunately for cue-theory logic, multiple meta-analyses just don't support the idea that stakes make much difference.[5]

In current legal and criminal psychology circles, the mediating psychological difference du jour is cognitive load. A critique of cognitive-load thinking was provided in chapters 5 and 8. For now, let's just say that TDT rejects the idea that deception is inherently more effortful than honesty and that from my reading of meta-analytic data, there is even less evidence for load cues than there is for arousal cues. I think that outside a controlled lab setting, adding cognitive load during an interrogation risks making honest senders appear deceptive.

TDT does not focus on communication media, either. TDT propositions apply to text messaging, tweeting, smoke signals, or whatever new or old medium over which some message might be sent. From the cue theory perspective, media is a crucial consideration, because different media have different affordances that limit the availability of certain cues. Vocal pitch or microexpressions, for example, are not available as cues in email. But that is not important in TDT.

The same is true for face-to-face interaction and the degree of interactivity. These don't matter much by themselves. There is a big caveat, however, in regard to both media and interactivity. If the medium precludes diagnostic questioning, then two potential paths to improved lie detection are precluded. But it is not interactivity per se that is important; it is properly exploiting the opportunity to prompt diagnostic information and to persuade a person to be honest that are critical.

A DIFFERENT UNDERSTANDING OF HUMAN NATURE

The preceding pages have hinted about some things that should be made explicit. TDT just sees us humans in our social world differently than do most other deception theories.

Many rival theories offer a cynical worldview where deception is everywhere, where people are hyper-Machiavellian, highly mindful of communicative nuance, and super strategic. Interaction is presumed to involve higher-order theory of mind, where people mentally represent others' thoughts about them and adjust on the fly to address contingencies upon contingencies. Specific verbal and nonverbal behaviors have specific meaning across individuals and situations. I, however, find such depictions difficult to reconcile with empirical findings suggesting low rates of deception relative to honest communication, pervasive truth-bias, and poor real-time truth–lie discrimination.

Putting together the themes raised so far, TDT sees most people as mostly honest. People lie only on an as-needed basis in situations where honesty won't work. When people do deceive others, they can do so convincingly both because most of us learned how to be deceptive as we grew up and also because those who get duped are not on guard for deception. This second reason is because most people believe most of what is said most of time. This works well because the passive presumption of honesty turns out to be right most of the time. Most people just aren't that Machiavellian most of time. Most of us don't approach human interaction with suspiciousness and vigilance. Instead, we often go through most of our communicative lives on autopilot. What we say pops out of our mouths without pre-scripting or strategic scheming, and we accept most of what other people tell us.

MOST LIES ARE DETECTED AFTER THE FACT

In TDT people do detect lies, but usually well after the fact. In cue theories, lies are detected when we notice behaviors indicative of deception and correctly conclude that those behaviors are indicative of deception. In TDT people passively believe others regardless of cues. If for some reason people are watching for cues as indicators of deception, then their cue-based judgments are only slightly-better-than-chance.

According to TDT, people detect most lies when information is later discovered that reveals deception for what it is. This deception-revealing information is of two basic types: some evidence comes to light that exposes the truth, or the liar later confesses the truth. Understanding how people actually detect deception suggests methods of improving lie detection accuracy.

THE FIVE KEYS TO IMPROVING LIE DETECTION

In TDT there are five ways to improve deception detection accuracy. I list them below and then discuss each. Much more detail is provided in chapter 14.

1. Correspondence of communication content with evidence
2. Content in context (situational familiarity)
3. Assessment of deception motives
4. Diagnostic questioning
5. Persuading honesty

In TDT, evidence-based lie detection is the most-preferred single approach. Using evidence is the best way to improve the probability of knowing the truth of some matter. We compare the content of some communication to the available evidence. To the extent that communication content corresponds with the evidence (i.e., it checks out), then we can have some confidence that what was said is indeed true. Content that is contradicted by evidence is suspect and, depending on the reliability of the evidence, might well be false. Not all false statements count as deception, but evidence-based lie detection has the advantage of getting at the truth of the matter.

Even absent compelling evidence, paying attention to communication content (i.e., what is said) is still useful when the communication can be understood in context in a situation familiar to the recipient. With an understanding of the context in which communication occurs, content plausibility becomes valuable in distinguishing truth from deception. We can ask ourselves, "Does it make sense?" and "Does it sound right?"

Another important aspect of context that comes with situational familiarity is the ability to estimate the likelihood of a deceptive motive. In TDT people try to deceive others only when the truth is a problem. When people have nothing to gain from deception, deception is improbable. Not all people with a motive for deception are deceptive, but understanding the motivation of communicators is useful in narrowing the field.

Fourth, in situations where interaction is possible, asking the right questions can dramatically improve deception detection accuracy. The key, however, is asking the right questions, those that make the previous three methods more useful. We can ask questions for which we know the answer but the interviewee does not know we know. We can ask questions that we can later fact-check. We can ask questions that better enable us to assess plausibility and motive. When something strikes us as suspicious, we can follow up.

The final path to improved lie detection is persuasion. We can persuade a liar to be honest and tell us the truth. This can be done in a variety of ways. We can bluff about what is already known. There is often little point in lying when the target already knows the truth. We can appeal to a person's character and morality. We can appeal to the incentive structure to motivate honesty rather than deceit. Regardless of the approach, however, there is one firm requirement. The goal must be to seek the truth not just to elicit a confession (which can be true or false). Seeking confessions as an effective lie detection strategy works only to the extent that false confessions are avoided.

TWO MYSTERIES SOLVED

Way back in the first chapter, two mysteries regarding prior research findings were described. These included (a) the mystery of normally distributed slightly-better-than-chance accuracy and (b) the mystery of deception accuracy in research that is not about deception. A viable social scientific theory of deception should be able to make sense of these otherwise odd sets of findings.

Chapter 13 is devoted to providing a nuanced explanation of slightly-better-than-chance-accuracy in deception detection research. The snarky macro-theoretical explanation is that reliably poor accuracy is the inevitable consequence of understanding deception detection through cue-theory blinders. Cues are by their nature ephemeral. Reliance on ephemeral indicators invariably pushes accuracy down toward chance. The more precise solution to the first mystery involves individual differences in senders. Massive variation in sender demeanor depresses accuracy, while the few transparent liars provide counterforce preventing the nil-null hypothesis of chance accuracy from fully obtaining. The result is high accuracy for a few people who can't lie well, chance accuracy for the majority of senders, and average accuracy that hovers just above chance.

The second mystery involved the discrepancy in findings between experiments investigating deception detection and research that involves deception but is not about deception. In studies of deception, the typical finding is that accuracy is better than chance, but not by much. In contrast, much social science research involves deception, and what research using deception finds is not accuracy just above chance, but instead accuracy near zero. Subjects are typically fooled by deceptive research designs. For example, in my cheating experiments, few real subjects suspect that their partner is a research confederate merely posing as a subject. So why the difference in the findings? Why do deception detection experiments provide such a different picture of deception detection accuracy than findings involving deception but not about deception detection accuracy?

This question was not directly and explicitly answered previously. Nevertheless, people who read chapters 10, 11, and 12 and who understand TDT should see the answer as obvious. The mystery of deception accuracy in research that is not about deception is no mystery from the vantage of TDT.

In deception detection experiments, subjects are primed (or even required) to consider the issue of deception by the very fact that they are in a deception detection experiment and that as part of the research, they are asked to assess honesty–deceit in some explicit way. When asked about deception, people are slightly-better-than-chance at distinguishing truth from lies. But, in research using deception, the research works only if the subjects are deceived. Researchers want the deception to be successful, so they don't prime or otherwise alert research subjects to the possibility of deception. Absent a researcher-induced trigger, the subject's truth-default remains intact. The deception is constant across subjects, so the base-rate is 100% deceptive, and accuracy for the deception approaches 0%. Mystery no more. It all makes good sense once you understand TDT.

EXPECTING MORE FROM THEORY

This book is about deception. It is also about social scientific theory. While I hope the book is successful in providing a new understanding of deception and deception detection, I also hope it makes a powerful and compelling statement about theory. The fifteen chapters of this book articulate a new theory of deception. I described where the ideas came from, how they evolved over time, and how I have sought to test my theory. I hope that TDT is a role model for how to develop theory and how to do programmatic theoretically important research. I hope too that TDT exemplifies the value of good theory. I think we need to expect more from theory, and I sincerely hope that TDT exceeds expectations.

Among many social scientists, theory is seen as the sine qua non of scholarship. Graduate students are typically asked, "What is your theory?" rather than the usually more appropriate question "Is there a viable theory that fits your purpose?" Otherwise, good research submitted for academic publication that lacks sufficient lip service to theory is often summarily rejected. Declarations of "it's not theoretical" are hurled as insults.

I do not hold a Pollyannaish view of theory, nor do I subscribe to the theory-is-a-must point of view. Some research objectives simply don't require theory. In those situations where theory is needed (or at least would be advantageous), often the right theory for the job just does not exist. It is my experience that poor or ill-fitting theory does more harm than good. It is my belief that theory-for-theory's-sake cheapens theory.

There are at least three problems with the state of theory in current social science practices. First, the words "theory" and "theoretical" are used in a wide variety of ways. For some, anything that is remotely conceptual counts as theory. Others use the terms narrowly to refer to conceptual frameworks meeting some set of requirements like testable and falsifiable predictions, logical coherence among propositions, and/or a unifying explanatory mechanism. Because the word is used in so many ways, it is often hard to know what, if anything, is meant by "theory."

Second, too often theory is seen as a prerequisite for inquiry rather than as the desirable but not essential outcome or goal of inquiry. I think it is perfectly fine for research to be driven by intellectual curiosity or by the need to solve a specific problem. Not all research needs theory to make a contribution. Of the work that is theoretical, the theory need not come first. Going from curiosity to data to theory has worked well for TDT. If I'd had to start with a theory that I accepted, TDT could not have been developed.

The third problem is that in many areas of social science there is a real lack of good, sound theory. Nevertheless, social scientists believe they need a theory to publish their research or to defend their thesis. So, what social scientists often do is just give mere lip service to theory. That is, they bullshit. Steve McCornack has long suggested this test: Take the theory out of the article or research project. Do the argument and research design still make sense? If the answer is yes, then the theory is just clutter. The superficial or deceptive use of the word "theory" detracts from the true value of good theory.

All this said, I see good theory as important, a huge asset in research. Obviously, I have invested much effort into developing and disseminating TDT. I don't believe I need TDT or some other theory to do meaningful research, but I think having TDT provides advantages that would be missed without the theory. To explain my opinion, we need to seriously consider what theory does for us. What do we get from a good theory that we miss absent theory? What does expecting more from theory entail?

Let's just stipulate that accurate prediction and insightful explanation are obvious functions of good theory. We should not downplay the importance of prediction and explanation, but let's instead focus on two other less often recognized functions of theory. I will call these functions (1) focus-prioritization and (2) generality.

Human cognition and behavior in social environments is undoubtedly complex. There is too much going on for a social observer to take it all in. The trick is to focus on the important things and not get lost in the minutiae. We need to prioritize. There are many, many ways to approach any given research topic, and theory provides much-needed guidance.

Here is an example that I think really illustrates this underappreciated function of theory. The previous chapter describes our expert questioning experiment (TDT experiment fifty-four). We brought federal agents into our lab and had them question subjects who had just completed the cheating game. Interestingly and unbeknownst to us at the time, IDT researchers Norah Dunbar, Judee Burgoon, and colleagues had previously done an experiment that was remarkably similar to ours in several ways.[6] Like us, they used a trivia-game cheating experiment where experts were brought in to question potential cheaters. More important for the current point, however, are the differences between the Dunbar experiment and TDT experiment fifty-four.

The experts in Dunbar's experiment questioned potential cheaters either face-to-face or mediated with video conferencing. Modality and interactivity are central to IDT, so this design decision follows directly from IDT. This is not the sort of thing a TDT-guided researcher would think to do. TDT thinking suggests that adding media as a variable is something unlikely to yield valuable results. As it turned out, modality did not have a big or consistent effect on accuracy.[7] Dunbar and colleagues also looked at ratings of interviewee dominance, involvement, relaxation, activity, and pleasantness. This is something we didn't bother to do either, because that is the stuff of cue theories, not TDT thinking.

Dunbar imposed scripted questions on the experts, whereas we did not. Our idea was that expertise lies in knowing what questions to ask, and we also wanted to see how the experts approached questioning, not how well they could do asking the questions we as researchers thought they should ask. Importantly, we scored believed honest confessions as accurate outcomes. Dunbar excluded confessions when scoring accuracy. The bottom line was 59% accuracy in the Dunbar expert experiment, compared to 98% accuracy in the TDT experiment.[8] The point here is not to brag about our results or to denigrate Dunbar's experiment. The point is that theories guide research priorities and research designs. Otherwise similar IDT and TDT experiments focused on different aspects of deception detection and consequently prioritized different variables and obtained different results. Theories tell us where to look for findings. This is not trivial, because the path to finding good, strong, reliable results requires knowing to look in the right place.

The second function of good theory is generality. Consumers of research findings typically want to know whether the findings of research apply beyond the specifics of the research design. If college students were subjects, we might wonder whether the findings generalize to older adults. If the findings came from a lab experiment, we wonder whether the findings apply to non-lab settings. If the findings came from a study conducted in the 1970s, we wonder whether the findings would still hold today. If the study involved a mock crime, we wonder whether the findings would apply to real crimes. We want to know how general the findings are. In social science lingo, we want to know about so-called external validity.

"External validity" is a term introduced by the famed methodologists Donald Campbell and Julian Stanley.[9] Their work had a huge and valuable impact, but their idea that external validity is achieved by research design was, in my opinion, horribly misguided. The issue is that all data are finite and that the types of generalizations research consumers want are not those provided by either inferential statistics or features of the research design.

Let's use TDT study one as an example. Study one used a nationally representative sample from the United States to ask people how often they lie. Presumably, using a large representative sample lets us statistically project our findings in a way we can't with smaller samples of college students, right? But project across what? Presumably, we can generalize to the population, in this case US adults. But we sampled subjects only, not cultures, methods, or time frames. What if we had asked the question differently? We did not randomly sample question wording or question order. What if we had done our survey on a different day? See my point? We just can't achieve the generality we want with method, data, and statistics. Fortunately, there is an alternative.

TDT propositions one and two make generalizations about lie prevalence. If these two propositions are right, lying is not normally distributed in any human population; most people are mostly honest most of the time, and most lies are told by a few prolific liars. TDT studies one through five tested these propositions. What we were doing was using theory to make generalizations and data to test generalizations.

We should hold theories to a high standard. Are our theories pointing us in the most fruitful directions? Are our theories leading to important new findings and steering us away from dead ends? Do our theories have the empirical adequacy and the specifics to help solve the problems of induction and provide us with the ability to generalize beyond our findings?

GOOD FINDINGS REPLICATE; UNRELIABLE FINDINGS DON'T

My first semester in graduate school, I had the good fortune to take a seminar from James C. McCroskey, who, as many people in my academic field know, was something of a character. On the syllabus for the class, the attendance policy simply read: "Good graduate students come to class, former graduate students don't." What a great line. I'll borrow that line to talk about how I feel about theory and research findings. Good theory aligns with research findings, bad theory doesn't. And good findings replicate, bad findings don't.

Looking back at TDT research, especially now that it has all been pulled together, I can proudly claim an obsession with replication. I am not obsessive-compulsive, but a reader might get that impression. In TDT study one, for example, a large, nationally representative sample wasn't enough. Study one was followed by studies two through five. Kim Serota and I hope to do more cross-cultural replications in the future. Pretty much all the TDT findings reported have been successfully replicated at least once. Most key TDT findings have been replicated several times.

There are two related points regarding replication. First, I want to restate the importance of replication in science. Second, I want to emphasize that the fact that TDT predictions replicate is a major bragging point for TDT. If empirical adequacy is the bottom in the evaluation of theory, and if replication is required for confidence in empirical adequacy, then TDT sure looks great.

THE FUTURE OF TDT

Something like ten years ago, I had a mid-academic-career crisis of confidence. I told Hee Sun Park that I was worried that I was out of good new ideas. Maybe I had already had my best ideas. I had just had a great run getting my ideas into one top journal after another. I didn't know how I was ever going to top the ideas I had already had. What was I going to do? Anyway, that was just before TDT came together in my head. This book, I think, proves that back then I was far from being permanently out of ideas. Back then, even though I didn't know it yet, another series of good ideas was just around the corner.

As I wrap up this book, I feel that way again. TDT, the research behind it, and this book have been a huge undertaking. Maybe this is the best work I will ever do. If so, I can live with that. Unlike last time, this time around I don't find the thought worrisome. Past experience has shown me that I can't predict what's next, but there are probably several things to keep me intellectually engaged just around the corner.

I do, however, have a vision for what's next for TDT. TDT ideas are taking off and gaining momentum. I can see it in citations of my articles and in the manuscripts I am reviewing for journals. Up until now, TDT was a guiding force for me and my small circle of close coauthors. That, I think and hope, is about to change. Now it is time to see how TDT holds up when tested by others. We will see in what directions others take TDT. Now we will see how TDT lives, dies, or, most likely, morphs. I don't know what the future holds for TDT. That is, as we scientists say, an empirical question. But I can honestly say that I am quite pleased with how TDT and this book turned out.

Notes

Chapter 1

1. Philip Houston and Michael Floyd, *Spy the Lie: Former CIA Officers Teach You How to Detect Deception* (New York: St. Martin's Press, 2012).

2. Not only that, but I actually published an experiment showing that if you told people beforehand that someone else was lying, people saw them as engaging in less eye contact than if they were told the person was honest. The causal direction was opposite to what is usually thought. The mere misperception of dishonesty can lead to "seeing" deception cues. Timothy R. Levine, Kelli Jean K. Asada, and Hee Sun Park, "The Lying Chicken and the Gaze Avoidant Egg: Eye Contact, Deception, and Causal Order," *Southern Communication Journal* 71, no. 4 (December 2006): 401–11.

3. For a detailed discussion, see Timothy R. Levine, "Ecological Validity and Deception Detection Research Design," *Communication Methods and Measures* 12, no. 1 (2018): 45–54, https://doi.org/10.1080/19312458.2017.1411471.

4. I did my master's in communication studies at West Virginia University studying under Buddy Wheeless and Jim McCroskey.

5. Steven A. McCornack and Malcolm R. Parks, "Deception Detection and Relationship Development: The Other Side of Trust," in *Communication Yearbook 9*, ed. Margaret L. McLaughlin (Beverly Hills: Sage, 1986), 377–89.

6. Mark E. Comadena, "Accuracy in Detecting Deception: Intimate and Friendship Relationships," in *Communication Yearbook 6*, ed. Michael Burgoon (Beverly Hills, CA: Sage, 1982), 446–72.

7. Timothy R. Levine and Steven A. McCornack, "The Dark Side of Trust: Conceptualizing and Measuring Types of Communicative Suspicion," *Communication Quarterly* 39, no. 4 (Fall 1991): 325–40; Timothy R. Levine and Steven A. McCornack, "Linking Love and Lies: A Formal Test of the McCornack and Parks Model of Deception Detection," *Journal of Social and Personal Relationships* 9, no. 1 (February 1992): 143–54; Timothy R. Levine and Steven A. McCornack, "Behavioral Adaptation, Confidence, and Heuristic-Based Explanations of the Probing Effect," *Human Communication Research* 27, no. 4 (October 2001): 471–502; Timothy R. Levine, Steven A. McCornack, and Penny Baldwin Avery, "Sex Differences in Emotional Reactions to Discovered Deception," *Communication Quarterly* 40, no. 3 (Summer 1992): 289–96; Steven A. McCornack and Timothy R. Levine, "When Lies Are Uncovered: Emotional and Relational Outcomes of Discovered Deception," *Communication Monographs* 57, no. 2 (March 1990): 119–38; Steven A. McCornack and Timothy R. Levine, "When Lovers Become Leery: The Relationship between Suspicion and Accuracy in Detecting Deception," *Communication Monographs* 57,

no. 3 (September 1990): 219–30; Steven A. McCornack, Timothy R. Levine, Kathleen A. Solow-czuk, Helen I. Torres, and Dedra M. Campbell, "When the Alteration of Information Is Viewed as Deception: An Empirical Test of Information Manipulation Theory," *Communication Monographs* 59, no. 2 (March 1992): 17–29.

8. Sixty-four percent of more than ten thousand people surveyed mentioned gaze aversion. No other answer was listed by more than 30% of respondents. Global Deception Research Team, "A World of Lies," *Journal of Cross-Cultural Psychology* 37, no. 1 (January 2006): 60–74, https://doi.org/10.1177/0022022105282295.

9. Gaze aversion was listed as the top answer in fifty-one of the fifty-eight countries surveyed. Global Deception Research Team, "World of Lies."

10. Across thirty-two studies, the average effect for deception in gaze is $d = 0.01$. Bella M. DePaulo, James J. Lindsay, Brian E. Malone, Laura Muhlenbruck, Kelly Charlton, and Harris Cooper, "Cues to Deception," *Psychological Bulletin* 129, no. 1 (January 2003): 74–118, https://dx.doi:10.1037/0033-2909.129.1.74.

11. There is also no evidence to suggest that liars or honest senders look in one direction or the other. Richard Wiseman, Caroline Watt, Leanne ten Brinke, Stephen Porter, Sara-Louise Couper, and Calum Rankin, "The Eyes Don't Have It: Lie Detection and Neuro-Linguistic Programming," *PLOS ONE* 7, no. 7 (July 2012): e40259, https://doi.org/10.1371/journal.pone.0040259.

12. Timothy R. Levine, Kim B. Serota, Hillary Shulman, David D. Clare, Hee Sun Park, Allison S. Shaw, Jae Chul Shim, and Jung Hyon Lee, "Sender Demeanor: Individual Differences in Sender Believability Have a Powerful Impact on Deception Detection Judgments," *Human Communication Research* 37, no. 3 (July 2011): 377–403. https://doi:10.1111/j.1468-2958.2011.01407.x.

13. Charles F. Bond Jr., Timothy R. Levine, and Maria Hartwig, "New Findings in Non-Verbal Lie Detection. In *Detecting Deception: Current Challenges and Cognitive Approaches*, ed. Pär Anders Granhag, Aldert Vrij, and Bruno Verschuere (Chichester: John Wiley and Sons, 2015), 37–58.

14. Timothy R. Levine, "Scientific Evidence and Cue Theories in Deception Research: Reconciling Findings from Meta-analyses and Primary Experiments," *International Journal of Communication* 12 (2018): 2461–79.

15. Charles F. Bond Jr. and Bella M. DePaulo, "Accuracy of Deception Judgments," *Personality and Social Psychology Review* 10, no. 3 (August 2006): 214–34, https://doi.org/10.1207/s15327957pspr1003_2.

16. Bond and DePaulo, "Accuracy of Deception Judgments."

17. Michael G. Aamodt and Heather Custer, "Who Can Best Catch a Liar?" *Forensic Examiner* 15, no. 1 (Spring 2006): 6–11; Bond and DePaulo, "Accuracy of Deception Judgments."

18. Bond and DePaulo, "Accuracy of Deception Judgments."

19. The mean is 53.66%, and the median and mode are both 54%. The standard deviation is 6.13%. The skewness is negligible, showing that extreme values are equally likely on both the high and low ends of distribution. The distribution is notably leptokurtic (kurtosis = .88, standard error of kurtosis = .29), indicating tighter clustering around the mean than expected in a normal distribution. To me, the symmetrical, leptokurtic distribution suggests little in the way of individual differences and a lack of moderators. All the 289 studies converge on a single finding plus or minus random error.

20. Stanley Milgram, *Obedience to Authority* (New York: Harper and Row, 1974).

21. Solomon Asch, "Studies of Independence and Conformity: I. A Minority of One against a Unanimous Majority," *Psychological Monographs: General and Applied* 70, no. 9 (1956): 1–70, http://dx.doi.org/10.1037/h0093718.

22. Asch, "Studies of Independence and Conformity, 29, 31.

Chapter 2

1. Bella M. DePaulo, James J. Lindsay, Brian E. Malone, Laura Muhlenbruck, Kelly Charlton, and Harris Cooper, "Cues to Deception," *Psychological Bulletin* 129, no. 1 (January 2003): 74–118, http://dx.doi: 10.1037/0033–2909.129.1.74

2. Valerie Hauch, Iris Blandón-Gitlin, Jaume Masip, and Siegfried L. Sporer, "Are Computers Effective Lie Detectors? A Meta-analysis of Linguistic Cues to Deception," *Personality and Social Psychology Review* 19, no. 4 (November 2015): 307–42, https://doi.org/10.1177/1088868314556539.

3. DePaulo, Lindsay, Malone, Muhlenbruck, Charlton, and Cooper, "Cues to Deception," 83.

4. Again, this assumes just one significance test is performed, which is rarely the case in cue research. As the number of tests increases, the more likely it is that one or more findings might obtain significance by chance. Chance results, however, tend not to replicate. Consequently, it is essential to consider results across individual studies. This is yet another reason meta-analysis is valuable.

5. "Wikipedia: Effect size," Wikimedia Foundation, http://en.wikipedia.org/wiki/Effect _size.

6. DePaulo, Lindsay, Malone, Muhlenbruck, Charlton, and Cooper, "Cues to Deception," 95.

7. Leanne ten Brinke, Dayna Stimson, and Dana R. Carney, "Some Evidence for Unconscious Lie Detection," *Psychological Science* 25, no. 5 (May 2014): 1098–105, https://doi.org/10.1177/0956797614524421.

8. James E. Driskell, "Effectiveness of Deception Detection Training: A Meta-analysis," *Psychology, Crime & Law* 18, no. 8 (2012): 713–31, https://doi.org/10.1080/1068316X.2010.535820.

9. Charles F. Bond Jr. and Bella M. DePaulo, "Accuracy of Deception Judgments," *Personality and Social Psychology Review* 10, no. 3 (August 2006): 214–34.

10. Mark G. Frank and Thomas Hugh Feeley, "To Catch a Liar: Challenges for Research in Lie Detection Training," *Journal of Applied Communication Research* 31, no. 1 (February 2003): 58–75, https://doi.org/10.1080/00909880305377.

11. Timothy R. Levine, Thomas Hugh Feeley, Steven A. McCornack, Mikayla Hughes, and Chad M. Harms, "Testing the Effects of Nonverbal Training on Deception Detection Accuracy with the Inclusion of a Bogus Training Control Group," *Western Journal of Communication* 69, no. 3 (July 2005): 203–17. https://doi.org/10.1080/10570310500202355.

12. Timothy R. Levine, "Direct and Indirect Measures of Lie Detection Tell the Same Story: A Reply to ten Brinke, Stimson, and Carney (2014)," *Psychological Science* 25, no. 10 (October 2014): 1960–61, https://doi.org/10.1177/0956797614536740.

13. For example, Maria Hartwig and Charles F. Bond Jr., "Why Do Lie-Catchers Fail? A Lens Model Meta-analysis of Human Lie Judgments," *Psychological Bulletin* 137, no. 4 (July 2011): 643–59, http://doi:10.1037/a0023589.

14. Timothy R. Levine, Kim B. Serota, Hillary Shulman, David D. Clare, Hee Sun Park, Allison S. Shaw, Jae Chul Shim, and Jung Hyon Lee, "Sender Demeanor: Individual Differ-

ences in Sender Believability Have a Powerful Impact on Deception Detection Judgments," *Human Communication Research* 37, no. 3 (July 2011): 377–403, https://doi:10.1111/j.1468 –2958.2011.01407.x.

15. The Global Deception Research Team, "A World of Lies," *Journal of Cross-Cultural Psychology* 37, no. 1 (January 2006): 60–74, https://doi.org/10.1177/0022022105282295.

16. The research leading to these conclusions is covered in chapters 10 and 14.

17. Levine, Serota, Shulman, Clare, Park, Shaw, Shim, and Lee, "Sender Demeanor."

18. Miron Zuckerman, Bella M. DePaulo, and Robert Rosenthal, "Verbal and Nonverbal Communication of Deception," in *Advances in Experimental Social Psychology* 14, ed. Leonard Berkowitz (New York: Academic Press, 1981), 1–59.

19. Hee Sun Park, Timothy R. Levine, Steven A. McCornack, Kelly Morrison, and Merissa Ferrara, "How People Really Detect Lies," *Communication Monographs* 69, no. 2 (June 2002): 144–57.

20. DePaulo, Lindsay, Malone, Muhlenbruck, Charlton, and Cooper, "Cues to Deception."

21. Hartwig and Bond, "Why Do Lie-Catchers Fail?"; Zuckerman, DePaulo, and Rosenthal, "Verbal and Nonverbal Communication of Deception."

22. Levine, Serota, Shulman, Clare, Park, Shaw, Shim, and Lee, "Sender Demeanor."

23. David Dryden Henningsen, Michael G. Cruz, and Mary Clair Morr, "Pattern Violations and Perceptions of Deception," *Communication Reports* 11, no. 1 (Winter 2000): 1–9.

24. Zuckerman, DePaulo, and Rosenthal, "Verbal and Nonverbal Communication of Deception."

25. DePaulo, Lindsay, Malone, Muhlenbruck, Charlton, and Cooper, "Cues to Deception."

26. Siegfried Ludwig Sporer and Barbara Schwandt, "Paraverbal Indicators of Deception: A Meta-analytic Synthesis," *Applied Cognitive Psychology* 20, no. 4 (May 2006): 421–46, https://doi.org/10.1002/acp.1190; Siegfried Ludwig Sporer and Barbara Schwandt, "Moderators of Nonverbal Indicators of Deception: A Meta-analytic Synthesis," *Psychology, Public Policy, and Law* 13, no. 1 (February 2007): 1–34, https://doi:10.1037/1076–8971.13.1.1.

27. The pupil dilation results are based on only four studies. The pitch findings are based on more data (twelve studies), but the effects were heterogeneous across studies. These considerations limit confidence in the utility of these two cues.

28. Credit and thanks to Sigi Sporer, who pointed this out to me in a conversation in July 2015. As a researcher myself and a user of others' research, I am not critical of the decisions on study inclusion. The problems were created by those reporting original findings, not by the meta-analysts making difficult decisions in an imperfect world. The fact that the different research teams made different choices is an asset to the careful and thoughtful reader because we can see the differences that follow from the different choices and interpret the results accordingly.

29. Mark A. deTurck and Gerald R. Miller, "Deception and Arousal: Isolating the Behavioral Correlates of Deception," *Human Communication Research* 12, no. 2 (Winter 1985): 181–201.

30. Zuckerman, DePaulo, and Rosenthal, "Verbal and Nonverbal Communication of Deception."

31. DePaulo, Lindsay, Malone, Muhlenbruck, Charlton, and Cooper, "Cues to Deception."

32. Jonah Lehrer, "The Truth Wears Off: Is There Something Wrong with the Scientific Method?" *New Yorker*, December 13, 2010, https://www.newyorker.com/magazine/2010/12/13/the-truth-wears-off.

33. Hartwig and Bond, "Why Do Lie-Catchers Fail?"

34. $r = -.43$, $p < .001$.

35. Charles F. Bond Jr., Timothy R. Levine, and Maria Hartwig, "New Findings in Non-Verbal Lie Detection. In *Detecting Deception: Current Challenges and Cognitive Approaches*, ed. Pär Anders Granhag, Aldert Vrij, and Bruno Verschuere (Chichester: John Wiley and Sons, 2015), 37–58.

36. Maria Hartwig and Charles F. Bond Jr., "Lie Detection from Multiple Cues: A Meta-Analysis," *Applied Cognitive Psychology* 28, no. 5 (October 2015): 661–76, https://doi.org/10.1002/acp.3052.

37. Timothy R. Levine, Thomas Hugh Feeley, Steven A. McCornack, Mikayla Hughes, and Chad M. Harms, "Testing the Effects of Nonverbal Training on Deception Detection Accuracy with the Inclusion of a Bogus Training Control Group," *Western Journal of Communication* 69, no. 3 (July 2005): 203–17, https://doi.org/10.1080/10570310500202355.

Chapter 3

1. Paul L. Fay and Warren C. Middleton, "The Ability to Judge Truth-Telling, or Lying, from the Voice as Transmitted over a Public Address System," *Journal of General Psychology* 24 (1941): 211–15, https://doi.org/10.1080/00221309.1941.10544369.

2. Michael G. Aamodt and Heather Custer, "Who Can Best Catch a Liar?" *Forensic Examiner* 15, no. 1 (Spring 2006): 6–11; Charles F. Bond Jr. and Bella M. DePaulo, "Accuracy of Deception Judgments," *Personality and Social Psychology Review* 10, no. 3 (August 2006): 214–34, https://doi.org/10.1207/s15327957pspr1003_2; Charles F. Bond Jr. and Bella M. DePaulo, "Individual Differences in Judging Deception: Accuracy and Bias," *Psychological Bulletin* 134, no. 4 (July 2008): 477–92, http://dx.doi.org/10.1037/0033-2909.134.4.477; Bella M. DePaulo, Kelly Charlton, Harris Cooper, James J. Lindsay, and Laura Muhlenbruck, "The Accuracy-Confidence Correlation in the Detection of Deception," *Personality and Social Psychology Review* 1, no. 4 (November 1997): 346–57, https://doi.org/10.1207/s15327957pspr0104_5; Bella M. DePaulo, Miron Zuckerman, and Robert Rosenthal, "Humans as Lie Detectors," *Journal of Communication* 30, no. 2 (June 1980): 129–39; Maria Hartwig and Charles F. Bond Jr., "Why Do Lie-Catchers Fail? A Lens Model Meta-analysis of Human Lie Judgments," *Psychological Bulletin* 137, no. 4 (July 2011): 643–59, http://dx.doi: 10.1037/a0023589; Robert Kraut, "Humans as Lie Detectors," *Journal of Communication* 30, no. 4 (December 1980): 209–18, https://doi.org/10.1111/j.1460–2466.1980.tb02030.x; Miron Zuckerman, Bella M. DePaulo, and Robert Rosenthal, "Verbal and Nonverbal Communication of Deception," in *Advances in Experimental Social Psychology* 14, ed. Leonard Berkowitz, 1–59 (New York: Academic Press, 1981).

3. An important exception is deception detection experiments in which judges each assess very few messages. For example, if each judge evaluates just one message, then their score will be either 0% or 100%. The variance is massive. What happens in experiments where judges evaluate more senders and/or messages is that as the judgments per judge increase, the more the average accuracy score for each individual judge approaches 54%. One of the least-appreciated findings from the Bond and DePaulo, "Accuracy of Deception Judgments," 222, meta-analysis is the role of mere reliability. Aberrant findings come from unreliable data (especially single-judgment data), and findings quickly converge as the reliability increases. In my experience, even four judgments per judge is sufficient, but eight to twelve is even better. Findings based on single-judgment data often do not replicate and can be misleading.

4. See, for example, Jeff Hancock, *The Future of Lying*, filmed September 2012 TEDxWinnipeg, Winnipeg, Canada, video, 18:25, https://www.ted.com/talks/jeff_hancock_3_types_of_digital_lies.

5. Norman R. F. Maier and James A. Thurber, "Accuracy of Judgments of Deception When an Interview Is Watched, Heard, and Read," *Personnel Psychology* 21 (March 1968): 23–30, https://doi.org/10.1111/j.1744-6570.1968.tb02283.x.

6. Zuckerman, DePaulo, and Rosenthal, "Verbal and Nonverbal Communication of Deception," 24–28. Their results were presented as effect sizes and significance tests rather than as percent correct.

7. There has been a slight decline in accuracy over time. DePaulo, Zuckerman, and Rosenthal, "Humans as Lie Detectors," 131, report that accuracy was better than chance at $d = 0.86$, and Kraut, "Humans as Lie Detectors," 209, noted that average accuracy was 57%. Although these values fall within the slightly-better-than-chance range, in the Bond and DePaulo, "Accuracy of Deception Judgments," 214, 222, analysis the average d dropped to 0.4, and raw accuracy dropped to 54%.

8. For example, Norah E. Dunbar, Matthew L. Jensen, Judee K. Burgoon, Katherine M. Kelley, Kylie J. Harrison, Bradley J. Adame, and Daniel Rex Bernard, "Effects of Veracity, Modality, and Sanctioning on Credibility Assessment during Mediated and Unmediated Interviews," *Communication Research* 42, no. 5 (July 2015): 649–74, https://doi.org/10.1177/0093650213480175.

9. Timothy R. Levine, Allison Shaw, and Hillary C. Shulman, "Increasing Deception Detection Accuracy with Strategic Questioning," *Human Communication Research* 36, no. 2 (April 2010): 216–31, https://doi.org/10.1111/j.1468-2958.2010.01374.x.

10. Kraut, "Humans as Lie Detectors," 209, pointed this out several decades ago. Hartwig and Bond, "Why Do Lie-Catchers Fail?" provide the most recent meta-analytic evidence. This point is critical to the rationale for TDT and offers a key departure from perspectives such as interpersonal deception theory.

11. Bond and DePaulo, "Accuracy of Deception Judgments," 227.

12. Bond and DePaulo, "Accuracy of Deception Judgments," 228.

13. Bond and DePaulo, "Accuracy of Deception Judgments," 228.

14. Bond and DePaulo, "Individual Differences."

15. Aamodt and Custer, "Who Can Best Catch a Liar?"

16. Bond and DePaulo, "Accuracy of Deception Judgments," 228.

17. Dunbar, Jensen, Burgoon, Kelley, Harrison, Adame, and Bernard, "Effects of Veracity, Modality, and Sanctioning"; Maria Hartwig, Pär Anders Granhag, Leif A. Strömwall, and Aldert Vrij, "Police Officers' Lie Detection Accuracy: Interrogating Freely versus Observing Video," *Police Quarterly* 7, no. 4 (December 2004): 429–56, https://doi.org/10.1177/1098611104264748. An exception to these findings is discussed in chapter 14.

18. For example, one experiment had friends lie to friends about issues such as occupation and religious beliefs. Friends might know their friends' religion and occupation, so strangers should have an advantage lying about such things. See Judee K. Burgoon, David B. Buller, Amy S. Ebesu, and Patricia Rockwell, "Interpersonal Deception: V. Accuracy in Deception Detection," *Communication Monographs* 61, no. 4 (December 1994): 303–25, https://doi.org/10.1080/03637759409376340.

19. Steven A. McCornack and Malcolm R. Parks, "Deception Detection and Relationship Development: The Other Side of Trust," in *Communication Yearbook 9*, ed. Margaret L. McLaughlin, 377–89 (Beverly Hills: Sage, 1986).

20. Timothy R. Levine and Steven A. McCornack, "Linking Love and Lies: A Formal Test of the McCornack and Parks Model of Deception Detection," *Journal of Social and Personal Relationships* 9, no. 1 (February 1992): 143–54.

21. DePaulo, Charlton, Cooper, Lindsay, and Muhlenbruck, "Accuracy-Confidence Correlation."

22. Steven A. McCornack and Timothy R. Levine, "When Lovers Become Leery: The Relationship between Suspicion and Accuracy in Detecting Deception," *Communication Monographs* 57, no. 3 (September 1990): 219–30.

23. Timothy R. Levine, David D. Clare, Tracie Green, Kim B. Serota, and Hee Sun Park, "The Effects of Truth–Lie Base Rate on Interactive Deception Detection Accuracy, *Human Communication Research* 40, no. 3 (July 2014): 350–72, https://doi.org/10.1111/hcre.12027. Other aspects of these studies are presented in chapter 12 under TDT experiments twenty and twenty-one.

24. There is a second catch too. In the model, truth-bias lowers accuracy. This is inconsistent with the veracity effect described in chapter 12. The issue is briefly discussed later in this chapter when discussing truth-bias and scoring truth and lie accuracy separately.

25. Bond and DePaulo, "Accuracy of Deception Judgments," 229.

26. David B. Buller, Jamie Comstock, R. Kelly Aune, and Krystyna D. Strzyzewski, "The Effect of Probing on Deceivers and Truthtellers," *Journal of Nonverbal Behavior* 13, no. 3 (Fall 1989): 155–70; David B. Buller, Krystyna D. Strzyzewski, and Jamie Comstock, "Interpersonal Deception I: Deceivers' Reactions to Receivers' Suspicions and Probing," *Communication Monographs* 58, no. 1 (March 1991): 1–24, https://doi.org/10.1080/03637759109376211; Timothy R. Levine and Steven A. McCornack, "Behavioral Adaptation, Confidence, and Heuristic-Based Explanations of the Probing Effect," *Human Communication Research* 27, no. 4 (October 2001): 471–502; James B. Stiff and Gerald R. Miller, "'Come to Think of It . . .': Interrogative Probes, Deceptive Communication, and Deception Detection," *Human Communication Research* 12, no. 3 (March 1986): 339–57, https://doi.org/10.1111/j.1468–2958.1986.tb00081.x.

27. Levine and McCornack, "Behavioral Adaptation."

28. James E. Driskell, "Effectiveness of Deception Detection Training: A Meta-analysis," *Psychology, Crime & Law* 18, no. 8 (2012): 713–31, https://doi.org/10.1080/1068316X.2010.535820; Mark G. Frank and Thomas Hugh Feeley, "To Catch a Liar: Challenges for Research in Lie Detection Training," *Journal of Applied Communication Research* 31, no. 1 (February 2003): 58–75, https://doi.org/10.1080/00909880305377; Valerie Hauch, Siegfried L. Sporer, Stephen W. Michael, and Christian A. Meissner, "Does Training Improve the Detection of Deception? A Meta-Analysis," *Communication Research* 43, no. 3 (April 2016): 283–343, https://doi.org/10.1177/0093650214534974.

29. Frank and Feeley, "To Catch a Liar."

30. Hauch, Sporer, Michael, and Meissner, "Does Training Improve."

31. Timothy R. Levine, Thomas Hugh Feeley, Steven A. McCornack, Mikayla Hughes, and Chad M. Harms, "Testing the Effects of Nonverbal Training on Deception Detection Accuracy with the Inclusion of a Bogus Training Control Group," *Western Journal of Communication* 69, no. 3 (July 2005): 203–17, https://doi.org/10.1080/10570310500202355.

32. Levine, Feeley, McCornack, Hughes, and Harms, "Testing the Effects." These experiments are described in more detail in chapter 13 as TDT experiments twenty-four and twenty-five.

33. Timothy R. Levine, Hee Sun Park, and Steven A. McCornack, "Accuracy in Detecting Truths and Lies: Documenting the 'Veracity Effect,'" *Communication Monographs* 66, no. 2 (June 1999): 125–44, https://doi.org/10.1080/03637759909376468; Rachel K. Kim and Timothy R.

Levine, "The Effect of Suspicion on Deception Detection Accuracy: Optimal Level or Opposing Effects?" *Communication Reports* 24, no. 2 (July–December 2011): 51–62, http://dx.doi.org/10 .1080/08934215.2011.615272.

34. Bond and DePaulo, "Accuracy of Deception Judgments," 221.

35. Bond and DePaulo, "Accuracy of Deception Judgments," 214.

36. Bond and DePaulo, "Accuracy of Deception Judgments," 224.

37. For an example of this assertion, see Burgoon, Buller, Ebesu, and Rockwell, "Interpersonal Deception: V. Accuracy in Deception Detection."

38. Bond and DePaulo, "Accuracy of Deception Judgments," 222.

39. Daniel Kahneman, *Thinking, Fast and Slow* (New York: Farrar, Straus and Giroux, 2011).

40. DePaulo, Charlton, Cooper, Lindsay, and Muhlenbruck, "Accuracy-Confidence Correlation," 355.

41. For example, Justin S. Albrechtsen, Christian A. Meissner, and Kyle J. Susa, "Can Intuition Improve Deception Detection Performance?" *Journal of Experimental Social Psychology* 45, no. 4 (July 2009): 1052–55, https://doi.org/10.1016/j.jesp.2009.05.017; Marc-André Reinhard, Greifeneder Rainer, and Martin Scharmach, "Unconscious Processes Improve Lie Detection," *Journal of Personality and Social Psychology* 105, no. 5 (November 2013): 721–39, http://dx.doi .org/10.1037/a0034352; Leanne ten Brinke, Dayna Stimson, and Dana R. Carney, "Some Evidence for Unconscious Lie Detection," *Psychological Science* 25, no. 5 (May 2014): 1098–105, https://doi.org/10.1177/0956797614524421; Aldert Vrij, Katherine Edward, and Ray Bull, "Police Officers' Ability to Detect Deceit: The Benefit of Indirect Deception Detection Measures," *Legal and Criminological Psychology* 6, no. 2 (September 2001): 185–96, https://doi.org/10.1348 /135532501168271.

42. Ten Brinke, Stimson, and Carney, "Some Evidence," 6.

43. Charles F. Bond Jr., Timothy R. Levine, and Maria Hartwig, "New Findings in Non-Verbal Lie Detection," in *Detecting Deception: Current Challenges and Cognitive Approaches*, ed. Pär Anders Granhag, Aldert Vrij, and Bruno Verschuere, 37–58 (Chichester: John Wiley and Sons, 2015).

44. Timothy R. Levine and Charles F. Bond Jr., "Direct and Indirect Measures of Lie Detection Tell the Same Story: A Reply to ten Brinke, Stimson, and Carney (2014)," *Psychological Science* 25, no. 10 (October 2014): 1960–61, https://doi.org/10.1177/0956797614536740.

45. The number of judgments is a function of the number of judges and the number of judgments per subject. Statistically, the number of judges (sample size) determines sampling error, while the number of judgments per judge determines reliability (random response error). Both types of error are random.

46. "Wikipedia: Law of Large Numbers," Wikimedia Foundation, http://en.wikipedia.org /wiki/Law_of_large_numbers.

47. See Timothy R. Levine, J. Pete Blair, and Christopher J. Carpenter, "A Critical Look at Meta-analytic Evidence for the Cognitive Approach to Lie Detection: A Re-examination of Vrij, Fisher, and Blank (2017)," *Legal and Criminological Psychology* 23, no. 1 (February 2018): 7–19, https://doi.org/10.1111/lcrp.12115.

48. Bond and DePaulo, "Individual Differences."

Chapter 4

1. Paul Ekman and Wallace V. Friesen, "Nonverbal Leakage and Clues to Deception," *Psychiatry* 32, no. 1 (1969): 88–106, https://doi.org/10.1080/00332747.1969.11023575.

11. Ekman and Friesen, "Nonverbal Leakage," 99–100.

12. Paul Ekman, "Lying and Nonverbal Behavior: Theoretical Issues and New Findings," *Journal of Nonverbal Behavior* 12, no. 3 (September 1988): 163–75, https://doi.org/10.1007 /BF00987486; Paul Ekman, "Deception, Lying, and Demeanor," in *States of Mind: American and Post-Soviet Perspectives on Contemporary Issues in Psychology,* ed. Diane F. Halpern and Aleksander E. Voiskounsky, 93–105 (New York: Oxford University Press, 1997); Paul Ekman, *Telling Lies* (New York: W. W. Norton, 1985, 1992, 2001, 2009).

13. For example, Ekman, "Telling Lies," 2001.

14. Ekman "Telling Lies," 2001.

15. Ekman "Telling Lies," 2001.

16. Ekman, "Lying and Nonverbal Behavior"; Ekman, "Telling Lies," 2001; Mark G. Frank and Paul Ekman, "The Ability to Detect Deceit Generalizes across Different Types of High-Stake Lies," *Journal of Personality and Social Psychology* 72, no. 6 (June 1997): 1429–39, http://dx .doi.org/10.1037/0022–3514.72.6.1429; Maureen O'Sullivan, Mark G. Frank, Carolyn M. Hurley, and Jaspreet Tiwana, "Police Lie Detection Accuracy: The Effect of Lie Scenario," *Law and Human Behavior* 33, no. 6 (December 2009): 530–38, https://doi.org/10.1007/s10979–008–9166–4.

17. Mark G. Frank and Paul Ekman, "Appearing Truthful Generalizes across Different Deception Situations," *Journal of Personality and Social Psychology* 86, no. 3 (March 2004): 486–95, http://dx.doi.org/10.1037/0022–3514.86.3.486, 486–487.

18. Ekman and Friesen, "Nonverbal Leakage."

19. Frank and Ekman, "Appearing Truthful."

20. Paul Ekman and Maureen O'Sullivan, "Who Can Catch a Liar?" *American Psychologist* 46, no. 9 (September 1991): 913–20, http://dx.doi.org/10.1037/0003–066X.46.9.913; Paul Ekman, Maureen O'Sullivan, and Mark G. Frank, "A Few Can Catch a Liar," *Psychological Science* 10, no. 3 (May 1999): 263–66, https://doi.org/10.1111/1467–9280.00147; Maureen O'Sullivan and Paul Ekman, "The Wizards of Deception Detection," in *The Detection of Deception in Forensic Contexts,* ed. Pär Anders Granhag and Leif A. Strömwall (Cambridge: Cambridge University Press), 269–86.

21. Ekman, "Telling Lies," 2001.

22. This approach is sometimes called "baselining." The efficacy of using baseline honest behaviors as a comparison was covered in chapter 3.

23. Ekman and O'Sullivan, "Who Can Catch a Liar?"

24. Ekman, O'Sullivan, and Frank, "Few Can Catch a Liar."

25. O'Sullivan and Ekman, "Wizards."

26. Gary D. Bond, "Deception Detection Expertise," *Law and Human Behavior* 34, no. 4 (August 2008): 339–51, https://doi.org/10.1007/s10979-007-9110-z.

27. O'Sullivan, Frank, Hurley, and Tiwana, "Police Lie Detection Accuracy."

28. O'Sullivan, Frank, Hurley, and Tiwana, "Police Lie Detection Accuracy," 530.

29. O'Sullivan, Frank, Hurley, and Tiwana, "Police Lie Detection Accuracy."

30. Ekman, "Deception, Lying, and Demeanor," 101.

31. Miron Zuckerman, Bella M. DePaulo, and Robert Rosenthal, "Verbal and Nonverbal Communication of Deception," in *Advances in Experimental Social Psychology 14*, edited by Leonard Berkowitz, 1–59 (New York: Academic Press, 1981).

32. Bella M. DePaulo, "Nonverbal Behavior and Self-Presentation," *Psychological Bulletin* 111, no. 2 (March 1992): 203–43, http://dx.doi.org/10.1037/0033-2909.111.2.203.

33. The series of bullet points is a mix of direct quotations, close paraphrasing, and condensing from DePaulo, "Nonverbal Behavior and Self-Presentation," 211–12.

34. This hypothesized willingness to accept others' performances is consistent with the work of Erving Goffman, and it marks a sharp contrast with the next theory discussed, in which people are depicted as vigilant and often deeply suspicious of others. Like Goffman and DePaulo, I believe people usually accept others' self-presentations, and that even when they don't, people usually "play along," so to speak. Erving Goffman, *The Presentation of Self in Everyday Life* (New York: Doubleday, 1959).

35. Bella M. DePaulo, James J. Lindsay, Brian E. Malone, Laura Muhlenbruck, Kelly Charlton, and Harris Cooper, "Cues to Deception," *Psychological Bulletin* 129, no. 1 (January 2003): 74–118. https://dx.doi:10.1037/0033-2909.129.1.74, 81.

36. DePaulo, Lindsay, Malone, Muhlenbruck, Charlton, and Cooper, "Cues to Deception," 106.

37. David B. Buller and Judee K. Burgoon, "Interpersonal Deception Theory," *Communication Theory* 6, no. 3 (August 1996): 203–42, https://doi.org/10.1111/j.1468-2885.1996.tb00127.x.

38. James B. Stiff and Gerald R. Miller, "'Come to Think of It . . .': Interrogative Probes, Deceptive Communication, and Deception Detection," *Human Communication Research* 12, no. 3 (March 1986): 339–57, https://doi.org/10.1111/j.1468-2958.1986.tb00081.x.

39. For example: Steven A. McCornack and Timothy R. Levine, "When Lovers Become Leery: The Relationship between Suspicion and Accuracy in Detecting Deception," *Communication Monographs* 57, no. 3 (September 1990): 219–30, https://doi.org/10.1080/03637759009376197; Steven A. McCornack, Timothy R. Levine, Kathleen A. Solowczuk, Helen I. Torres, and Dedra M. Campbell, "When the Alteration of Information Is Viewed as Deception: An Empirical Test of Information Manipulation Theory," *Communication Monographs* 59, no. 1 (March 1992): 17–29, https://doi.org/10.1080/03637759209376246.

40. Stiff and Miller, "'Come to Think of It.'"

41. Jim Stiff and G. R. Miller were both professors of mine at Michigan State. I took multiple classes from each.

42. This is an example of what Hee Sun Park, Steve McCornack, and I call "the veracity effect," which is discussed in chapter 12.

43. Timothy R. Levine and Steven A. McCornack, "A Critical Analysis of the Behavioral Adaptation Explanation of the Probing Effect," *Human Communication Research* 22, no. 4 (June 1996): 575–88, https://doi.org/10.1111/j.1468-2958.1996.tb00380.x.

44. Buller and Burgoon, "Interpersonal Deception Theory."

45. I did my best to accurately portray the basic theoretical flow of IDT. As I will argue in the next chapter, clarity and IDT are, I believe, incompatible.

46. The following description of IDT's structure and propositions is from Buller and Burgoon, "Interpersonal Deception Theory."

47. The exact wording is "Proposition 1: Sender and receiver cognitions and behaviors vary systematically as deceptive communication contexts vary in (a) access to social cues, (b) immediacy, (c) relational engagement, (d) conversational demands, and (e) spontaneity." Buller and Burgoon, "Interpersonal Deception Theory," 214.

48. This proposition places IDT in contrast to DePaulo's self-presentation perspective and is consistent with the earlier four-factor theory.

49. Aldert Vrij and Pär Anders Granhag, "Eliciting Cues to Deception and Truth: What Matters Are the Questions Asked," *Journal of Applied Research in Memory and Cognition* 1, no. 2 (June 2012): 110–17, https://doi.org/10.1016/j.jarmac.2012.02.004, 110.

50. Vrij and Granhag, "Eliciting Cues," 111.

51. Vrij and Granhag, "Eliciting Cues," 113.

52. Vrij and Granhag, "Eliciting Cues," 112.

53. Vrij and Granhag, "Eliciting Cues," 113.

Chapter 5

1. The efficiency criteria might also be called the explanatory-power-to-parsimony ratio.

2. See, for example, Steven A. McCornack, "The Generation of Deceptive Messages: Laying the Groundwork for a Viable Theory of Interpersonal Deception," in *Message Production: Advances in Communication Theory*, ed. John O. Green, 91–126 (Mahwah, NJ: Erlbaum, 1997).

3. For more detail, see Timothy R. Levine, "Scientific Evidence and Cue Theories in Deception Research: Reconciling Findings from Meta-Analyses and Primary Experiments," *International Journal of Communication* 12 (2018): 2461–79.

4. According to TDT, cues and demeanor do play a role in what people see as honest, and reliance on cues and demeanor tends to push accuracy down toward chance, as described in chapter 13.

5. DePaulo, Lindsay, Malone, Muhlenbruck, Charlton, and Cooper, "Cues to Deception."

6. The metaphor is adapted from Christopher J. Ferguson and Moritz Heene, "A Vast Graveyard of Undead Theories: Publication Bias and Psychological Science's Aversion to the Null," *Perspectives in Psychological Science* 7, no. 6 (November 2012): 555–61, https://doi.org/10.1177/1745691612459059. Deception theory, in my view, provides an excellent example of Ferguson and Heene's concerns with psychological science. Many of the questionable research practices described in the same issue of *Perspectives on Psychological Science* (vol. 7, no. 6) apply to research on the theories I am describing in this chapter.

7. Recall the 2014 findings from Hartwig and Bond reviewed in chapter 2, in which the average effect for the strongest cue in a given cue study was $r = .43$ ($d = 0.95$).

8. According to a Wikipedia entry (http://en.wikipedia.org/wiki/Overfitting): "In statistics and machine learning, overfitting occurs when a statistical model describes random error or noise instead of the underlying relationship. Overfitting generally occurs when a model is excessively complex, such as having too many parameters relative to the number of observations. A model which has been overfit will generally have poor predictive performance, as it can exaggerate minor fluctuations in the data."

9. See Five-Thirty-Eight (http://fivethirtyeight.com/features/science-isnt-broken/#part1) for an explanation and demonstration.

10. Imre Lakatos, *The Methodology of Scientific Research Programmes*, Cambridge: Cambridge University Press, 1978.

11. For example, see Maureen O'Sullivan, Mark G. Frank, Carolyn M. Hurley, and Jaspreet Tiwana, "Police Lie Detection Accuracy: The Effect of Lie Scenario," *Law and Human Behavior* 33, no. 6 (December 2009): 530–38, https://doi.org/10.1007/s10979–008–9166–4.

12. Robert Kraut, "Humans as Lie Detectors," *Journal of Communication* 30, no. 4 (December 1980): 209–18, https://doi.org/10.1111/j.1460–2466.1980.tb02030.x.

13. Kraut, "Humans as Lie Detectors," 209.

14. He put the average at 57.0% based on ten studies at the time.

15. Kraut, "Humans as Lie Detectors," 209.

16. Kraut, "Humans as Lie Detectors," 213. These observations are very much in line with TDT but predate it by decades.

17. Kraut, "Humans as Lie Detectors," 213.

18. Kraut, "Humans as Lie Detectors," 214. The observation of the importance of sender variation is central to TDT and is discussed in chapter 13.

19. McCornack, "Generation of Deceptive Messages."

20. Quoted from McCornack, "Generation of Deceptive Messages," 94–95.

21. These observations are consistent with DePaulo's self-presentation approach and her work on everyday lies. See, for example, Bella M. DePaulo, Deborah A. Kashy, Susan E. Kirkendol, Melissa M. Wyer, and Jennifer A. Epstein, "Lying in Everyday Life," *Journal of Personality and Social Psychology* 70, no. 5 (May 1996): 979–95, http://dx.doi.org/10.1037/0022–3514.70.5.979.

22. Interested readers are directed to McCornack's 1997 chapter and its 2014 update under the label IMT2. Some of his arguments are summarized in chapter 8.

23. Stephen Porter and Leanne ten Brinke, "Reading Between the Lies: Identifying Concealed and Falsified Emotions in Universal Facial Expressions," *Psychological Science* 19, no. 5 (May 2008): 508–14, https://doi.org/10.1111/j.1467–9280.2008.02116.x

24. Sharon Weinberger, "Intent to Deceive? Can the Science of Deception Detection Help to Catch Terrorists?" *Nature* 465, no. 7297 (May 2010): 412–15, https://doi:10.1038/465412a, https://www.nature.com/news/2010/100526/full/465412a.html.

25. Hartwig and Bond, "Lie Detection."

26. Mark G. Frank and Paul Ekman, "Appearing Truthful Generalizes across Different Deception Situations," *Journal of Personality and Social Psychology* 86, no. 3 (March 2004): 486–95, http://dx.doi.org/10.1037/0022–3514.86.3.486, footnote 2, 488.

27. Charles F. Bond Jr. and Bella M. DePaulo, "Accuracy of Deception Judgments," *Personality and Social Psychology Review* 10, no. 3 (August 2006): 214–34, https://doi.org/10.1207/s15327957pspr1003_2

28. Bella M. DePaulo, Susan E. Kirkendol, John Tang, and Thomas P. O'Brien, "The Motivational Impairment Effect in the Communication of Deception: Replications and Extensions," *Journal of Nonverbal Behavior* 12, no. 3 (Fall 1988): 177–202, https://doi.org/10.1007/BF00987487.

29. Bond and DePaulo, "Accuracy of Deception Judgments."

30. Timothy R. Levine, J. Pete Blair, and David D. Clare, "Diagnostic Utility: Experimental Demonstrations and Replications of Powerful Question Effects in High-Stakes Deception Detection," *Human Communication Research* 40, no. 2 (April 2014): 262–89, https://doi.org/10.1111/hcre.12021; Timothy R. Levine, Kim B. Serota, Hillary Shulman, David D. Clare, Hee Sun Park, Allison S. Shaw, Jae Chul Shim, and Jung Hyon Lee, "Sender Demeanor: Individual Differences in Sender Believability Have a Powerful Impact on Deception Detection Judgments," *Human Communication Research* 37, no. 3 (July 2011): 377–403, https://doi.org/10.1111/j.1468-2958.2011.01407.x.

31. Levine, Blair, and Clare, "Diagnostic Utility"; Timothy R. Levine, Rachel K. Kim, and J. Pete Blair, "(In)accuracy at Detecting True and False Confessions and Denials: An Initial Test of a Projected Motive Model of Veracity Judgments," *Human Communication Research* 36, no. 1 (January 2010): 82–102, https://doi.org/10.1111/j.1468-2958.2009.01369.x.

32. Charles F. Bond Jr. and Bella M. DePaulo, "Individual Differences in Judging Deception: Accuracy and Bias," *Psychological Bulletin* 134, no. 4 (July 2008): 477–92, http://dx.doi.org/10.1037/0033-2909.134.4.477.

33. Internal validity is the extent to which causal inferences can unambiguously be drawn from an experimental design; external validity refers to the generality of findings; construct validity refers to the extent to which measures or experimental inductions capture or produce variation in the intended theoretical constructs; and grant validity refers to the extent to which research is successful in garnering and spending large amounts of money. The first three types of validity are often credited to Campbell and Stanley, and Cronback and Meehl. The fourth type, grant validity, is my own cynical creation and a reaction to the observation that in today's academic culture, research funding is more important in many circles than good scholarship and scientific progress. Donald T. Campbell and Julian C. Stanley, *Experimental and Quasi-experimental Designs for Research* (Boston: Houghton Mifflin, 1963); Lee J. Cronbach and Paul E. Meehl, "Construct Validity in Psychological Tests," *Psychological Bulletin* 52, no. 4 (July 1955): 281–302, http://dx.doi.org/10.1037/h0040957.

34. Published critiques include: Bella M. DePaulo, Matthew E. Ansfield, and Kathy L. Bell, "Theories about Deception and Paradigms for Studying It: A Critical Appraisal of Buller and Burgoon's Interpersonal Deception Theory," *Communication Theory* 6, no. 3 (August 1996): 297–310, https://doi.org/10.1111/j.1468-2885.1996.tb00131.x; Timothy R. Levine, David D. Clare, Tracie Green, Kim B. Serota, and Hee Sun Park, "The Effects of Truth–Lie Base Rate on Interactive Deception Detection Accuracy," *Human Communication Research* 40, no. 3 (July 2014): 350–72, https://doi.org/10.1111/hcre.12027; Timothy R. Levine and Steven A. McCornack, "A Critical Analysis of the Behavioral Adaptation Explanation of the Probing Effect," *Human Communication Research* 22, no. 4 (June 1996): 575–88, https://doi.org/10.1111/j.1468-2958.1996.tb00380.x; Timothy R. Levine and Steven A. McCornack, "Can Behavioral Adaptation Explain the Probing Effect? Rejoinder to Buller et al.," *Human Communication Research* 22, no. 4 (June 1996): 604–13, https://doi.org/10.1111/j.1468-2958.1996.tb00382.x; Timothy R. Levine and Steven A. McCornack, "Behavioral Adaptation, Confidence, and Heuristic-Based Explanations of the Probing Effect," *Human Communication Research* 27, no. 4 (October 2001): 471–502,

https://doi.org/10.1111/j.1468–2958.2001.tb00790.x; Hee Sun Park and Timothy R. Levine, "Base Rates, Deception Detection, and Deception Theory: A Reply to Burgoon (2015)," *Human Communication Research* 41, no. 3 (July 2015): 350–66, https://doi.org/10.1111/hcre.12066; James B. Stiff, "Theoretical Approaches to the Study of Deceptive Communication: Comments on Interpersonal Deception Theory," *Communication Theory* 6, no. 3 (August 1996): 289–96, https://doi.org/10.1111/j.1468–2885.1996.tb00130.x.

35. David B. Buller and Judee K. Burgoon, "Interpersonal Deception Theory," *Communication Theory* 6, no. 3 (August 1996): 203–42, https://doi.org/10.1111/j.1468–2885.1996.tb00127.x., 214.

36. Bond and DePaulo, "Accuracy of Deception Judgments." See also Table 3.1 in chapter 3.

37. Timothy R. Levine, David D. Clare, J. Pete Blair, Steve McCornack, and Kelly Morrison, "Expertise in Deception Detection Involves Actively Prompting Diagnostic Information rather than Passive Behavioral Observation," *Human Communication Research* 40, no. 4 (October 2014): 442–62, https://doi.org/10.1111/hcre.12032; see chapter 14.

38. Buller and Burgoon, "Interpersonal Deception Theory," 281.

39. Bond and DePaulo, "Accuracy of Deception Judgments."

40. Hartwig and Bond, "Lie Detection from Multiple Cues."

41. David B. Buller, Krystyna D. Strzyzewski, and Frank G. Hunsaker, "Interpersonal Deception: II. The Inferiority of Conversational Participants as Deception Detectors," *Communication Monographs* 58, no. 1 (1991): 25–40, https://doi.org/10.1080/03637759109376212.

42. Buller and Burgoon, "Interpersonal Deception Theory," 223.

43. Bond and DePaulo, "Accuracy of Deception Judgments"; see table 3 and text on page 226.

44. Judee K. Burgoon, David B. Buller, Leesa Dillman, and Joseph B. Walther, "Interpersonal Deception: IV. Effects of Suspicion on Perceived Communication and Nonverbal Behavior Dynamics," *Human Communication Research* 22, no. 2 (December 1995): 165, https://doi.org/10.1111/j.1468–2958.1995.tb00365.x. This claim is also repeated in Buller and Burgoon, "Interpersonal Deception Theory" (228), along with a string of self-citations as support.

45. Judee K. Burgoon, "Rejoinder to Levine, Clare et al.'s Comparison of the Park–Levine Probability Model versus Interpersonal Deception Theory: Application to Deception Detection," *Human Communication Research* 41, no. 3 (July 2015): 327–49, https://doi.org/10.1111/hcre.12065.

46. DePaulo, Ansfield, and Bell, "Theories about Deception," made this argument.

47. Judee K. Burgoon, David B. Buller, Amy S. Ebesu, and Patricia Rockwell, "Interpersonal Deception: V. Accuracy in Deception Detection," *Communication Monographs* 61, no. 4 (December 1994): 303–25, https://doi.org/10.1080/03637759409376340.

48. Burgoon, Buller, Ebesu, and Rockwell, "Interpersonal Deception: V," 305.

49. Burgoon, Buller, Ebesu, and Rockwell, "Interpersonal Deception: V," 315.

50. Burgoon, Buller, Ebesu, and Rockwell, "Interpersonal Deception: V," 315, report that "F (1, 21) = 3.50, $p < .05$ one-tailed." The critical value of F with those df is 4.32. Since 3.50 is less than 4.32, F cannot be statistically significant at $p < .05$.

51. Burgoon, Buller, Ebesu, and Rockwell, "Interpersonal Deception: V," 318.

52. See Levine and Banas for numerous examples of questionable one-tailed tests in IDT, and Levine and Hullett for commentary on the misreporting of effect sizes. Both the Levine and Banas and Levine and Hullett articles were inspired by statistical shenanigans in IDT articles such as Burgoon, Buller, Ebesu, and Rockwell, "Interpersonal Deception: V." But Burgoon is not alone in the use of questionable statistical practices. Footnote 4 on p. 507 of Vrij,

Mann, Kristen, and Fisher (2007) reports so-called one-tailed *F*-tests. Timothy R. Levine and John Banas, "One-Tailed *F*-Tests in Communication Research," *Communication Monographs* 69, no. 2 (2002): 132–43, https://doi.org/10.1080/714041709; Timothy R. Levine and Craig R. Hullett, "Eta Squared, Partial Eta Squared, and Misreporting of Effect Size in Communication Research," *Human Communication Research* 28, no. 4 (October 2002): 612–25, https://doi.org /10.1111/j.1468–2958.2002.tb00828.x; Aldert Vrij, Samantha Mann, Susanne Kristen, and Ronald P. Fisher, "Cues to Deception and Ability to Detect Lies as a Function of Police Interview Styles," *Law and Human Behavior* 31, no. 5 (October 2007): 499–518, https://doi.org /10.1007/s10979–006–9066–4.

53. For example, Aldert Vrij and Pär Anders Granhag, "Eliciting Cues to Deception and Truth: What Matters Are the Questions Asked," *Journal of Applied Research in Memory and Cognition* 1, no. 2 (June 2012): 110–17, https://doi.org/10.1016/j.jarmac.2012.02.004, 110.

54. Aldert Vrij, Samantha A. Mann, Ronald P. Fisher, Rebecca Milne, and Ray Bull, "Increasing Cognitive Load to Facilitate Lie Detection: The Benefit of Recalling an Event in Reverse Order," *Law and Human Behavior* 32, no. 3 (June 2008): 253–65, https://doi.org/10.1007 /s10979–007–9103-y.

55. Aldert Vrij, Samantha Mann, Sharon Leal, and Ronald Fisher, "'Look into My Eyes': Can an Instruction to Maintain Eye Contact Facilitate Lie Detection?" *Psychology, Crime & Law* 16, no. 4 (2010): 327–48, https://doi.org/10.1080/10683160902740633.

56. Meiling Liu, Pär Anders Granhag, Sara Landstrom, Emma Roos af Hjelmsater, Leif Strömwall, and Aldert Vrij, "'Can You Remember What Was in Your Pocket When You Were Stung by a Bee?' Eliciting Cues to Deception by Asking the Unanticipated," *Open Criminology Journal* 3, no. 3 (June 2010): 31–36, doi: 10.2174/1874917801003010031.

57. For example, Aldert Vrij, Sharon Leal, Pär Anders Granhag, Samantha Mann, Ronald P. Fisher, Jackie Hillman, and Kathryn Sperry, "Outsmarting the Liars: The Benefit of Asking Unanticipated Questions," *Law and Human Behavior* 33, no 2 (April 2009): 159–66, https://doi.org /10.1007/s10979–008–9143-y.

58. Timothy R. Levine, J. Pete Blair, and Christopher J. Carpenter, "A Critical Look at Meta-analytic Evidence for the Cognitive Approach to Lie Detection: A Re-examination of Vrij, Fisher, and Blank (2017)," *Legal and Criminological Psychology* 23, no. 1 (February 2018): 7–19, https:// doi.org/10.1111/lcrp.12115.

59. James Honeycutt, *Imagine That: Studies in Imagined Interactions* (Cresskill, NJ: Hampton Press, 2009).

60. Also see Siegfried L. Sporer, "Deception and Cognitive Load: Expanding Our Horizon with a Working Memory Model," *Frontiers in Psychology* 7 (April 2016), https://doi.org/10.3389 /fpsyg.2016.00420.

61. James B. Stiff and Gerald R. Miller, "'Come to Think of It . . .': Interrogative Probes, Deceptive Communication, and Deception Detection." *Human Communication Research* 12, no. 3 (March 1986): 339–57, https://doi.org/10.1111/j.1468–2958.1986.tb00081.x. See also Levine and McCornack, "Critical Analysis."

62. Aldert Vrij, Samantha Mann, Susanne Kristen, and Ronald P. Fisher, "Cues to Deception and Ability to Detect Lies as a Function of Police Interview Styles," *Law and Human Behavior* 31, no. 5 (October 2007): 499–518, https://doi.org/10.1007/s10979–006–9066–4.

63. Timothy R. Levine, Hillary C. Shulman, Christopher J. Carpenter, David C. DeAndrea, and J. Pete Blair, "The Impact of Accusatory, Non-Accusatory, Bait, and False Evidence Ques-

tioning on Deception Detection," *Communication Research Reports* 30, no. 2 (April 2013): 169–74, https://doi.org/10.1080/08824096.2012.762905.

64. Aldert Vrij, Ronald P. Fisher, and Hartmut Blank, "A Cognitive Approach to Lie Detection: A Meta-Analysis," *Legal and Criminological Psychology* 22, no. 1 (February 2017): 1–21, https://doi.org/10.1111/lcrp.12088.

65. Timothy R. Levine, J. Pete Blair, and Christopher J. Carpenter, "A Critical Look at Meta-analytic Evidence for the Cognitive Approach to Lie Detection: A Re-examination of Vrij, Fisher, and Blank (2017)," *Legal and Criminological Psychology* 23, no. 1 (February 2018): 7–19, https://doi.org/10.1111/lcrp.12115.

66. For example, Pär Anders Granhag and Leif A. Strömwall, "Deception Detection: Examining the Consistency Heuristic," in *New Trends in Criminal Investigation and Evidence II*, ed. C. M. Breur, M. M. Kommer, J. F. Nijboer, and J. M. Reintjes, 309–21 (Antwerpen: Intersentia, 2000).

67. Maria Hartwig, Pär Anders Granhag, Leif A. Strömwall, and Ola Kronkvist, "Strategic Use of Evidence during Police Interviews: When Training to Detect Deception Works," *Law and Human Behavior* 30, no. 5 (October 2006): 603–19, https://doi.org/10.1007/s10979–006–9053–9.

68. Pär Anders Granhag, Sebastian C. Montecinos, and Simon Oleszkiewicz, "Eliciting Intelligence from Sources: The First Scientific Test of the Scharff Technique," *Legal and Criminological Psychology* 20, no. 1 (February 2015): 96–113, https://doi.org/10.1111/lcrp.12015.

69. https://www.google.com/webhp?hl=en&tab=mw#hl=en&q=cult.

Chapter 6

1. The information in this chapter is also presented in Timothy R. Levine, "Truth-Default Theory (TDT): A Theory of Human Deception and Deception Detection," *Journal of Language and Social Psychology* 33, no. 4 (September 2014): 378–92, https://doi.org/10.1177/0261927X14535916. Although this chapter and the 2014 publication are not identical, there is considerable overlap, and both provide a general outline and summary of TDT.

2. This definition is explained in chapter 7.

3. I will sometimes use "lie" and "deception" interchangeably, although they are not the same thing. Lies are one type of deception, but not all deception involves a lie. I use them interchangeably for mere convenience when the difference between deception and lie is unimportant. The distinction is discussed in chapter 7 on definitions and chapter 8 on information manipulation.

Chapter 7

1. Much of the discussion in this section is reproduced, paraphrased, or reworked from a 2010 book chapter I authored with Rachel Kim. However, my opinion has changed somewhat since writing the 2010 chapter, and this chapter reflects my current thinking, and my move toward a more functional perspective and away from conscious intent. This chapter, too, provides a much more expanded exploration into the issue of defining deception than I have offered previously. Timothy R. Levine and Rachel K. Kim, "Some Considerations for a New Theory of Deceptive Communication," in *The Interplay of Truth and Deception: New Agendas in Theory and Research*, ed. Matt S. McGlone and Mark L. Knapp, (New York: Routledge, 2010), 16–34.

2. Paul Ekman, *Telling Lies* (New York: W. W. Norton, 2001), 28.

3. David B. Buller and Judee K. Burgoon, "Interpersonal Deception Theory," *Communication Theory* 6, no. 3 (August 1996): 205, https://doi.org/10.1111/j.1468-2885.1996.tb00127.x.

4. Aldert Vrij, *Detecting Lies and Deceit: Pitfalls and Opportunities* (West Sussex: John Wiley and Sons, 2008), 15.

5. My approach to definitions was influenced by a book by Gerald R. Miller and Henry E. Nicholson, *Communication Inquiry* (Reading, MA: Addison-Wesley, 1976).

6. Levine and Kim, "Some Considerations," 16.

7. I understand the word "intent" as implying conscious forethought. The intention to deceive precedes a deceptive action in time, and the deceiver has awareness and is deliberate in seeking to deceive. Knowing, in contrast, can occur after the fact.

8. Miller and Nicholson, *Communication Inquiry*.

9. Glenn Kessler, Salvador Rizzo, and Meg Kelly, "President Trump Has Made More than 5,000 False or Misleading Claims," *Washington Post*, September 13, 2018, https://www.washingtonpost.com/politics/2018/09/13/president-trump-has-made-more-than-false-or-misleading-claims.

10. Robert Trivers, *The Folly of Fools: The Logic of Deceit and Self-Deception in Human Life* (New York: Basic, 2011).

11. This footnote is a rant about what I call the cult of self-efficacy. Some people will argue that self-deception is adaptive because there is value in unrealistic self-appraisals and self-efficacy. What is important, according to this view, is thinking you can do something and feeling good about yourself. Delusion is empowering and healthy. We need a strong psychological immune system to protect our self-esteem and to ensure motivation. In my academic field of human communication, high self-efficacy is almost always seen as desirable. In my view, however, an unrealistic assessment of the self leads to social problems and ill-advised risk taking. I don't accept the self-efficacy-is-always-good view. I see value in realistic appraisals.

12. Daniel Kahneman, *Thinking, Fast and Slow* (New York: Farrar, Straus and Giroux, 2011).

13. Leon Festinger, Henry W. Rieken, and Stanley Schachter, *When Prophecy Fails: A Social and Psychological Study of a Modern Group That Predicted the Destruction of the World* (Minneapolis: University of Minnesota Press, 1956).

14. For an excellent discussion of these issues in primates, see A. Whiten and Richard W. Byrne, "Tactical Deception in Primates," *Behavioral and Brain Sciences* 11, no. 2 (June 1988): 233–44, https://doi.org/10.1017/S0140525X00049682.

15. "Wikipedia: Hanns Scharff," Wikimedia Foundation, http://en.wikipedia.org/wiki/Hanns_Scharff.

16. This is the idea behind the strategic use of evidence (SUE) approach to lie detection; see Maria Hartwig, Pär Anders Granhag, Leif A. Strömwall, and Ola Kronkvist, "Strategic Use of Evidence during Police Interviews: When Training to Detect Deception Works," *Law and Human Behavior* 30, no. 5 (October 2006): 603–19, https://doi.org/10.1007/s10979-006-9053-9.

17. Joan Peskin, "Ruse and Representation: On Children's Ability to Conceal Information," *Developmental Psychology* 28, no. 1 (January 1992): 84–89, http://dx.doi.org/10.1037/0012-1649.28.1.84.

18. For those interested in the development of deception in children, a topic beyond the scope of this book, I suggest the outstanding work of Victoria Talwar, for example, Victoria Talwar and Angela Crossman, "From Little White Lies to Filthy Liars: The Evolution of Honesty

and Deception in Young Children," *Advancement in Child Development and Behavior* 40, (January 2011): 139–79, https://doi.org/10.1016/B978-0-12-386491-8.00004-9.

19. This may raise an additional problem for intent-based definitions. Even though we all know that fiction is fiction, good fiction often strives to be believable. The word "transported" is sometimes used in describing especially engaging fiction. So, is a fiction author, or a movie actor who is striving to be believable, being deceptive? I want to say no, but I think it might be deceptive under many definitions of deception.

20. David C. DeAndrea, Stephanie Tom Tong, Yuhua Jake Liang, Timothy R. Levine, and Joseph B. Walther, "When Do People Misrepresent Themselves to Others? The Effects of Social Desirability, Ground Truth, and Accountability on Deceptive Self-Presentations," *Journal of Communication* 62, no. 3 (June 2012): 400–17, https://doi.org/10.1111/j.1460-2466.2012.01646.x.

21. For many incredible examples, see Michael Farquhar, *A Treasury of Deception: Liars, Misleaders, Hoodwinkers, and the Extraordinary True Stories of History's Greatest Hoaxes, Fakes and Frauds* (New York: Penguin Books, 2005).

22. Fortunately, the researcher of the month lasted only a few months. Unfortunately, efforts to spur more grants shifted from incentive-based to downright punitive. Further, the superficial similarity of researcher of the month to *Playboy*'s Playmate of the Month greatly amused some sexist old male professors and offended many of the more politically correct members of the college.

23. The poster now hangs in my office at UAB, easily in sight of unwary visitors. A graduate student was duped by it this week. A parent on a college scouting visit fell for it last week. For the record, I have no musical or basketball talent.

Chapter 8

1. Steven A. McCornack, "The Generation of Deceptive Messages: Laying the Groundwork for a Viable Theory of Interpersonal Deception," in *Message Production: Advances in Communication Theory*, ed. John O. Green (Mahwah, NJ: Erlbaum, 1997), 91–126; Steven A. McCornack, Kelly Morrison, Jihyun Esther Paik, Amy M. Wisner, and Xun Zhu, "Information Manipulation Theory 2: A Propositional Theory of Deceptive Discourse Production," *Language and Social Psychology* 33, no. 4 (September 2014): 348–77, https://doi.org/10.1177/0261927X14534656.

2. Steven A. McCornack, "Information Manipulation Theory," *Communication Monographs* 59, no. 1 (1992): 1–16, https://doi.org/10.1080/03637759209376245; Steven A. McCornack, Timothy R. Levine, Kathleen A. Solowczuk, Helen I. Torres, and Dedra M. Campbell, "When the Alternation of Information Is Viewed as Deception: An Empirical Test of Information Manipulation Theory," *Communication Monographs* 59, no. 2 (March 1992): 17–29, https://doi.org/10.1080/03637759209376246.

3. Peter Meijes Tiersma, "The Language of Perjury: Literal Truth, Ambiguity, and the False Statement Requirement," *Southern California Law Review* 63 (1989): 373–431.

4. Dariusz Galasinski, *The Language of Deception: A Discourse Analytical Study* (Thousand Oaks, CA: Sage, 2000).

5. See Judee K. Burgoon, David B. Buller, Laura K. Guerrero, Walid A. Afifi, and Clyde M. Feldman, "Interpersonal Deception: XII. Information Management Dimensions Underlying Deceptive and Truthful Messages," *Communication Monographs* 63, no. 1 (1996): 50–69, https://doi.org/10.1080/03637759609376374. In IDT, information manipulation is changed to information management, quantity becomes completeness, quality becomes veridicality, relevance be-

comes directness/relevance, and manner becomes clarity. A fifth dimension, personalization, is added in IDT. Steve and I jokingly referred to the IDT version as IMT + 1. Buller and Burgoon nevertheless distance their view from Grice, criticize the application of Grice's cooperation principle (CP) to deception, and assert the originality of their own ideas. See David B. Buller and Judee K. Burgoon, "Another Look at Information Management: A Rejoinder to McCornack, Levine, Morrison, and Lapinski," *Communication Monographs* 63, no. 1 (1996): 92–98, https://doi.org/10.1080/03637759609376377.

6. Paul Grice, *Studies in the Way of Words* (Cambridge: Harvard University Press, 1989).

7. Edward T. Hall, *Beyond Culture* (New York: Anchor Books, 1976).

8. The writings of both Grice and Hall influenced TDT, especially the importance of understanding what is said in context; see chapter 14. Note that things that are implicated or highly contextualized are not deception, although people lacking contextual nuance may well be misled. The sender says what he or she does do presuming the reviewer will get the message.

9. Grice, *Studies in the Way of Words*, 26.

10. Grice, *Studies in the Way of Words*, 26–27.

11. Grice, *Studies in the Way of Words*, 30.

12. An alternative interpretation is that the violation of quantity was meant to be, or just heard as, covert; that is, no one realized that he thought the quality was low. In such cases, "they publish a lot" might be heard as "I think they are well qualified," and the message would be deceptive as explained in the discussion of IMT.

13. McCornack, "Information Manipulation Theory," 8, Table 1, Deception Provoking Situations.

14. The exception is what might be called a false implicature. An example is false sarcasm. The maxims are literally followed, but the listener is tricked into thinking there is a flout, thereby being deceived by a literally truthful statement. McCornack (1992) recognized this possibility in his original article. This sort of deceptive message that falls outside IMT is exceptionally rare in practice, but I have seen occasional examples in real discourse.

15. McCornack, Levine, Solowczuk, Torres, and Campbell, "When the Alternation."

16. Timothy R. Levine, "Dichotomous and Continuous Views of Deception: A Reexamination of Deception Ratings in Information Manipulation Theory," *Communication Research Reports* 18, no. 3 (2001): 230–40, https://doi.org/10.1080/08824090109384803. A 1996 experiment by Jacobs and colleagues provides an independent replication reporting results that were very similar to the first IMT study. Discrepancies were likely attributable to a minor methodological error in the Jacobs replication. The conference paper version of Jacobs's study listed the situation-message combinations used, and in one condition, they used a faulty message example. I discovered this in a re-analysis of the Jacob's data. Once the error was detected and corrected, IMT study 1, IMT study 2, and Jacobs's findings cohere. Scott Jacobs, Edwin J. Dawson, and Dale Brashers, "Information Manipulation Theory: A Replication and Assessment," *Communication Monographs* 63, no. 1 (1996): 70–82, https://doi.org/10.1080/03637759609376375.

17. I have no explanation for the 13% who said the lie was honest. I don't think it is simply errors of not paying attention because that did not seem to be happening in the base honest condition. It is hard to imagine that the truth-default could be this strong with some people.

18. Timothy R. Levine, Kelli Jean Asada, and Lisa L. Massi Lindsey, "The Relative Impact of Violation Type and Lie Severity on Judgments of Message Deceptiveness," *Communication Research Reports* 20, no. 3 (2003): 208–18, https://doi.org/10.1080/08824090309388819.

19. STD stands for sexually transmitted disease.

20. Human immunodeficiency virus (HIV) causes AIDs (acquired immunodeficiency syndrome), a particularly serious STD; see http://en.wikipedia.org/wiki/HIV.

21. Timothy R. Levine, "Modeling the Psychometric Properties of Information Manipulation Ratings," *Communication Research Reports* 15, no. 2 (1998): 218–25, https://doi.org/10.1080/08824099809362116.

22. Jacobs, Dawson, and Brashers, "Information Manipulation."

23. The data were originally reported by Steven A. McCornack, Timothy R. Levine, Kelly Morrison, and Maria Lapinski, "Speaking of Information Manipulation: A Critical Rejoinder," *Communication Monographs* 63, no. 1 (1996): 83–92, https://doi.org/10.1080/03637759609376376; and Jacobs, Dawson, and Brashers, "Information Manipulation."

24. For example, McCornack, "Generation of Deceptive Messages." I think he is too hard on himself and IMT. IMT does make a testable prediction. Covert violations of the four maxims are deceptive, and research on IMT has borne that out. IMT, in my view, is not a grand theory; it is small in scope. But it meets my criteria for social scientific theory I mentioned in chapter 5.

25. Steven A. McCornack, *Reflect and Relate* (Boston: Bedford/St. Martin's, 2006); Steven A. McCornack, *Interpersonal Communication and You* (Boston: Bedford/St. Martin's, 2015); Steven A. McCornack and Joseph Ortiz, *Choices & Connections: An Introduction to Human Communication* (Boston: Bedford/St. Martin's, 2015).

26. Timothy R. Levine and Steven A. McCornack, "Theorizing about Deception," *Journal of Language and Social Psychology* 33, no. 4 (September 2014): 431–40, https://doi.org/10.1177/0261927X14536397.

27. McCornack, Morrison, Paik, Wisner, and Zhu, "Information Manipulation Theory 2," 355.

28. McCornack, Morrison, Paik, Wisner, and Zhu, "Information Manipulation Theory 2," 362.

29. Quoted from Steven A. McCornack, Kelly Morrison, Jihyun Esther Paik, Amy M. Wisner, and Xun Zhu, "Information Manipulation Theory 2: A Propositional Theory of Deceptive Discourse Production," *Language and Social Psychology* 33, no. 4 (September 2014): 348–77, https://doi.org/10.1177/0261927X14534656.

30. McCornack, Morrison, Paik, Wisner, and Zhu, "Information Manipulation Theory 2," 365.

31. McCornack, Morrison, Paik, Wisner, and Zhu, "Information Manipulation Theory 2," 367.

32. McCornack, Morrison, Paik, Wisner, and Zhu, "Information Manipulation Theory 2," 368–69.

33. McCornack, Morrison, Paik, Wisner, and Zhu, "Information Manipulation Theory 2," 269. I did some minor editing.

Chapter 9

1. Paul Rozin, "Social Psychology and Science: Some Lessons from Solomon Asch," *Personality and Social Psychology Review* 5, no. 1 (February 2001): 2–14, https://doi.org/10.1207/S15327957PSPR0501_1.

2. Steven A. McCornack, "The Generation of Deceptive Messages: Laying the Groundwork for a Viable Theory of Interpersonal Deception," in *Message Production: Advances in Communication Theory*, ed. John O. Green, 91–126 (Mahwah, NJ: Erlbaum, 1997).

3. Notable examples of descriptive work include Steve McCornack's original message data from IMT, Bella DePaulo's work on everyday lies, DePaulo and Bell's art study, and Hee Sun Park's "how people really detect lies" study. Steven A. McCornack, "Information Manipula-

tion Theory," *Communication Monographs* 59, no. 1 (1992): 1–16, https://doi.org/10.1080 /03637759209376245; Bella M. DePaulo, Deborah A. Kashy, Susan E. Kirkendol, Melissa M. Wyer, and Jennifer A. Epstein, "Lying in Everyday Life," *Journal of Personality and Social Psychology* 70, no. 5 (May 1996): 979–95, http://dx.doi.org/10.1037/0022-3514.70.5.979; Bella M. DePaulo and Kathy L. Bell, "Truth and Investment: Lies Are Told to Those Who Care," *Journal of Personality and Social Psychology* 71, no. 4 (October 1996): 703–16, http://dx.doi.org/10.1037 /0022-3514.71.4.703; Hee Sun Park, Timothy R. Levine, Steven A. McCornack, Kelly Morrison, and Merissa Ferrara, "How People Really Detect Lies," *Communication Monographs* 69, no. 2 (June 2002): 144–57, https://doi.org/10.1080/714041710.

4. This is an underappreciated point. Establishing prevalence involves sampling communication, not people! Knowing what proportion of communication is honest and what proportion is deceptive requires knowing first how often people communicate, and second, the portion of that communication that is deceptive. Sampling people is necessary because there are individual differences in honesty, but sampling people is insufficient, because situations matter a great deal too. The critical unit of analysis is some unit of communication, not the person. There is no way I know of to representatively sample communication units across the population of all instances of human communication.

5. Steven A. McCornack, Kelly Morrison, Jihyun Esther Paik, Amy M. Wisner, and Xun Zhu, "Information Manipulation Theory 2: A Propositional Theory of Deceptive Discourse Production," *Language and Social Psychology* 33, no. 4 (September 2014): 348–77, https://doi.org /10.1177/0261927X14534656. See the discussion of IMT2 at the end of the previous chapter for more detail.

6. Elizabeth B. Ford, "Lie Detection: Historical, Neuropsychiatric and Legal Dimensions," *International Journal of Law and Psychiatry* 29, no. 3 (May–June 2006): 159, https://doi.org /10.1016/j.ijlp.2005.07.001.

7. Pamela Meyer, *How to Spot a Liar*. TED Talk (October 2011). https://www.ted.com/talks /pamela_meyer_how_to_spot_a_liar. For the record, I have been unable to find a source for the claim. As we will see, there is plenty of evidence that contradicts Meyer's assertion.

8. David B. Buller and Judee K. Burgoon, "Interpersonal Deception Theory," *Communication Theory* 6, no. 3 (August 1996): 203, https://doi.org/10.1111/j.1468-2885.1996.tb00127.x.

9. Ronny E. Turner, Charles Edgley, and Glen Olmstead, "Information Control in Conversations: Honesty Is Not Always the Best Policy, *Kansas Journal of Sociology* 11, no. 1 (Spring 1975): 72, https://www.jstor.org/stable/23255229.

10. Robert S. Feldman, James A. Forrest, and Benjamin R. Happ, "Self-Presentation and Verbal Deception: Do Self-Presenters Lie More?" *Basic and Applied Social Psychology* 24, no. 2 (2002): 170, https://doi.org/10.1207/S15324834BASP2402_8.

11. DePaulo and Bell, "Truth and Investment," 703.

12. Jeffrey T. Hancock, Jennifer Thom-Santelli, and Thompson Ritchie, "Deception and Design: The Impact of Communication Technology on Lying Behavior," *Chi Letters* 6: 129, doi: 10.1145/985692.985709.

13. DePaulo, Kashy, Kirkendol, Wyer, and Epstein, "Lying in Everyday Life," 979.

14. *NBC Nightly News* (August 18, 2014).

15. Turner, Edgley, and Olmstead, "Information Control," 82.

16. Turner, Edgley, and Olmstead, "Information Control," 82. Note that this parallels McCornack's distinction between bald-faced truths and packaged truths.

17. DePaulo, Kashy, Kirkendol, Wyer, and Epstein, "Lying in Everyday Life."

18. This is a critical point overlooked by subsequent works citing the study as evidence that people lie in one out of every three, four, or five conversations. The data do not allow that kind of comparison, since lies were reported in conversations of any length, while honest conversations were counted only if they lasted at least ten minutes.

19. There were a number of important findings that are not directly relevant to the issue of prevalence but are important to deception theory. Most lies were not considered big deals; most were not especially arousing and not especially guilt- or fear-producing. Most lies were self-serving, and most were successful. In general, everyday lies can be described as pretty casual.

20. Joey F. George and Alistair Robb, "Deception and Computer-Mediated Communication in Daily Life," *Communication Reports* 21, no. 2 (2008): 92–103, https://doi.org/10.1080/08934210802298108; Hancock, Thom-Santelli, and Ritchie, "Deception and Design."

21. Study 1 in Kim B. Serota, Timothy R. Levine, and Franklin J. Boster, "The Prevalence of Lying in America: Three Studies of Self-Reported Lies," *Human Communication Research* 36, no. 1 (January 2010): 2–25, https://doi.org/10.1111/j.1468-2958.2009.01366.x.

22. The mode is the most frequently occurring response, and the median is the response at the 50th percentile. A mode of zero means that people answered zero more than any other single response. The median of zero means that when all responses are ordered from zero to the highest, zero is the middle score.

23. The question was asked: "True or False: *Most adults in America lie less frequently than average.*" The answer is that in addition to the 60% of the respondents reporting telling no lies, another 15% reported just one lie. Thus, 75% of the respondents were below the average of 1.65. Thus, the correct answer is "true." These percentages are weighted to be representative of the population. Unweighted, 62% told no lies, and 14.6% told one lie. Either way, most adults in America lie less frequently than average.

24. The plots in the figures in this chapter are based on the raw data, not weighted to be representative of the population. The conclusions and patterns are the same regardless of weighting, but the numbers are slightly different. For example, overall, 62.0% of the respondents reported telling no lies, but the value drops slightly, to 59.9%, when weighted. Also note that the "small bumps" at twenty lies per day in figures 9.1 and 9.2 are because all responses over twenty are just plotted there. Otherwise, there are very long tails.

25. Rony Halevy, Shaul Shalvi, and Bruno Verschuere, "Being Honest about Dishonesty: Correlating Self-Reports and Actual Lying," *Human Communication Research* 40, no. 1 (January 2014): 54–72, https://doi.org/10.1111/hcre.12019; Timothy R. Levine, Kim B. Serota, Frankie Carey, and Doug Messer, "Teenagers Lie a Lot: A Further Investigation into the Prevalence of Lying," *Communication Research Reports* 30, no. 3 (2013): 211–20, https://doi.org/10.1080/08824096.2013.806254; Kim B. Serota and Timothy R. Levine, "A Few Prolific Liars: Variation in the Prevalence of Lying," *Journal of Language and Social Psychology* 34, no. 2 (March 2015): 138–57, https://doi.org/10.1177/0261927X14528804.

26. Halevy, Shalvi, and Verschuere, "Being Honest."

27. Serota, Levine, and Boster, "Prevalence of Lying in America," study two.

28. Serota, Levine, and Boster, "Prevalence of Lying in America," study three.

29. Levine, Serota, Carey and Messer, "Teenagers Lie a Lot."

30. Serota and Levine, "Few Prolific Liars."

31. "Wikipedia: Confirmation bias," Wikimedia Foundation, http://en.wikipedia.org/wiki/Confirmation_bias.

32. Halevy, Shalvi, and Verschuere, "Being Honest."

33. Imagine that everyone lies a lot and that liars lie on surveys and say they don't lie. If this were the case, we would expect dishonesty in the experimental task by those people who claimed honesty in the self-report data (because it is those who say they didn't lie who are the big liars). But this is not what happened. The people who said on the survey that they lied a lot were more likely to later cheat on the experimental task, and the people who reported honesty in communication demonstrated more honest behaviors in the experiment.

34. Demographic correlates of lying are reported in both Serota, Levine, and Boster, "Prevalence of Lying in America," and Serota and Levine, "Few Prolific Liars." In our first study, those findings were added at the request of the journal editor, and my preference was to not report them because I thought the effects were too small and that it was possible that findings $p < .05$ with a sample size of one thousand could be misinterpreted.

Chapter 10

1. "Wikipedia: Sissela Bok," Wikimedia Foundation, http://en.wikipedia.org/wiki/Sissela_Bok.

2. Sissela Bok, *Lying: Moral Choice in Public and Private Life* (New York: Vintage Books, 1999).

3. Steven A. McCornack, Kelly Morrison, Jihyun Esther Paik, Amy M. Wisner, and Xun Zhu, "Information Manipulation Theory 2: A Propositional Theory of Deceptive Discourse Production," *Language and Social Psychology* 33, no. 4 (September 2014): 369, https://doi.org/10.1177/0261927X14534656.

4. Joan Peskin, "Ruse and Representation: On Children's Ability to Conceal Information," *Developmental Psychology* 28, no. 1 (January 1992): 84–89, http://dx.doi.org/10.1037/0012-1649.28.1.84.

5. There are a couple exceptions that will be discussed later. False confessions can and do happen. Interestingly, however, they have never happened in my research on cheating. I am very curious as to why this is the case.

6. This is how I think about pathological lying. My expertise is not clinical. I lack clinical training or experience.

7. For example, see Elizabeth F. Loftus and Jacqueline E. Pickrell, "The Formation of False Memories," *Psychiatric Annals* 25, no. 12 (December 1995): 720–25, https://doi.org/10.3928/0048-5713-19951201-07.

8. Experiments six through eight were previously published in Timothy R. Levine, Rachel K. Kim, and Lauren M. Hamel, "People Lie for a Reason: Three Experiments Documenting the Principle of Veracity," *Communication Research Reports* 27, no. 4 (2010): 271–85, https://doi.org/10.1080/08824096.2010.496334.

9. The five X^2 tests were significant, and the Φ effect sizes ranged from .59 to .94.

10. Again all the X^2 tests were significant, and the effect sizes ranged from .64 to .92.

11. For example, see my work on verbal aggression and argumentativeness where there is little correlation between self-reports and observations of actual behavior. Michael R. Kotowski, Timothy R. Levine, Colin R. Baker, and Jeffrey M. Bolt, "A Multitrait–Multimethod Validity Assessment of the Verbal Aggressiveness and Argumentativeness Scales," *Communication Monographs* 76, no. 4 (2009): 443–62, https://doi.org/10.1080/03637750903300247; Timothy R.

Levine, Michael R. Kotowski, Michael J. Beatty, and Martijn J. Van Kelegom, "A Meta-Analysis of Trait–Behavior Correlations in Argumentativeness and Verbal Aggression," *Journal of Language and Social Psychology* 31, no. 1 (March 2012): 95–111, https://doi.org/10.1177/0261927X11425037.

12. Paul L. Fay and Warren C. Middleton, "The Ability to Judge Truth-Telling, or Lying, from the Voice as Transmitted over a Public Address System," *Journal of General Psychology* 24 (1941): 211–15, https://doi.org/10.1080/00221309.1941.10544369. Details about this experiment were provided in chapter 4.

13. Paul Ekman and Wallace V. Friesen, "Detecting Deception from the Body or Face," *Journal of Personality and Social Psychology* 29, no. 3 (March 1974): 288–98. http://dx.doi.org/10.1037/h0036006.

14. The research design appears confounded. The experiment compared lies + unpleasant images to honest messages + pleasant images, so any differences might be attributed to the honesty or dishonesty of the communication or seeing pleasant or unpleasant images.

15. Also see Timothy R. Levine, "Ecological Validity and Deception Detection Research Design," *Communication Methods and Measures* 12, no. 1 (2018): 45–54, https://doi.org/10.1080/19312458.2017.1411471.

16. Judee K. Burgoon, "Rejoinder to Levine, Clare et al.'s Comparison of the Park–Levine Probability Model versus Interpersonal Deception Theory: Application to Deception Detection," *Human Communication Research* 41, no. 3 (July 2015): 327–49, https://doi.org/10.1111/hcre.12065.

17. Norah E. Dunbar, Matthew L. Jensen, Judee K. Burgoon, Katherine M. Kelley, Kylie J. Harrison, Bradley J. Adame, and Daniel Rex Bernard, "Effects of Veracity, Modality, and Sanctioning on Credibility Assessment during Mediated and Unmediated Interviews," *Communication Research* 42, no. 5 (July 2015): 649–74, https://doi.org/10.1177/0093650213480175; Thomas H. Feeley and Mark A. deTurck, "The Behavioral Correlates of Sanctioned and Unsanctioned Deceptive Communication," *Journal of Nonverbal Behavior* 22, no. 3 (September 1998): 189–204, https://doi.org/10.1023/A:1022966505471.

18. Gerald R. Miller and James B. Stiff, *Deceptive Communication* (Newbury Park, CA: Sage, 1993).

19. Feeley and deTurck, "Behavioral Correlates."

20. Dunbar, Jensen, Burgoon, Kelley, Harrison, Adame, and Bernard, "Effects of Veracity."

21. In terms of types of research validity, I think of ground truth as an issue of construct validity.

22. Funded by the National Science Foundation (grant number SBE0725685).

23. X^2 (1, N = 126) = 42.4, p < .001, Φ = .58.

24. Ronny E. Turner, Charles Edgley, and Glen Olmstead, "Information Control in Conversations: Honesty Is Not Always the Best Policy," *Kansas Journal of Sociology* 11, no. 1 (Spring 1975): 69–89, https://www.jstor.org/stable/23255229.

25. Paul Ekman, *Why Kids Lie* (New York: Penguin, 1991).

26. Dale Hample, "Purpose and Effects of Lying," *Southern Speech Communication Journal* 46, no. 1 (1980): 33–47, https://doi.org/10.1080/10417948009372474; Sandra Metts, "An Exploratory Investigation of Deception in Close Relationships," *Journal of Social and Personal Relationships* 6, no. 2 (May 1969): 159–79, https://doi.org/10.1177/026540758900600202.

27. Carl Camden, Michael T. Motley, and Ann Wilson, "White Lies in Interpersonal Com-

munication: A Taxonomy and Preliminary Investigation of Social Motivations," *Western Journal of Speech Communication* 48, no. 4 (1984): 309–25, https://doi.org/10.1080/10570318409374167.

28. Timothy R. Levine, Mohamed Vaqas Ali, Marleah Dean, Rasha A. Abdulla, and Karina Garia-Ruano, "Toward a Pan-cultural Typology of Deception Motives," *Journal of Intercultural Communication Research* 45, no. 1 (2016): 1–12, doi: 10.1080/17475759.2015.1137079.

29. Inter-coder reliability was kappa = .91.

30. Elaine Walster, Elliot Aronson, and Darcy Abrahams, "On Increasing the Persuasiveness of a Low Prestige Communicator," *Journal of Experimental Social Psychology* 2, no. 4 (October 1966): 325–42, https://doi.org/10.1016/0022-1031(66)90026-6.

31. Bertram F. Malle, *How the Mind Explains Behavior: Folk Explanations, Meaning, and Social Interaction* (Cambridge, MA: MIT Press, 2004).

32. Steven Fein, James L. Hilton, and Dale T. Miller, "Suspicion of Ulterior Motivation and the Correspondence Bias," *Journal of Personality and Social Psychology* 58, no. 5 (May 1990): 753–64, http://dx.doi.org/10.1037/0022-3514.58.5.753.

33. All three experiments were reported in Timothy R. Levine, Rachel K. Kim, and J. Pete Blair, "(In)accuracy at Detecting True and False Confessions and Denials: An Initial Test of a Projected Motive Model of Veracity Judgments," *Human Communication Research* 36, no. 1 (January 2010): 82–102, https://doi.org/10.1111/j.1468-2958.2009.01369.x.

34. A complete accounting of all the versions of the cheating experiment is provided in chapter 14.

35. We eventually learned a trick to get more lying cheaters. We typically started a run of the cheating experiment fairly early in a semester and continued until just before finals. Early in a semester, the good students sign up to get their research credits out of the way. These students are less motivated by the cash incentive, they tend not to cheat even with temptation, and when they do, they are more likely to confess. Toward the end of the semester, the procrastinators sign up. The students who wait until the last minute are more likely to cheat and lie. After a while, we noticed the trend. Early in the semester, almost everyone was honest. Late in the semester, cheating and lying increase. As I said, lying isn't random (unless researchers make it so).

36. Unfortunately, the design is confounded. Not only did we use instructed lies. In one condition, instruction to lie was confounded with actual guilt–innocence. That is, the deception conditions involve a comparison between instructed lies + actual innocence with non-instructed lies + actual guilt. Although such confounding is less than ideal, the solution of using instructed truths and lies in all four conditions was considered an even less desirable choice. While the confounding does open us up to criticism of the knee-jerk "look, a flaw!" sort, the two lie cells are not the critical comparison in the experiment, and the confounding does not really offer a rival explanation for the findings. Thus, this confounding is fodder for "gotcha" criticism but not indicative of bad science.

37. $F(1, 126) = 555$, $p < .001$, $d = 2.67$.

38. Repeated measures designs typically have greater statistical power, they offer a more efficient use of research subjects, and subjects serve as their own controls, typically making error terms smaller and controlling for individual differences better than random assignment. Repeated measures designs are also sometimes called within subjects designs while independent groups designs are sometimes called between subjects.

39. $p < .001$.

40. The first place I recall seeing this claim in print is Judee K. Burgoon, David B. Buller, Amy S. Ebesu, and Patricia Rockwell, "Interpersonal Deception: V. Accuracy in Deception Detection," *Communication Monographs* 61, no. 4 (December 1994): 303–25, https://doi.org /10.1080/03637759409376340. Similar claims appear in the following: Jaume Masip, Hernán Alonso, Eugenio Garrido, and Concha Antón, "Generalized Communicative Suspicion (GCS) among Police Officers: Accounting for the Investigator Bias Effect," *Journal of Applied Social Psychology* 35, no. 5 (May 2005): 1046–66, https://doi.org/10.1111/j.1559-1816.2005.tb02159.x; Christian A. Meissner and Saul M. Kassin, "He's Guilty: Investigator Bias in Judgments of Truth and Deception," *Law and Human Behavior* 26, no. 5 (October 2002): 469–80, https://doi .org/10.1023/A:1020278620751.

41. Meta-analysis does not support a lie-bias for professionals. A correct interpretation is that truth-bias is lower, but still in the direction of truth. See Charles F. Bond Jr. and Bella M. DePaulo, "Accuracy of Deception Judgments," *Personality and Social Psychology Review* 10, no. 3 (August 2006): 214–34, https://doi.org/10.1207/s15327957pspr1003_2.

42. Timothy R. Levine, J. Pete Blair, and David D. Clare, "Diagnostic Utility: Experimental Demonstrations and Replications of Powerful Question Effects in High-Stakes Deception Detection," *Human Communication Research* 40, no. 2 (April 2014): 262–89, https://doi.org/10.1111 /hcre.12021.

43. Charles F. Bond Jr., Amanda R. Howard, Joanna L. Hutchison, and Jaume Masip, "Overlooking the Obvious: Incentives to Lie," *Basic and Applied Social Psychology* 35, no. 2 (2013): 212–21, https://doi.org/10.1080/01973533.2013.764302.

Chapter 11

1. For example, as scored in interpersonal deception theory research, people cannot be truth-biased with honest people. In IDT studies, truth-bias is a signed discrepancy score; that is, it is the extent to which a receiver judges a sender as more honest than the sender rates himself or herself. When scored in the IDT way, truth-bias is identical to the false-negative error rate and therefore is confounded with inaccuracy. Further, given the IDT conceptualization and scoring, if most people are honest most of the time, people are seldom truth-biased. TDT avoids this conflation by defining and scoring truth-bias independent from sender honesty.

2. Examples include: David B. Buller and Judee K. Burgoon, "Interpersonal Deception Theory," *Communication Theory* 6, no. 3 (August 1996): 203–42, https://doi.org/10.1111/j .1468-2885.1996.tb00127.x; Judee K. Burgoon, "Rejoinder to Levine, Clare et al.'s Comparison of the Park–Levine Probability Model versus Interpersonal Deception Theory: Application to Deception Detection," *Human Communication Research* 41, no. 3 (July 2015): 327–49, https:// doi.org/10.1111/hcre.12065; Steven A. McCornack and Timothy R. Levine, "When Lovers Become Leery: The Relationship between Suspicion and Accuracy in Detecting Deception," *Communication Monographs* 57, no. 3 (September 1990): 219–30, https://doi.org/10.1080 /03637759009376197; Steven A. McCornack and Malcolm R. Parks, "Deception Detection and Relationship Development: The Other Side of Trust," in *Communication Yearbook 9*, ed. Margaret L. McLaughlin, 377–89 (Beverly Hills, CA: Sage, 1986).

3. Daniel Kahneman, Paul Slovic, and Amos Tversky, *Judgment under Uncertainty: Heuristics and Bias* (Cambridge: Cambridge University Press, 1992); Gerd Gigerenzer, Peter M. Todd, and the ABC Research Group, *Simple Heuristics That Make Us Smart* (New York: Oxford University Press, 1999).

4. Gerd Gigerenzer, *Rationality for Mortals* (Oxford: Oxford University Press. 2008); Gerd Gigerenzer and Reinhard Selten, *Bounded Rationality: The Adaptive Toolbox* (Cambridge, MA: MIT Press, 2001); Gigerenzer, Todd, and ABC Research Group, *Simple Heuristics That Make Us Smart*.

5. McCornack and Parks, "Deception Detection and Relationship Development." See previous mention in chapters 1 and 3 and figure 3.1.

6. This is the operational definition of truth-bias.

7. McCornack and Levine, "When Lovers Become Leery."

8. Charles F. Bond Jr. and Bella M. DePaulo, "Accuracy of Deception Judgments," *Personality and Social Psychology Review* 10, no. 3 (August 2006): 214–34, https://doi.org/10.1207/s15327957pspr1003_2; See also TDT experiment twelve in chapter 10.

9. Certain prison inmates may be an exception. Gary Bond reported evidence that prison inmates are typically lie-biased, especially when they have little contact with the outside word. Outside of incarcerated individuals, meta-analysis shows that truth-bias scores dip below the 50% honest threshold in about one in five lab experiments, although finding a substantial lie-bias is less frequent. Less than 10% of prior experiments report truth-bias scores below 45%, and truth-bias scores below 40% occur less than 4% of the time. In contrast, truth-bias above 80% also occurs about 4% of the time, the upper 10% of scores fall above 70%, and the upper 20% are at 65% and above. Slight lie-bias findings happen, as do findings of extreme truth-bias. Gary D. Bond, Daniel M. Mally, Elizabeth A. Arias, Shannon N. Nunn, and Laura A. Thompson, "Lie-Biased Decision Making in Prison," *Communication Reports* 18, no. 1–2 (2005): 9–19, https://doi.org/10.1080/08934210500084180; Bond and DePaulo, "Accuracy of Deception Judgments."

10. Burgoon, Buller, Ebesu, and Rockwell, "Interpersonal Deception: V," for example, score truth-bias as the signed discrepancy between senders and judges. Senders rate how honest they are, judges rate how honest they think the senders are, and sender ratings are subtracted from judge ratings. Subjects are truth-biased to the extent that they judge a sender as more honest than the senders say they are. Other researchers use bias calculations in signal-deception theory. So my approach to defining and scoring truth-bias is not universally accepted. My approach has the advantages of being both simpler and true to the original use of the term. The real theoretical payoff from defining truth-bias as independent of actual honesty, however, should become apparent in the next chapter on base-rates. Readers interested in this issue are directed to a debate between Judee Burgoon and Hee Sun Park and me in *Human Communication Research* in 2015. Our reply to Burgoon (2015) makes the case for the advantages of the TDT approach using Burgoon's own data. Judee K. Burgoon, David B. Buller, Amy S. Ebesu, and Patricia Rockwell, "Interpersonal Deception: V. Accuracy in Deception Detection," *Communication Monographs* 61, no. 4 (December 1994): 303–25, https://doi.org/10.1080/03637759409376340; Burgoon, "Rejoinder to Levine, Clare et al.'s Comparison of the Park–Levine Probability Model"; Hee Sun Park and Timothy R. Levine, "Base Rates, Deception Detection, and Deception Theory: A Reply to Burgoon (2015)," *Human Communication Research* 41, no. 3 (July 2015): 350–66, https://doi.org/10.1111/hcre.12066.

11. McCornack and Levine, "When Lovers Become Leery."

12. McCornack and Parks, "Deception Detection and Relationship Development."

13. This was back in the days before Hee Sun Park came up with the veracity effect, and when I still viewed truth-bias as flawed reasoning. For reasons explained in the article version

of experiment 14 and the next chapter, once the veracity effect is understood, the flaws in our thinking back then become apparent. In TDT, truth-bias impairs accuracy only in environments where lies are more prevalent than honest communication.

14. This is a low-suspicion condition, not a no-suspicion condition. Just being in a lab experiment creates suspicion, and we tried to minimize that. As we will see later in this chapter, even asking about honesty is enough to kick people out of truth-default. There is an important lesson here for deception researchers. The trick in suspicion experiments is not in making subjects suspicious. That is easy. The art is minimizing suspicion in the low-suspicion conditions. Researchers studying suspicion often have difficulty getting suspicion inductions to work (e.g., the 1994 IDT experiment cited previously), and this may be one reason. Looking back, our realization of this issue in creating our research design is a subtle but important strength of the design of which I am quite proud.

15. At the same time we were doing this study, we were working on another study looking at the negative impact of deception on relationships. That study, cited at the end of this note, is beyond the scope of this book, but doing that study made us especially sensitive to the ethical implications of the suspicion study. By the way, this and every other study reported in this book were reviewed and approved by a university human-subjects review (IRB, Internal Review Board). My coauthors and I take research ethics, including protection of human subjects, very seriously. Steven A. McCornack and Timothy R. Levine, "When Lies Are Uncovered: Emotional and Relational Outcomes of Discovered Deception," *Communication Monographs* 57, no. 2 (March 1990): 119–38, https://doi.org/10.1080/03637759009376190.

16. Rachel K. Kim and Timothy R. Levine, "The Effect of Suspicion on Deception Detection Accuracy: Optimal Level or Opposing Effects?" *Communication Reports* 24, no. 2 (July–December 2011): 51–62, http://dx.doi.org/10.1080/08934215.2011.615272.

17. Among the differences were a reconceptualization of suspicion and that the predictions were grounded in the veracity effect.

18. Contrasts show that the effects of suspicion on truth-bias are linear in both studies. The linear contrasts fit very nicely, and the deviations from linearity are trivial and not statistically significant.

19. McCornack and Parks, "Deception Detection and Relationship Development"; Replication: Timothy R. Levine and Steven A. McCornack, "Linking Love and Lies: A Formal Test of the McCornack and Parks Model of Deception Detection," *Journal of Social and Personal Relationships* 9, no. 1 (February 1992): 143–54, https://doi.org/10.1177/0265407592091008.

20. Bond and DePaulo, "Accuracy of Deception Judgments."

21. Timothy R. Levine and Steven A. McCornack, "Behavioral Adaptation, Confidence, and Heuristic-Based Explanations of the Probing Effect," *Human Communication Research* 27, no. 4 (October 2001): 471–502, https://doi.org/10.1111/j.1468–2958.2001.tb00790.x.

22. Bond and DePaulo, "Accuracy of Deception Judgments."

23. Timothy R. Levine, Kim B. Serota, Hillary Shulman, David D. Clare, Hee Sun Park, Allison S. Shaw, Jae Chul Shim, and Jung Hyon Lee, "Sender Demeanor: Individual Differences in Sender Believability Have a Powerful Impact on Deception Detection Judgments," *Human Communication Research* 37, no. 3 (July 2011): 377–403, https://doi.org/10.1111/j.1468–2958 .2011.01407.x.

24. For reasons explained in the next chapter, increases or decreases in truth-bias do not affect accuracy when there is an equal number of truths and lies.

25. Credit for using the word "trigger" to capture the idea goes to Professor Torsten Reimer. Thanks, Torsten!

26. Conrad Trump, a student from West Virginia University, recently e-mailed me and asked how long it takes to revert back to the truth-default. TDT does not specify a time frame. My guess is that there is no set amount of time and that it will vary depending on individual and situational differences.

27. Walter Weiss, "A Sleeper Effect in Opinion Change," *Journal of Abnormal and Social Psychology* 48, no. 2 (1953): 173–80, http://dx.doi.org/10.1037/h0063200.

28. Daniel T. Gilbert, "How Mental Systems Believe," *American Psychologist* 46, no. 2 (February 1991): 107–19, http://dx.doi.org/10.1037/0003-066X.46.2.107.

29. Daniel T. Gilbert, Douglas S. Krull, and Patrick S. Malone, "Unbelieving the Unbelievable: Some Problems in the Rejection of False Information," *Journal of Personality and Social Psychology* 59, no. 4 (October 1990): 601–13, http://dx.doi.org/10.1037/0022-3514.59.4.601; Daniel T. Gilbert, Romin W. Tafordi, and Patrick S. Malone, "You Can't Not Believe Everything You Read," *Journal of Personality and Social Psychology* 65, no. 2 (August 1993): 221–33, http://dx.doi.org/10.1037/0022-3514.65.2.221.

30. Bruce Schneier, *Liars and Outliers: Enabling the Trust That Society Needs to Thrive* (Indianapolis: John Wiley and Sons, 2012).

31. David D. Clare and Timothy R. Levine, "Documenting the Truth-Default: The Low Frequency of Spontaneous Unprompted Veracity Assessments in Deception Detection." *Human Communication Research*, in press.

32. Maria Hartwig and Charles F. Bond Jr., "Why Do Lie-Catchers Fail? A Lens Model Meta-analysis of Human Lie Judgments," *Psychological Bulletin* 137, no. 4 (July 2011): 643–59, http://dx.doi: 10.1037/a0023589.

33. See, for example, one of my all-time favorite studies: Muzafer Sherif, O. J. Harvey, William R. Hood, Carolyn W. Sherif, and Jack White, *The Robbers Cave Experiment: Intergroup Conflict and Cooperation* (Middletown, CT: Wesleyan University Press, 1988).

34. Thanks to Conrad Trump for prompting me to include the section on intergroup interaction.

Chapter 12

1. Timothy R. Levine, Hee Sun Park, and Steven A. McCornack, "Accuracy in Detecting Truths and Lies: Documenting the 'Veracity Effect,'" *Communication Monographs* 66, no. 2 (June 1999): 125–44, https://doi.org/10.1080/03637759909376468.

2. There is one study (seventy truth-bias and twenty veracity effect) that does not fall along the line formed by the rest of the studies. There are two unusual features of that study that might explain why it did not fall in line, so to speak. Overall accuracy was unusually high (70% overall, 72% truth accuracy, and 52% lie accuracy), and the base-rate was heavily tilted toward honest senders (approximately 90% honest).

3. For example, see Timothy R. Levine, David D. Clare, Tracie Green, Kim B. Serota, and Hee Sun Park, "The Effects of Truth–Lie Base Rate on Interactive Deception Detection Accuracy," *Human Communication Research* 40, no. 3 (July 2014): 350–72, https://doi.org/10.1111/hcre.12027; Judee K. Burgoon, "Rejoinder to Levine, Clare et al.'s Comparison of the Park–Levine Probability Model versus Interpersonal Deception Theory: Application to Deception Detection," *Human Communication Research* 41, no. 3 (July 2015): 327–49, https://doi.org/10.1111

/hcre.12065; Hee Sun Park and Timothy R. Levine, "Base Rates, Deception Detection, and Deception Theory: A Reply to Burgoon (2015)," *Human Communication Research* 41, no. 3 (July 2015): 350–66, https://doi.org/10.1111/hcre.12066.

4. Atlanta Airport, http://www.atlanta-airport.com/Airport/ATL/ATL_FactSheet.aspx.

5. Levine, Park, and McCornack, "Accuracy in Detecting Truths and Lies," experiment 4.

6. Hee Sun Park and Timothy R. Levine, "A Probability Model of Accuracy in Deception Detection Experiments," *Communication Monographs* 68, no. 2 (2001): 201–210, https://doi.org/10.1080/03637750128059.

7. Readers interested in a deeper explanation, a critique of NHST, and alternatives are directed to a pair of essays I authored; see Timothy R. Levine, René Weber, Hee Sun Park, and Craig R. Hullett, "A Communication Researchers' Guide to Null Hypothesis Significance Testing and Alternatives," *Human Communication Research* 34, no. 2 (April 2008): 188–209, https://doi.org/10.1111/j.1468–2958.2008.00318.x; Timothy R. Levine, René Weber, Craig R. Hullett, Hee Sun Park, and Lisa Lindsey, "A Critical Assessment of Null Hypothesis Significance Testing in Quantitative Communication Research," *Human Communication Research* 34, no. 2 (April 2008): 171–87, https://doi.org/10.1111/j.1468–2958.2008.00317.x.

8. Timothy R. Levine, Rachel K. Kim, Hee Sun Park, and Mikayla Hughes, "Deception Detection Accuracy Is a Predictable Linear Function of Message Veracity Base-Rate: A Formal Test of Park and Levine's Probability Model," *Communication Monographs* 73, no. 3 (2006): 243–60, https://doi.org/10.1080/03637750600873736.

9. Open Science Collaboration, "Estimating the Reproducibility of Psychological Science," *Science* 349, no. 6251 (August 2015): aac4716. https://doi: 10.1126/science.aac4716.

10. Levine, Clare, Green, Serota, and Park, "The Effects of Truth–Lie Base Rate."

11. Hee Sun Park and Timothy R. Levine, "The Effects of Truth–Lie Base-Rates on Deception Detection Accuracy in Korea," *Asian Journal of Communication* 27, no. 5 (2017): 554–62, https://doi.org/10.1080/01292986.2017.1334074.

12. Timothy R. Levine and Kim B. Serota, "Truth-Bias: Who Is Biased, Subjects or Deception Researchers?" Talk given at SARMAC. Victoria, Canada, 2015.

Chapter 13

1. Charles F. Bond Jr. and Bella M. DePaulo, "Accuracy of Deception Judgments," *Personality and Social Psychology Review* 10, no. 3 (August 2006): 214–34, https://doi.org/10.1207/s15327957pspr1003_2.

2. Bond and DePaulo, "Accuracy of Deception Judgments."

3. A technical qualification is needed here. Small standard errors occur only with multiple judgments per judge. When each judge makes a single judgment, standard errors are huge. This too is part of the mystery. Why is it that judgments per judge rather than number of judges (i.e., sample size) is critical for standard error?

4. Charles F. Bond Jr. and Bella M. DePaulo, "Individual Differences in Judging Deception: Accuracy and Bias," *Psychological Bulletin* 134, no. 4 (July 2008): 477–92, http://dx.doi.org/10.1037/0033–2909.134.4.477.

5. See Robert Kraut, "Humans as Lie Detectors," *Journal of Communication* 30, no. 4 (December 1980): 209–18, https://doi.org/10.1111/j.1460–2466.1980.tb02030.x.

6. The Global Deception Research Team, "A World of Lies," *Journal of Cross-Cultural Psychology* 37, no. 1 (January 2006): 60–74, https://doi.org/10.1177/0022022105282295.

7. Bella M. DePaulo, James J. Lindsay, Brian E. Malone, Laura Muhlenbruck, Kelly Charl-

ton, and Harris Cooper, "Cues to Deception," *Psychological Bulletin* 129, no. 1 (January 2003): 74–118, http://dx.doi:10.1037/0033–2909.129.1.74.

8. Maria Hartwig and Charles F. Bond Jr., "Why Do Lie-Catchers Fail? A Lens Model Meta-analysis of Human Lie Judgments," *Psychological Bulletin* 137, no. 4 (July 2011): 643–59, http://dx.doi: 10.1037/a0023589.

9. Mark G. Frank and Thomas Hugh Feeley, "To Catch a Liar: Challenges for Research in Lie Detection Training," *Journal of Applied Communication Research* 31, no. 1 (February 2003): 58–75, https://doi.org/10.1080/00909880305377; Valerie Hauch, Siegfried L. Sporer, Stephen W. Michael, and Christian A. Meissner, "Does Training Improve the Detection of Deception? A Meta-Analysis," *Communication Research* 43, no. 3 (April 2016): 283–343, https://doi.org/10.1177/0093650214534974; Timothy R. Levine, Thomas Hugh Feeley, Steven A. McCornack, Mikayla Hughes, and Chad M. Harms, "Testing the Effects of Nonverbal Training on Deception Detection Accuracy with the Inclusion of a Bogus Training Control Group," *Western Journal of Communication* 69, no. 3 (July 2005): 203–17, https://doi.org/10.1080/10570310500202355.

10. Levine, Feeley, McCornack, Hughes, and Harms, "Testing the Effects of Nonverbal Training."

11. Timothy R. Levine, Kim B. Serota, and Hillary C. Shulman, "The Impact of *Lie to Me* on Viewers' Actual Ability to Detect Deception," *Communication Research* 37, no. 6 (December 2010): 847–56, https://doi.org/10.1177/0093650210362686.

12. Frank and Feeley, "To Catch a Liar"; Hauch, Sporer, Michael, and Meissner, "Does Training Improve."

13. All three accuracies were statistically different from each other, $p < .05$. The effect size for the omnibus effect was $\eta^2 = .06$.

14. Valid training = bogus training > control, $p < .05$. The effect size for the omnibus effect was $\eta^2 = .09$.

15. See show information on the Internet Movie Database, http://www.imdb.com/title/tt1235099/.

16. The tapes from the second set were used with Lauren Hamel as the interviewer.

17. The differences were not significantly different at $p < .05$.

18. $p < .05$.

19. Hartwig and Bond, "Why Do Lie-Catchers Fail?"

20. DePaulo, Lindsay, Malone, Muhlenbruck, Charlton, and Cooper, "Cues to Deception."

21. Hartwig and Bond, "Why Do Lie-Catchers Fail?"

22. Maria Hartwig and Charles F. Bond Jr., "Lie Detection from Multiple Cues: A Meta-analysis," *Applied Cognitive Psychology* 28, no. 5 (September–October 2014): 661–76, https://doi.org/10.1002/acp.3052.

23. For example, see Maureen O'Sullivan, Mark G. Frank, Carolyn M. Hurley, and Jaspreet Tiwana, "Police Lie Detection Accuracy: The Effect of Lie Scenario," *Law and Human Behavior* 33, no. 6 (December 2009): 530–38, https://doi.org/10.1007/s10979–008–9166–4.

24. For example, see Judee K. Burgoon, "Rejoinder to Levine, Clare et al.'s Comparison of the Park–Levine Probability Model versus Interpersonal Deception Theory: Application to Deception Detection," *Human Communication Research* 41, no. 3 (July 2015): 327–49, https://doi.org/10.1111/hcre.12065.

25. Bond and DePaulo, "Accuracy of Deception Judgments"; Hartwig and Bond, "Lie Detection from Multiple Cues." See chapters 3 and 5 for details.

26. Timothy R. Levine, Allison Shaw, and Hillary C. Shulman, "Increasing Deception De-

NOTES

tection Accuracy with Strategic Questioning," *Human Communication Research* 36, no. 2 (April 2010): 216–31, https://doi.org/10.1111/j.1468–2958.2010.01374.x.

27. Mark G. Frank and Paul Ekman, "Appearing Truthful Generalizes across Different Deception Situations, *Journal of Personality and Social Psychology* 86, no. 3 (March 2004): 486–95, http://dx.doi.org/10.1037/0022–3514.86.3.486; Timothy R. Levine, "Examining Sender and Judge Variability in Honesty Assessments and Deception Detection Accuracy: Evidence for a Transparent Liar but No Evidence of Deception-General Ability," *Communication Research Reports* 33, no. 3 (2016): 188–94, https://doi.org/10.1080/08824096.2016.1186629; Gordon R. T. Wright, Christopher J. Berry, and Geoffrey Bird, "You Can't Kid a Kidder: Association between Production and Detection of Deception in an Interactive Deception Task," *Frontiers in Human Neuroscience* (April 2012), https://doi.org/10.3389/fnhum.2012.00087; Gordon R. T. Wright, Christopher J. Berry, Carline Catmur, and Geoffrey Bird. "Good Liars Are Neither 'Dark' nor Self-Deceptive." *PLOS ONE* 10, no. 6 (June 2015): e0127315. https://doi.org/10.1371/journal .pone.0127315.

28. This is where I disagree with a recent series of articles by Wright and colleagues (Wright, Berry, and Bird, "You Can't Kid a Kidder," and Wright, Berry, Catmur, and Bird, "Good Liars"). Good liars aren't just nontransparent; they are credible. Signal detection math makes accuracy and bias independent. Being a good liar, however, involves both judge error and a specific direction of judge error. Good liars aren't poker-faced (low-transparency or inscrutable); they are authentic and sincere. This exemplifies yet another reason why I am not a big fan of signal detection thinking applied to deception detection.

29. Timothy R. Levine, "A Few Transparent Liars Explaining 54% Accuracy in Deception Detection Experiments," *Annals of the International Communication Association* 34 (formerly *Communication Yearbook*), no. 1 (2010): 41–61, https://doi.org/10.1080/23808985.2010.11679095.

30. This is also the approach taken with the application of the Brunswik Lens Model; see, for example: Klaus Fiedler and Isabella Walka, "Training Lie Detectors to Use Nonverbal Cues Instead of Global Heuristics," *Human Communication Research* 20, no. 2 (December 1993): 199–223, https://doi.org/10.1111/j.1468–2958.1993.tb00321.x; Hartwig and Bond, "Why Do Lie-Catchers Fail?" But note that with the lens model (or any model with multiple mediators), the predictive power from multiple independent mediated links adds up, and thus the model should produce higher predicted accuracy.

31. False. It is the tenth-longest (1,230 miles). The Rio Negro (1,400 miles) is the correct answer; "Wikipedia: Amazon River," Wikimedia Foundation, https://en.wikipedia.org/wiki /Amazon_River#Major_tributaries.

32. Bond and DePaulo, "Individual Differences."

33. Levine, "Examining Sender and Judge Variability."

34. Viewing demeanor as a constellation of interrelated behaviors has big implications for the cue research discussed back in chapter 2. Almost all cue-related studies treat cues as statistically independent (i.e., uncorrelated). If I am right about the strong interrelationship between cues, cue studies have big problems with violated statistical assumptions and spurious relationships stemming from correlated cues.

35. Erving Goffman, "The Nature of Deference and Demeanor," *American Anthropologist* 58, no. 3 (June 1956): 473–502, https://doi.org/10.1525/aa.1956.58.3.02a00070.

36. Miron Zuckerman, Richard S. DeFrank, Judith A. Hall, Deborah T. Larrance, and Robert Rosenthal, "Facial and Vocal Cues of Deception and Honesty," *Journal of Experimental Social Psychology* 15, no. 4 (July 1979): 378–96, https://doi.org/10.1016/0022–1031(79)90045–3.

37. Frank and Ekman, "Appearing Truthful Generalizes."

38. Bond and DePaulo, "Individual Differences in Judging Deception."

39. Bond and DePaulo, "Individual Differences in Judging Deception"; Frank and Ekman, "Appearing Truthful Generalizes"; Zuckerman, DeFrank, Hall, Larrance, and Rosenthal, "Facial and Vocal Cues."

40. I speculate that outside the lab or when people have a choice in the matter, honestly demeanored people are more likely to lie. These people tend to get away with lying. Some but not all of them may exploit that. I have some experimental evidence that this is the case; see Levine, Shaw, and Shulman, "Increasing Deception Detection Accuracy with Strategic Questioning."

41. This idea of the believability quotient, or demeanor index, and the eleven behaviors were created and copyrighted by the author (Timothy R. Levine) and are considered proprietary. Use of the materials in scales, behavioral coding, training, and other applications is permissible only with the prior written permission of the author, who owns the intellectual property rights and copyright to this demeanor index or believability quotient.

42. Bernard Barber and Renée C. Fox, "The Case of the Floppy-Eared Rabbits: An Instance of Serendipity Gained and Serendipity Lost," *American Journal of Sociology* 64, no. 2 (September 1958): 128–36, https://doi.org/10.1086/222420.

Chapter 14

1. The first two paragraphs are an excerpt from a recent essay of mine: Timothy R. Levine, "New and Improved Accuracy Findings in Deception Detection Research," *Current Opinion in Psychology* 6 (December 2015): 1–5, https://doi.org/10.1016/j.copsyc.2015.03.003. The experiments finding above 90% accuracy are reported toward the end of the chapter as TDT experiments fifty-one through fifty-five.

2. If I were to say what he denied saying, readers might guess whom I was talking about. I want to preserve the anonymity of that researcher here, because who he is and what he said are not important to the point I am making.

3. The Asch experiments are described in chapter 1 with regard to the mystery of deception accuracy in research that is not about deception. The Asch study examined conformity by having fake subjects offer obviously false judgments to sway the judgments of real subjects. Solomon E. Asch, "Studies of Independence and Conformity: I. A Minority of One against a Unanimous Majority," *Psychological Monographs: General and Applied* 70, no. 9 (1956): 1–70. http://dx.doi.org/10.1037/h0093718.

4. I find Princeton philosopher Harry Frankfurt's *On Bullshit* intriguing. Frankfurt argues that for the bullshit artist, the truth is just irrelevant. In the case of this example, I find bullshit more plausible than delusion or honest mistake, but who knows? I don't. Harry G. Frankfurt, *On Bullshit* (Princeton: Princeton University Press, 2005).

5. Hee Sun Park, Timothy R. Levine, Steven A. McCornack, Kelly Morrison, and Merissa Ferrara, "How People Really Detect Lies," *Communication Monographs* 69, no. 2 (June 2002): 144–57, https://doi.org/10.1080/714041710.

6. Jaume Masip and Carmen Herrero, "Police Detection of Deception: Beliefs about Behavioral Cues to Deception Are Strong Even Though Contextual Evidence Is More Useful," *Journal of Communication* 65, no. 1 (February 2015): 125–45, https://doi.org/10.1111/jcom.12135.

7. Paul Ekman, "Deception, Lying, and Demeanor," in *States of Mind: American and Post-Soviet Perspectives on Contemporary Issues in Psychology*, ed. Diane F. Halpern and Aleksander E. Voiskounsky, 101 (New York: Oxford University Press, 1997).

8. J. Pete Blair, Torsten O. Reimer, and Timothy R. Levine, "The Role of Consistency in Detecting Deception: The Superiority of Correspondence over Coherence," *Communication Studies* 69, no. 5 (September 2018): 483–98, https://doi.org/10.1080/10510974.2018.1447492.

9. E.g., see Pär Anders Granhag and Leif A. Strömwall, "Repeated Interrogations—Stretching the Deception Detection Paradigm," *Expert Evidence* 7, no. 3 (September 1999): 163–74, https://doi.org/10.1023/A:1008993326434; Pär Anders Granhag and Leif A. Strömwall, "Deception Detection: Examining the Consistency Heuristic," in *New Trends in Criminal Investigation and Evidence II*, ed. C. M. Breur, M. M. Kommer, J. F. Nijboer, and J. M. Reintjes, 309–21 (Antwerpen: Intersentia, 2000); Pär Anders Granhag and Leif A. Strömwall, "Deception Detection: Interrogators' and Observers' Decoding of Consecutive Statements," *Journal of Psychology* 135, no. 6 (2001): 603–20, https://doi.org/10.1080/00223980109603723.

10. Timothy R. Levine and Steven A. McCornack, "A Critical Analysis of the Behavioral Adaptation Explanation of the Probing Effect," *Human Communication Research* 22, no. 4 (June 1996): 575–88, https://doi.org/10.1111/j.1468–2958.1996.tb00380.x, study 2.

11. This was part of a series of experiments Steve and I did on the probing effect, which led to one of our first debates with Judee Burgoon over IDT. See David B. Buller, James B. Stiff, and Judee K. Burgoon, "Behavioral Adaptation in Deceptive Transactions: Fact or Fiction: Reply to Levine and McCornack," *Human Communication Research* 22, no. 4 (June 1996): 589–603, https://doi.org/10.1111/j.1468–2958.1996.tb00381.x; Timothy R. Levine and Steven A. McCornack, "A Critical Analysis of the Behavioral Adaptation Explanation of the Probing Effect," *Human Communication Research* 22, no. 4 (June 1996): 575–88, https://doi.org/10.1111/j.1468–2958.1996.tb00380.x; Timothy R. Levine and Steven A. McCornack, "Can Behavioral Adaptation Explain the Probing Effect? Rejoinder to Buller et al.," *Human Communication Research* 22, no. 4 (June 1996): 604–13, https://doi.org/10.1111/j.1468–2958.1996.tb00382.x.

12. By the way, senders were not better liars on familiar topics. Familiarity did not affect the extent to which senders were believed.

13. Marc-André Reinhard, Siegfried L. Sporer, and Martin Scharmach, "Perceived Familiarity with a Judgmental Situation Improves Lie Detection Ability," *Swiss Journal of Psychology* 72, no. 1 (January 2013): 43–52, https://doi.org/10.1024/1421–0185/a000098; Marc-André Reinhard, Siegfried L. Sporer, Martin Scharmach, and Mamara Marksteiner, "Listening, Not Watching: Situational Familiarity and the Ability to Detect Deception," *Journal of Personality and Social Psychology* 101, no. 3 (September 2011): 467–84, http://dx.doi.org/10.1037/a0023726.

14. Reid and Associates. http://www.reid.com/.

15. Edward T. Hall, *Beyond Culture* (New York: Anchor Books, 1976).

16. J. Pete Blair, Timothy R. Levine, and Allison S. Shaw, "Content in Context Improves Deception Detection Accuracy," *Human Communication Research* 36, no. 3 (July 2010): 423–42, https://doi.org/10.1111/j.1468–2958.2010.01382.x.

17. The standard errors were about 1%, so any difference in the across-study means of 2% or more is statistically significant at $p < .05$.

18. I'm using the Park–Levine base-rate formula from chapter 12 to make these projections.

19. Charles F. Bond Jr. and Bella M. DePaulo, "Accuracy of Deception Judgments," *Personality and Social Psychology Review* 10, no. 3 (August 2006): 214–34, https://doi.org/10.1207/s15327957pspr1003_2.

20. The differences between the 53%, 54%, and 52% averages were statistically significant at $p < .001$. The margin of error around the estimates is less than one-third of 1% percent for the larger sets of findings and less than 2% for the eighteen interactive studies. Accuracies,

however, were 53%, 53%, 54% when weighting for sample size. There were also no significant differences in ten experiments involving head-to-head comparisons of interaction with senders versus passive observation of interaction with third parties. To my eye, this is a difference of little consequence in spite of statistical significance.

21. For more on the probing effect, see Levine and McCornack, "Behavioral Adaptation."

22. This was where our 2001 findings departed from the Stiff and Miller 1986 findings that first documented the probing effect; see James B. Stiff and Gerald R. Miller, "'Come to Think of It . . .': Interrogative Probes, Deceptive Communication, and Deception Detection," *Human Communication Research* 12, no. 3 (March 1986): 339–57, https://doi.org/10.1111/j.1468-2958.1986.tb00081.x.

23. Levine and McCornack, "Behavioral Adaptation."

24. Aldert Vrij, Samantha Mann, Susanne Kristen, and Ronald P. Fisher, "Cues to Deception and Ability to Detect Lies as a Function of Police Interview Styles," *Law and Human Behavior* 31, no. 5 (October 2007): 499–518, https://doi.org/10.1007/s10979-006-9066-4.

25. Information gathering is a nonaccusatory style involving the structured, open-ended questioning that is favored in the criminal-legal psychology literature. The Behavior Analysis Interview (BAI) is a creation of John Reid and Associates, who train American police and investigators. The accusatory questioning is just that; it involves direct accusations.

26. Vrij, Mann, Kristen, and Fisher also analyzed the data for truth-bias, hits, and false positives. They make the claim that information gathering produced a lower rate of false positives; "$F (1, 67) = 3.31, p < .05$" (513). Of course, the F statistic with 1 and 67 degrees of freedom is not statistically significant when $F = 3.31$ and therefore is not $p < .05$. This appears to be a case of a statistical sleight of hand I call a one-tailed F; see Timothy R. Levine and John Banas, "One-Tailed F-Tests in Communication Research," *Communication Monographs* 69, no. 2 (2002): 132–43, https://doi.org/10.1080/714041709.

27. Timothy R. Levine, Hillary C. Shulman, Christopher J. Carpenter, David C. DeAndrea, and J. Pete Blair, "The Impact of Accusatory, Non-Accusatory, Bait, and False Evidence Questioning on Deception Detection," *Communication Research Reports* 30, no. 2 (April 2013): 169–74. https://doi.org/10.1080/08824096.2012.762905.

28. TDT experiment forty-five prompted me to write and publish an essay titled, "A Defense of Publishing Nonsignificant (Ns) Results." See Timothy R. Levine, "A Defense of Publishing Nonsignificant (Ns) Results," *Communication Research Reports* 30, no. 3 (2013): 270–74, https://doi.org/10.1080/08824096.2013.806261.

29. My NSF grant that funded the creation of the first five sets of cheating tapes was part of a larger consortium of research teams led by Judee Burgoon. Our relationship had been rocky since the early 1990s, and this was an attempt at collaboration. We had a complete falling out following the completion of the second set of cheating interviews. The blow-up was sparked by a different project with a different funding agency. We have not collaborated since. Nevertheless, Judee contributed intellectually to the creation of the first two sets of cheating interviews. It is also the case that she was central to obtaining the initial funding from NSF for the cheating tapes.

30. Timothy R. Levine, J. Pete Blair, and David D. Clare, "Diagnostic Utility: Experimental Demonstrations and Replications of Powerful Question Effects in High-Stakes Deception Detection," *Human Communication Research* 40, no. 2 (April 2014): 262–89, https://doi.org/10.1111/hcre.12021.

31. Experiments forty-nine and fifty were reported in Levine, Blair, and Clare, "Diagnostic

Utility." Experiment fifty-one was published as Timothy R. Levine, "Strong Diagnostic Questioning Effects on Deception Detection Accuracy with U.S. Customs Agents," *Communication Research Reports* 34, no. 1 (2017): 84–87, https://doi.org/10.1080/08824096.2016.1240075.

32. Both IDT and TDT explanations involve changes in sender behavior accounting for the below-chance accuracy. In the IDT version, liars (more than honest senders) act strategically when they realize they are under suspicion. In the explanation I am providing, it is poorly worded questions that make honest senders seem less honest.

33. Michael G. Aamodt and Heather Custer, "Who Can Best Catch a Liar?," *Forensic Examiner* 15, no. 1 (Spring 2006): 6–11; Bond and DePaulo, "Accuracy of Deception Judgments."

34. Bond and DePaulo, "Accuracy of Deception Judgments." Note that the finding is that experts are less truth-biased, not that they are lie-biased.

35. David Clare put together the tapes so that we did not know which senders were which.

36. We added a condition where the partner went ahead and cheated even without the subject and asked the subject to cover for them. We did this to increase the number of instances of cheating. Whenever the subject cheated, their partner helped them cheat. Consequently, there were three possibilities regarding ground truth; both cheated, only the partner cheated, or neither cheated.

37. Aldert Vrij, Christian A. Meissner, and Saul M. Kassin, "Problems in Expert Deception Detection and the Risk of False Confessions: No Proof to the Contrary in Levine et al. (2014)," *Psychology, Crime, & Law* 21, no. 9 (2015): 901–9, https://doi.org/10.1080/1068316X.2015.1054389.

38. The number of questions is not as diagnostic as one might expect. Most people who cheat only cheat a little bit. Many cheaters inflate their performance by just a question or two. Originally, we thought this was an effort not to seem suspicious. But in line with Dan Ariely's work, maybe cheaters cheat only a little bit because they don't want to think of themselves as unethical. Dan Ariely, *The Honest Truth about Dishonesty: How We Lie to Everyone—Especially Ourselves* (New York: HarperCollins, 2012).

Chapter 15

1. John T. Cacioppo and William Patrick, *Loneliness: Human Nature and the Need for Social Connection* (New York: W. W. Norton, 2008).

2. See the first several pages of chapter 9 for examples.

3. For a similar line of reasoning, see Siegfried L. Sporer, "Deception and Cognitive Load: Expanding Our Horizon with a Working Memory Model," *Frontiers in Psychology* 7 (April 2016): 420, https://doi.org/10.3389/fpsyg.2016.00420.

4. For example, Galit Nahari, Aldert Vrij, and Ronald P. Fisher, "Exploiting Liars' Verbal Strategies by Examining the Verifiability of Details," *Legal and Criminological Psychology* 19, no. 2 (September 2014): 227–39, https://doi.org/10.1111/j.2044-8333.2012.02069.x; Galit Nahari, Aldert Vrij, and Ronald P. Fisher, "The Verifiability Approach: Countermeasures Facilitate Its Ability to Discriminate between Truths and Lies," *Applied Cognitive Psychology* 28, no. 1 (January–February 2014): 122–28, https://doi.org/10.1002/acp.2974; Galit Nahari, Sharon Leal, Aldert Vrij, Lara Warmelink, and Zarah Vernham, "Did Somebody See It? Applying the Verifiability Approach to Insurance Claim Interviews," *Journal of Psychology and Offender Profiling* 11, no. 3 (October 2014): 237–43, https://doi.org/10.1002/jip.1417.

5. See chapters 2, 3, and 5. Also, Charles F. Bond Jr. and Bella M. DePaulo, "Accuracy of

Deception Judgments," *Personality and Social Psychology Review* 10, no. 3 (August 2006): 214–34, https://doi.org/10.1207/s15327957pspr1003_2. Maria Hartwig and Charles F. Bond Jr., "Lie Detection from Multiple Cues: A Meta-analysis," *Applied Cognitive Psychology* 28, no. 5 (September–October 2014): 661–76, https://doi.org/10.1002/acp.3052.

6. Norah E. Dunbar, Matthew L. Jensen, Judee K. Burgoon, Katherine M. Kelley, Kylie J. Harrison, Bradley J. Adame, and Daniel Rex Bernard, "Effects of Veracity, Modality, and Sanctioning on Credibility Assessment during Mediated and Unmediated Interviews," *Communication Research* 42, no. 5 (July 2015): 649–74, https://doi.org/10.1177/0093650213480175.

7. There were four experts. One expert was much better in video, two experts were better face-to-face, and one expert performed similarly in face-to-face and video conferencing. Because of the wide expert-by-modality swings, no firm conclusion about accuracy and modality can be made.

8. There were two important findings both experiments had in common. Both experiments found high rates of honest confessions, and there were no false confessions.

9. Donald T. Campbell and Julian C. Stanley, *Experimental and Quasi-experimental Designs for Research* (Boston: Houghton Mifflin, 1963).

Bibliography

Aamodt, Michael G., and Heather Custer. "Who Can Best Catch a Liar?" *Forensic Examiner* 15, no. 1 (Spring 2006): 6–11.

Albrechtsen, Justin S., Christian A. Meissner, and Kyle J. Susa. "Can Intuition Improve Deception Detection Performance?" *Journal of Experimental Social Psychology* 45, no. 4 (July 2009): 1052–55. https://doi.org/10.1016/j.jesp.2009.05.017.

Ariely, Dan. *The Honest Truth about Dishonesty: How We Lie to Everyone—Especially Ourselves.* New York: HarperCollins, 2012.

Asch, Solomon E. "Studies of Independence and Conformity: I. A Minority of One against a Unanimous Majority." *Psychological Monographs: General and Applied* 70, no. 9 (1956): 1–70. http://dx.doi.org/10.1037/h0093718.

Barber, Bernard, and Renée C. Fox. "The Case of the Floppy-Eared Rabbits: An Instance of Serendipity Gained and Serendipity Lost." *American Journal of Sociology* 64, no. 2 (September 1958): 128–36. https://doi.org/10.1086/222420.

Bok, Sissela. *Lying: Moral Choice in Public and Private Life.* New York: Vintage Books, 1999.

Blair, J. Pete, Timothy R. Levine, and Allison S. Shaw. "Content in Context Improves Deception Detection Accuracy." *Human Communication Research* 36, no. 3 (July 2010): 423–42. https://doi.org/10.1111/j.1468-2958.2010.01382.x.

Blair, J. Pete, Torsten O. Reimer, and Timothy R. Levine. "The Role of Consistency in Detecting Deception: The Superiority of Correspondence over Coherence." *Communication Studies* 69, no. 5 (September 2018): 483–98. https://doi.org/10.1080/10510974.2018.1447492.

Bond, Charles F., Jr., and Bella M. DePaulo. "Accuracy of Deception Judgments." *Personality and Social Psychology Review* 10, no. 3 (August 2006): 21–234. https://doi.org/10.1207/s15327957pspr1003_2.

———. "Individual Differences in Judging Deception: Accuracy and Bias." *Psychological Bulletin* 134, no. 4 (July 2008): 477–92. http://dx.doi.org/10.1037/0033-2909.134.4.477.

Bond, Charles F., Jr., Amanda R. Howard, Joanna L. Hutchison, and Jaume Masip. "Overlooking the Obvious: Incentives to Lie." *Basic and Applied Social Psychology* 35, no. 2 (2013): 212–21. https://doi.org/10.1080/01973533.2013.764302.

Bond, Charles F., Jr., Timothy R. Levine, and Maria Hartwig. "New Findings in Non-Verbal Lie Detection. In *Detecting Deception: Current Challenges and Cognitive Approaches,* edited by Pär Anders Granhag, Aldert Vrij, and Bruno Verschuere, 37–58. Chichester: John Wiley and Sons, 2015.

Bond, Gary D. "Deception Detection Expertise." *Law and Human Behavior* 34, no. 4 (August 2008): 339–51. https://doi.org/10.1007/s10979-007-9110-z.

Bond, Gary D., Daniel M. Mally, Elizabeth A. Arias, Shannon N. Nunn, and Laura A. Thompson. "Lie-Biased Decision Making in Prison." *Communication Reports* 18, no. 1–2 (2005): 9–19. https://doi.org/10.1080/08934210500084180.

Buller, David B., and Judee K. Burgoon. "Interpersonal Deception Theory." *Communication Theory* 6, no. 3 (August 1996): 203–42. https://doi.org/10.1111/j.1468-2885.1996.tb00127.x.

———. "Another Look at Information Management: A Rejoinder to McCornack, Levine, Morrison, and Lapinski." *Communication Monographs* 63, no. 1 (1996): 92–98. https://doi.org/10.1080/03637759609376377.

Buller, David B., Jamie Comstock, R. Kelly Aune, and Krystyna D. Strzyzewski. "The Effect of Probing on Deceivers and Truthtellers." *Journal of Nonverbal Behavior* 13, no. 3 (Fall 1989): 155–70. https://doi.org/10.1007/BF00987047.

Buller, David B., James B. Stiff, and Judee K. Burgoon. "Behavioral Adaptation in Deceptive Transactions: Fact or Fiction: Reply to Levine and McCornack." *Human Communication Research* 22, no. 4 (June 1996): 589–603. https://doi.org/10.1111/j.1468-2958.1996.tb00381.x.

Buller, David B., Krystyna D. Strzyzewski, and Jamie Comstock. "Interpersonal Deception: I. Deceivers' Reactions to Receivers' Suspicions and Probing." *Communication Monographs* 58, no. 1 (March 1991): 1–24. https://doi.org/10.1080/03637759109376211.

Buller, David B., Krystyna D. Strzyzewski, and Frank G. Hunsaker. "Interpersonal Deception: II. The Inferiority of Conversational Participants as Deception Detectors." *Communication Monographs* 58, no. 1 (1991): 25–40. https://doi.org/10.1080/03637759109376212.

Burgoon, Judee K. "Rejoinder to Levine, Clare et al.'s Comparison of the Park–Levine Probability Model versus Interpersonal Deception Theory: Application to Deception Detection." *Human Communication Research* 41, no. 3 (July 2015): 327–49. https://doi.org/10.1111/hcre.12065.

Burgoon, Judee K., David B. Buller, Leesa Dillman, and Joseph B. Walther. "Interpersonal Deception: IV. Effects of Suspicion on Perceived Communication and Nonverbal Behavior Dynamics." *Human Communication Research* 22, no. 2 (December 1995): 163–96. https://doi.org/10.1111/j.1468-2958.1995.tb00365.x.

Burgoon, Judee K., David B. Buller, Amy S. Ebesu, and Patricia Rockwell. "Interpersonal Deception: V. Accuracy in Deception Detection." *Communication Monographs* 61, no. 4 (December 1994): 303–25. https://doi.org/10.1080/03637759409376340.

Burgoon, Judee K., David B. Buller, Laura K. Guerrero, Walid A. Afifi, and Clyde M. Feldman. "Interpersonal Deception: XII. Information Management Dimensions Underlying Deceptive and Truthful Messages." *Communication Monographs* 63, no. 1 (1996): 50–69. https://doi.org/10.1080/03637759609376374.

Cacioppo, John T., and William Patrick. *Loneliness: Human Nature and the Need for Social Connection.* New York: W. W. Norton, 2008.

Campbell, Donald T., and Julian C. Stanley. *Experimental and Quasi-experimental Designs for Research.* Boston: Houghton Mifflin, 1963.

Camden, Carl, Michael T. Motley, and Ann Wilson. "White Lies in Interpersonal Communication: A Taxonomy and Preliminary Investigation of Social Motivations." *Western Journal of Speech Communication* 48, no. 4 (1984): 309–25. https://doi.org/10.1080/10570318409374167.

Clare, David, and Timothy Levine. "Documenting the Truth-Default: The Low Frequency of Spontaneous Unprompted Veracity Assessments in Deception Detection." *Human Communication Research.* In press.

Comadena, Mark E. "Accuracy in Detecting Deception: Intimate and Friendship Relationships." In *Communication Yearbook 6*, edited by Michael Burgoon, 446–72. Beverly Hills: Sage, 1982.

Cronbach, Lee J., and Paul E. Meehl. "Construct Validity in Psychological Tests." *Psychological Bulletin* 52, no. 4 (July 1955): 281–302. http://dx.doi.org/10.1037/h0040957.

DeAndrea, David C., Stephanie Tom Tong, Yuhua Jake Liang, Timothy R. Levine, and Joseph B. Walther. "When Do People Misrepresent Themselves to Others? The Effects of Social Desirability, Ground Truth, and Accountability on Deceptive Self-Presentations." *Journal of Communication* 62, no. 3 (June 2012): 400–417. https://doi.org/10.1111/j.1460-2466.2012 .01646.x.

DePaulo, Bella M. "Nonverbal Behavior and Self-Presentation." *Psychological Bulletin* 111, no. 2 (March 1992): 203–43. http://dx.doi.org/10.1037/0033-2909.111.2.203.

DePaulo, Bella M., Matthew E. Ansfield, and Kathy L. Bell. "Theories about Deception and Paradigms for Studying It: A Critical Appraisal of Buller and Burgoon's Interpersonal Deception Theory. *Communication Theory* 6, no. 3 (August 1996): 297–310. https://doi.org /10.1111/j.1468-2885.1996.tb00131.x.

DePaulo, Bella M., and Kathy L. Bell. "Truth and Investment: Lies Are Told to Those Who Care." *Journal of Personality and Social Psychology* 71, no. 4 (October 1996): 703–16. http:// dx.doi.org/10.1037/0022-3514.71.4.703.

DePaulo, Bella M., Kelly Charlton, Harris Cooper, James J. Lindsay, Laura Muhlenbruck. "The Accuracy-Confidence Correlation in the Detection of Deception." *Personality and Social Psychology Review* 1, no. 4 (November 1997): 346–57. https://doi.org/10.1207/s15327957pspr0104_5.

DePaulo, Bella M., Deborah A. Kashy, Susan E. Kirkendol, Melissa M. Wyer, and Jennifer A. Epstein. "Lying in Everyday Life." *Journal of Personality and Social Psychology* 70, no. 5 (May 1996): 979–95. http://dx.doi.org/10.1037/0022-3514.70.5.979.

DePaulo, Bella M., Susan E. Kirkendol, John Tang, and Thomas P. O'Brien. "The Motivational Impairment Effect in the Communication of Deception: Replications and Extensions." *Journal of Nonverbal Behavior* 12, no. 3 (Fall 1988): 177–202. https://doi.org/10.1007/BF00987487.

DePaulo, Bella M., James J. Lindsay, Brian E. Malone, Laura Muhlenbruck, Kelly Charlton, and Harris Cooper. "Cues to Deception." *Psychological Bulletin* 129, no. 1 (January 2003): 74–118. http://dx.doi:10.1037/0033-2909.129.1.74.

DePaulo, Bella M., Miron Zuckerman, and Robert Rosenthal. "Humans as Lie Detectors." *Journal of Communication* 30, no. 2 (June 1980): 129–39. https://doi.org/10.1111/j.1460-2466 .1980.tb01975.x.

DeTurck, Mark A., and Gerald R. Miller. "Deception and Arousal: Isolating the Behavioral Correlates of Deception." *Human Communication Research* 12, no. 2 (Winter 1985): 181–201. https://doi.org/10.1111/j.1468-2958.1985.tb00072.x.

Driskell, James E. "Effectiveness of Deception Detection Training: A Meta-analysis." *Psychology, Crime & Law* 18, no. 8 (2012): 713–31. https://doi.org/10.1080/1068316X.2010.535820.

Dunbar, Norah E., Matthew L. Jensen, Judee K. Burgoon, Katherine M. Kelley, Kylie J. Harrison, Bradley J. Adame, Daniel Rex Bernard. "Effects of Veracity, Modality, and Sanctioning on Credibility Assessment during Mediated and Unmediated Interviews." *Communication Research* 42, no. 5 (July 2015): 649–74. https://doi.org/10.1177/0093650213480175.

Ekman, Paul. "Deception, Lying, and Demeanor." In *States of Mind: American and Post-Soviet Perspectives on Contemporary Issues in Psychology*, edited by Diane F. Halpern and Aleksander E. Voiskounsky, 93–105. New York: Oxford University Press, 1997.

———. "Lying and Nonverbal Behavior: Theoretical Issues and New Findings." *Journal of Nonverbal Behavior* 12, no. 3 (September 1988): 163–75. https://doi.org/10.1007/BF00987486.

———. *Telling Lies.* New York: W. W. Norton, 1985, 1992, 2001, 2009.

———, Ekman, M. A., and Ekman, T. *Why Kids Lie.* New York: Penguin, 1991.

Ekman, Paul, and Wallace V. Friesen. "Nonverbal Leakage and Clues to Deception." *Psychiatry* 32, no. 1 (1969): 88–106. https://doi.org/10.1080/00332747.1969.11023575.

———. "Detecting Deception from the Body or Face." *Journal of Personality and Social Psychology* 29, no. 3 (March 1974): 288–98. http://dx.doi.org/10.1037/h0036006.

Ekman, Paul, and Maureen O'Sullivan. "Who Can Catch a Liar?" *American Psychologist* 46, no. 9 (September 1991): 913–20. http://dx.doi.org/10.1037/0003-066X.46.9.913.

Ekman, Paul, Maureen O'Sullivan, and Mark G. Frank. "A Few Can Catch a Liar." *Psychological Science* 10, no. 3 (May 1999): 263–66. https://doi.org/10.1111/1467-9280.00147.

Exline, Ralph V., John Thibaut, Carole B. Hickey, and Peter Gumpert. "Visual Interaction in Relation to Machiavellianism and an Unethical Act." In *Studies in Machiavellianism*, edited by Richard Christie and Florence L. Geis, 53–76. New York: Academic Press, 1970.

Farquhar, Michael. *A Treasury of Deception: Liars, Misleaders, Hoodwinkers, and the Extraordinary True Stories of History's Greatest Hoaxes, Fakes, and Frauds.* New York: Penguin Books, 2005.

Fay, Paul L., and Warren C. Middleton. "The Ability to Judge Truth-Telling, or Lying, from the Voice as Transmitted over a Public Address System." *Journal of General Psychology* 24 (1941): 211–15. https://doi.org/10.1080/00221309.1941.10544369.

Feeley, Thomas H., and Mark A. deTurck. "The Behavioral Correlates of Sanctioned and Unsanctioned Deceptive Communication." *Journal of Nonverbal Behavior* 22, no. 3 (September 1998): 189–204. https://doi.org/10.1023/A:1022966505471.

Fein, Steven, James L. Hilton, and Dale T. Miller. "Suspicion of Ulterior Motivation and the Correspondence Bias." *Journal of Personality and Social Psychology* 58, no. 5 (May 1990): 753–64. http://dx.doi.org/10.1037/0022-3514.58.5.753.

Feldman, Robert S., James A. Forrest, and Benjamin R. Happ. "Self-Presentation and Verbal Deception: Do Self-Presenters Lie More?" *Basic and Applied Social Psychology* 24, no. 2 (2002): 163–70. https://doi.org/10.1207/S15324834BASP2402_8.

Ferguson, Christopher J., and Moritz Heene. "A Vast Graveyard of Undead Theories: Publication Bias and Psychological Science's Aversion to the Null." *Perspectives in Psychological Science* 7, no. 6 (November 2012): 555–61. https://doi.org/10.1177/1745691612459059.

Festinger, Leon, Henry W. Rieken, and Stanley Schachter. *When Prophecy Fails: A Social and Psychological Study of a Modern Group That Predicted the Destruction of the World.* Minneapolis: University of Minnesota Press, 1956.

Fiedler, Klaus, and Isabella Walka. "Training Lie Detectors to Use Nonverbal Cues Instead of Global Heuristics." *Human Communication Research* 20, no. 2 (December 1993): 199–223. https://doi.org/10.1111/j.1468-2958.1993.tb00321.x.

Ford, Elizabeth B. "Lie Detection: Historical, Neuropsychiatric and Legal Dimensions." *International Journal of Law and Psychiatry* 29, no. 3 (May–June 2006): 159–77. https://doi.org/10.1016/j.ijlp.2005.07.001.

Frank, Mark G., and Paul Ekman. "The Ability to Detect Deceit Generalizes across Different Types of High-Stake Lies." *Journal of Personality and Social Psychology* 72, no. 6 (June 1997): 1429–39. http://dx.doi.org/10.1037/0022-3514.72.6.1429.

———. "Appearing Truthful Generalizes across Different Deception Situations." *Journal of Per-

sonality and Social Psychology 86, no. 3 (March 2004): 486–95. http://dx.doi.org/10.1037 /0022–3514.86.3.486.

Frank, Mark G., and Thomas Hugh Feeley. "To Catch a Liar: Challenges for Research in Lie Detection Training." *Journal of Applied Communication Research* 31, no. 1 (February 2003): 58–75. https://doi.org/10.1080/00909880305377.

Frankfurt, Harry G. *On Bullshit.* Princeton: Princeton University Press, 2005.

Galasinski, Dariusz. *The Language of Deception: A Discourse Analytical Study.* Thousand Oaks, CA: Sage, 2000.

George, Joey F., and Alistair Robb. "Deception and Computer-Mediated Communication in Daily Life." *Communication Reports* 21, no. 2 (2008): 92–103. https://doi.org/10.1080 /08934210802298108.

Gigerenzer, Gerd. *Rationality for Mortals.* Oxford: Oxford University Press. 2008.

Gigerenzer, Gerd, and Reinhard Selten. *Bounded Rationality: The Adaptive Toolbox.* Cambridge, MA: MIT Press, 2001.

Gigerenzer, Gerd, Peter M. Todd, and ABC Research Group. *Simple Heuristics That Make Us Smart.* New York: Oxford University Press, 1999.

Gilbert, Daniel T. "How Mental Systems Believe." *American Psychologist* 46, no. 2 (February 1991): 107–19. http://dx.doi.org/10.1037/0003–066X.46.2.107.

Gilbert, Daniel T., Douglas S. Krull, and Patrick S. Malone. "Unbelieving the Unbelievable: Some Problems in the Rejection of False Information." *Journal of Personality and Social Psychology* 59, no. 4 (October 1990): 601–13. http://dx.doi.org/10.1037/0022–3514.59.4.601.

Gilbert, Daniel T., Romin W. Tafordi, and Patrick S. Malone. "You Can't Not Believe Everything You Read." *Journal of Personality and Social Psychology* 65, no. 2 (August 1993): 221–33. http://dx.doi.org/10.1037/0022–3514.65.2.221.

Global Deception Research Team. "A World of Lies." *Journal of Cross-Cultural Psychology* 37, no. 1 (January 2006): 60–74. https://doi.org/10.1177/0022022105282295.

Goffman, Erving. "The Nature of Deference and Demeanor." *American Anthropologist* 58, no. 3 (June 1956): 473–502. https://doi.org/10.1525/aa.1956.58.3.02a00070.

———. *The Presentation of Self in Everyday Life.* New York: Doubleday, 1959.

Granhag, Pär Anders, Sebastian C. Montecinos, and Simon Oleszkiewicz. "Eliciting Intelligence from Sources: The First Scientific Test of the Scharff Technique." *Legal and Criminological Psychology* 20, no. 1 (February 2015): 96–113. https://doi.org/10.1111/lcrp.12015.

Granhag, Pär Anders, and Leif A. Strömwall. "Repeated Interrogations–Stretching the Deception Detection Paradigm." *Expert Evidence* 7, no. 3 (September 1999): 163–74. https://doi.org /10.1023/A:1008993326434.

———. "Deception Detection: Examining the Consistency Heuristic." In *New Trends in Criminal Investigation and Evidence II,* edited by C. M. Breur, M. M. Kommer, J. F. Nijboer, and J. M. Reintjes, 309–21. Antwerpen: Intersentia, 2000.

———. "Deception Detection: Interrogators' and Observers' Decoding of Consecutive Statements." *Journal of Psychology* 135, no. 6 (2001): 603–20. https://doi.org/10.1080/00223980109603723.

Grice, Paul. *Studies in the Way of Words.* Cambridge: Harvard University Press, 1989.

Halevy, Rony, Shaul Shalvi, and Bruno Verschuere. "Being Honest about Dishonesty: Correlating Self-Reports and Actual Lying." *Human Communication Research* 40, no. 1 (January 2014): 54–72. https://doi.org/10.1111/hcre.12019.

Hall, Edward T. *Beyond Culture.* New York: Anchor Books, 1976.

Hample, Dale. "Purpose and Effects of Lying." *Southern Speech Communication Journal* 46, no. 1 (1980): 33–47. https://doi.org/10.1080/10417948009372474.

Hancock, Jeff. *The Future of Lying*. Filmed September 2012 TEDxWinnipeg, Winnipeg, Canada, video, 18:25, https://www.ted.com/talks/jeff_hancock_3_types_of_digital_lies.

Hancock, Jeffrey T., Jennifer Thom-Santelli, and Thompson Ritchie. "Deception and Design: The Impact of Communication Technology on Lying Behavior." *Chi Letters* 6: 129–34. https://doi:10.1145/985692.985709.

Hartwig, Maria, and Charles F. Bond Jr. "Why Do Lie-Catchers Fail? A Lens Model Meta-analysis of Human Lie Judgments." *Psychological Bulletin* 137, no. 4 (July 2011): 643–59. http://dx.doi.org:10.1037/a0023589.

———. "Lie Detection from Multiple Cues: A Meta-analysis." *Applied Cognitive Psychology* 28, no. 5 (September–October 2014): 661–76. https://doi.org/10.1002/acp.3052.

Hartwig, Maria, Pär Anders Granhag, Leif A. Strömwall, and Ola Kronkvist. "Strategic Use of Evidence during Police Interviews: When Training to Detect Deception Works." *Law and Human Behavior* 30, no. 5 (October 2006): 603–19. https://doi.org/10.1007/s10979–006–9053–9.

Hartwig, Maria, Pär Anders Granhag, Leif A. Strömwall, and Aldert Vrij. "Police Officers' Lie Detection Accuracy: Interrogating Freely versus Observing Video." *Police Quarterly* 7, no. 4 (December 2004): 429–56. https://doi.org/10.1177/1098611104264748.

Hauch, Valerie, Iris Blandón-Gitlin, Jaume Masip, and Siegfried L. Sporer. "Are Computers Effective Lie Detectors? A Meta-analysis of Linguistic Cues to Deception." *Personality and Social Psychology Review* 19, no. 4 (November 2015): 307–42. https://doi.org/10.1177/1088868314556539.

Hauch, Valerie, Siegfried L. Sporer, Stephen W. Michael, and Christian A. Meissner. "Does Training Improve the Detection of Deception? A Meta-analysis." *Communication Research* 43, no. 3 (April 2016): 283–43. https://doi.org/10.1177/0093650214534974.

Henningsen, David Dryden, Michael G. Cruz, and Mary Clair Morr. "Pattern Violations and Perceptions of Deception." *Communication Reports* 11, no. 1 (Winter 2000): 1–9. https://doi.org/10.1080/08934210009367718.

Honeycutt, James. *Imagine That: Studies in Imagined Interactions*. Cresskill, NJ: Hampton Press, 2009.

Houston, Philip, and Michael Floyd. *Spy the Lie: Former CIA Officers Teach You How to Detect Deception*. New York: St. Martin's Press, 2012.

Jacobs, Scott, Edwin J. Dawson, and Dale Brashers. "Information Manipulation Theory: A Replication and Assessment." *Communication Monographs* 63, no. 1 (1996): 70–82. https://doi.org/10.1080/03637759609376375.

Kahneman, Daniel. *Thinking, Fast and Slow*. New York: Farrar, Straus and Giroux, 2011.

Kahneman, Daniel, Paul Slovic, and Amos Tversky. *Judgment under Uncertainty: Heuristics and Bias*. Cambridge: Cambridge University Press, 1992.

Kessler, Glenn, Salvador Rizzo, and Meg Kelly. "President Trump Has Made More than 5,000 False or Misleading Claims." *Washington Post*, September 13, 2018. https://www.washingtonpost.com/politics/2018/09/13/president-trump-has-made-more-than-false-or-misleading-claims.

Kim, Rachel K., and Timothy R. Levine. "The Effect of Suspicion on Deception Detection Accuracy: Optimal Level or Opposing Effects?" *Communication Reports* 24, no. 2, (July–December 2011): 51–62. http://dx.doi.org/10.1080/08934215.2011.615272.

Kotowski, Michael R., Timothy R. Levine, Colin R. Baker, and Jeffrey M. Bolt. "A Multitrait–Multimethod Validity Assessment of the Verbal Aggressiveness and Argumentativeness Scales." *Communication Monographs* 76, no. 4 (2009): 443–62. https://doi.org/10.1080/03637750903300247.

Kraut, Robert. "Humans as Lie Detectors." *Journal of Communication* 30, no. 4 (December 1980): 209–18. https://doi.org/10.1111/j.1460-2466.1980.tb02030.x.

Lakatos, Imre. *The Methodology of Scientific Research Programmes.* Cambridge: Cambridge University Press, 1978.

Lehrer, Jonah. "The Truth Wears Off: Is There Something Wrong with the Scientific Method?" *New Yorker,* December 13, 2010. https://www.newyorker.com/magazine/2010/12/13/the-truth-wears-off.

Levine, Timothy R. "A Defense of Publishing Nonsignificant (ns) Results." *Communication Research Reports* 30, no. 3 (2013): 270–74. https://doi.org/10.1080/08824096.2013.806261.

———. "Dichotomous and Continuous Views of Deception: A Reexamination of Deception Ratings in Information Manipulation Theory." *Communication Research Reports* 18, no. 3 (2001): 230–40. https://doi.org/10.1080/08824090109384803.

———. "Ecological Validity and Deception Detection Research Design." *Communication Methods and Measures* 12, no. 1 (2018): 45–54. https://doi.org/10.1080/19312458.2017.1411471.

———. "Examining Sender and Judge Variability in Honesty Assessments and Deception Detection Accuracy: Evidence for a Transparent Liar but No Evidence of Deception-General Ability." *Communication Research Reports* 33, no. 3 (2016): 188–94. https://doi.org/10.1080/08824096.2016.1186629.

———. "A Few Transparent Liars Explaining 54% Accuracy in Deception Detection Experiments." *Annals of the International Communication Association* 34 (formerly *Communication Yearbook* 34), no. 1 (2010): 41–61. https://doi.org/10.1080/23808985.2010.11679095.

———. "Modeling the Psychometric Properties of Information Manipulation Ratings." *Communication Research Reports* 15, no. 2 (1998): 218–25. https://doi.org/10.1080/08824099809362116.

———. (2007–2010). MSU trivia game interviews. Unpublished videotapes. East Lansing: Michigan State University.

———. "Truth-Default Theory (TDT): A Theory of Human Deception and Deception Detection." *Journal of Language and Social Psychology* 33, no. 4 (September 2014): 378–92. https://doi.org/10.1177/0261927X14535916.

Levine, Timothy R., Mohamed Vaqas Ali, Marleah Dean, Rasha A. Abdulla, and Karina Garia-Ruano. "Toward a Pan-cultural Typology of Deception Motives." *Journal of Intercultural Communication Research* 45, no. 1 (2016): 1–12. https://doi:10.1080/17475759.2015.1137079.

Levine, Timothy R., Kelli Jean Asada, and Lisa L. Massi Lindsey. "The Relative Impact of Violation Type and Lie Severity on Judgments of Message Deceptiveness." *Communication Research Reports* 20, no. 3 (2003): 208–18. https://doi.org/10.1080/08824090309388819.

Levine, Timothy R., Kelli Jean K. Asada, and Hee Sun Park. "The Lying Chicken and the Gaze Avoidant Egg: Eye Contact, Deception, and Causal Order." *Southern Communication Journal* 71, no. 4 (December 2006): 401–11. https://doi:10.1080/10417940601000576.

Levine, Timothy R., and John Banas. "One-Tailed F-Tests in Communication Research." *Communication Monographs* 69, no. 2 (2002): 132–43. https://doi.org/10.1080/714041709.

Levine, Timothy R., J. Pete Blair, and Christopher J. Carpenter. "A Critical Look at Meta-analytic Evidence for the Cognitive Approach to Lie Detection: A Re-examination of Vrij, Fisher, and

Blank (2017)." *Legal and Criminological Psychology* 23, no. 1 (February 2018): 7–19. https://doi.org/10.1111/lcrp.12115.

Levine, Timothy R., J. Pete Blair, and David D. Clare. "Diagnostic Utility: Experimental Demonstrations and Replications of Powerful Question Effects in High-Stakes Deception Detection." *Human Communication Research* 40, no. 2 (April 2014): 262–89. https://doi.org/10.1111/hcre.12021.

Levine, Timothy R., and Charles F. Bond Jr. "Direct and Indirect Measures of Lie Detection Tell the Same Story: A Reply to ten Brinke, Stimson, and Carney (2014)." *Psychological Science* 25, no. 10 (October 2014): 1960–61. https://doi.org/10.1177/0956797614536740.

Levine, Timothy R., David D. Clare, J. Pete Blair, Steve McCornack, and Kelly Morrison. "Expertise in Deception Detection Involves Actively Prompting Diagnostic Information rather than Passive Behavioral Observation." *Human Communication Research* 40, no. 4 (October 2014): 442–62. https://doi.org/10.1111/hcre.12032.

Levine, Timothy R., David D. Clare, Tracie Green, Kim B. Serota, and Hee Sun Park. "The Effects of Truth–Lie Base Rate on Interactive Deception Detection Accuracy. *Human Communication Research* 40, no. 3 (July 2014): 350–72. https://doi.org/10.1111/hcre.12027.

Levine, Timothy R., Thomas Hugh Feeley, Steven A. McCornack, Mikayla Hughes, and Chad M. Harms. "Testing the Effects of Nonverbal Training on Deception Detection Accuracy with the Inclusion of a Bogus Training Control Group." *Western Journal of Communication* 69, no. 3 (July 2005): 203–17. https://doi.org/10.1080/10570310500202355.

Levine, Timothy R., and Craig R. Hullett. "Eta Squared, Partial Eta Squared, and Misreporting of Effect Size in Communication Research." *Human Communication Research* 28, no. 4 (October 2002): 612–25. https://doi.org/10.1111/j.1468–2958.2002.tb00828.x.

Levine, Timothy R., and Rachel K. Kim. "Some Considerations for a New Theory of Deceptive Communication." In *The Interplay of Truth and Deception: New Agendas in Theory and Research*, edited by Matt S. McGlone and Mark L. Knapp, 16–34. New York: Routledge, 2010.

Levine, Timothy R., Rachel K. Kim, and J. Pete Blair. "(In)accuracy at detecting True and False Confessions and Denials: An Initial Test of a Projected Motive Model of Veracity Judgments. *Human Communication Research*, 36, no. 1 (January 2010): 82–102. https://doi.org/10.1111/j.1468–2958.2009.01369.x.

Levine, Timothy R., Rachel K. Kim, and Lauren M. Hamel. "People Lie for a Reason: Three Experiments Documenting the Principle of Veracity." *Communication Research Reports* 27, no 4 (2010): 271–85. https://doi.org/10.1080/08824096.2010.496334.

Levine, Timothy R., Rachel K. Kim, Hee Sun Park, and Mikayla Hughes. "Deception Detection Accuracy is a Predictable Linear Function of Message Veracity Base-Rate: A Formal Test of Park and Levine's Probability Model." *Communication Monographs* 73, no. 3 (2006): 243–60. https://doi.org/10.1080/03637750600873736.

Levine, Timothy R., Michael R. Kotowski, Michael J. Beatty, and Martijn J. Van Kelegom. "A Meta-Analysis of Trait–Behavior Correlations in Argumentativeness and Verbal Aggression." *Journal of Language and Social Psychology* 31, no 1 (March 2012): 95–111. https://doi.org/10.1177/0261927X11425037.

Levine, Timothy R., and Steven A. McCornack. "Behavioral Adaptation, Confidence, and Heuristic-Based Explanations of the Probing Effect." *Human Communication Research* 27, no. 4 (October 2001): 471–502. https://doi.org/10.1111/j.1468–2958.2001.tb00790.x.

———. "Can Behavioral Adaptation Explain the Probing Effect? Rejoinder to Buller et al." *Human *Communication Research* 22, no 4 (June 1996): 604–13. https://doi.org/10.1111/j.1468 -2958.1996.tb00382.x.

———. "A Critical Analysis of the Behavioral Adaptation Explanation of the Probing Effect." *Human Communication Research* 22, no 4 (June 1996): 575–88. https://doi.org/10.1111/j.1468 -2958.1996.tb00380.x.

———. "The Dark Side of Trust: Conceptualizing and Measuring Types of Communicative Suspicion." *Communication Quarterly* 39, no. 4 (Fall 1991): 325–40. https://doi.org/10.1177 /0265407592091008.

———. "Linking Love and Lies: A Formal Test of the McCornack and Parks Model of Deception Detection." *Journal of Social and Personal Relationships* 9, no. 1 (February 1992): 143–54. https://doi.org/10.1177/0265407592091008.

———. "Theorizing about Deception." *Journal of Language and Social Psychology* 33, no. 4 (September 2014): 431–40. https://doi.org/10.1177/0261927X14536397.

Levine, Timothy R., Steven A. McCornack, and Penny Baldwin Avery. "Sex Differences in Emotional Reactions to Discovered Deception." *Communication Quarterly* 40, no. 3 (Summer 1992): 289–96. https://doi.org/10.1080/01463379209369843.

Levine, Timothy R., Hee Sun Park, and Steven A. McCornack. "Accuracy in Detecting Truths and Lies: Documenting the 'Veracity Effect.'" *Communication Monographs* 66, no. 2 (June 1999): 125–44. https://doi.org/10.1080/03637759909376468.

Levine, Timothy R., and Kim B. Serota. "Truth-Bias: Who Is Biased, Subjects or Deception Researchers?" Talk given at SARMAC. Victoria, Canada, 2015.

Levine, Timothy R., Kim B. Serota, Frankie Carey, and Doug Messer. "Teenagers Lie a Lot: A Further Investigation into the Prevalence of Lying." *Communication Research Reports* 30, no. 3 (2013): 211–20. https://doi.org/10.1080/08824096.2013.806254.

Levine, Timothy R., Kim B. Serota, and Hillary C. Shulman. "The Impact of *Lie to Me* on Viewers' Actual Ability to Detect Deception." *Communication Research* 37, no. 6 (December 2010): 847–56. https://doi.org/10.1177/0093650210362686.

Levine, Timothy R., Kim B. Serota, Hillary Shulman, David D. Clare, Hee Sun Park, Allison S. Shaw, Jae Chul Shim, and Jung Hyon Lee. "Sender Demeanor: Individual Differences in Sender Believability Have a Powerful Impact on Deception Detection Judgments." *Human Communication Research* 37, no. 3 (July 2011): 377–403. https://doi.org/10.1111/j.1468 -2958.2011.01407.x.

Levine, Timothy R., Allison Shaw, and Hillary C. Shulman. "Assessing Deception Detection Accuracy with Dichotomous Truth–Lie Judgments and Continuous Scaling: Are People Really More Accurate When Honesty Is Scaled?" *Communication Research Reports* 27, no. 2 (2010): 112–22. https://doi.org/10.1080/08824090903526638.

———. "Increasing Deception Detection Accuracy with Strategic Questioning." *Human Communication Research* 36, no. 2 (April 2010): 216–31. https://doi.org/10.1111/j.1468-2958.2010 .01374.x.

Levine, Timothy R., Hillary C. Shulman, Christopher J. Carpenter, David C. DeAndrea, and J. Pete Blair. "The Impact of Accusatory, Non-Accusatory, Bait, and False Evidence Questioning on Deception Detection." *Communication Research Reports* 30, no. 2 (April 2013): 169–74. https://doi.org/10.1080/08824096.2012.762905.

Levine, Timothy R., René Weber, Craig R. Hullett, Hee Sun Park, and Lisa Lindsey. "A Critical Assessment of Null Hypothesis Significance Testing in Quantitative Communication Research." *Human Communication Research* 34, no. 2 (April 2008): 171–87. https://doi.org /10.1111/j.1468–2958.2008.00317.x.

Levine, Timothy R., René Weber, Hee Sun Park, and Craig R. Hullett. "A Communication Researchers' Guide to Null Hypothesis Significance Testing and Alternatives." *Human Communication Research* 34, no. 2 (April 2008): 188–209. https://doi.org/10.1111/j.1468–2958 .2008.00318.x.

Lie to Me. Television series (2009–2011). Los Angeles: Fox Broadcasting Company.

Liu, Meiling, Pär Anders Granhag, Sara Landstrom, Emma Roos af Hjelmsater, Leif Strömwall, and Aldert Vrij. "'Can You Remember What Was in Your Pocket When You Were Stung by a Bee?' Eliciting Cues to Deception by Asking the Unanticipated." *Open Criminology Journal* 3, no. 3 (June 2010): 31–36. https://doi:10.2174/1874917801003010031.

Loftus, Elizabeth F., and Jacqueline E. Pickrell. "The Formation of False Memories." *Psychiatric Annals* 25, no. 12 (December 1995): 720–25. https://doi.org/10.3928/0048-5713-19951201-07.

Maier, Norman R. F., and James A. Thurber. "Accuracy of Judgments of Deception When an Interview Is Watched, Heard, and Read." *Personnel Psychology* 21 (March 1968): 23–30. https:// doi.org/10.1111/j.1744–6570.1968.tb02283.x.

Malle, Bertram F. *How the Mind Explains Behavior: Folk Explanations, Meaning, and Social Interaction.* Cambridge, MA: MIT Press, 2004.

Masip, Jaume, Hernán Alonso, Eugenio Garrido, and Concha Antón. "Generalized Communicative Suspicion (GCS) among Police Officers: Accounting for the Investigator Bias Effect." *Journal of Applied Social Psychology* 35, no. 5 (May 2005): 1046–66. https://doi.org/10.1111 /j.1559–1816.2005.tb02159.x.

Masip, Jaume, and Carmen Herrero. "Police Detection of Deception: Beliefs about Behavioral Cues to Deception Are Strong Even Though Contextual Evidence Is More Useful." *Journal of Communication* 65, no. 1 (February 2015): 125–45. https://doi.org/10.1111/jcom.12135.

McCornack, Steven A. "The Generation of Deceptive Messages: Laying the Groundwork for a Viable Theory of Interpersonal Deception." In *Message Production: Advances in Communication Theory*, edited by John O. Green, 91–126. Mahwah, NJ: Erlbaum, 1997.

———. "Information Manipulation Theory." *Communication Monographs* 59, no. 1 (1992): 1–16. https://doi.org/10.1080/03637759209376245.

———McCornack, Steven A. *Interpersonal Communication and You.* 1st ed. Boston: Bedford/St. Martin's, 2015.

———. *Reflect and Relate.* 1st ed. Boston: Bedford/St. Martin's, 2006.

McCornack, Steven A., and Timothy R. Levine. "When Lies Are Uncovered: Emotional and Relational Outcomes of Discovered Deception." *Communication Monographs* 57, no. 2 (March 1990): 119–38. https://doi.org/10.1080/03637759009376190.

———. "When Lovers Become Leery: The Relationship between Suspicion and Accuracy in Detecting Deception." *Communication Monographs* 57, no. 3 (September 1990): 219–30. https:// doi.org/10.1080/03637759009376197.

McCornack, Steven A., Timothy R. Levine, Kelly Morrison, and Maria Lapinski. "Speaking of Information Manipulation: A Critical Rejoinder." *Communication Monographs* 63, no. 1 (1996): 83–92. https://doi.org/10.1080/03637759609376376.

McCornack, Steven A., Timothy R. Levine, Kathleen A. Solowczuk, Helen I. Torres, and Dedra M. Campbell. "When the Alteration of Information Is Viewed as Deception: An Empirical Test of Information Manipulation Theory. *Communication Monographs* 59, no. 2 (March 1992): 17–29. https://doi.org/10.1080/03637759209376246.

McCornack, Steven A., Kelly Morrison, Jihyun Esther Paik, Amy M. Wisner, and Xun Zhu. "Information Manipulation Theory 2: A Propositional Theory of Deceptive Discourse Production." *Language and Social Psychology* 33, no. 4 (September 2014): 348–77. https://doi.org /10.1177/0261927X14534656.

McCornack, Steven A., and Joseph Ortiz. *Choices & Connections: An Introduction to Human Communication*, 1st ed. Boston: Bedford/St. Martin's, 2015.

McCornack, Steven A., and Malcolm R. Parks. "Deception Detection and Relationship Development: The Other Side of Trust." In *Communication Yearbook 9*, edited by Margaret L. McLaughlin, 377–89. Beverly Hills: Sage, 1986.

Meissner, Christian A., and Saul M. Kassin. "He's Guilty: Investigator Bias in Judgments of Truth and Deception." *Law and Human Behavior* 26, no. 5 (October 2002): 469–80. https:// doi.org/10.1023/A:1020278620751.

Metts, Sandra. "An Exploratory Investigation of Deception in Close Relationships." *Journal of Social and Personal Relationships* 6, no. 2 (May 1969): 59–179. https://doi.org/10.1177 /026540758900600202.

Meyer, Pamela. *How to Spot a Liar*. TED Talk (October 2011). https://www.ted.com/talks/pamela _meyer_how_to_spot_a_liar.

Milgram, Stanley. *Obedience to Authority*. New York: Harper and Row, 1974.

Miller, Gerald R., and Henry E. Nicholson. *Communication Inquiry*. Reading, MA: Addison-Wesley, 1976.

Miller, Gerald R., and James B. Stiff. *Deceptive Communication*. Newbury Park, CA: Sage, 1993.

Nahari, Galit, Sharon Leal, Aldert Vrij, Lara Warmelink, and Zarah Vernham. "Did Somebody See It? Applying the Verifiability Approach to Insurance Claim Interviews." *Journal of Psychology and Offender Profiling* 11, no. 3 (October 2014): 237–43. https://doi.org/10.1002 /jip.1417.

Nahari, Galit, Aldert Vrij, and Ronald P. Fisher. "Exploiting Liars' Verbal Strategies by Examining the Verifiability of Details." *Legal and Criminological Psychology* 19, no. 2 (September 2014): 227–39. https://doi.org/10.1111/j.2044–8333.2012.02069.x.

———. "The Verifiability Approach: Countermeasures Facilitate Its Ability to Discriminate between Truths and Lies." *Applied Cognitive Psychology* 28, no. 1 (January–February 2014): 122–28. https://doi.org/10.1002/acp.2974.

NBC Nightly News (August 18, 2014). Businesses rely on honor system to collect funds.

Open Science Collaboration. "Estimating the Reproducibility of Psychological Science." *Science* 349, no. 6251 (August 2015): aac4716. https://doi:10.1126/science.aac4716.

O'Sullivan, Maureen, and Paul Ekman. "The Wizards of Deception Detection." In *The Detection of Deception in Forensic Contexts*, ed. Pär Anders Granhag and Leif A. Strömwall (Cambridge: Cambridge University Press, 2004), 269–86.

O'Sullivan, Maureen, Mark G. Frank, Carolyn M. Hurley, and Jaspreet Tiwana. "Police Lie Detection Accuracy: The Effect of Lie Scenario." *Law and Human Behavior* 33, no. 6 (December 2009): 530–38. https://doi.org/10.1007/s10979–008–9166–4.

Park, Ernest S., Timothy R. Levine, Chad M. Harms, and Merissa H. Ferrara. "Group and Individual Accuracy in Deception Detection." *Communication Research Reports* 19, no. 2 (2002): 99–106. https://doi.org/10.1080/08824090209384837.

Park, Hee Sun, and Timothy R. Levine. "Base Rates, Deception Detection, and Deception Theory: A Reply to Burgoon (2015)." *Human Communication Research* 41, no. 3 (July 2015): 350–66. https://doi.org/10.1111/hcre.12066.

———. "The Effects of Truth–Lie Base-Rates on Deception Detection Accuracy in Korea." *Asian Journal of Communication* 27, no. 5 (2017): 554–62. https://doi.org/10.1080/01292986.2017.1334074.

———. "A Probability Model of Accuracy in Deception Detection Experiments." *Communication Monographs* 68, no. 2 (2001): 201–10. https://doi.org/10.1080/03637750128059.

Park, Hee Sun, Timothy R. Levine, Steven A. McCornack, Kelly Morrison, and Merissa Ferrara. "How People Really Detect Lies." *Communication Monographs* 69, no. 2 (June 2002): 144–57. https://doi.org/10.1080/714041710.

Peskin, Joan. "Ruse and Representation: On Children's Ability to Conceal Information. *Developmental Psychology* 28, no. 1 (January 1992): 84–89. http://dx.doi.org/10.1037/0012–1649.28.1.84.

Porter, Stephen, and Leanne ten Brinke. "Reading between the Lies: Identifying Concealed and Falsified Emotions in Universal Facial Expressions." *Psychological Science* 19, no. 5 (May 2008): 508–14. https://doi.org/10.1111/j.1467–9280.2008.02116.x

Reid and Associates. http://www.reid.com/.

Reinhard, Marc-André, Greifeneder Rainer, and Martin Scharmach. "Unconscious Processes Improve Lie Detection." *Journal of Personality and Social Psychology* 105, no. 5 (November 2013): 721–39. http://dx.doi.org/10.1037/a0034352.

Reinhard, Marc-André, Siegfried L. Sporer, and Martin Scharmach. "Perceived Familiarity with a Judgmental Situation Improves Lie Detection Ability." *Swiss Journal of Psychology* 72, no. 1 (January 2013): 43–52. https://doi.org/10.1024/1421–0185/a000098.

Reinhard, Marc-André, Siegfried L. Sporer, Martin Scharmach, and Mamara Marksteiner. "Listening, Not Watching: Situational Familiarity and the Ability to Detect Deception." *Journal of Personality and Social Psychology* 101, no. 3 (September 2011): 467–84. http://dx.doi.org/10.1037/a0023726.

Rozin, Paul. "Social Psychology and Science: Some Lessons from Solomon Asch." *Personality and Social Psychology Review* 5, no. 1 (February 2001): 2–14. https://doi.org/10.1207/S15327957PSPR0501_1.

Schneier, Bruce. *Liars and Outliers: Enabling the Trust That Society Needs to Thrive.* Indianapolis: John Wiley and Sons, 2012.

Serota, Kim B., and Timothy R. Levine. "A Few Prolific Liars: Variation in the Prevalence of Lying." *Journal of Language and Social Psychology* 34, no. 2 (March 2015): 138–57. https://doi.org/10.1177/0261927X14528804.

Serota, Kim B., Timothy R. Levine, and Franklin J. Boster. "The Prevalence of Lying in America: Three Studies of Self-Reported Lies." *Human Communication Research* 36, no. 1 (January 2010): 2–25. https://doi.org/10.1111/j.1468–2958.2009.01366.x.

Sherif, Muzafer, O. J. Harvey, William R. Hood, Carolyn W. Sherif, and Jack White. *The Robbers Cave Experiment: Intergroup Conflict and Cooperation.* Middletown, CT: Wesleyan University Press, 1988.

Sporer, Siegfried L. "Deception and Cognitive Load: Expanding Our Horizon with a Working Memory Model." *Frontiers in Psychology* 7 (April 2016). https://doi.org/10.3389/fpsyg.2016.00420.

Sporer, Siegfried Ludwig, and Barbara Schwandt. "Moderators of Nonverbal Indicators of Deception: A Meta-analytic Synthesis." *Psychology, Public Policy, and Law* 13, no. 1 (February 2007): 1–34. https://doi.org/10.1037/1076–8971.13.1.1.

————. "Paraverbal Indicators of Deception: A Meta-analytic Synthesis." *Applied Cognitive Psychology* 20, no. 4 (May 2006): 421–46. https://doi.org/10.1002/acp.1190.

Stiff, James B. "Theoretical Approaches to the Study of Deceptive Communication: Comments on Interpersonal Deception Theory." *Communication Theory* 6, no. 3 (August 1996): 289–96. https://doi.org/10.1111/j.1468–2885.1996.tb00130.x.

Stiff, James B., and Gerald R. Miller. "'Come to Think of It . . .': Interrogative Probes, Deceptive Communication, and Deception Detection." *Human Communication Research* 12, no. 3 (March 1986): 339–57. https://doi.org/10.1111/j.1468–2958.1986.tb00081.x.

Strömwall, Leif A., Pär Anders Granhag, and A. Jonsson. "Deception among Pairs: 'Let's Say We Had Lunch and Hope They Will Swallow It!'" *Psychology Crime & Law* 9 (2003): 109–24. https://doi.org/10.1080/1068316031000116238" \t "_blank" \o.

Talwar, Victoria, and Angela Crossman. "From Little White Lies to Filthy Liars: The Evolution of Honesty and Deception in Young Children." In *Advancement in Child Development and Behavior* 40, edited by Janette B. Benson, 139–79. London: Elsevier, 2011. https://doi.org /10.1016/B978–0–12–386491–8.00004–9.

ten Brinke, Leanne, Dayna Stimson, and Dana R. Carney. "Some Evidence for Unconscious Lie Detection." *Psychological Science* 25, no. 5 (May 2014): 1098–105. https://doi.org/10.1177 /0956797614524421.

Tiersma, Peter Meijes. "The Language of Perjury: Literal Truth, Ambiguity, and the False Statement Requirement." *Southern California Law Review* 63 (1989): 373–431.

Trivers, Robert. *The Folly of Fools: The Logic of Deceit and Self-Deception in Human Life.* New York: Basic, 2011.

Turner, Ronny E., Charles Edgley, and Glen Olmstead. "Information Control in Conversations: Honesty Is Not Always the Best Policy." *Kansas Journal of Sociology* 11, no. 1 (Spring 1975): 69–89. https://www.jstor.org/stable/23255229.

Vrij, Aldert. "A Cognitive Approach to Lie Detection." In *Detecting Deception: Current Challenges and Cognitive Approaches*, edited by Pär Anders Granhag, Aldert Vrij, and Bruno Verschuere, 205–30. Chichester: John Wiley and Sons, 2015.

————. *Detecting Lies and Deceit: Pitfalls and Opportunities.* West Sussex: John Wiley and Sons, 2008.

Vrij, Aldert, Katherine Edward, and Ray Bull. "Police Officers' Ability to Detect Deceit: The Benefit of Indirect Deception Detection Measures." *Legal and Criminological Psychology* 6, no. 2 (September 2001): 185–96. https://doi.org/10.1348/135532501168271.

Vrij, Aldert, Ronald P. Fisher, and Hartmut Blank. "A Cognitive Approach to Lie Detection: A Meta-analysis." *Legal and Criminological Psychology* 22, no. 1 (February 2017): 1–21. https:// doi.org/10.1111/lcrp.12088.

Vrij, Aldert, and Pär Anders Granhag. "Eliciting Cues to Deception and Truth: What Matters Are the Questions Asked." *Journal of Applied Research in Memory and Cognition* 1, no. 2 (June 2012): 110–17. https://doi.org/10.1016/j.jarmac.2012.02.004.

Vrij, Aldert, Sharon Leal, Pär Anders Granhag, Samantha Mann, Ronald P. Fisher, Jackie Hillman, and Kathryn Sperry. "Outsmarting the Liars: The Benefit of Asking Unanticipated Questions." *Law and Human Behavior* 33, no. 2 (April 2009): 159–66. https://doi.org/10.1007 /s10979–008–9143-y.

Vrij, Aldert, Samantha A. Mann, Ronald P. Fisher, Rebecca Milne, and Ray Bull. "Increasing Cognitive Load to Facilitate Lie Detection: The Benefit of Recalling an Event in Reverse

Order." *Law and Human Behavior* 32, no. 3 (June 2008): 253–65. https://doi.org/10.1007
/s10979–007–9103-y.

Vrij, Aldert, Samantha Mann, Susanne Kristen, and Ronald P. Fisher. "Cues to Deception and
Ability to Detect Lies as a Function of Police Interview Styles." *Law and Human Behavior* 31,
no. 5 (October 2007): 499–518. https://doi.org/10.1007/s10979–006–9066–4.

Vrij, Aldert, Samantha Mann, Sharon Leal, and Ronald Fisher. "'Look into My Eyes': Can an Instruction to Maintain Eye Contact Facilitate Lie Detection?" *Psychology, Crime & Law* 16, no. 4
(2010): 327–48. https://doi.org/10.1080/10683160902740633.

Vrij, Aldert, Christian A. Meissner, and Saul M. Kassin. "Problems in Expert Deception Detection and the Risk of False Confessions: No Proof to the Contrary in Levine et al. (2014)."
Psychology, Crime, & Law 21, no. 9 (2015): 901–9. https://doi.org/10.1080/1068316X.2015
.1054389.

Walster, Elaine, Elliot Aronson, and Darcy Abrahams. "On Increasing the Persuasiveness of
a Low Prestige Communicator." *Journal of Experimental Social Psychology* 2, no 4 (October
1966): 325–42. https://doi.org/10.1016/0022–1031(66)90026–6.

Weinberger, Sharon. "Intent to Deceive? Can the Science of Deception Detection Help to Catch
Terrorists?" *Nature* 465, no. 7297 (May 2010): 412–15. https://doi:10.1038/465412a. https://
www.nature.com/news/2010/100526/full/465412a.html.

Weiss, Walter. "A Sleeper Effect in Opinion Change." *Journal of Abnormal and Social Psychology*
48, no. 2 (1953): 173–80. http://dx.doi.org/10.1037/h0063200.

Whiten, A., and Richard W. Byrne. "Tactical Deception in Primates." *Behavioral and Brain Sciences* 11, no. 2 (June 1988): 233–44. https://doi.org/10.1017/S0140525X00049682.

Wiseman, Richard, Caroline Watt, Leanne ten Brinke, Stephen Porter, Sara-Louise Couper, and
Calum Rankin. "The Eyes Don't Have It: Lie Detection and Neuro-Linguistic Programming."
PLOS ONE 7, no. 7 (July 2012): e40259. https://doi.org/10.1371/journal.pone.0040259.

Wright, Gordon R. T., Christopher J. Berry, and Geoffrey Bird. "'You Can't Kid a Kidder': Association between Production and Detection of Deception in an Interactive Deception Task."
Frontiers in Human Neuroscience (April 2012). https://doi.org/10.3389/fnhum.2012.0008 7.

Wright, Gordon R. T., Christopher J. Berry, Carline Catmur, and Geoffrey Bird. "Good Liars Are
Neither 'Dark' nor Self-Deceptive." *PLOS ONE* 10, no. 6 (June 2015): e0127315. https://doi
.org/10.1371/journal.pone.0127315.

Zuckerman, Miron, Richard S. DeFrank, Judith A. Hall, Deborah T. Larrance, and Robert
Rosenthal. "Facial and Vocal Cues of Deception and Honesty." *Journal of Experimental Social
Psychology* 15, no. 4 (July 1979): 378–96. https://doi.org/10.1016/0022–1031(79)90045–3.

Zuckerman, Miron, Bella M. DePaulo, and Robert Rosenthal. "Verbal and Nonverbal Communication of Deception." In *Advances in Experimental Social Psychology* 14, edited by Leonard
Berkowitz, 1–59. New York: Academic Press, 1981.

Zuckerman, Miron, Nancy H. Spiegel, Bella M. DePaulo, and Robert Rosenthal. "Nonverbal
Strategies for Decoding Deception." *Journal of Nonverbal Behavior* 6, no. 3 (1982): 171–87.
https://doi.org/10.1007/BF00987066.

Index

aberrant controls, 87–88

ability to detect deception, 44, 47, 52–53, 61–63, 79, 188, 232, 239–40, 289

ability to lie convincingly, 291. *See also* transparency

abductive (approach to truth-default theory), xii

accuracy (in deception detection): below-chance, 100, 172, 244, 247, 278, 280, 388n32; by experts, 44, 62, 82, 133, 184, 207, 247, 265, 272, 275, 277, 279–87, 299–300, 388n34; 54% accuracy, 10–11, 13–14, 21–22, 38–53, 87, 208–11, 222–29, 234, 237, 244, 246, 266, 268–69, 272, 276, 278, 284, 304n19, 307n3, 308n7; improved, 37, 100, 225, 253–87; lie accuracy and truth accuracy, 37, 47–48, 202–4, 206–9, 211, 213–16, 224, 309n24; by media, 39–42, 83, 227, 293–94, 300; slightly-better-than-chance accuracy, 10–12, 16, 22, 36–46, 50–53, 62, 79, 86, 99, 180, 205, 208, 223, 225–54, 258, 265–66, 269, 287, 295, 297, 308n7. *See also* deception detection wizard; negative utility; training to detect deception

active questioning, 268–69

adaptors, 23, 26, 28, 31, 57–58. *See also* cues

affect displays, 57

affirming the consequence, 201

age and prevalence of lying, 148. *See also* lying in children

Ariely, Dan, 338n38

arousal, 31, 63–64, 69, 72, 76, 79, 80, 84, 86, 109, 127, 294

Asada, Kelli, xiv, 124

Asch, Solomon, 13–14

Asch conformity experiment, 13–14, 254, 335n3

Atlanta Hartsfield-Jackson Airport, 210

attempted behavioral control, 64

attributions, 168

audio-only communication, 40, 42, 184, 227. *See also* accuracy: by media

avoidance lies, 166

bait question, 270, 276. *See also* behavioral analysis interview

bald-faced lies (BFL), 80–81, 101–2, 104–6, 116, 120, 124, 126–27, 129–33, 159,

bald-faced truths (BFT), 80–81, 101, 116, 120, 126–29, 131–32, 323n16

baseline honest behaviors. *See* baselining

baselining, 34, 40, 43–44, 61, 312n22

base-rates. *See* truth-lie base-rates

behavioral analysis interview (BAI), 72, 88, 269, 270, 337n25

believability quotient (BQ), 34, 97, 247–52, 270–71, 291

Beyond Culture, 117

biology, xii, 135

Blair, Pete, xiii, 170, 200, 210, 258, 261–62, 264, 272, 274, 281–83

body language, xi, 42, 230, 260. *See also* cues

bogus training experiments, 22, 33, 47, 229–30

Bok, Sissela, 153–54

Bond, Charles (Charlie), 11, 22, 24–25, 37–38, 40, 42, 50–51, 173, 226, 230, 231, 243, 307n3, 308n7, 313n7. *See also* meta-analysis

Bond, Gary, 62, 329n9